P9-CET-025

Discover
Turkey

Contents

Throughout this book, we use these icons to highlight special recommendations:

The Best...
Lists for everything from bars to wildlife – to make sure you don't miss out

Don't Miss
A must-see – don't go home until you've been there

Local Knowledge
Local experts reveal their top picks and secret highlights

Detour
Special places a little off the beaten track

If you like...
Lesser-known alternatives to world-famous attractions

These icons help you quickly identify reviews in the text and on the map:

Sights

Eating

Drinking

Sleeping

Information

This edition written and researched by

James Bainbridge
Brett Atkinson, Chris Deliso, Steve Fallon, Will Gourlay,
Jessica Lee, Virginia Maxwell, Tom Spurling

İstanbul
p51

p105 Gallipoli
& the North
Aegean

Cappadocia &
Central Anatolia

p233

p285

Eastern
Anatolia

p143 **p185** Antalya & the
Mediterranean
Ephesus, Bodrum Coast
& the South Aegean

Contents

On the Road

Contents

On the Road

In Focus

Survival Guide

This is Turkey

Turkey's dramatic landscape is a fitting canvas for the country's long history. It sweeps from Europe to Asia, from sun-baked Aegean beaches to expansive steppe, and from Mediterranean bays to snowy mountains.

A succession of empires, armies, pilgrims and traders have passed through Anatolia (Asian Turkey). Ottoman sultans, Byzantine emperors, whirling dervishes and Christian saints have all left clues, monuments, ciphers and ruins that add lyricism and romance to Turkey's scenery. Lycian tombs poke above the waterline in Mediterranean coves, fresco-filled cave churches survey Cappadocia's surreal fairy chimneys, and the marble streets of Ephesus (Efes) glint in the Aegean sun.

Contemporary Turkey's rich culture combines these diverse historical influences. Here you can start the day in the bazaar, lunch on a kebap or *köfte* (meatballs) and spend the afternoon touring ruins, before hearing the sunset call to prayer and hitting a seafood restaurant or *meyhane* (Turkish tavern). Reflecting Turkish society's mix of Islamic, secular, traditional and modern elements, the country's cities range from breathtaking, continent-straddling İstanbul to southeastern outposts where minarets shimmer in the heat haze.

There are countless ways to enjoy Turkey's charms. It's an extraordinary cauldron of Eastern mystique, Mediterranean *joie de vivre*, urban sophistication and slow-paced rural life. Soak in the hamam, have a meze-and-rakı (aniseed brandy) session, seek out wind-whipped ruins or tour İstanbul's palaces: Turkey offers more than the keenest Grand Bazaar shopkeeper.

For physical activities, southwest Turkey reigns supreme. It is lined with beaches and dive spots, white-water rapids roar out of mountain ranges and walking trails lead to villages and ruins. You can kayak over the submerged remains of a city or paraglide from a 2000m-high peak; either way, don't miss the Turkish ritual of sipping a tulip-shaped glass of sweet black çay.

> **Turkey offers more than the keenest Grand Bazaar shopkeeper**

Hot-air ballooning in Göreme (p251), Cappadocia

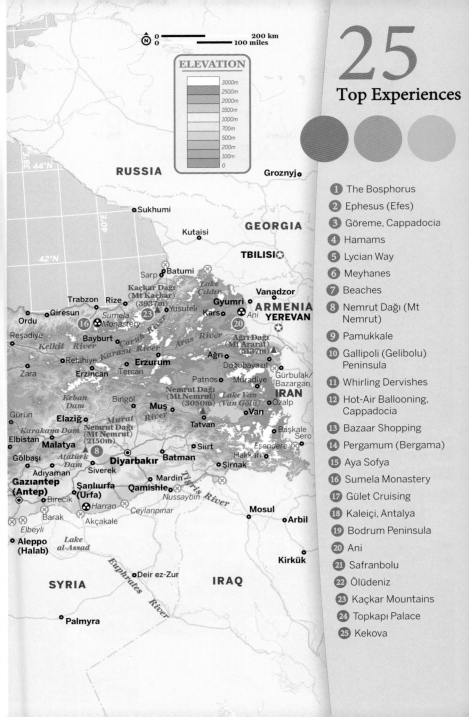

25

Top Experiences

25
Turkey's Top Experiences

Crossing Between Continents

In İstanbul, you can board a commuter ferry (p85) and flit between Europe and Asia in under an hour. Every day, a flotilla takes locals across the Bosphorus and over the Sea of Marmara, sounding sonorous horns as it goes. Morning services share the waterways with diminutive fishing boats and massive container ships. At sunset, the tapering minarets and Byzantine domes of the Old City are thrown into relief against a dusky pink sky – it's the city's most magical sight. İstanbul

KEN WELSH/GETTY IMAGES ©

2

Ephesus (Efes)

Undoubtedly Turkey's most famous ancient site, and considered the best-preserved ruins in the Mediterranean, Ephesus (p156) is a powerful tribute to Greek artistry and Roman architectural prowess. A stroll down the marble-coated Curetes Way provides myriad photo opportunities; at the bottom are the pillared facade of the Library of Celsus and, offering incredible insight into the daily lives of the city's elite, the Terraced Houses complex. Library of Celsus (p160)

Göreme, Cappadocia

The hard-set honeycomb landscape surrounding Göreme (p248) looks sculpted by a swarm of genius bees. The truth – the cooling effects of a major volcanic eruption – is only slightly less cool. Humans have also left their mark on this fantastical area: colourful Byzantine frescoes decorate the rock-cut churches clustered at open-air museums; and the Underground Cities are hideouts forged by early Christians. These days, Cappadocia is all about good times: fine wine, Anatolian cuisine, five-star caves, valley hikes and trail rides. There's enough to keep you buzzing for days. Byzantine frescoes in Karanlık Kilise (p253)

GIANNI DAGLI ORTI/GETTY IMAGES ©

The Best...
Boutique Hotels

HOTEL IBRAHIM PASHA
Ottoman style, contemporary decor, a terrace bar and Blue Mosque views. (p88)

TUVANA HOTEL
Compound of Ottoman houses in Kaleiçi, Antalya. (p214)

KELEBEK HOTEL & CAVE PENSION
Rock-cut rooms and Cappadocian views. (p252)

SU OTEL
Epitomises Bodrum's sunny, white-and-bright-blue style. (p172)

CENTAUERA
Brings boutique style to Alanya's heritage neighbourhood. (p219)

HERA BOUTIQUE HOTEL
Occupies a pair of 200-year-old Greek houses in Bergama. (p133)

The Best...
Hamams

AYASOFYA HÜRREM SULTAN HAMAMI
Hit the restored 16th-century Ottoman bathhouse after touring the Aya Sofya. (p86)

CINCI HAMAM
One of Turkey's best, located in Safranbolu's Ottoman old town. (p239)

ELIS KAPADOKYA HAMAM
Soothe those sore legs after a day walking in Cappadocia's valleys. (p252)

BALIK PAZARI HAMAMI
The 700-year-old Fish Market Hamam in Kaleiçi, Antalya. (p189)

YALI HAMAM
Unwind after a Gallipoli tour at Çanakkale's 17th-century hamam. (p123)

IZZET KERIBAR/GETTY IMAGES ©

Hamams

4

At most of the traditional hamams in Turkey, plenty of extras are on offer: bath treatments, facials, pedicures and the like. However, we recommend you stick with the tried and true hamam experience – a soak and a scrub followed by a good (and optional) pummelling. The world (and your body) will never feel quite the same again. For a truly memorable experience, take a soak in a centuries-old hamam in Antalya's old quarter (p213) or historic Sultanahmet (p86). Cağaloğlu Hamamı (p86)

ROBERT HARDING PRODUCTION/GETTY IMAGES ©

Lycian Way

5

One of the world's top long-distance walks, the Lycian Way (p191) follows signposted paths for 500km between Fethiye and Antalya. This is the Teke peninsula, birthplace of the ancient and mysterious Lycian civilisation. The route leads through forests in the shadow of mountains rising almost 3000m, past villages, coastal vistas and ruins at such ancient cities as Xanthos, Patara and Olympos. You can also tackle sections of the trail as day walks. Lycian ruins, Xanthos (p208)

Meyhanes

Say *şerefe* (cheers) to Efes-drinking Turks in a *meyhane* (tavern). A raucous night mixing meze with rakı (aniseed brandy) and live music is a time-honoured Turkish activity. The soundtrack ranges from romantic ballads to *fasıl* (lively local gypsy music). A great place to sample Turkish nightlife is Beyoğlu, İstanbul, where the *meyhane* precincts (p94) around İstiklal Caddesi heave with people on Friday and Saturday nights. Nightlife in Beyoğlu (p79), İstanbul

Beaches

Turkey's *plajlar* (beaches) are world-famous, offering a reliable summer mix of sun, sand and azure waters. Heading the list are beauties such as Kaputaş (p206), a tiny cove with dazzling shallows, and Patara (p204), Turkey's longest beach. Many of the finest Mediterranean beaches are on the ruin-dotted Teke peninsula and linked by the Lycian Way footpath. Other stretches of sand are pleasingly remote – the Aegean isle of Bozcaada (p127) has a string of quiet beaches, offering undemanding activities such as trying the local *dondurma* (ice cream). Butterfly Valley (p198)

Nemrut Dağı (Mt Nemrut)

One man's megalomania echoes across the centuries atop Nemrut Dağı's exposed and rugged summit (p315). A gently emerging sunrise coaxes stark shadows from the mountain's giant sculpted heads, and as dawn breaks, the finer details of the immense landscape below are gradually added. Huddling against the chill of a new morning, a warming glass of çay could not be more welcome. And when your time on the summit is complete, don't miss the graceful Roman bridge crossing the nearby Cendere River.

The Best...
Water Sports

KAŞ
Mediterranean diving centre; also canyoning and sea kayaking over Kekova's sunken ruins. (p207)

KAÇKAR MOUNTAINS
Gnarly white-water rafting on mountain rapids. (p303)

AYVALIK
Dive to deep-sea red coral in the north Aegean. (p128)

FETHIYE
Sea kayaking, diving, rafting and parasailing on the Med. (p199)

PATARA
Canoe down the Xanthos River to Turkey's longest beach. (p205)

IZZET KERIBAR/GETTY IMAGES ©

Pamukkale

Famed for its intricate series of travertines (calcite shelves) and crowned by the ruined Roman and Byzantine spa city of Hierapolis, the 'Cotton Castle' (p263) – a bleach-white mirage by day and alien ski slope by night – is one of the most unusual treasures in Turkey. Gingerly tiptoe through the crystal travertines and, when you reach the top, reward yourself with a refreshing dunk in Hierapolis' Antique Pool amid toppled marble columns and dramatic friezes.

The Best...
Mosques

BLUE MOSQUE
İstanbul's famous mosque has voluptuous domes, six minarets and İznik tiles. (p64)

SELIMIYE CAMII
Edirne's grandest mosque is the Ottoman architect Mimar Sinan's finest work. (p123)

SÜLEYMANIYE MOSQUE
Another Sinan-designed mosque, towering above İstanbul's Golden Horn. (p72)

ULU CAMII
Bursa's monumental 14th-century mosque has 20 domes. (p259)

RIZVANIYE VAKFI CAMII & MEDRESESI
Şanlıurfa's elegant mosque and *medrese* (seminary) complex has a much-photographed arcaded wall. (p311)

DAJ/GETTY IMAGES ©

10 Gallipoli (Gelibolu) Peninsula

The narrow stretch of land guarding the entrance to the much-contested Dardanelles is a beautiful area (p118), where pine trees roll across hills above Eceabat's fish restaurants and Kilitbahir's castle. Touring the peaceful countryside is a poignant experience for many: memorials (p120) and cemeteries mark where young men from far away fought and died in gruelling conditions. The passionate guides evoke the futility and tragedy of the Gallipoli campaign, one of WWI's worst episodes. Çanakkale Şehitleri Anıtı (Martyrs Memorial; p121)

Whirling Dervishes

Over 700 years after the foundation of the Mevlevi brotherhood of whirling dervishes, you can see *semas* (whirling dervish ceremonies) in locations including İstanbul (see boxed text, p87) and Cappadocia. *Semas* crackle with spiritual energy as the robe-clad constellation of dancers perform this trancelike ritual. The ceremony begins and ends with chanted passages from the Koran and is rich with symbolism; the dervishes' conical felt hats represent their tombstones, as the dance signifies relinquishing earthly life to be reborn in mystical union with God.

Hot-Air Ballooning, Cappadocia

A dawn hot-air balloon ride (p251) over Cappadocia's rocky dreamscape is a serene start to the day, giving a sweeping overview of the fairy chimneys (rock formations). Gaze at the flowing valleys far below and feel the invigorating Anatolian breeze as snowy Erciyes Dağı (Mt Erciyes) sparkles in the early-morning sunshine. The best companies change their launch pad according to the wind, ensuring you float over Cappadocia's scenic valleys. Back on terra firma, toast your pilot with a Cloud Nine cocktail.

Bazaar Shopping

Turkey's çarşıs (markets) range from İstanbul's famously clamorous bazaars – look out for the Arasta Bazaar (p99), for carpets, jewellery, textiles and ceramics – to the traditional shadow puppets in Bursa's *bedesten* (covered market; p266) and silk scarves in Şanlıurfa's ancient caravanserai (p311). Find something you like, drink some çay with the shopkeeper, and accept that you might not bag the world's best deal but you'll hone your haggling skills. Grand Bazaar (p72), İstanbul

Pergamum (Bergama)

In the hills above this unassuming north Aegean town are the ruins of the Asclepion (p131), ancient Rome's pre-eminent medical centre, and the acropolis, with its dramatic Greek theatre. A cable car now climbs to the acropolis from near the ruined Red Basilica, where the Byzantines built a basilica inside the hulking temple to Egyptian gods. Bergama can be visited in a day from Ayvalık or İzmir; alternatively, overnight in an atmospheric boutique hotel and watch life slope along in this low-key town. Temple of Trajan (p138)

14

The Best...
Bazaars

GRAND BAZAAR
Lose yourself in the hidden caravanserais and labyrinthine lanes of İstanbul's famous bazaar. (p72)

SPICE BAZAAR
Stalls upon stalls of spices, herbs and *lokum* (Turkish delight) near İstanbul's Galata Bridge. (p78)

ŞANLIURFA (URFA) BAZAAR
The 16th-century jumble of streets and shady courtyards has a Middle Eastern feel. (p311)

MARDIN BAZAAR
Donkeys are still a form of transport in the ancient city's hillside commercial hub. (p317)

The Best...
Museums

MUSEUM OF ANATOLIAN CIVILISATIONS
Ancient finds from the steppe. (p275)

KARIYE MUSEUM
Like the Aya Sofya, a former church and mosque with Byzantine mosaics. (p93)

GÖREME OPEN-AIR MUSEUM
A valley of fresco-filled rock-cut churches. (p253)

ANTALYA MUSEUM
Covers Mediterranean history back to the Stone Age. (p216)

MUSEUM OF TURKISH & ISLAMIC ARTS
Antique carpets fit for palaces. (p65)

HIERAPOLIS ARCHAEOLOGY MUSEUM
Sarcophagi in former Roman baths. (p264)

LEFT: JEAN-PIERRE LESCOURRET/GETTY IMAGES ©; RIGHT: JOHN JONES SINGING BOWL MEDIA/GETTY IMAGES ©

Aya Sofya

Even in mighty İstanbul, nothing beats the Church of the Divine Wisdom (p69), which was the greatest church in Christendom, until the Ottomans took Constantinople. Emperor Justinian had it built in the 6th century and it's hard to believe this fresco-covered marvel didn't single-handedly revive Rome's fortunes. Entering the ancient interior, covered in mosaics and messages left by generations of rulers, leaves an impression that few buildings can equal.

Sumela Monastery

The improbable cliff-face location of Sumela Monastery (p301) is more than matched by the surrounding verdant scenery. The gently winding roads to the Byzantine monastery twist past rustic riverside fish restaurants, and your journey from nearby Trabzon may be pleasantly hindered by a herd of fat-tailed sheep en route to fresh pastures. The last few kilometres afford tantalising glimpses across pine-covered valleys, and once inside the rock-cut retreat you will see colourful 9th- to 19th-century frescoes.

Gület Cruising

Known locally as a blue voyage (*mavi yolculuk*), a cruise lasting four days and three nights on a *gület* (traditional wooden sailing boat) along the western Mediterranean's Turquoise Coast is the highlight of many a trip to Turkey (see boxed text, p202). The cruises offer opportunities to explore isolated beaches, watch sunsets and get away from it all out at sea. The usual route is Fethiye–Olympos, but aficionados say Fethiye–Marmaris is even prettier. A *gület* off the coast of Fethiye (p198)

Kaleiçi, Antalya

Antalya's old town is a heritage labyrinth of restored Ottoman houses, many containing pensions, boutique hotels and shops. With Antalya Museum a few tram stops away and boat trips departing from the Roman harbour, Kaleiçi (p213) is an ideal base for exploring the Turquoise Coast. The hillside neighbourhood doesn't trade on its past alone; restaurants such as Vanilla and Seraser excel at international dishes with a Mediterranean twist, and you can see live *türkü* (Turkish folk music) or drink an Efes beer with a view. Street scene, Kaleiçi

18

The Best...
Scenic Strolls

CAPPADOCIA
Explore the maze of valleys and fairy chimneys (rock formations). (p251)

KAÇKAR MOUNTAINS
Wander across alpine *yaylalar* (mountain pastures) to bucolic villages. (p303)

İSTIKLAL CADDESI
Promenade down modern İstanbul's thoroughfare, through Galata and over the Galata Bridge. (p79)

SUMELA MONASTERY
Climb to the cliff-side monastery and back along forest paths. (p301)

KAYAKÖY
Walk the trail from Ölüdeniz to the abandoned Greek town. (p205)

Bodrum Peninsula

For Turkey's glitterati, celebs and fashionistas, this Aegean peninsula (p177) is *the* place to see and be seen during summer. The gateway to the peninsula's villages and beaches, seafood restaurants and boutique hotels is Bodrum town (p171), a whitewashed holiday hang-out devoted to the good life. From Bodrum, you can embark on boat trips, or just absorb the cosmopolitan ambience. The town has come a long way since being besieged by Alexander the Great around 335 BC and shelled by the French during WWI. Castle of St Peter (p173), Bodrum

JON ARNOLD/GETTY IMAGES ©

The Best...
Mosaics, Frescoes & Reliefs

AYA SOFYA
The glittering mosaics show Byzantine emperors and empresses. (p69)

KARANLIK KILISE
Cappadocian rock-cut church with colourful Byzantine frescoes. (p253)

HATAY ARCHAEOLOGY MUSEUM
Antakya's superb collection of Roman and Byzantine mosaics. (p227)

AKDAMAR KILISESI
The 10th-century island church's biblical relief carvings are Armenian masterworks. (p319)

TERRACED HOUSES
Colourful mosaics, frescoes and graffiti give insights into the lives of Ephesus' upper crust. (p161)

20 Ani

Ani (p308) is a truly exceptional site. Historically intriguing, culturally compelling and scenically magical, this ghost city floating in a sea of grass looks like a movie set. Lying in blissful isolation right at the Armenian border, the site exudes an eerie ambience. Before it was deserted in 1239 after a Mongol invasion, Ani was a thriving city and a capital of both the Urartian and Armenian kingdoms. The ruins include several notable churches, plus a cathedral built between 987 and 1010.

IZZET KERIBAR/GETTY IMAGES ©

Safranbolu

Listed for eternal preservation by Unesco in 1994, Safranbolu (p277) is Turkey's prime example of an Ottoman town brought back to life. Domestic tourists descend here, full of sentiment, to stay in half-timbered houses that seem torn from the pages of a children's storybook. Sweets and saffron vendors line the cobblestone alleyways, and artisans ply their centuries-old trades beneath medieval mosques. When the summer storms light up the night sky, the fantasy is complete.

Ölüdeniz

With its sheltered lagoon lying between a spit of sandy beach, lush national park and Baba Dağ (Mt Baba), it's easy to see why this beach town is a major cog in the Turquoise Coast's tourist machine. A boat trip to Ölüdeniz (p203; pronounced 'eu-leu-den-eez') from Fethiye, or a walk from the Greek ghost town of Kayaköy, is highly recommended. The curving beach and green slopes are a dramatic sight, and 1960m-high Mt Baba is capped with snow until April.

Kaçkar Mountains

Rippling along between the Black Sea coast and the Çoruh River, the Kaçkars (p302) rise to almost 4000m, affording superb hiking when the snow melts in summer. The day walks and longer treks in the *yaylalar* (mountain pastures) around mountain hamlets like Olgunlar and Ayder are some of Turkey's top hiking experiences, and the lower slopes offer cultural encounters. The local Hemşin people are welcoming, serving their beloved, fondue-like *muhlama* (cornmeal cooked in butter) in villages with Ottoman bridges and Georgian churches.

The Best...
Fish Restaurants

AHIRKAPI BALIKÇISI
Sultanahmet local favourite near the Sea of Marmara. (p92)

BODRUM FISH MARKET
Restaurants cook your pick from the adjoining fishmongers' tables. (p172)

SANDAL RESTAURANT
Alfresco seafood and mezes on Bozcaada island. (p127)

İSKELE SOFRASI
Güveç (seafood casserole) and Alanya harbour views. (p220)

REIS
Have your choice from Fethiye's fishmongers cooked here. (p200)

BALIKÇI
Pair *balık* (fish) with *rakı* (aniseed brandy) in Ayvalık. (p130)

23

Topkapı Palace

You could easily spend a day looking around İstanbul's sprawling palace (p73); after all, the Ottoman sultans spent four centuries, from the great days of Süleyman the Magnificent to later eras, when the empire was declining. As you poke around the palace's many corners and courtyards, you'll sense the echoes of the princes, courtiers, eunuchs and concubines who also walked these corridors. To get a feel for 16th-century İstanbul, when palace life was in full swing, read Orhan Pamuk's novel *My Name is Red*. Topkapı Palace interior

The Best...
Boat Trips

KEKOVA
From Kaş to the ruined Lycian Batık Şehir (Sunken City). (p210)

BOSPHORUS
A few hours cruising between continents towards the Black Sea. (p85)

AYVALIK
Across the bay to Alibey Island or Assos. (p128)

ANTALYA
Trips head along the Turquoise Coast from the Roman harbour. (p213)

BUTTERFLY VALLEY
From Fethiye via Ölüdeniz's mountain and lagoon. (p199)

KNIDOS
Cruise from Datça to the Dorian port city. (p180)

MARK HORN/GETTY IMAGES ©

25

Kekova

Overlooking the glittering stretch of sea between the isle of Kekova (see boxed text, p210) and the Mediterranean mainland are rocky peninsulas, vertiginous slopes and fishing villages. What's more, if you shift your gaze from these stunning surroundings and peer over the side of your boat or sea kayak, you will see the submerged shapes of ancient ruins. This was once a residential neighbourhood in the Lycian city of Simena, consigned to a watery grave by a series of severe earthquakes in the 2nd century AD. Kekova village

Turkey's
Top Itineraries

İstanbul to Ephesus
Classic Turkey

5 DAYS

This tour of Turkish highlights leads from the great city of İstanbul across the Sea of Marmara to the north Aegean, where the ruined Roman capital at Ephesus makes an excellent double bill with the laid-back town of Selçuk.

Map labels: BULGARIA · GREECE · Black Sea · Aegean Sea · ① İSTANBUL · ② SELÇUK · ③ EPHESUS (EFES)

① İstanbul (p51)

Ahh, İstanbul. The former capital of the Byzantine and Ottoman empires is like a country in itself, with enough size, swagger and diversity to outshine a dozen small nations. Exploring the world-famous sights alone takes a couple of days: the Byzantine splendour of the **Aya Sofya**, with its seemingly floating dome; the neighbouring **Blue Mosque's** voluptuous domes and six minarets; the labyrinthine Harem and glittering Treasury in the **Topkapı Palace**; and the winding lanes of the **Grand Bazaar**. Leave time to cross between Europe and Asia on a **ferry** across the Bosphorus.

İSTANBUL ➲ SELÇUK
✈ **Three hours** Fly to İzmir and catch the train.
⚓ **Nine hours** Ferry to Bandırma, then train or drive.

② Selçuk (p161)

In this amiable country town, stay in a family-run pension and wander around the historic core, **Ayasuluk Hill**. Here you'll find the **Basilica of St John**, built by order of the Byzantine Emperor Justinian, and **Ayasuluk Fortress**. There's also a **Roman aqueduct**; one of the Seven Wonders of the Ancient World, the **Temple of Artemis**, now a solitary pillar; and the **Ephesus Museum**, displaying artefacts from your next stop.

SELÇUK ➲ EPHESUS (EFES)
🚌 Half- and full-day tours available (see p156).
🚕 **Ten minutes** Take a taxi to the Upper Gate (₺20).

③ Ephesus (Efes) (p156)

The capital of the Roman province of Asia Minor, Ephesus' marble streets lead between ruined temples and fountains. Imagining the other tourists are clad in togas will help to evoke the days when Anthony and Cleopatra strolled down the **Curetes Way**. The Aegean sunshine glints off the pillared facade of the **Library of Celsus** and, in the neighbouring **Terraced Houses**, mosaics, frescoes and graffiti reveal the Roman aristocracy's daily concerns.

İstanbul cityscape (p51)

5 DAYS

Antalya to Bodrum
Coast to Coast

This roam around the western Mediterranean, western Anatolia and southern Aegean focuses on Turkey's glorious coastline and surreal rock formations.

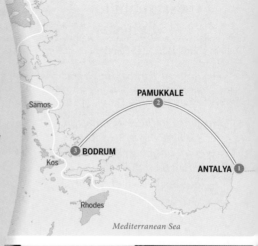

Samos

PAMUKKALE 2

③ **BODRUM**

Kos

ANTALYA ①

Rhodes

Mediterranean Sea

① Antalya (p212)

Get off to a stylish start in the Turkish Mediterranean's most attractive and vibrant city, where boutique hotels and pensions occupy restored Ottoman houses in the old town, **Kaleiçi**. Stroll down to the **Roman-era harbour**, now a modern marina, for **boat trips** along the Turquoise Coast. In the city itself, Kaleiçi is dotted with monuments such as the 13th-century Yivli Minare (Fluted Minaret), the city's symbol; the **Antalya Museum's** exhibits include statues of Olympian gods. At the end of the Mediterranean day, enjoy the slick bars, local hang-outs and classy restaurants serving modern Turkish cuisine. You can fly to Antalya from İstanbul.

ANTALYA ⚪ PAMUKKALE

🚌 **Five hours** Via Denizli (hotels in Pamukkale offer transfers from Denizli).

② Pamukkale (p263)

This Anatolian town's name, 'Cotton Castle', comes from its incredible mountain of glittering white **travertines** (calcite shelves). You can take a dip in the mineral-rich waters inside the saucer-shaped formations. Remarkably, atop this troglodytes' ski slope is the 2200-year-old spa resort of **Hierapolis**, which had large Jewish and Orthodox communities during the Byzantine era. The well-kept ruins evoke life in ancient times, while the **Hierapolis Archaeology Museum** exhibits sarcophagi, statuary and friezes in a former Roman bathhouse. Fancy another curative dip? The **Antique Pool's** water (a balmy 36°C) is abundant in minerals and has submerged sections of original fluted marble columns. Pamukkale is also a good base for visiting the ruins of **Afrodisias**, once a 150,000-strong Roman provincial capital.

PAMUKKALE ⚪ BODRUM

🚌 **5½ hours** Via Denizli; hotels in Pamukkale offer transfers to Denizli.

③ Bodrum (p171)

Despite its success as an Aegean tourist destination, whitewashed Bodrum has retained its arty sophistication and charm. In the 1940s, the town overlooked by the 15th-century **Castle of St Peter** became a haven for dissidents and intellectuals, writers and artists. Make a beeline for the castle, with its harbour views and **Museum of Underwater Archaeology**. As well as ancient sights such as the **Mausoleum** (built for a Carian king), Bodrum offers boat trips, as well as excellent restaurants and nightlife. At the **Fish Market** choose between the catches on the fishmongers' tables and get your pick cooked at a neighbouring restaurant. For more opportunities to take lingering looks at the coast over mezes and cold beer, take a day trip to the **Bodrum Peninsula**. The area's villages, beaches and bays are the summer playground of Turkey's jet set, and the peninsula's chic restaurants offer beachfront dining. You can fly back to İstanbul from Bodrum.

Ottoman buildings in Kaleiçi (p213), Antalya's old town
PHOTOGRAPHER: NIGEL HICKS/GETTY IMAGES ©

10 DAYS

Cappadocia to Van
Eastern Wander

Starting in Cappadocia's famously dreamy landscape, this itinerary explores Turkey's southeastern spaces. From Arab-influenced Antakya (Hatay), continue east to mystical Şanlıurfa, Mardin's mosques, and the magnificent steppe around Van.

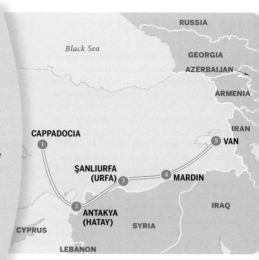

RUSSIA

Black Sea

GEORGIA

AZERBAIJAN

ARMENIA

IRAN

CAPPADOCIA
❶

❺ **VAN**

ŞANLIURFA (URFA) ❸

❹ **MARDIN**

❷ **ANTAKYA (HATAY)**

SYRIA

IRAQ

CYPRUS

LEBANON

1 Cappadocia (p246)

This magical area of central Anatolia – its valleys dotted with **cave hotels** and **fairy chimneys** (rock formations) – is a dreamscape created by volcanic eruptions. Spend a couple of days in the village of **Göreme**, walking and horse riding in the surrounding valleys. Learn about the area's history at the nearby **Göreme Open-Air Museum**, a rock-cut Byzantine monastic settlement with fresco-filled chapels; and the **underground cities**, where the persecuted early Christians went to earth.

Between amazing experiences such as **hot-air ballooning** and watching a *sema* (whirling dervish ceremony), Cappadocia offers innumerable simple pleasures, from tasting Anatolian food and wine to pottering between tiny villages on foot or by scooter.

You can fly to Cappadocia from İstanbul.

CAPPADOCIA ➲ ANTAKYA (HATAY)

🚌 **8½ hours** Via Adana. 🚗 Car hire available in Cappadocia.

2 Antakya (Hatay) (p227)

At the Mediterranean Sea's northeastern corner, near the Syrian border, Arabic influence is writ large on this ancient city. Just try **local dishes** such as *oruk*, a fried croquette of spicy minced beef in bulgur wheat flour (similar to Lebanese *kibbeh*). Antakya is the site of the biblical Antioch, and sights such as the **Church of St Peter** and **Hatay Archaeology Museum** evoke its long history.

ANTAKYA (HATAY) ➲ ŞANLIURFA (URFA)

🚌 **Seven hours.**

Sunset over Göreme (p248), Cappadocia
PHOTOGRAPHER: DAN WICKLAND/GETTY IMAGES ©

3 Şanlıurfa (Urfa) (p309)

Urfa has been an Islamic pilgrimage site for centuries and its venerated mosques, sacred pools and bazaar lanes all exude a certain mystique. This being multifaceted Turkey, you can take in the devout activities over a cold beer on a rooftop terrace. The city is a good base for visiting **Göbekli Tepe**, the mysterious Neolithic stone circles, and **Nemrut Dağı** (Mt Nemrut), a mountaintop funerary mound in the Anti-Taurus Range.

ŞANLIURFA (URFA) ➲ MARDIN

🚌 **Three hours.** 🚗 Car hire available in Şanlıurfa.

4 Mardin (p316)

Mardin has been inhabited by Assyrian Christians since the 5th century and its baked-brown lanes overlook the Mesopotamian plains. You can try the city's **Syriac wine** and wander its honey-coloured streets between churches and mosques. The **Sakıp Sabancı Mardin City Museum** unravels the history of Mardin, controlled at times by Arabs, Seljuks, Kurds, Mongols, Persians and Ottomans.

MARDIN ➲ VAN

🚌 **8½ hours** Via Diyarbakır.

5 Van (p320)

Lake Van is a dramatic break in the steppe, covering 3750 sq km of mountainous southeastern Anatolia. On its eastern shore, the city of Van is a pleasant base for visiting sights such as **Akdamar Kilisesi**, the 10th-century island church. The city itself does a good line in *kahvaltı* (Turkish breakfast) and has the hilltop **Van Castle** (Van Kalesi). You can fly back to İstanbul from Van.

Ankara to Kars
Across the Steppe

This journey takes you to northeastern Anatolia's stunning plateaus and peaks. The area is a long way from western Turkey's tourist territory, and this itinerary requires a little adventurous spirit. However, the trip is doable by both car and Turkey's comfortable buses, with plenty of good hotels and restaurants along the way.

① Ankara (p270)

The capital is a convenient hub for central Turkey, with flights from İstanbul and buses travelling far and wide from its huge otogar (bus station). While here, hop on the metro to Ulus and see the **Museum of Anatolian Civilisations**, displaying finds from Anatolia's many significant archaeological sites. Staying overnight here is not as awful as İstanbullus will tell you: **Kızılay's** cafe culture shows modern Turkey at its vibrant best.

ANKARA ➲ AMASYA
🚌 **Five hours**. 🚗 Car hire available in Ankara.

② Amasya (p280)

One of two restored Ottoman towns within a few hours' drive of Ankara (Safranbolu is the other), Amasya is a handy staging post en route to northeastern Anatolia. With gingerbread-like **Ottoman houses** on one side of the Yeşilırmak River and **mosques and museums** on the other, Amasya's setting is superb. Above its minarets looms a rocky bluff, carved with **Pontic tombs** and crowned by lofty **Harşena Castle**.

AMASYA ➲ TRABZON
🚌 **8½ hours** Via Samsun.

③ Trabzon (p298)

Come to the Black Sea coast's largest city to visit the remarkable **Sumela Monastery**, 46km south of town. Easily reached on buses from central Trabzon, the abandoned Orthodox monastery clings to the cliffs above a forested mountain valley. Trabzon is a pleasant place to spend a night, with some reasonable eating options on its main square and pedestrianised walkways.

Women carrying hay in the Kaçkar Mountains (p302)
PHOTOGRAPHER: IMAGES & STORIES/ALAMY ©

TRABZON ➲ KAÇKAR MOUNTAINS
🚌 **Two/eight hours** Ayder via Pazar/Yusufeli via Hopa or Artvin. 🚗 Car hire available in Trabzon.

④ Kaçkar Mountains (p302)

This beautiful area of snowy peaks, alpine lakes and *yaylalar* (mountain pastures) offers some of Turkey's best **walking** and **white-water rafting**. When it's time to just put your feet up, both sides of the range (around Ayder and Yusufeli) are great places to experience traditional village life.

KAÇKAR MOUNTAINS ➲ KARS
🚌 **Two/eight hours** From Yusufeli/Ayder via Pazar.

⑤ Kars (p306)

The Russians occupied this distinctive city from 1878 to 1920 and built many of its grand buildings. A slow-paced outpost in the steppe with two excellent *ocakbaşıs* (grill houses), Kars is the gateway to incredible **Ani**, 45km east on the Armenian border. In this ancient Silk Road entrepôt and Armenian capital, ruined churches romantically scatter a windblown field. From Kars, you can fly back to İstanbul or Ankara.

İstanbul to Datça & Bozburun Peninsulas
South to the Med

This journey across the Sea of Marmara and western Anatolia, followed by a cruise along the Mediterranean coast to one of the Aegean region's loveliest corners, combines glossy-brochure highlights and hidden gems.

1 İstanbul (p51)

Atatürk made Ankara the Turkish capital, but İstanbul remains one of the world's most exciting cities. Begin with a look at Sultanahmet's monumental buildings and historic sites (in addition to the obvious Byzantine and Ottoman sites, check out the intriguing subterranean **Basilica Cistern**). Next, get a feel for the sheer energy of this booming metropolis, best experienced on a wander down **İstiklal Caddesi** and a night in **Beyoğlu's** rooftop bars and *meyhanes* (taverns).

İSTANBUL ⟶ BURSA
🚢 **Three to four hours** To Mudanya or Yalova, then bus. 🚌 **Four to five hours** Around the Sea of Marmara.

2 Bursa (p258)

After crossing the Sea of Marmara, spend a night in the first Ottoman capital. In the centre is a diverting mix of mosques, including Sultan Beyazıt I's 20-dome **Ulu Camii**, and **markets**, where you can buy Bursa's traditional products, shadow puppets and silk, in age-old caravanserais.

BURSA ⟶ EĞIRDIR
🚌 **Eight hours** Direct or via Isparta. 🚗 Car hire available in Bursa.

3 Eğirdir (p267)

This waterfront town in western Anatolia's Lake District offers a pleasant slice of rural Turkish life. There are 13th-century **Seljuk buildings** to explore and a peninsula to wander down, stopping at **beaches** and at the **Eğirdir Outdoor Center**. The centre rents out bikes, organises boat trips and runs tours to the mystical mountaintop ruins of **Sagalassos**.

EĞIRDIR ⟶ OLYMPOS & ÇIRALI
🚌 **Five hours** Via Antalya.

4 Olympos & Çıralı (p211)

On the slopes of Mt Olympos, witness the eternal flame of the **Chimaera**: dozens of naturally occurring flames, which are clearly visible from the sea at night. It's easy to see why ancient peoples attributed these extraordinary flames to the breath of a monster. More prosaically, nearby

Ruins of ancient Olympos (p211)
PHOTOGRAPHER: BRANDON SAWAYA/GETTY IMAGES ©

⑥ Fethiye (p198)

Say goodbye to the Teke peninsula in Fethiye, another great launch pad for Mediterranean **boat trips**. Local destinations include **Ölüdeniz**, where Baba Dağ (Mt Baba) overshadows the beach and lagoon; three-night *gület* (traditional wooden yacht) **cruises** are also available. The town nestles in the southern reaches of a bay scattered with islands, which featured in the James Bond film *Skyfall*. Activities here include parasailing, rafting, horse riding, diving, nocturnal sea kayaking and ogling the ancient **rock-cut tombs**.

FETHIYE ➔ DATÇA & BOZBURUN PENINSULAS
🚌 **Four to five hours** Via Marmaris. 🚗 Car hire available in Fethiye.

Çıralı is a beach haven for families and anyone who wants to relax, while ancient **Olympos** was a major, fire-worshipping Lycian city.

OLYMPOS & ÇIRALI ➔ KAŞ
🚌 **2½ hours** Combined with accommodation transfer to highway. 🚌 **2½ hours** Direct on a dolmuş (minibus).

⑤ Kaş (p205)

In the heart of the blissful Teke peninsula, this low-key harbour town is **activities** central. Diving, sea kayaking, paragliding, canyoning and mountain biking are on offer, and a boat trip to **Kekova** island's submerged Lycian ruins is a Mediterranean highlight. This being the ancient Lycians' stomping ground, the 4th-century BC **King's Tomb** stands among the fish restaurants in the pretty backstreets.

KAŞ ➔ FETHIYE
🚌 **2½ hours**. 🚗 Stop en route at Kaputaş beach.

⑦ Datça & Bozburun Peninsulas (p180)

These adjoining peninsulas are the perfect place to reflect on your Turkish journey, with forested peaks and rugged coves overlooking the Aegean. At the tip of the Datça Peninsula are the ruins of **Knidos**, a 4th-centruy BC Dorian port city. The best thing to do in this raw landscape is slow to the local pace and spend your days pottering between villages and beaches, trying the local seafood and olives. From the Dalaman Airport (three hours from the peninsulas) you can fly back to İstanbul (1½ hours).

Turkey Month by Month

Top Events

- **Mountain Walking,** July
- **Ski Season,** December
- **Kaçkar Mountains Festivals,** June
- **Nevruz,** March
- **Historic Kırkpınar Oil Wrestling Festival,** June

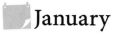

January

New Year's Day

A surrogate Christmas takes place across the Islamic country, with the usual decorations, exchange of gifts and greeting cards. Christmas and New Year are an exception to the low season; prices rise and accommodation fills up.

March

Nevruz

Kurds and Alevis celebrate the ancient Middle Eastern spring festival with much jumping over bonfires and general jollity. Banned until a few years ago, Nevruz (21 March) is now an official holiday with huge all-night parties, particularly in Diyarbakır and southeastern Anatolia.

Çanakkale Deniz Zaferi

Turks descend on the Gallipoli (Gelibolu) Peninsula and the towns across the Dardanelles on 18 March to celebrate what they call the Çanakkale Naval Victory – and commemorate the WWI campaign's 130,000 fatalities. The area, particularly the Turkish memorials in the southern peninsula (p121), is busy with busloads of people.

April

Anzac Day, Gallipoli Peninsula

The WWI battles for the Dardanelles are commemorated again on 25 April, this time with more emphasis on the Allied soldiers. Antipodean pilgrims sleep at Anzac Cove (p120) before the dawn services; another busy time on the peninsula.

(left) December Skiing at Mt Uludağ (p258)

İstanbul Film Festival

For a filmic fortnight, Beyoğlu's wonderful vintage cinemas host a packed program of Turkish and international films and events (see http://film.iksv.org/en), with cheap-as-çay tickets available. An excellent crash course in Turkish cinema, but book ahead.

İstanbul Tulip Festival

İstanbul's parks and gardens are resplendent with tulips, which originated in Turkey before being exported to the Netherlands during the Ottoman era. Multicoloured tulips are often planted to resemble the Turks' cherished 'evil eye'. Flowers bloom from late March or early April.

 May

Windsurfing

In Turkey's windsurfing centre, Alaçatı (www.alacati.info; p361), the season begins in mid-May. The protected Aegean bay hosts the Windsurf World Cup in August and the season winds down in early November, when many of the resident schools close.

Ruins, Mosques, Palaces & Museums

This is your last chance until September to see the main attractions at famous Aegean and Mediterranean sights such as Ephesus (Efes; p156) without major crowds, which can become almost unbearable at the height of summer.

 June

Cherry Season

June is the best month to gobble Turkey's delicious cherries. On the Sea of Marmara's north shore, en route from İstanbul to the Gallipoli Peninsula, Tekirdağ's Kiraz Festivalı (Cherry Festival) in early June celebrates the juicy wonders.

Kaçkar Mountains Festivals

In the second week of June, the Çamlıhemşin Ayder Festival celebrates the northern Kaçkars' Hemşin culture (see p353). If you visit Ayder on any summer weekend, look out for groups of Hemşin holidaymakers dancing the *horon*, a cross between the conga and the hokey-cokey set to the distinctive whining skirl of the *tulum*, a goatskin bagpipe.

Historic Kırkpınar Oil Wrestling Festival, Edirne

In a sport dating back 650 years, brawny *pehlivan* (wrestlers) from across Turkey rub themselves from head to foot with olive oil and grapple in late June or early July (p126).

 July

Mountain Walking

In northeastern Anatolia, the snow clears from atop the Kaçkar Mountains (Kaçkar Dağları) and Mt Ararat (Ağrı Dağı, 5137m), Turkey's highest peak, allowing sublime day walks and *yaylalar* (highland pastures; p302) views in July and August. See www.cultureroutesinturkey.com for more.

Kültür Sanat ve Turizm Festivalı, Doğubayazıt

The Kurdish town (p314) between Mt Ararat and İshak Paşa Palace hosts its Culture and Arts Festival, allowing you to immerse yourself in Kurdish heritage through music, dance and theatre performances. The festival is held in June or July.

Music Festivals

Turkey hosts a string of summer music jamborees in June and July, including İstanbul, İzmir and Bursa's highbrow festivals, Aspendos Opera & Ballet Festival, plus multiple pop, rock, jazz and dance music events in İstanbul and other cities. For more, see http://muzik.iksv.org/en.

 # September

 ### Diving

The water is warmest between May to October and you can expect water temperatures of 25°C in September. Turkey's scuba diving centres include Kuşadası and Ayvalık (p128) on the Aegean, and Kaş (p207) on the Mediterranean.

 ### İstanbul Biennial

The city's major visual-arts shindig (http://bienal.iksv.org/en), considered to be one of the world's most prestigious biennials, takes place from early September to early November in odd-numbered years. It typically features more than 100 projects by artists from dozens of countries.

 # October

 ### Walking

The weather in eastern Anatolia has already become challenging by this time of year, but in the southwest, autumn and spring are the best seasons to enjoy the scenery without too much sweat on your brow. For more, see www.trekkinginturkey.com.

Akbank Jazz Festival

From mid-September to early October, İstanbul celebrates its love of jazz with this eclectic line-up of local and international performers (www.akbank sanat.com). The older sibling of July's İstanbul Jazz Festival, it celebrated its 21st in 2011.

Efes Pilsen Blues Festival

Between late September and late October, American blues twangers tour İstanbul and a varying selection of other Turkish cities. For more, see www.pozitif-ist.com.

 # August

 ### Cappadocian Festivals

A summer series of chamber music concerts are held in Cappadocia's valleys and, for three days in mid-August, sleepy Hacıbektaş comes alive with the annual pilgrimage of Bektaşı dervishes (www.klasikkeyifler.org).

International Bodrum Ballet Festival

The 15th-century Castle of St Peter is an atmospheric location for the fortnight-long festival (www.bodrumballetfestival.gov.tr), which features Turkish and international ballet and opera performances.

November

 Karagöz Festival, Bursa

Five days of festivities and performances celebrate the city's Karagöz shadow-puppetry heritage, with local and international puppeteers and marionette performers. Originally a Central Asian Turkic tradition, the camel-hide puppet theatre developed in Bursa and spread through the Ottoman Empire.

December

 Ski Season

The Turkish ski season begins at half a dozen resorts across the country, including Cappadocia's Erciyes Dağı (Mt Erciyes), Uludağ (near Bursa), Palandöken (near Erzurum, northeastern Anatolia) and Sarıkamış, near Kars. The season runs from late November to April.

 Snow in Anatolia

If you're really lucky, after skiing on Erciyes Dağı, you could head west and see central Cappadocia's fairy chimneys (rock formations) looking even more magical under a layer of snow. A white blanket also covers eastern Anatolia, but temperatures get brutally low.

Far left: April İstanbul Tulip Festival **Left: September** Diving near Kaş (p207)

What's New

For this new edition of Discover Turkey, our authors have hunted down the fresh, the transformed, the hot and the happening. These are some of our favourites. For up-to-the-minute recommendations, see lonelyplanet.com/turkey.

1 AYA SOFYA
The 17-year restoration of the world's greatest Byzantine edifice, İstanbul's Aya Sofya, has finished to rapturous applause, and nearby Ayasofya Hürrem Sultan Hamamı has reopened after a US$13 million restoration. (p69 and p86)

2 GÖBEKLI TEPE
Their fame was a long time coming (about 12,000 years), but Şanlıurfa's Neolithic megaliths featured on a *National Geographic* cover in 2011.

3 CULINARY İSTANBUL
İstanbul has bolstered its gastronomic offering with culinary walks led by food bloggers, coffee workshops at the Museum of Turkish & Islamic Arts, and new Ottoman restaurant Matbah. (Map p66; ☎ 212-514 6151; www.matbahrestaurant.com; Ottoman Imperial Hotel, Caferiye Sokak 6/1; mezes ₺10-22, mains ₺28-48; ☺ lunch & dinner; ☒ Sultanahmet)

4 HISTORICAL DEVELOPMENTS
Improvements at historic sites include Boğazkale Museum's Hittite sphinxes, returned from Berlin and İstanbul, the cable car to Pergamum acropolis and Seljuk's Ayasuluk Fortress, reopened after a 20-year excavation.

5 KAÇKAR MOUNTAINS (KAÇKAR DAĞLARI)
On the range's southern side, day walks have been marked around the villages and a new package with East Turkey Expeditions makes summiting Mt Kaçkar affordable for independent travellers.

6 ISTANBUL
Exciting openings include writer Orhan Pamuk's whimsical Museum of Innocence, SALT cultural centres and the Galata Mevlevi Museum, the dervish museum in Galata's renovated 15th-century *tekke* (dervish lodge).

7 TROY MUSEUM
A national archaeological and history museum is set to open near Troy in 2015, giving another reason to visit the site from nearby Çanakkale or the Gallipoli Peninsula.

8 EVLIYA ÇELEBI WAY
Turkey's first long-distance walking and riding route follows the Ottoman traveller through Western Anatolia. Culture Routes in Turkey is developing several other trails.

9 PERA PALACE HOTEL
A US$23 million renovation has improved the famous İstanbul hotel's opulent late-Ottoman interiors, and its Golden Horn views remain. (Map p80; ☎ 212-377 4000; www.perapalace.com; Meşrutiyet Caddesi 52, Tepebaşı; r €205-325, ste €350-2600; ✻ @ ☎; ☒ Karaköy, then funicular to Tünel)

10 ANCIENT PATARA
Patara's *bouleuterion* (council chamber) reopened in 2012 following a ₺8.5 million reconstruction. It was the centre of the Lycian League, often cited as history's first proto-democratic union. (p204)

11 CAVE CUISINE
Join Cappadocia's slow-food revolution, based around traditional village dishes, at Göreme's recent openings Köy Evi and Topdeck Cave Restaurant. (p254 and p254)

Get Inspired

Books

o **Yashim novels** (Jason Goodwin; 2006–11) Eunuch detective in Ottoman İstanbul.

o **Honour** (Elif Şafak; 2011) Kurdish family saga set in southeastern Anatolia, İstanbul and London.

o **Portrait of a Turkish Family** (Irfan Orga; 1950) Memoir of İstanbul in the late Ottoman/early Republican era.

o **The Museum of Innocence** (Orhan Pamuk; 2008) Businessman obsesses over shop girl; inspired a museum in İstanbul.

Films

o **Skyfall** (2012) James Bond visits İstanbul and the Mediterranean.

o **Once Upon a Time in Anatolia** (2011) Murder mystery on the steppe.

o **Bal** (Honey; 2010) Coming-of-age story set in the Black Sea countryside.

o **Kosmos** (Cosmos; 2010) Allegory about Turkish–Armenian relations, set in a snowy border town.

o **Babam ve Oğlum** (My Father and My Son; 2005) Portrays the generation gap in an Aegean village.

Music

o **Turkish Groove** (compilation) Putumayo introduction.

o **Crossing the Bridge: The Sound of İstanbul** (compilation) Soundtrack to a documentary about İstanbul's music scene.

o **Işık Doğdan Yükselir** (Sezen Aksu) Contemporary folk from Turkey's pop queen.

o **Nefes** (Mercan Dede) Sufi-electronic-techno fusion.

o **Keçe Kurdan** (Aynur) Kurdish folk chanteuse.

Websites

o **Turkey Travel Planner** (www.turkeytravelplanner.com) Travel information.

o **İstanbul Eats** (istanbuleats.com) Culinary guide.

o **Tulumba** (www.tulumba.com) US-based emporium of Turkish music, books and paraphernalia.

o **Today's Zaman** (www.todayszaman.com) Travel articles.

o **Cornucopia** (www.cornucopia.net/blog) Cultural listings.

Short on time?

This list will give you an instant insight into the country.

Read *Birds Without Wings* (Louis de Bernières), a lyrical epic set during the early 20th century and featuring characters that ring true today.

Watch *Vizontele* (2001), a black comedy about the first family to get a TV in a southeastern Anatolian town (with a sequel, *Vizontele Tuuba*).

Listen *Duble Oryantal* (BaBa ZuLa), mixed by British dub master Mad Professor, is a fusion classic.

Log On *Hürriyet Daily News* (www.hurriyetdailynews.com) is the secularist newspaper's English-language website.

Museum of Innocence (p88), İstanbul
REFIK ANADOL/INNOCENCE FOUNDATION ©

Need to Know

Currency
Türk Lirası (Turkish lira; ₺)

Language
Turkish and Kurdish

ATMs
Widely available in towns; not as common in villages.

Credit Cards
Visa and MasterCard more widely accepted than Amex.

Visas
To stay for up to 90 days, most Western nationalities either don't require a visa or can purchase one on arrival (from €15).

Mobile Phones
Foreign phones work on roaming.

Wi-Fi
Most accommodation and many cafes offer free wi-fi.

Internet Access
Internet cafes widespread; typically charge around ₺1.50 an hour (İstanbul ₺3).

Driving
Drive on the right; steering wheel is on the left.

Tipping
Customary in restaurants, taxis and hotels; 10% to 15% in restaurants; a few coins in budget eateries.

When to Go

İstanbul
GO Apr–May, Sep

Eastern Anatolia
GO May–Jun, Sep

Cappadocia
GO May, Sep–Oct

Aegean
GO May–Jun, Sep

Mediterranean
GO Apr, Sep–Oct

Desert, dry climate
Warm to hot summers, mild winters
Mild to hot summers, cold winters

High Season
(Jun–Aug)
○ Hot weather

○ Expect crowds; book ahead

○ İstanbul's high season April, May, September and October

○ Christmas–New Year and Easter also busy, expensive periods

Shoulder
(May & Sep)
○ Fewer crowds

○ Most businesses open; prices drop

○ Warm spring/ autumn temperatures likely, especially in the southwest

○ İstanbul's shoulder season June to August

Low Season
(Oct–Apr)
○ Few travellers

○ Accommodation in tourist areas may close

○ Accommodation discounts of 20% or more

○ İstanbul's low season November to March

Advance Planning

○ **Three months before** Book accommodation for popular areas. Check your passport will be valid for six months minimum after entering Turkey.

○ **One month before** Update travel vaccinations. Book cultural activities – performances, festivals, cooking classes and walking tours.

○ **One week before** Check if visa needed on arrival and how much it costs. If visiting southeastern Anatolia, check news about the Kurdish issue and Syrian unrest. Check if any public or Islamic holidays are happening.

Your Daily Budget

Budget less than ₺135

○ Budget hotel double: less than ₺80 (İstanbul ₺165)

○ Rooms often include breakfast

○ Take night buses and trains to skip accommodation costs

○ Minimise your time in pricey İstanbul

Midrange ₺135–350

○ Midrange hotel double: ₺80–420

○ Licensed eateries more expensive

○ Buses, trains and flights often cheaper than hire cars

Top End more than ₺350

○ Top-end hotel double: from ₺170 (İstanbul ₺420)

○ Top-end restaurant main: more than ₺17.50 (İstanbul ₺25)

○ Hot-air balloon flight in Cappadocia: about ₺405

Exchange Rates

Australia	A$1	₺1.88
Canada	C$1	₺1.81
Europe	€1	₺2.35
Japan	¥100	₺2.13
New Zealand	NZ$1	₺1.51
UK	£1	₺2.89
USA	US$1	₺1.78

For current exchange rates see www.xe.com.

What to Bring

○ **Credit cards** Often needed for hiring cars; you may prefer to withdraw money using a debit card.

○ **Euros/dollars** To buy visitor visas and use in İstanbul and tourist areas.

○ **Handwash, soap and toilet roll** Budget accommodation options often don't provide soap and toilet rolls in bathrooms.

○ **Oral rehydration salts** Hot weather and spicy food mean traveller's diarrhoea is not uncommon.

○ **Demure clothing** For visiting mosques and wearing around staunchly Islamic cities.

Arriving in Turkey

○ **İstanbul Atatürk & Sabiha Gökçen International Airports**

Havataş (Havaş) Airport Bus To Taksim Sq every 30 minutes (₺10 to ₺12)

Metro From Atatürk to Zeytinburnu, then tram to centre (₺4)

Taxi From Atatürk/Sabiha Gökçen to Sultanahmet ₺40/120

Getting Around

○ **Air** Extensive domestic networks from İstanbul and Ankara. A good option for long journeys.

○ **Boat** Ferry across Sea of Marmara convenient from İstanbul to Bursa, Çanakkale and İzmir.

○ **Bus** Fast, comfortable and efficient; extensive network throughout the country.

○ **Hired transport** Metered taxis plentiful in cities. Hire cars widely available.

○ **Public transport** Buses and dolmuşes (minibuses) plentiful in cities. Several cities have trams, metros and taksi dolmuşes (shared taxis).

○ **Train** Slow, apart from high-speed Ankara–Konya line. Trains to eastern Anatolia depart from Ankara, not İstanbul, at least to 2014.

Accommodation

○ **Boutique hotels** Renovated properties with mod cons and bags of character.

○ **Pensions** Family-run guesthouses offering local charm.

○ **Hotels** Range from budget to palatial top-end establishments.

Be Forewarned

○ **Southeastern Anatolia** Affected by fighting in Syria and between Turkish army and Kurdish rebels.

○ **Relationships** Do not be overly tactile in public. Women should beware miscommunications with local men and preconceptions about female Westerners.

○ **Holidays** Many businesses close over major public holidays. Muslims fast during Ramazan.

○ **Criticising Atatürk** Criticising Atatürk and Turkish nationalism is illegal.

İstanbul

Some ancient cities are the sum of their monuments. But others, such as İstanbul, factor a lot more into the equation. In the former Byzantine and Ottoman capital, you can start the day visiting the churches and mosques left by the two empires, shop in chic boutiques during the afternoon and party all night at glamorous clubs. In the space of a few minutes you can hear the evocative strains of the call to prayer issuing from the Old City's tapering minarets, the sonorous horn of a crowded commuter ferry crossing between Europe and Asia, and the strident cries of street hawkers selling fresh seasonal produce.

Ask locals to describe what they love about İstanbul and they'll shrug, give a small smile and say merely that there is no other place like it. Spend a few days in this marvellous metropolis, and you'll know exactly what they mean.

Aya Sofya (p69) and downtown İstanbul

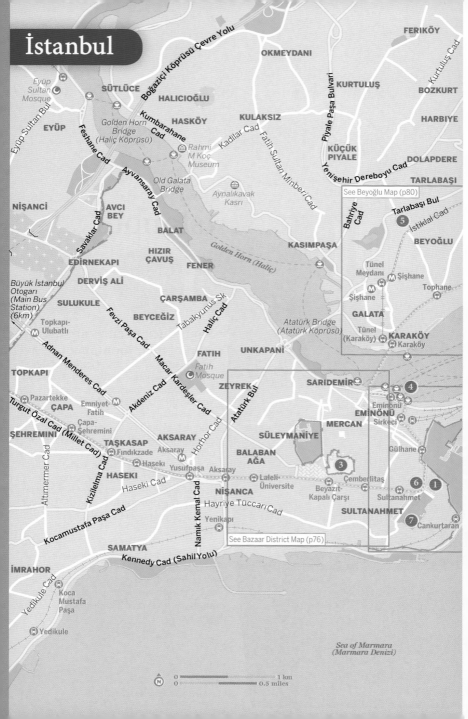

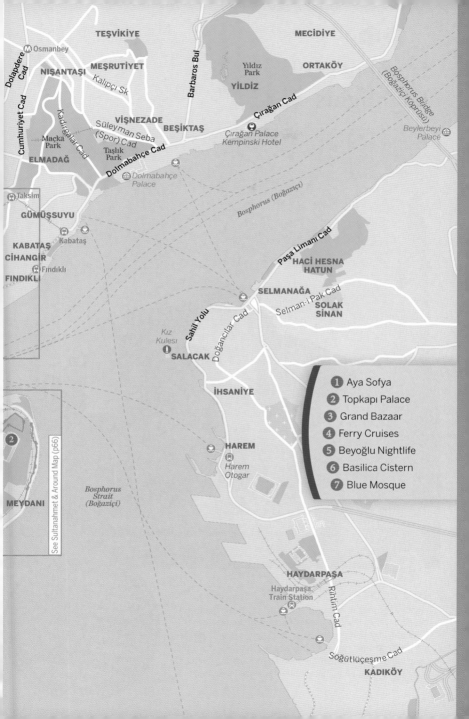

TEŞVİKİYE

Osmanbey

Dolapdere Cad

NIŞANTAŞI

MEŞRUTİYET

Kalıpçı Sk

VİŞNEZADE

Barbaros Bul

MECIDİYE

Yıldız Park

ORTAKÖY

YİLDİZ

Çırağan Cad

Bosphorus Bridge (Boğaziçi Köprüsü)

Cumhuriyet Cad

Kadırgalar Cad

Maçka Park

ELMADAĞ

Süleyman Seba (Spor) Cad

BEŞİKTAŞ

Çırağan Palace Kempinski Hotel

Beylerbeyi Palace

Taşlık Park

Dolmabahçe Cad

Dolmabahçe Palace

Taksim

GÜMÜŞSUYU

Bosphorus (Boğaziçi)

KABATAŞ

Kabataş

CİHANGİR

Paşa Limanı Cad

FINDIKLI

Fındıklı

HACİ HESNA HATUN

SELMANAĞA

Selman-i Pak Cad

SOLAK SİNAN

Kız Kulesi

Sahil Yolu

Doğancılar Cad

SALACAK

İHSANİYE

See Sultanahmet & Around Map (p66)

MEYDANI

HAREM

Harem Otogar

Bosphorus Strait (Boğaziçi)

1 Aya Sofya

2 Topkapı Palace

3 Grand Bazaar

4 Ferry Cruises

5 Beyoğlu Nightlife

6 Basilica Cistern

7 Blue Mosque

HAYDARPAŞA

Haydarpaşa Train Station

Rıhtım Cad

Söğütlüçeşme Cad

KADIKÖY

İstanbul's Highlights

① Aya Sofya

History resonates when you visit this majestic Byzantine basilica (p69). Built by order of Emperor Justinian in the 6th century AD, its soaring dome, huge nave and glittering gold mosaics make it both İstanbul's most revealing time capsule and one of the world's most beautiful buildings. Top Right: Last Judgement mosaic; Bottom Right: Omphalion

Need to Know

TOP TIP Museum Pass İstanbul (www.muze.gov.tr/museum_pass) gives discounted entrance. **CROWDS** Go early or late to avoid the hordes. **For further coverage, see p69**

Aya Sofya Don't Miss List

BY GAMZE ARTAMAN,
PROFESSIONAL TOUR GUIDE

1 'FLOATING' DOME

This dome changed the history of architecture. In a wholly original manner, they applied a circular plan on top of a rectangular plan; the cupola resting on four triangular pendentives implements the transition from the dome's circular base to the rectangular base below. For almost a thousand years there was no building better than this. To exceed the Aya Sofya was the dream of all architects and engineers, their inspiration to build higher domes and larger churches.

2 APSE

The beautiful mosaic in the apse of Child Jesus in the lap of his mother, Mary, is flanked by Arabic inscriptions relating to Allah and Mohammed. It's amazing to find two religions together, and to see this kind of composition in a 99% Muslim country.

3 DEESIS (LAST JUDGEMENT) MOSAIC

This scene in the south gallery upstairs has some interesting features, such as the way Mary and John the Baptist are depicted. Their emotions are clearly visible, which is very unusual for the 12th century, especially before the Renaissance. Maybe the artists of Constantinople were about to start their own Renaissance, but alas, the Ottomans arrived! Indeed, early Renaissance art has a considerable amount of Byzantine influence.

4 OMPHALION (CORONATIONS AREA)

The church was not simply a place of worship, and many important ceremonies happened here: on this ornate floor, Byzantine emperors were crowned. It's a unique section of flooring, composed of circles of granite, red and green porphyry and verd antique (serpentine) in a technique called *opus sectile* (cutting thin sections of coloured stone to make elaborate inlaid floors).

5 'PRESENTATION' MOSAIC

As you leave the building, be sure to look back to admire this 10th-century scene, in which the Byzantine emperor Justinian, who built the Aya Sofya, presents the church to Mary, and Constantine the Great offers her the city.

Topkapı Palace

The secrets of Ottoman royalty are revealed in this opulent palace (p73) complex at Seraglio Point. A series of mad, sad and downright bad sultans lived here with their concubines and courtiers between 1465 and 1830, leaving extravagant relics of their folly, intrigue, excess, patronage, diplomacy and war. Below: Palace interior; Top Right: Spoon Maker's Diamond in the Treasury; Bottom Right: Marble Terrace

Need to Know

TOP TIP The Harem is well worth the extra ₺15. GUIDES Organise a tour in advance or opt for the rudimentary audio guide (₺10). For further coverage, see p73

2

Topkapı Palace Don't Miss List

BY ATILLA TUNA, CHIEF GUIDE AT İSTANBUL WALKS

1 HAREM

This is not only the most fascinating place in the palace, but in all İstanbul: the home of the Ottoman sultans. The sultan's office was here, so he spent much of his time here when in İstanbul. The Harem remained largely secret despite the interest of the outside world, and once you step into the labyrinthine corridors of this amazing structure, you will find yourself in an unknown world full of stories. Just imagine that, once upon a time, between the silent walls of this extraordinary building, the sounds of laughter and tears of concubines, eunuchs and sultans were heard.

2 TREASURY

An exhibition not to be missed, this spectacular collection includes emeralds, pearls and jade – an endless variety of precious stones. Watch the movie *Topkapi* (with Melina Mercouri and Peter Ustinov) before visiting the Treasury, and remember your 'spiritual spectacles' – or your glittering eyes will be overcome with excitement.

3 DIVANHANE

The Divanhane is the best illustration of the modesty and simplicity of the Ottoman world. This was the administration building of one of the most powerful empires in history, yet it doesn't try to show the power of the emperor, but rather his spiritual simpleness. Inside, you won't find a throne for the sultan, but a gold-plated iron frame where he would watch government meetings. A simple window was the symbol of his power.

4 STABLES

In front of the stables, look around you: there is nothing to see but walls. However, careful eyes will notice a little mosque built by a chief eunuch, the walls of the dormitory of the guardians of the Harem, and the stable building itself. There are normally temporary exhibitions about Ottoman history in this peaceful section of the palace.

5 MARBLE TERRACE (MECIDIYE KIOSK)

The views of the Bosphorus and Sea of Marmara will take your breath away!

57

Grand Bazaar

You could spend a day buying souvenirs or just getting lost in this atmospheric bazaar (p72), which has been open for business since 1461. Peep through doorways to discover hidden *hans* (caravanserais), explore narrow laneways to watch artisans at work, and wander the thoroughfares to differentiate the treasures from the tourist tack. It's obligatory to drink lots of tea, compare prices and try your hand at bargaining.

3

YAĞLIKÇILAR CAD.
FERACECILER SK.
ZENNECİLER SK.
SARIHACIHASAN SK.
HALICILAR CAD.
SİPAHİ SK.
KALPAKÇILAR CAD.

ŞARK
KAHVESİ

Ferry Cruises

4

Straddling Europe and Asia, İstanbul is the only city in the world where you can board a commuter ferry and, 20 minutes later, arrive on another continent. A quick return trip to Üsküdar or Kadıköy on the Asian shore is thrilling, with seagulls screeching around the boat as it crosses the strait. For the full Bosphorus experience, cruise up to the Black Sea, past Ottoman palaces and waterfront mansions (p85). Ferry on the Bosphorus passing Dolmabahçe Palace (p94)

Beyoğlu Nightlife

5

Sultanahmet may have the Aya Sofya and Blue Mosque, but Beyoğlu has enough rooftop bars, *meyhanes* (Turkish taverns), nargile (water pipe) cafes, restaurants and nightclubs to satisfy the hardiest night owl. Wander the lanes leading off İstiklal Caddesi (p79) between the dusk and dawn calls to prayer and you'll see that even after 1700 years of existence, İstanbul is a city that never stops. Bars on Nevizade Sokak (p94)

6

7

Basilica Cistern

İstanbul's largest surviving Byzantine cistern (p65) provides cool relief on a hot day. Walking between the pillars on raised wooden platforms, you'll feel water dripping from the vaulted ceiling and see ghostly carp patrolling the water. A scholar rediscovered the cistern in 1545, after locals told him they could miraculously obtain water (and even catch fish) by lowering buckets into a dark space below their basement floors.

Blue Mosque

The wonderfully curvaceous exterior of İstanbul's signature building (p64), Sultan Ahmet I's grand project, features a cascade of domes and six tapering minarets. Inside, the huge space is encrusted with thousands of blue İznik tiles, which give the Sultan Ahmet Camii its unofficial name. Beloved of tourists and locals alike, the 17th-century mosque and Aya Sofya bookend Sultanahmet Park in a truly extraordinary fashion.

Istanbul's Best...

People Watching

○ **İstiklal Caddesi** (p79) Window-shopping locals stream along modern İstanbul's thoroughfare.

○ **Tophane Nargile Cafes** (p102) Apple tobacco smoke scents the air as televised football matches fire everyone up.

○ **Nevizade Sokak** (p94) Beyoğlu's outdoor drinking enclave hosts boisterous crowds on weekend evenings.

○ **Divan Yolu** (p76) Traders, tourists and touts flow between Sultanahmet and the Grand Bazaar.

Ottoman Palaces

○ **Topkapı Palace** (p73) Centuries of court intrigue writ large in the sprawling Harem.

○ **Dolmabahçe Palace** (p94) The imperial dynasty's final, 19th-century flourish.

○ **Çırağan Palace** (p85) Next to the Dolmabahçe and now a luxury hotel.

○ **Beylerbeyi Palace** (p85) Baroque-style, with whimsical marble bathing pavilions.

○ **Küçüksu Kasrı** (p85) Rococo summer palace, with ornate cast-iron fence, boat dock and wedding-cake exterior.

Rooftop Bars

○ **360** (p97) The name summarises the view from this stylish Beyoğlu bar-restaurant.

○ **Leb-i Derya** (p97) Off İstiklal Caddesi, with Bosphorus and Old City views.

○ **Mikla** (p97) Atop a towering hotel above the Golden Horn.

○ **Litera** (p97) Views of the city's Asian side from the 5th floor.

○ **X Bar** (p99) Golden Horn vistas from atop a cultural centre.

Need to Know

Mimar Sinan Buildings

○ **Mihrimah Sultan Mosque** (p84) One of the great Ottoman architect's best works.

○ **Ayasofya Hürrem Sultan Hamamı** (p86) Still-functioning 16th-century hamam opposite Aya Sofya.

○ **Rüstem Paşa Mosque** (p78) Showcases supreme architecture and İznik tilework.

○ **Süleymaniye Mosque** (p72) One of the grandest imperial mosques.

○ **Sokollu Şehit Mehmet Paşa Mosque** (p84) Has some of the finest İznik tiles ever made.

RESOURCES

○ **Culinary Backstreets** (www.culinarybackstreets.com)

○ **İstanbul Beat** (www.istanbulbeatblog.com)

○ **Sirkeci Restaurants** (sirkecirestaurants.com)

GETTING AROUND

○ **Airport shuttle** Havataş (Havaş) buses travel in from both airports.

○ **Funicular** Climbs from Karaköy (near Galata Bridge) to Tünel Meydanı (for İstiklal Caddesi), and from Kabataş to Taksim Meydanı.

○ **Taxi** Sultanahmet to Taksim Meydanı costs around ₺15.

○ **Tram** Connects Zeytinburnu (for metro to Atatürk airport), Aksaray (for metro to bus station), Beyazıt-Kapalı Çarşı (for Grand Bazaar), Sultanahmet, Karaköy and Kabataş.

BE FOREWARNED

○ **Costs** Prices are similar to Europe; much higher than the rest of Turkey.

○ **Accommodation** Book ahead May to September and for the Christmas–New Year period.

○ **Noise** Accommodation in Cankurtaran (near Sultanahmet) can be noisy, with music from hostels and bars on Akbıyık Caddesi, and calls to prayer from the İşak Paşa Mosque behind Adliye Sokak.

○ **Taxi** Ignore drivers who insist on a fixed rate; these are generally pricier than using the meter.

○ **Roads** Avoid during rush hours (7am to 10am and 3pm to 7pm Monday to Saturday) when traffic is nightmarish, particularly on Bosphorus bridges.

○ **Driving** When leaving İstanbul, hire a car from one of the airports, thus avoiding the city centre's manic roads.

Left: Leb-i Derya (p97);
Above: Dolmabahçe Palace (p94)

İstanbul Walking Tour

This historical stroll around the Old City's highlights starts with Byzantine finery and proceeds past Ottoman tombs and minarets to the Grand Bazaar, in business since 1461. Cafes and çay bahçesi (tea gardens) are never far away.

WALK FACTS

- **Start** Aya Sofya
- **Finish** Grand Bazaar
- **Distance** 2km
- **Duration** Four to five hours

1 Aya Sofya

Take a deep breath and enter this overwhelming Byzantine basilica, its glittering **mosaics** depicting emperors and empresses alongside Jesus and Mary. When Justinian first entered the masterwork he had commissioned, he exclaimed, 'Glory to God that I have been judged worthy of such a work. Oh Solomon! I have outdone you!' Almost 1500 years later, stepping beneath the seemingly **floating dome**, you will share the emperor's excitement.

2 Aya Sofya Tombs

Look out for these ornate tombs, the final resting places of five Ottoman sultans. The great Ottoman architect Mimar Sinan designed two, and many royal children, including 19 of Murad III's sons, are buried here. It was customary for Ottoman heirs to kill their younger brothers in order to safeguard their accession; later, junior siblings were confined to the *kafes* (cage) in Topkapı Palace (Topkapı Sarayı).

3 Blue Mosque

The exterior of Sultan Ahmet's grand mosque, with its cascade of domes and six slender minarets, was an Ottoman retort to the Aya Sofya's wham-bam interior. Its courtyard is the largest of all Ottoman mosques and the thousands of blue **İznik tiles** inside, lit by 260 windows, give the Sultan Ahmet Camii its unofficial name. On busy days, you may prefer to admire the facade without joining the long queue.

Hippodrome

This promenade was a Byzantine chariot racing arena, and the centre of Constantinople life for 1400 years. Wander its length, passing ancient relics such as the well-preserved pink granite **Obelisk of Theodosius**, carved in Egypt around 1500 BC and brought here by Theodosius the Great in AD 390. South of the obelisk, the **Spiral Column** emerges from a hole in the ground. It stood in front of the temple of Apollo at Delphi until AD 330, when Constantine the Great brought it to his new capital city.

5 Grand Bazaar

To reach the famous Grand Bazaar (Kapalı Çarşı), catch the tram two stops from Sultanahmet to Beyazıt-Kapalı Çarsı, or wander through the backstreets from the Hippodrome to Divan Yolu (Ordu) Caddesi, the thoroughfare leading west. En route, you can't miss the tall column known as **Çemberlitaş**, erected to celebrate the dedication of Constantinople as capital of the Roman Empire in AD 330. Wander the bazaar's colourful maze of stalls, checking out the prices, and then prepare to drink some çay and haggle. From here, you can easily continue to the Süleymaniye Mosque or Spice Bazaar (Mısır Çarşısı).

Istanbul in...

TWO DAYS

On day one, follow our walking tour and then relax in Sultanahmet's *çay bahçesis*. For dinner, head over the **Galata Bridge** to the modern side of town, **Beyoğlu**.

Day two should be devoted to **Topkapı Palace** and the Bosphorus. Spend the morning at the palace, then board one of the private excursion boats at Eminönü for a **Bosphorus cruise**. Afterwards, walk up through Galata to **İstiklal Caddesi**, have a drink at a rooftop bar and enjoy dinner at a *meyhane*.

FOUR DAYS

On your third day visit the **İstanbul Archaeology Museums** or **Museum of Turkish & Islamic Arts** in the morning and the **Süleymaniye Mosque** in the afternoon. For dinner, sample the succulent **kebaps** at Hamdi Restaurant or Zübeyir Ocakbaşı.

On day four, descend to the **Basilica Cistern**'s dank depths, before heading to the Golden Horn (Haliç) to explore the **Spice Bazaar** and **Rüstem Paşa Mosque**. Back in Sultanahmet, shop for souvenirs at the **Arasta Bazaar** before hitting **Beyoğlu**'s bar, restaurant and club scenes.

Süleymaniye Mosque (p72)

Discover İstanbul

Sights

The Bosphorus strait, between the Black and Marmara Seas, divides Europe from Asia and Anatolia. On its western shore, European İstanbul is further divided by the Golden Horn (Haliç) into the Old City (aka the Historical Peninsula) and the New City.

At the tip of the Historical Peninsula is Sultanahmet, the centre of İstanbul's Unesco-designated World Heritage Site, where you'll find most of the city's famous monuments. Over Galata Bridge (Galata Köprüsü) on the northern side of the Golden Horn is Beyoğlu.

Sultanahmet & Around

BLUE MOSQUE Mosque
(Sultan Ahmet Camii; Map p66; Hippodrome; ⊙9am-12.15pm, 2-4.30pm & 5.30-6.30pm Sat-Thu, 9-11.15am, 2.30-4.30pm & 5.30-6.30pm Fri; 🚋Sultanahmet) İstanbul's most photogenic building was the grand project of Sultan Ahmet I (r 1603–17), whose **tomb** (Map p66; Kabasakal Caddesi; ⊙9.30am-4.30pm) is located on the north side of the site facing Sultanahmet Park. The mosque's wonderfully curvaceous exterior features a cascade of domes, six slender minarets, and the biggest courtyard of all of Ottoman mosques. Blue İznik tiles adorn the interior and give the building its unofficial but commonly used name.

The mosque's architect, Sedefhar Mehmet Ağa, managed to orchestrate the sort of visual wham-bam effect with the mosque's exterior that Aya Sofya achieved with its interior. The interior has a similarly grand scale, with İznik tiles

Aya Sofya tombs
CINDY HOPKINS/ALAMY ©

in the tens of thousands, 260 windows and huge central prayer space. In the courtyard, which is the same size as the interior, you'll appreciate the building's perfect proportions.

Admission is controlled so as to preserve the mosque's sacred atmosphere. Tourists must use the north door (follow the signs).

GREAT PALACE MOSAIC MUSEUM   Museum

(Map p66; Torun Sokak; admission ₺8; ⏰9am-6.30pm Tue-Sun Apr-Oct, to 4.30pm Nov-Mar; 🚇Sultanahmet) When archaeologists excavated around the Arasta Bazaar at the rear of the Blue Mosque, they uncovered a stunning early Byzantine mosaic pavement featuring hunting and mythological scenes. It was restored and is now preserved in this museum.

Thought to have been added by Justinian to the Great Palace of Byzantium, the pavement is estimated to have measured from 3500 to 4000 sq metres in its original form. The 250-sq-metre section here is the largest discovered remnant.

FREE AYA SOFYA TOMBS   Tombs

(Aya Sofya Müzesi Padişah Türbeleri; Map p66; Kabasakal Caddesi; ⏰9am-5pm; 🚇Sultanahmet) Part of the Aya Sofya complex but entered via Kabasakal Caddesi, these tombs are the final resting places of five Ottoman sultans. The ornate interior decoration features supreme Ottoman tilework, calligraphy and decorative paintwork.

Next to Murad III's tomb is that of his five children; this was designed by the great Ottoman architect Mimar Sinan, as was Selim II's tomb. The fifth tomb is Aya Sofya's original baptistry, converted to a mausoleum for sultans İbrahim I and Mustafa I during the 17th century.

HIPPODROME   Park

(Atmeydanı; Map p66; 🚇Sultanahmet) The Byzantine emperors loved nothing more than an afternoon at the chariot races, and this rectangular arena was their venue of choice. In its heyday, it was decorated by obelisks and statues, some of which remain in place today. Recently relandscaped, it is one of İstanbul's most popular promenades.

The Hippodrome was the centre of Byzantium's life for 1000 years and of Ottoman life for another 400 years, and has been the scene of many popular uprisings.

MUSEUM OF TURKISH & ISLAMIC ARTS   Museum

(Türk ve Islam Eserleri Müzesi; Map p66; www.tiem.gov.tr; Atmeydanı Caddesi 46; admission ₺10; ⏰9am-6.30pm Tue-Sun Apr-Oct, to 4.30pm Nov-Mar; 🚇Sultanahmet) This Ottoman palace was built in 1524 for İbrahim Paşa, Süleyman the Magnificent's childhood friend, brother-in-law and grand vizier. It's now home to a magnificent collection of artefacts, including exquisite examples of calligraphy and a collection of antique carpets that is generally held to be the best in the world.

You can enjoy an expertly prepared Turkish coffee in the courtyard.

BASILICA CISTERN   Cistern

(Yerebatan Sarnıçı; Map p66; www.yerebatan.com; Yerebatan Caddesi 13; admission ₺10; ⏰9am-6.30pm; 🚇Sultanahmet) This atmospheric subterranean structure, İstanbul's largest surviving Byzantine cistern, was commissioned by Emperor Justinian and built in 532. It was constructed using 336 columns, many salvaged from ruined temples, and featuring fine carved capitals. Its symmetry and sheer grandeur of conception are quite breathtaking, and its cavernous depths make a great retreat on summer days.

Designed to service the Great Palace and surrounding buildings, the cistern was able to store up to 80,000 cu metres of water delivered via 20km of aqueducts from a reservoir near the Black Sea, but was closed when the Byzantine emperors relocated from the Great Palace. Forgotten by the city authorities some time before the Conquest, it was rediscovered in 1545.

Sultanahmet & Around

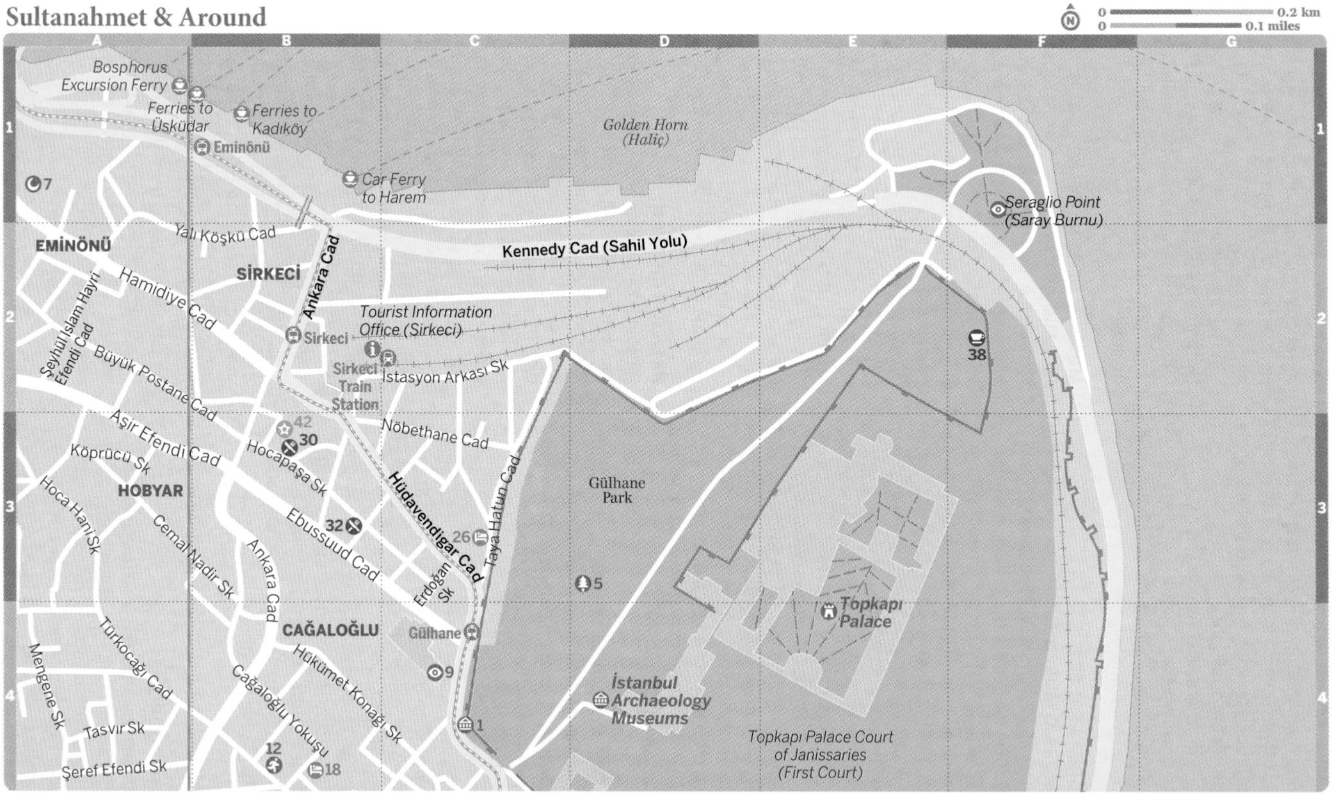

N

0   0.2 km
0   0.1 miles

Golden Horn
(Haliç)

Seraglio Point
(Saray Burnu)

Kennedy Cad (Sahil Yolu)

Bosphorus
Excursion Ferry
Ferries To
Üsküdar
Ferries to
Kadıköy
Eminönü
Car Ferry
to Harem

7

EMINÖNÜ

Şeyhül İslam Hayri
Efendi Cad

Büyük Postane Cad

Hamidiye Cad

Yalı Köşkü Cad

Ankara Cad

SIRKECI

Sirkeci

Tourist Information
Office (Sirkeci)

Sirkeci
Train
Station

İstasyon Arkası Sk

Nöbethane Cad

Taya Hatun Cad

Gülhane
Park

5

Topkapı Palace Court
of Janissaries
(First Court)

Topkapı
Palace

İstanbul
Archaeology
Museums

Hüdavendigar Cad

Erdoğan
Sk

26

Gülhane

9

38

Hocapaşa Sk

42
30

Ebussuud Cad

32

Aşir Efendi Cad

Köprücü Sk

Cemal Nadir Sk

HOBYAR

Hoca Hanı Sk

Ankara Cad

CAĞALOĞLU

Hükümet Konağı Sk

Cağaloğlu Yokuşu

12

18

Türkocağı Cad

Tasvir Sk

Mengene Sk

Şeref Efendi Sk

1

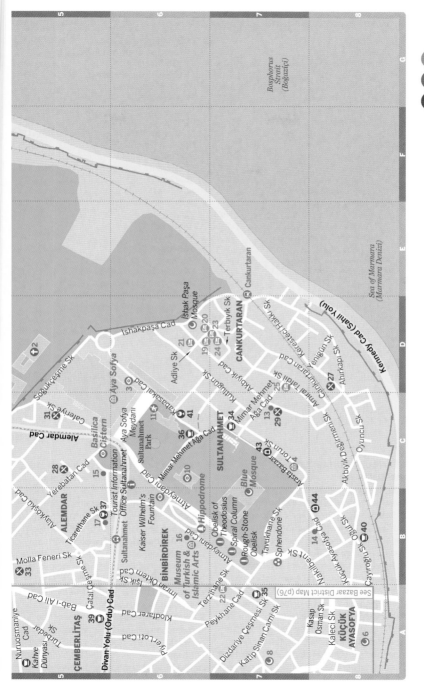

İSTANBUL

Bosphorus Strait (Boğaziçi)

Sea of Marmara (Marmara Denizi)

Kennedy Cad (Sahil Yolu)

Cankurtaran

CANKURTARAN

SULTANAHMET

ÇEMBERLİTAŞ

ALEMDAR

BİNBİRDİREK

KÜÇÜK AYASOFYA

See Bazaar District Map (p76)

Divan Yolu (Ordu) Cad

Aya Sofya

Aya Sofya Meydanı

Sultanahmet Park

Basilica Cistern

Blue Mosque

Hippodrome

Museum of Turkish & Islamic Arts

Kaiser Wilhelm's Fountain

Tourist Information Office Sultanahmet

Ishak Paşa Mosque

Obelisk of Theodosius

Spiral Column

Rough-Stone Obelisk

Sphendone

67

Sultanahmet & Around

İSTANBUL ARCHAEOLOGY MUSEUMS
Museum

(Map p66; www.istanbularkeologi.gov.tr; Osman Hamdi Bey Yokuşu, Gülhane; admission ₺10; ◷9am-6pm Tue-Sun mid-Apr–Sep, to 4pm Oct–mid-Apr; ☐Gülhane) This superb museum houses archaeological and artistic treasures from the Topkapı collections. Its exhibits include ancient artefacts, classical statuary and objects showcasing Anatolian history.

The complex can be easily reached by walking down the slope from Topkapı's First Court, or by walking uphill from the main gate of Gülhane Park. It has three main parts, housing the palace collections formed during the late 19th century.

Located immediately on the left after you enter the complex, the **Museum of the Ancient Orient** has a collection of pre-Islamic items collected from the expanse of the Ottoman Empire.

On the opposite side of the courtyard is the **Archaeology Museum**, with an extensive collection of classical statuary and sarcophagi plus a sprawling exhibit documenting İstanbul's history. After entering, in the second of the dimly lit rooms on the left, is the famous marble **Alexander Sarcophagus**, one of the most accomplished of all classical artworks. On the floor above the famed Statuary Galleries (closed for renovation at the time of publication), accessed

BJORN HOLLAND/GETTY IMAGES ©

Don't Miss Aya Sofya

This venerable structure – commissioned by the great Byzantine emperor Justinian, consecrated as a church in 537, converted to a mosque by Mehmet the Conqueror in 1453 and declared a museum by Atatürk in 1935 – stands out even among İstanbul's many important monuments, with its innovative architectural form, rich history, religious importance and extraordinary beauty. See p55 for more information.

As you enter and walk into the inner narthex, look up to see a brilliant mosaic of *Christ as Pantocrator (Ruler of All)* above the third and largest door (the Imperial Door). Through this is the building's main space, famous for its dome, huge nave and gold mosaics.

Ottoman additions include a *mimber* (pulpit), *mihrab* (prayer niche indicating the direction of Mecca) and the *hünkar mahfili* elevated kiosk.

In the side aisle to the northeast of the Imperial Door is the **Weeping Column**, with a worn copper facing pierced by a hole. Legend has it that the pillar was blessed by St Gregory the Miracle Worker and that putting one's finger into the hole can lead to ailments being healed if the finger emerges moist.

At the top of the switchback ramp at the northern end of the inner narthex, a large circle of green marble marks the spot where the throne of the empress once stood. In the upstairs galleries, look out for the Byzantine mosaics depicting the emperors and empresses with Christ and Mary.

Exit through the magnificent bronze Beautiful Gate (2nd century BC). Just before you exit the building, a doorway on the left leads into a small courtyard, which was part of a 6th-century baptistry – converted in the 17th century to a tomb for two sultans.

NEED TO KNOW

Hagia Sophia; Map p66; www.ayasofyamuzesi.gov.tr; Aya Sofya Meydanı 1; adult/under 12yr ₺25/free; ⊗9am-6pm Tue-Sun mid-Apr–Sep, to 4pm Oct–mid-Apr; 🚇Sultanahmet

Aya Sofya

Timeline

537 Emperor Justinian, depicted in one of the church's famous **mosaics** ❶, presides over the consecration of Byzantium's new basilica, Hagia Sophia (Church of the Holy Wisdom).

557 The huge **dome** ❷, damaged during an earthquake, collapses and is rebuilt.

843 The second Byzantine Iconoclastic period ends and figurative **mosaics** ❸ begin to be added to the interior. These include a depiction of the Empress Zoe and her third husband, Emperor Constantine IX Monomakhos.

1204 Soldiers of the Fourth Crusade led by the Doge of Venice, Enrico Dandolo, conquer and ransack Constantinople. Dandolo's **tomb** ❹ is eventually erected in the church whose desecration he presided over.

1453 The city falls to the Ottomans; Mehmet II orders that Hagia Sophia be converted to a mosque and renamed Aya Sofya.

1577 Sultan Selim II is buried in a specially designed tomb, which sits alongside the **tombs** ❺ of four other Ottoman Sultans in Aya Sofya's grounds.

1847–49 Sultan Abdül Mecit I orders that the building be restored and redecorated; the huge **Ottoman Medallions** ❻ in the nave are added.

1935 The mosque is converted into a museum by order of Mustafa Kemal Atatürk, president of the new Turkish Republic.

2009 The face of one of the four **seraphs** ❼ is uncovered during major restoration works in the nave.

2012 Restoration of the exterior walls and western upper gallery commences.

TOP TIPS

● Bring binoculars if you want to properly view the mosaic portraits in the apse and under the dome.

KIMBERLEY COOLE/GETTY IMAGES ©

Ottoman Medallions
These huge medallions are inscribed with gilt Arabic letters giving the names of God (Allah), Mohammed and the early caliphs Ali and Abu Bakr.

Imperial Loge

Omphalion

Imperial Door

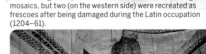

Seraph Figures
The four huge seraphs at the base of the dome were originally mosaics, but two (on the western side) were recreated as frescoes after being damaged during the Latin occupation (1204–61).

EYE UBIQUITOUS/ALAMY ©

Dome
Soaring 56m from ground level, the dome was originally covered in gold mosaics but was decorated with calligraphy during the 1847–49 restoration works overseen by Swiss-born architects Gaspard and Giuseppe Fossati.

Christ Enthroned with Empress Zoe and Constantine IX Monomakhos
This mosaic portrait in the upper gallery depicts Zoe, one of only three Byzantine women to rule as empress in their own right.

Ottoman Tombs
The tombs of five Ottoman sultans and their families are located in Aya Sofya's southern corner and can be accessed via Kabasakal Caddesi. One of these occupies the church's original Baptistry.

Aya Sofya Tombs

Former Baptistry

Astronomer's House & Workshop

Ablutions Fountain

Exit

Primary School

Main Entrance

Grave of Enrico Dandolo
The Venetian doge died in 1205, only one year after he and his Crusaders had stormed the city. A 19th-century marker in the upper gallery indicates the probable location of his grave.

Constantine the Great, the Virgin Mary and the Emperor Justinian
This 11th-century mosaic shows Constantine (right) offering the Virgin Mary the city of Constantinople. Justinian (left) is offering her Hagia Sophia.

behind the cloakroom, is the fascinating exhibition **İstanbul Through the Ages**, which traces the city's history through its neighbourhoods, during periods from Archaic to Ottoman. The exhibition continues downstairs, where an impressive gallery showcases Byzantine artefacts.

Built in 1472 as an outer pavilion of Topkapı Palace (with an 18th-century portico), the **Tiled Pavilion** holds Turkey's best collection of Seljuk, Anatolian and Ottoman tiles and ceramics; these date from the end of the 12th century to the beginning of the 20th century.

GÜLHANE PARK   Park
(Gülhane Parkı; Map p66; 🚇Gülhane) Gülhane Park was once the outer garden of Topkapı Palace, accessed only by the royal court. These days, locals come here to picnic under the trees, promenade past the formally planted flowerbeds and enjoy views over the Golden Horn and Sea of Marmara from the Set Üstü Çay Bahçesi (p102).

Bazaar District

GRAND BAZAAR   Market
(Kapalı Çarşı, Covered Market; Map p76; www.kapalicarsi.org.tr; ⏰9am-7pm Mon-Sat; 🚇Beyazıt-Kapalı Çarşı) This colourful and chaotic bazaar has been the heart of the Old City for centuries. Starting as a small vaulted *bedesten* (warehouse) in 1461, it grew to cover a vast area as laneways between the *bedesten*, neighbouring shops and *hans* (caravanserais) were roofed and the market assumed the sprawling, labyrinthine form that it retains today. Allow at least three hours for your visit; some travellers spend days!

SÜLEYMANIYE MOSQUE   Mosque
(Map p76; Prof Sıddık Sami Onar Caddesi; 🚇Beyazıt-Kapalı Çarşı) This local landmark crowns one of İstanbul's seven hills and dominates the Golden Horn. Though it's not the largest Ottoman mosque, it is one of the grandest, and retains many of its original *külliye* (mosque complex) buildings.

Commissioned by Süleyman the Magnificent and designed by the great Mimar Sinan, the Süleymaniye was the fourth imperial mosque constructed in İstanbul (built between 1550 and 1557). The four minarets with 10 *şerefes* (balconies) are said to symbolise that Süleyman was the fourth Osmanlı sultan to rule the city and the 10th sultan after the establishment of the empire.

In the garden behind the mosque is a terrace offering lovely views. Inside, the building is breathtaking in its size and pleasing in its simplicity. Sinan incorporated the four buttresses into the walls; the result is wonderfully 'transparent' (open and airy) and reminiscent of the Aya Sofya, with a dome nearly as large as the Byzantine basilica's.

Süleymaniye Mosque
GEORGE TSAFOS/GETTY IMAGES ©

MURAT TANER/GETTY IMAGES ©

Don't Miss **Topkapı Palace**

Libidinous sultans, ambitious courtiers, beautiful concubines and scheming eunuchs lived and worked here between the 15th and 19th centuries, when Topkapı was the court of the Ottoman empire. Visiting the palace's opulent pavilions, jewel-filled Treasury and sprawling Harem gives a fascinating glimpse into their lives. See p57 for more information.

Through the Imperial Gate is the **First Court**. Buy tickets to the palace at the main ticket office just outside the Middle Gate, which leads to the **Second Court**. Here, the Palace Kitchens exhibit Chinese celadon porcelain, and the Outer Treasury displays arms and armour.

The entrance to the **Harem** is on the court's western side. Far from being a place of debauchery, these were the imperial family quarters, governed by tradition, obligation and ceremony. The sumptuous 300-room complex has six floors; only one floor can be visited.

The **Third Court**, the sultan's private domain, is entered through the Gate of Felicity. The Dormitory of the Expeditionary Force houses imperial robes, talismanic shirts, kaftans and uniforms worked in silver and gold thread. The Sacred Safekeeping Rooms house relics of the Prophet, and sultans' portraits hang in the Dormitory of the Privy Chamber. On the court's eastern edge, the **Treasury** features an incredible collection of objects made from or decorated with gold, silver, rubies, emeralds, jade, pearls and diamonds. The most famous is the Topkapı Dagger. Be sure to admire the Bosphorus views from the terrace.

Pleasure pavilions occupy the **Fourth Court**, including the Mecidiye Köşkü. Up the stairs at the end of the nearby Tulip Garden is the Marble Terrace.

NEED TO KNOW

Topkapı Sarayı; Map p66; www.topkapisarayi.gov.tr; Babıhümayun Caddesi; palace ₺25, Harem ₺15; ⏰9am-6pm Wed-Mon mid-Apr–Sep, to 4pm Oct–mid-Apr, Harem closes 4.30pm Apr-Oct, 3.30pm Nov-Mar; 🚇Sultanahmet

Topkapı Palace

Daily Life in the Imperial Court

A visit to this opulent palace compound, with its courtyards, harem and pavilions, offers a fascinating glimpse into the lives of the Ottoman sultans. During its heyday, royal wives and children, concubines, eunuchs and servants were among the 4000 people living within Topkapı's walls.

The sultans and their families rarely left the palace grounds, relying on courtiers and diplomats to bring them news of the outside world. Most visitors would go straight to the magnificent Imperial **Council Chamber** ❶, where the sultan's grand vizier and *dîvân* (council) regularly met to discuss affairs of state and receive foreign dignitaries. Many of these visitors brought lavish gifts and tributes to embellish the **Imperial Treasury** ❷.

After receiving any guests and meeting with the *dîvân*, the grand vizier would make his way through the ornate **Gate of Felicity** ❸ into the Third Court, the palace's residential quarter. Here, he would brief the sultan on the deliberations and decisions of the *dîvân* in the ornate **Audience Chamber** ❹.

Meanwhile, day-to-day domestic chores and intrigues would be underway in the **Harem** ❺ and servants would be preparing feasts in the massive **Palace Kitchens** ❻. Amid all this activity, the **Marble Terrace** ❼ was a tranquil retreat where the sultan would come to relax, look out over the city and perhaps regret his sequestered lifestyle.

DON'T MISS

○ There are spectacular views from the terrace behind the Imperial Treasury and from the Marble Terrace in the Fourth Court.

Harem
The sultan, his mother and the crown prince had sumptuously decorated private apartments in the harem. The most beautiful of these are the Twin Kiosks (pictured), which were used by the crown prince.

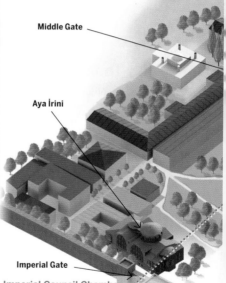

Harem Ticket Office

Middle Gate

Aya İrini

Imperial Gate

Imperial Council Chamber
This is where the Dîvân (Council) made laws, citizens presented petitions and foreign dignitaries were presented to the court. The sultan sometimes eavesdropped on proceedings through the window with the golden grill.

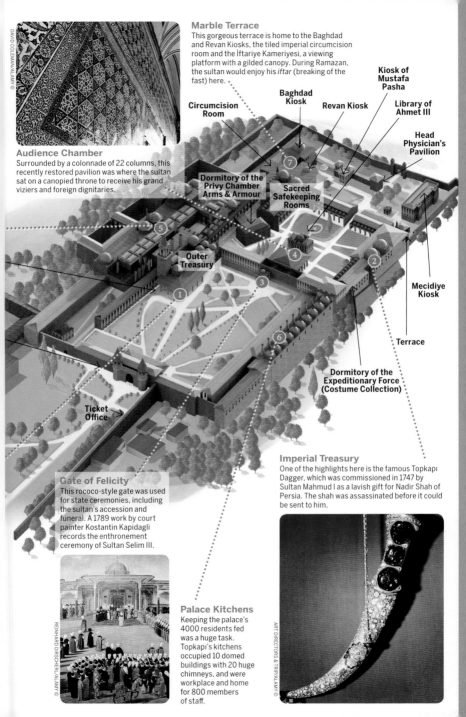

Marble Terrace
This gorgeous terrace is home to the Baghdad and Revan Kiosks, the tiled imperial circumcision room and the İftariye Kameriyesi, a viewing platform with a gilded canopy. During Ramazan, the sultan would enjoy his *iftar* (breaking of the fast) here.

Kiosk of Mustafa Pasha

Baghdad Kiosk

Revan Kiosk

Library of Ahmet III

Circumcision Room

Head Physician's Pavilion

Audience Chamber
Surrounded by a colonnade of 22 columns, this recently restored pavilion was where the sultan sat on a canopied throne to receive his grand viziers and foreign dignitaries.

Dormitory of the Privy Chamber Arms & Armour

Sacred Safekeeping Rooms

Outer Treasury

Mecidiye Kiosk

Terrace

Dormitory of the Expeditionary Force (Costume Collection)

Ticket Office

Gate of Felicity
This rococo-style gate was used for state ceremonies, including the sultan's accession and funeral. A 1789 work by court painter Kostantin Kapidagli records the enthronement ceremony of Sultan Selim III.

Imperial Treasury
One of the highlights here is the famous Topkapı Dagger, which was commissioned in 1747 by Sultan Mahmud I as a lavish gift for Nadir Shah of Persia. The shah was assassinated before it could be sent to him.

Palace Kitchens
Keeping the palace's 4000 residents fed was a huge task. Topkapı's kitchens occupied 10 domed buildings with 20 huge chimneys, and were workplace and home for 800 members of staff.

DAVID COLEMAN/ALAMY ©

REINHARD DIRSCHERL/ALAMY ©

ART DIRECTORS & TRIP/ALAMY ©

Bazaar District

76

200 m
0.1 miles

See Sultanahmet &
Around Map (p66)

Turyol Ferries to
Kadıköy & Üsküdar
Turyol Bosphorus Ferry

EMİNÖNÜ

HOBYAR

Hamidiye Cad
Büyük Postane Cad
Aşır Efendi Cad
Hoca Hanı Sk

Çeşnici Sk
Tarakçı Cafer Sk
Bezciler Sk

Yenicami Sk
Yenicami Cad
Mahmutpaşa Yokuşu
Çarkçılar Sk

TAYA HATUN

Çakmakçılar Yokuşu

SARIDEMIR
Ragıp Gümüşpala Cad

YENİ CAMİ
MEYDANI

Tahmis Sk
Spice/Egyptian
Bazaar
Çiçek Pazarı Sk
Tahtakale Cad
Sabuncu Hanı Cad

Rüstem Paşa
Mosque

Hasırcılar Cad
Tahtakale Sk
Tomruk Sk
Uzunçarşı Cad
Kutucular Cad

TAHTAKALE

MERCAN

Vasıf Çınar Cad
Havancı Sk
Nargileci Sk
Semaver Sk
Mercan Cad

Ragıp Gümüşpala Cad

Prof Cemil Birsel Cad

Şahande Sk

Siyavuşpaşa Sk

Fuat Paşa Cad

Kible Çeşme Cad
Kepenekçi Sabunhanesi Sk
Hayriye Hanım Sk

DEMİRTAŞ

Fetva Yokuşu

Mimar Sinan Cad

Süleymaniye
Mosque

Prof Sıddık Sami
Onar Cad

İstanbul
University

Beyazıt
Tower

Şemsettin Sk

Besim Ömer Paşa Cad

Oluk Sk

Süleymaniye Cad

Kazıl Mescit Sk

Yoğurtçuoğlu Sk

Tavanlı Çeşme Sk

KÜÇÜKPAZAR

Hacı Kadın Cad
Fıızı Külhanı Sk
Sarı Beyazıt Cad
Vefa Cad
Katip Çelebi Sk
Yeri Türhüsü Sk

VEFA

MOLLA
HÜSREV

Cüce Çeşmesi Sk

Vezneciler Cad

Cemal Yener Tosyalı Cad
Dede Efendi Cad
Darülelhan Sk

BALABAN AĞA

Feyziye Cad

Himmet Sk

Monastery
of Christ Pantokrator

İbadethane Sk

Zeyrek Cad

İtfaiye Cad

Atatürk Bul

Revani Çelebi Sk

Aqueduct
of Valens

İslin Sk
Kendir Sk

KALENDERHANE

Şehzade
Mehmet Mosque

Şehzadebaşı Cad

Gençtürk Cad

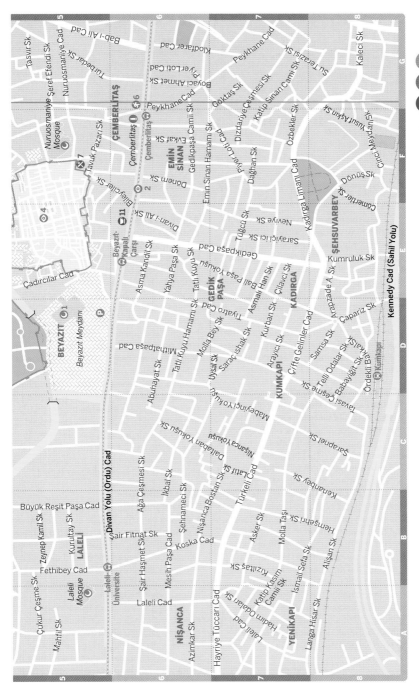

İSTANBUL

Kaleci Sk
Su Terazisi Sk
Katip Sinan Camii Sk
Peykhane Cad
Kloofarer Cad
Boyacı Ahmet Sk
Piyer Loti Cad
Göktaş Sk
Dizdariye Çeşmesi Sk
Özbekler Sk
Yusuf Aşkın Sk
Cinci Meydanı

Tasvir Sk
Şeref Efendi Sk
Bab-ı Ali Cad
Nuruosmaniye Cad
Turbedar Sk

Nuruosmaniye
Mosque

ÇEMBERLİTAŞ
Çemberlitaş
Peykhane Cad
EMİN
SİNAN
Evkaf Sk
Dönem Sk
Gedikpaşa Camii Sk
Emin Sinan Hamamı Sk
Piyer Loti Cad
Dağhan Sk
Kadırga Limanı Cad
Dönüş Sk
Cömertler Sk

ŞEHSUVARBEY

Tavuk Pazarı Sk
Biliycyiler Sk
Divan-ı Ali Sk
Nevriye Sk
Tüğcü Sk
Sarayiçiçi Sk
Kumruluk Sk

Beyazıt
Kapalı
Çarşı
Asma Kandil Sk
Yahya Paşa Sk
Tatlı Kuyu Sk
Gedikpaşa Cad
Balı Paşa Yokuşu Sk
Çılavcı Sk
Asmalı Han Sk

Çadırcılar Cad

BEYAZIT
Beyazıt Meydanı
Mithatpaşa Cad
Tatlı Kuyu Hamamı Sk
Tiyatro Cad
GEDİK
PAŞA
KADIRGA
Arabzade A. Sk
Çapariz Sk

Büyük Reşit Paşa Cad
Zeynep Kamil Sk
Kurultay Sk
LALELİ
Divan Yolu (Ordu) Cad
Laleli
Mosque
Fethibey Cad
Çukur Çeşme Sk
Mahfil Sk

Şair Fitnat Sk
Ağa Çeşmesi Sk
Abuhayat Sk
Molla Bey Sk
Uysal Sk
Saraç İshak Sk
Kurban Sk
Arayıcı Sk
Çifte Gelinler Cad
Samsa Sk
Telli Odalar
Babayiğit Sk
Ördekli Bostan Sk
KALE Sk
Kumkapı

KUMKAPI
Tavası Çeşme Sk
Mabeyinci Yokuşu
Şarapnel Sk
Kenanbey Sk

İkbal Sk
Şehnameci Sk
Koska Cad
Balaban Yokuşu Sk
Nişanca Yokuşu
Latif Sk
Türkeli Cad
Asker Sk
Molla Taşı
Hemşehri Sk
Alişan Sk

Şair Haşmet Sk
Mesih Paşa Cad
Nişanca Bostan Sk
Kızıltaş Sk
İsmail Sefa Sk

NİSANCA
Azimkar Sk
Laleli Cad
Hayriye Tüccarı Cad
Hadım Odaları Sk
Katip Kasım
Camii Sk
YENİKAPI
Langa Hisar Sk

Üniversite
Laleli Cad

Kennedy Cad (Sahil Yolu)

77

İSTANBUL SIGHTS

Today the *imaret* (soup kitchen), with its charming garden courtyard, houses a restaurant: a lovely place for a çay. On its left-hand side is Lale Bahçesi (p102), set in a sunken courtyard where the the *darüşşifa* (hospital) was located; an atmospheric venue for çay and nargile.

The main entrance to the mosque is accessed via Prof Sıddık Sami Onar Caddesi. To the right (southeast) of the main entrance is the cemetery, home to the **tombs** (Map p76) of Süleyman and his wife Roxelana.

RÜSTEM PAŞA MOSQUE   Mosque
(Rüstem Paşa Camii; Map p76; Hasırcılar Caddesi, Rüstem Paşa; ⊞Eminönü) Nestled in the Tahtakale shopping district, this diminutive mosque is a gem. It dates from 1560, and was designed by Mimar Sinan for Rüstem Paşa, son-in-law and grand vizier of Süleyman the Magnificent. A showpiece of the best Ottoman architecture and tilework, it is thought to have been the prototype for Sinan's greatest work, the Selimiye in Edirne.

The mosque is not at street level. There's a set of stairs on Hasırcılar Caddesi and another on the small street running right (north) off Hasırcılar Caddesi towards the Golden Horn. The preponderance of tiles was Rüstem Paşa's way of signalling his wealth and influence, İznik tiles being particularly expensive and desirable.

SPICE BAZAAR   Market
(Mısır Çarşısı, Egyptian Market; Map p76; ⊙8am-6pm Mon-Sat, 9am-6pm Sun; ⊞Eminönü) Vividly coloured spices are displayed alongside jewel-like *lokum* (Turkish delight) at this Ottoman-era marketplace, providing eye candy for the thousands of tourists and locals who make their way here every day. Stalls also sell dried herbs, caviar, nuts, honey in the comb, dried fruits and *pestil* (fruit pressed into sheets and dried). The well-preserved building is home to one of the city's oldest restaurants, **Pandeli** (Map p76; www.pandeli.com.tr; Spice Bazaar, Eminönü; ⊙noon-4pm Mon-Sat; ⊞Eminönü). Have a tea or coffee here after the tourist crush at lunchtime to see its richly decorated salons. Constructed in the 1660s, in its heyday the bazaar was the last stop for the camel caravans that travelled the Silk Routes from China, India and Persia.

GALATA BRIDGE   Bridge
(Galata Köprüsü; Map p76; ⊞Eminönü or Karaköy) Walk over this bridge at sunset, when the Galata Tower is surrounded by shrieking seagulls, the mosques atop the seven hills of the city are silhouetted against a soft red-pink sky and the evocative scent of apple tobacco wafts out of the nargile cafes under the bridge.

During the day, locals fish and sell everything imaginable on this bridge between Beyoğlu and Eminönü. Underneath are restaurants and cafes; enjoy a beer and nargile while watching the ferries approaching the nearby ferry docks.

Beyoğlu & Around

The suburb of Beyoğlu, rising from the shoreline north of Galata Bridge, was known in the mid-19th century as Pera and acknowledged as the 'European' quarter. After the republic was formed, embassies moved to Ankara and the grand buildings crumbled. However, the '90s brought about a rebirth and Beyoğlu is once again the heart of modern İstanbul.

The best way to see this side of town is to explore by foot. From Sultanahmet, catch the tram to Kabataş and the connecting funicular up to Taksim Meydanı. Then work your way down İstiklal Caddesi, exploring its many side streets. At the foot of the boulevard is Tünel Meydanı; follow Galipdede Caddesi downhill and you will be able to explore the historic Galata neighbourhood before walking across Galata Bridge to Eminönü.

GALATA TOWER   Landmark

(Galata Kulesi; Map p80; www.galatatower. net; Galata Meydanı, Galata; admission ₺12; ⏰9am-8pm; 🚇Karaköy) The cylindrical Galata Tower stands sentry over the approach to 'new' İstanbul. Constructed in 1348, it was the tallest structure in the city for centuries, and it still dominates the skyline north of the Golden Horn. Its vertiginous upper balcony offers 360-degree views.

İSTIKLAL CADDESI   Street

(Independence Ave; Map p80) Beyoğlu's premier boulevard, once called the Grand Rue de Pera, was renamed İstiklal (Independence) in the early years of the Republic. A long pedestrianised strip full of shops, cafes, cinemas and cultural centres, it showcases İstanbul's Janus-like personality, embracing modernity one minute and happily bowing to tradition the next.

At its northern end is the frantically busy square **Taksim Meydanı** (Map p80; 🚇Kabataş, then funicular to Taksim), the modern city's symbolic heart. At its southern end is the relatively tranquil district of Galata, home to crooked

If You Like…
Byzantine History

With the notable exception of the Aya Sofya, the Byzantines' stamp on the city they called Constantinople is fainter than the Ottoman mark. However, there are Byzantine buildings still standing, and remnants of the Bucoleon Palace, Magnaura Palace and Great Palace of Byzantium are intermittently uncovered. The latter, built by Constantine the Great soon after he founded Constantinople in AD 324, once had hundreds of buildings, stretching from the Hippodrome to the Aya Sofya and down the slope. For virtual reconstructions of the city's Byzantine monuments, visit www. byzantium1200.com.

1 LITTLE AYA SOFYA
(Küçük Aya Sofya Camii, SS Sergius & Bacchus Church; Map p66; Küçük Ayasofya Caddesi; 🚇Sultanahmet or Çemberlitaş) Justinian and his wife Theodora built this little church around 530, and it was converted into a mosque around 1500. It is one of İstanbul's most beautiful Byzantine structures, with fine green and red marble columns. Named after Sergius and Bacchus, the patron saints of Christians in the Roman army, it has been known as Küçük (Little) Aya Sofya for much of its existence.

2 AYA İRINI
(Hagia Eirene, Church of the Divine Peace; Map p66; 1st Court, Topkapı Palace; 🚇Sultanahmet) This Byzantine church is on your left as you enter the Topkapı Palace's First Court through the Imperial Gate.

3 FETHIYE MUSEUM
(Fethiye Müzesi, Church of Pammakaristos; Fethiye Caddesi, Çarşamba; admission ₺5; ⏰9am-4.30pm Thu-Tue; 🚌33ES, 90, 44B, 36C, 399B & C from Eminönü, 55T from Taksim) This 13th-century church and 14th-century chapel, visited by Mehmet the Conqueror, are decorated with gold mosaics, and were later converted to a mosque.

cobblestone lanes and traces of a fortified settlement built by 13th-century Genoese merchants.

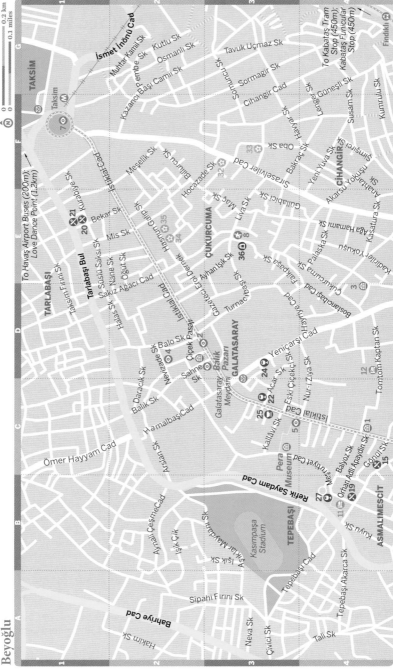

İSTANBUL

Beyoğlu

80

Map labels

TAKSİM

TARLABAŞI

TEPEBAŞI

ASMALIMESCİT

GALATASARAY

ÇUKURCUMA

CİHANGİR

Pera Museum

Galatasaray Meydanı

Balık Pazarı

Çiçek Pasajı

Kasımpaşa Stadium

To Havaş Airport Buses (200m);
Love Dance Point (1.2km)

To Kabataş Tram Stop (450m); Kabataş Funicular Stop (450m)

Fındıklı

Taksim

0.2 km
0.1 miles

Streets:

İsmet İnönü Cad
Muhtar Kamil Sk
Kutlu Sk
Osmanlı Sk
Tavuk Uçmaz Sk
Kazancı Başı Pembe Sk
Kazancı Başı Camii Sk
Sormagır Sk
Sormagır Sk
Cihangir Cad
Lenger Güneşli Sk
Susam Sk
Simsirci Sk
Kumrulu Sk
Oba Sk
Bakraç Sk
Yeni Yuva Sk
Akarsu Yokuşu
Hayvar Sk
Sıraselviler Cad
Ağa Hamamı Sk
Kaşatura Sk
Anahtar Sk
Kadirliler Yokuşu
Gülbahçe Sk
Palaska Sk
Çukurcuma Cad
Çukurcuma Sk
Bostancıbaşı Cad
Hayriye Cad
Yeniçarşı Cad
Eski Çiçekçi Sk
Acar Sk
Nur-i Ziya Sk
Tomtom Kaptan Sk
Kallavi Sk
İstiklal Cad
Büyük Parmakkapı Sk
Liva Sk
Maç Sk
Hocazade Sk
Bilim çık Sk
Meşelik Sk
Kurabiye Sk
Bekar Sk
İstiklal Cad
Meşrutiyet Cad
Refik Saydam Cad
Balyoz Sk
Orhan Adli Apaydın Sk
Gönül Sk
Kuyu Sk
Mis Sk
Öğüt Sk
Sakız Ağacı Cad
Sakız Nane Sk
Süslü Saksı Sk
Halas Sk
Taksim Fırını Sk
Tarlabaşı Bul
Hasnun Galip Sk
Nevizade Sk
Balo Sk
Sahne Sk
Daracık Sk
Balık Sk
Hamalbaşı Cad
Gazeteci Erol Dernek Sk
Turnacıbaşı Sk
Falıkbaşa Sk
Nuru Ziya Sk
Ömer Hayyam Cad
Aynalı Çeşme Cad
Arslan Sk
Işık Çık
Işık Sk
Aşıklar Meydanı
Sipahi Fırını Sk
Neva Sk
Çivici Sk
Bahriye Cad
Hakim Sk
Tali Sk
Tepebaşı Cad
Tepebaşı Akarca Sk

Numbered points:

2, 3, 4, 5, 7, 8, 11, 12, 15, 19, 20, 21, 22, 24, 25, 27, 32, 33, 34, 35, 36

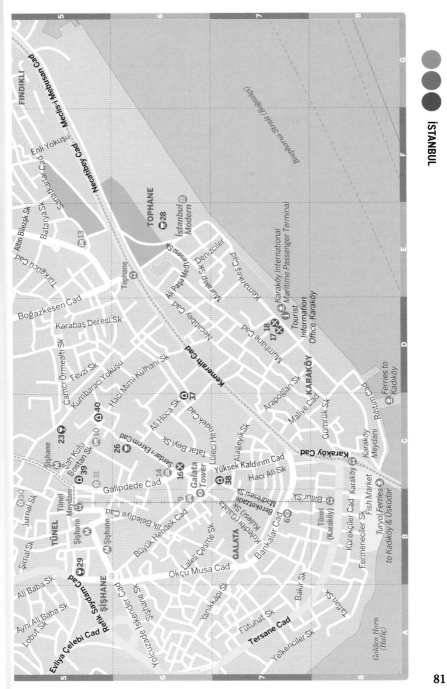

FINDIKLI

Meclis-i Mebusan Cad
Necatibey Cad
Enli Yokuşu
Sanatkarlar Cad
Batarya Sk
Altın Bileзik Sk
Türkücü Cad

TOPHANE

İstanbul Modern
28
13

Boğazkesen Cad
Karabaş Deresi Sk
Fevzi Sk
Camcı Ormealtı Sk
Kumbaracı Yokuşu

Ali Paşa Medresesi Sk
Murakıp Sk
Denizciler

Necatibey Cad
Kemeraltı Cad

Karaköy International
Maritime Passenger Terminal

Kemankeş Cad

Tourist
Information
Office Karaköy

18
17

Hacı Mimi Külhanı Sk
Ali Hoca Sk
37

Münhane Cad

Arapoğlan Sk

KARAKÖY

23
40
10
26
39
31
30

Galipdede Cad

Tatar Beyi Sk
Serdar-ı Ekrem Cad
Lüleci Hendek Cad
Alageyik Sk

14
16
Galata
Tower
Yüksek Kaldırım Cad
38
9

Maliye Cad
Gümrük Sk

Şah Kulu
Bostan Sk

Şişhane
Tünel
Meydanı

Karaköy
Meydanı

Ferries to
Kadıköy

Rıhtım Cad
Karaköy Cad

TÜNEL
Şişhane
Şişhane

İlk Belediye Cad
Büyük Hendek Cad

GALATA

Hacı Ali Sk
Berkeketzade
Madresesi Sk
Kuledibi (Galata
Kulesi) Cad
Bankalar Cad

Tünel
(Karaköy)

6

Kürekçiler Sk
Karaköy
Fish Market
Turyol Ferries
to Kadıköy & Üsküdar

Fermeneciler Sk

Şima Sk
Jurnal Sk

Yolcuzade İskender Cad
Şişhane Cad

Okçu Musa Cad

Yanıkkapı Sk

Bilur Sk

Bakır Sk

Tatlan Sk

Ali Baba Sk
Ayni Ali Baba Sk
Lobut Sk

Evliya Celebi Cad
Refik Saydam Cad
ŞİŞHANE
29

Fütuhat Sk
Tersane Cad
Yelkenciler Sk

Golden Horn
(Haliç)

Bosphorus Strait (Boğaziçi)

81

Beyoğlu

Promenading along the length of İstiklal is the most popular activity in town; huge crowds head here in the early evening and at weekends to browse in boutiques and bookshops, see exhibitions at galleries, listen to the street buskers, drink coffee in chain cafes and party in *meyhanes* (taverns).

PERA MUSEUM   Museum
(Pera Müzesi; Map p80; www.peramuzesi.org.tr; Meşrutiyet Caddesi 65, Tepebaşı; adult/student/child under 12yr ₺10/7/free; ⏱10am-7pm Tue-Sat, noon-6pm Sun; 🚇Karaköy, then funicular to Tünel) Contains a splendid collection of paintings featuring Turkish Orientalist themes. Exhibitions provide fascinating glimpses into the Ottoman world from the 17th to the early 20th century. The most beloved painting in the Turkish canon, *The Tortoise Trainer* (1906), is the standout,

but there's plenty more to see, including Kütahya tiles and ceramics.

Along the Bosphorus

KIZ KULESI   Tower
(🚇Üsküdar) This squat 18th-century tower on a small island on the Asian side of the Bosphorus near Üsküdar featured in the 1999 Bond film *The World is Not Enough*.

KANLICA   Neighbourhood
(🚇Kanlıca) The charming suburb of Kanlıca is famous for its rich and delicious yoghurt, which can be sampled at the two cafes in front of the Kanlıca ferry stop. It's past the Bosphorus Bridge on the Asian side.

FREE **HIDIV KASRI**   Notable Building
(Khedive's Villa; www.beltur.com.tr; Çubuklu Yolu 32, Çubuklu; ⏱9am-10pm; 🚇Kanlıca)

High on a promontory above Kanlıca is Hıdıv Kasrı, an art nouveau villa built by the last khedive of Egypt as a summer residence. Restored after decades of neglect, it now functions as a **restaurant** (mains ₺10-20.50) and **garden cafe** (tosts ₺4-4.50, cake ₺6). The villa is an architectural gem, and the extensive garden is superb, particularly during the İstanbul Tulip Festival in April. To get here from the Kanlıca ferry stop, turn left into Halide Edip Adivar Caddesi and then turn right into the second street (Kafadar Sokak). Turn left into Haci Muhittin Sokağı and walk up the hill until you come to a fork in the road. Take the left fork and follow the 'Hadiv Kasrí' signs to the villa's car park and garden.

SADBERK HANIM MUSEUM   Museum
(☎212-242 3813; www.sadberkhanimmuzesi. org.tr; Piyasa Caddesi 27-29; adult/student ₺7/2; ☺10am-5pm Thu-Tue; ⛴Sarıyer) This museum on the European shore is named after the wife of the late Vehbi Koç, founder of Turkey's foremost commercial empire. There's an eclectic collection here, including beautiful İznik and Kütahya ceramics, Ottoman silk textiles, and Ro-

man coins and jewellery. The museum is in the village of Büyükdere, which is also notable for its churches and the old summer embassies of foreign powers. When the heat and fear of disease increased in the warm months, foreign ambassadors and their staff would retire to these palatial residences, complete with lush gardens. To get here, walk south from the Sarıyer ferry dock for approximately 10 minutes.

ANADOLU KAVAĞI   Neighbourhood
(⛴Anadolu Kavağı) Here, on the Asian shore, the Bosphorus meets the Black Sea. Once a fishing village, Anadolu Kavağı's local economy now relies on the tourism trade and its main square is full of mediocre fish restaurants and their touts.

Perched above the village are the ruins of the medieval castle **Anadolu Kavağı Kalesi** (Yoros Kalesi). First built by the Byzantines, it was restored and reinforced by the Genoese and the Ottomans. Unfortunately, the castle is in such a serious state of disrepair that it has been fenced so that no one can enter and enjoy its spectacular Black Sea views.

Galata Bridge (p78)

If You Like...
Ottoman Architecture

İstanbul's Ottoman history are written on every corner, minaret, dome and doorway.

1 **NEW MOSQUE**
(Yeni Camii; Map p66; Yenicamii Meydanı Sokak, Eminönü; 🚇Eminönü) Dating from 1597; decorated inside with gold leaf, İznik tiles and carved marble.

2 **MIHRIMAH SULTAN MOSQUE**
(Mihrimah Sultan Camii; Ali Kuşçu Sokak, Edirnekapı; 🚌31E, 32, 36K & 38E from Eminönü, 87 from Taksim) This 16th-century mosque features stained-glass windows and 'birdcage' chandelier.

3 **ALAY KÖŞKÜ**
(Parade Kiosk; Map p66; Gülhane Park; 🚇Gülhane) Sultans sat here to watch parades of troops and trade guilds commemorating holidays and military victories.

4 **SUBLIME PORTE**
(Map p66; 🚇Gülhane) Rococo gate leading into the precincts of what was once the grand vizierate (Ottoman prime ministry).

5 **FATIH MOSQUE**
(Fatih Camii, Mosque of the Conqueror; Fevzi Paşa Caddesi, Fatih; 🚌31E, 32, 336E, 36KE & 38E from Eminönü, 87 from Taksim) This 18th-century mosque was constructed after an earthquake toppled the original, İstanbul's first great imperial mosque.

6 **SOKOLLU ŞEHIT MEHMET PAŞA MOSQUE**
(Sokollu Mehmet Paşa Camii; Map p66; cnr Şehit Çeşmesi & Katip Sinan Camii Sokaks, Kadırga; 🚇Sultanahmet or Çemberlitaş) Sinan-designed mosque; decorated with İznik tiles and fragments from the sacred Black Stone in the Kaaba at Mecca.

7 **BEYAZIT MOSQUE**
(Beyazıt Camii, Mosque of Sultan Beyazıt II; Map p76; Beyazıt Meydanı, Beyazıt; 🚇Beyazıt-Kapalı Çarşı) Imperial mosque, with fine stone including marble, verd antique and rare granite.

 Activities

Ferry Cruises

The mighty Bosphorus strait runs from the Sea of Marmara (Marmara Denizi) to the Black Sea (Karadeniz), located 32km north of the city centre. On one side is Asia; on the other, Europe.

A ferry journey – whether a short return trip on a commuter ferry to Kadıköy or Üsküdar, on which you cross from Europe to Asia and back again, or a longer cruise – is an essential activity while you are in İstanbul.

LONG TOURS

Most day-trippers take the *Uzun Boğaz Turu* (Long Bosphorus Tour) operated by **Istanbul Şehir Hatları** (İstanbul City Routes; www.sehirhatlari.com.tr). This travels the entire length of the strait in a 90-minute one-way trip and departs from the Boğaz İskelesi at Eminönü daily at 10.35am. From April to October, there is usually an extra service at 1.35pm, and during summer there is an extra service at noon. A ticket costs ₺25 return (*çift*), ₺15 one way (*tek yön*). The ferry stops at Beşiktaş, Kanlıca, Sarıyer, Rumeli Kavağı and Anadolu Kavağı (the turnaround point). It is not a hop-on, hop-off service; if you disembark, it is not possible to get back on the ferry and continue in the same direction on the same ticket. If you have a return ticket, you can get back to Eminönü from all the ferry stops along the way.

The ferry returns from Anadolu Kavağı at 3pm (plus 4.15pm from April to October).

From April to October, Istanbul Şehir Hatları also operates a two-hour Kısa Boğaz Turu (Short Bosphorus Tour) cruise that leaves Eminönü daily at 2.30pm. It travels as far as the Fatih Bridge before returning to Eminönü. Tickets cost ₺10.

Ferry Trips along the Bosphorus

A ferry trip is a great way to experience the Bosphorus. Hop onto a boat on the Eminönü quay. It's always a good idea to arrive 30 minutes or so before the scheduled departure time and manoeuvre your way to the front of the queue; when the doors open and the boat can be boarded, you'll need to move fast to score a good seat. The best spots are on the sides of the upper deck near the bow.

As you start your trip, you'll see Kız Kulesi (p82) on the Asian side near Üsküdar. Continuing up the Bosphorus you'll pass Ottoman palaces, mansions and summer getaways; keep a look out for the grandiose Dolmabahçe Palace (p94), **Çırağan Palace** (Çırağan Sarayı; Çırağan Caddesi 84, Ortaköy; 🚇 Çırağan), the 19th-century **Beylerbeyi Palace** (Beylerbeyi Sarayı; www.millisaraylar.gov.tr; Abdullah Ağa Caddesi, Beylerbeyi; admission ₺20; ⏰ 8.30am-4.30pm Tue, Wed & Fri-Sun; 🚇 Beylerbeyi Sarayı) with bathing pavilions on the shore, and the 19th-century **Küçüksu Kasrı** (✆ 216-332 3303; Küçüksu Caddesi, Beykoz; admission ₺5; ⏰ 9.30am-4pm Tue, Wed & Fri-Sun; 🚇 Küçüksu), featuring an ornate wedding-cake exterior. You're also sure to see *yalı* (waterside wooden summer residences, built by Ottoman aristocracy and foreign ambassadors in the 17th, 18th and 19th centuries) – including the 1698 **Köprülü Amcazade Hüseyin Paşa Yalı** (Rumeli Hisarı; 🚢 Eminönü-Kavaklar tourist ferry), the oldest on the Bosphorus – plus mosques such as the pretty **Ortaköy Mosque** (Ortaköy Camii, Büyük Mecidiye Camii; Ortaköy Meydanı, Ortaköy; 🚇 Ortaköy), and affluent suburbs. Keep an eye out for the fortifications of **Rumeli Hisarı** (Fortress of Europe; ✆ 212-263 5305; Yahya Kemal Caddesi 42; admission ₺3; ⏰ 9am-noon & 12.30-4.30pm Thu-Tue; 🚇 Rumeli Hisarı), built in just four months in 1452 in preparation for the Ottoman siege of Constantinople.

Short tours turn around here. Long tours continue to Kanlıca (p82), Sarıyer, Rumeli Kavağı and Anadolu Kavağı (p83).

Check www.sehirhatlari.com.tr for timetable and fare updates for all services, as these often change.

SHORT TOUR

A shorter option is a cruise on a private excursion boat to Rumeli Hisarı/Anadolu Hisarı (just before the Fatih Bridge) and back (without stopping). The boats are smaller so you travel closer to the shoreline and see a lot more. The entire trip takes about 90 minutes and tickets cost ₺10. Turyol boats leave from the dock on the western side of the Galata Bridge every hour from 11am to 6pm on weekdays and every 45 minutes or so from 11am to 7.15pm on weekends. Boats operated by other companies leave from near the Boğaz İskelesi.

COMMUTER FERRIES

Jetons (transport tokens) for most trips cost ₺2. Routes operated by İstanbul Şehir Hatları (p84):

● **Beşiktaş (near Dolmabahçe Palace)– Kadıköy** Every 30 minutes from 7.45am to 9.15pm.

● **Eminönü–Kadıköy** Approximately every 15 to 20 minutes from 7.30am to 9.10pm.

● **Eminönü–Üsküdar** Approximately every 20 minutes from 6.35am to 11pm.

● **Karaköy–Kadıköy** Approximately every 20 minutes from 6.10am to 11pm.

Hamams

The tourist hamams in historic Old City buildings are pricey, and their massages generally short and not particularly good, but you'll be in gorgeous historic surrounds.

AYASOFYA HÜRREM SULTAN HAMAMI
Hamam

(Map p66; ☎212-517 3535; www.ayasofya hamami.com; Aya Sofya Meydanı; bath treatments €70-165, massages €40-75; ☺8am-11pm; 🚊Sultanahmet) This restored twin 16th-century hamam offers the Old City's most luxurious traditional bath experience.

CAĞALOĞLU HAMAMI
Hamam

(Map p66; ☎212-522 2424; www.cagaloglu hamami.com.tr; Yerebatan Caddesi 34; bath, scrub & massage packages €50-110; ☺8am-10pm; 🚊Sultanahmet) Undoubtedly the most atmospheric İstanbul hamam. Built in 1741, it offers separate baths for men and women and a range of (overpriced) bath services. Consider signing up for the self-service treatment (€30) only.

ÇEMBERLITAŞ HAMAMI
Hamam

(Map p76; ☎212-522 7974; Vezir Han Caddesi 8; bath, scrub & soap massage €29; ☺6am–mid-night; 🚊Çemberlitaş) This twin 16th-century hamam designed by Mimar Sinan is among the city's most beautiful. Give the perfunctory massages and treatments a miss. Tips are meant to be covered in the treatment price.

AĞA HAMAMI
Hamam

(Map p80; ☎212-249 5027; www.agahamami. com; Turnacıbaşı Sokak 48b, Çukurcuma; bath ₺30, soap/oil massage ₺5/30, skin-peeling scrub ₺5; ☺10am-10pm; 🚊Kabataş, then funicular to Taksim) This low-key 16th-century hamam allows communal bathing for both genders, although scrubs and massages are conducted by same-sex masseurs in private spaces. Prices are relatively reasonable, but standards of cleanliness could be higher.

 Courses

COOKING ALATURKA
Cooking

(Map p66; ☎0536 338 0896; www.cooking alaturka.com; Akbıyık Caddesi 72a, Cankurtaran; cooking class per person €60; 🚊Sultanahmet) Dutch-born Eveline Zoutendijk's hands-on classes offer an introduction to Turkish cuisine; suitable for both novices and experienced cooks. The results are enjoyed over a five-course meal in the school's restaurant (p92).

MÜZENIN KAHVESI
Coffee

(Map p66; ☎212-517 4580; Museum of Turkish & Islamic Arts, Atmeydanı Caddesi 46; ☺9am-6.30pm Tue-Sun Apr-Oct, to 4.30pm Nov-Mar; 🚊Sultanahmet) The 30-minute 'Treasures of Turkey' coffee experience (₺20) demonstrates roasting, grinding, brewing and service techniques. Bookings essential.

Whirling dervishes
MARK HORN/GETTY IMAGES ©

TURKISH FLAVOURS Cooking

(☎ 0532 218 0653; www.turkishflavours.com; apartment 3, Vali Konağı Caddesi 14; per person tours US$100-145, cooking classes US$100)
As well as her foodie tour (US$145 per person) of the Spice Bazaar and Kadıköy markets, which includes lunch at award-winning **Çiya Sofrası** (www.ciya.com.tr; Güneşlibahçe Sokak 43; portions ₺10-15; ⊙11am-11pm; 🚇Kadıköy), Selin Rozanes conducts small-group cooking classes in her elegant Nişantaşı home (US$100 per person). The results are enjoyed over a four-course lunch with drinks.

LES ARTS TURCS Cultural Tour

(Map p66; ☎212-527 6859; www.lesartsturcs.com; 3rd fl, İncili Çavuş Sokak 19; workshops ₺100-150, tours from ₺150, dervish ceremony ₺60; 🚇Sultanahmet) This small cultural tourism company organises a range of tours and workshops, including visits to Sufi *tekke*s where the whirling-dervish ceremony is held, ebru (marbling) and calligraphy workshops, belly-dancing lessons, synagogue and photography tours.

 Tours

İSTANBUL WALKS Walking & Cultural Tours

(Map p66; ☎212-516 6300; www.istanbulwalks.net; 2nd fl, Şifa Hamamı Sokak 1; walking tours €25-75, child under 6yr free; 🚇Sultanahmet) This small cultural tourism company offers guided walking tours conducted by knowledgeable English-speaking guides. Tours concentrate on İstanbul's various neighbourhoods, but there are also tours to major monuments including Topkapı Palace, the İstanbul Archaeology Museums and Dolmabahçe Palace.

CULINARY BACKSTREETS Walking Tour

(www.culinarybackstreets.com) Full-day walking tours of the Old CIty and Beyoğlu (with lunch) as well as an evening spent tasting dishes from southeastern Anatolia in a progression of eateries. The foodie guides produce the blog of the same name.

Seeing the Dervishes Whirl

Those sultans of spiritual spin known as the whirling dervishes have been twirling their way to a higher plane since the 13th century. There are a number of opportunities to see a *sema* (whirling-dervish ceremony) in İstanbul; probably the best is the weekly **ceremony** (Galata Mevlevihanesi Müzesi; Map p80; Galipdede Caddesi 15, Tünel; per person ₺40; ⊙performances 4pm Sun; 🚇Karaköy, then funicular to Tünel) at the Galata Mevlevi Museum. Tickets are only available on the day of the performance and often sell out; head to the museum and purchase tickets well ahead of the performance. The Hocapaşa Culture Centre (p98) offers a more touristy experience.

URBAN ADVENTURES Walking & Cultural Tours

(Map p66; ☎212-512 7144; www.urbanadventures.com; 1st fl, Ticarethane Sokak 11; all tours ₺50; ⊙8.30am-5.30pm; 🚇Sultanahmet) International tour company Intrepid offers tours including a popular four-hour guided walk around Sultanahmet and the Bazaar District. The 'Home Cooked İstanbul' tour includes a no-frills dinner with a local family in their home and a visit to a neighbourhood teahouse.

🛏 Sleeping

Every accommodation style is available in İstanbul. You can live like a sultan in a world-class luxury hotel, or relax in a boutique establishment.

During low season (October to April, but not around Christmas or Easter) you should be able to negotiate a discount of at least 20% on the price. Before you confirm any booking, ask if the hotel will

If You Like...
Modern Art

Beyoğlu's slew of contemporary galleries perfectly complements Sultanahmet's ancient sights.

1 İSTANBUL MODERN
(İstanbul Modern Sanat Müzesi; Map p80; www.istanbulmodern.org; Meclis-i Mebusan Caddesi, Tophane; adult/student/under 12yr ₺15/8/free; ⏲10am-6pm Tue, Wed & Fri-Sun, to 8pm Thu; 🚇Tophane) In a stunning location on the Bosphorus, with a 20th-century art collection and exhibitions by local and international artists.

2 SALT GALATA
(Map p80; www.saltonline.org/en; Bankalar Caddesi 11, Karaköy; ⏲noon-8pm Tue-Sat, 10.30am-6pm Sun; 🚇Karaköy) Housed in a magnificent 1892 bank, this cutting-edge institution offers an exhibition space, auditorium, arts research library, cafe and glamorous rooftop restaurant.

3 ARTER
(Map p80; www.arter.org.tr; İstiklal Caddesi 211; ⏲11am-7pm Tue-Thu, noon-8pm Fri-Sun; 🚇Karaköy, then funicular to Tünel) This four-floor contemporary arts space is an exciting new arts venue.

4 SALT BEYOĞLU
(Map p80; www.saltonline.org/en; İstiklal Caddesi 136; ⏲noon-8pm Tue-Sat, 10.30am-6pm Sun; 🚇Karaköy, then funicular to Tünel) An exhibition space, a bookshop, a cinema and cafe occupy a 19th-century apartment building, where SALT shows high-profile and emerging international and local artists.

5 MUSEUM OF INNOCENCE
(Map p80; www.masumiyetmuzesi.org; Dalgıç Çıkmazı 2, off Çukurcuma Caddesi, Çukurcuma; admission ₺25; ⏲10am-6pm Tue-Sun, to 9pm Fri; 🚇Tophane) Despite the whopping entrance fee, Nobel laureate Orhan Pamuk's museum/piece of conceptual art is worth a visit, particularly if you have read his novel of the same name. Displaying found objects in a 19th-century house, it evokes what Pamuk describes as 'the melancholy of the period' in which the novel is set.

give you a discount for cash payment (usually 5% or 10%), whether a pick-up from the airport is included (it often is if you stay more than three nights) and whether there are discounts for extended stays.

Check the following for short-term furnished apartment rentals (many with three- or four-day minimum rental periods):

○ **1001 Nites** (www.1001nites.com; Sultanahmet apt for 2 people per night €100, Çukurcuma apt for 4 people 120€, 10% discount for weekly stays)

○ **Istanbul Apartments** (📞212-249 5065; www.istanbulapt.com; d €70-80, tr €85-95, q €110-120; ❄@)

○ **İstanbul Holiday Apartment** (📞212-251 8530; www.istanbulholidayapartments.com; apt per night €115-260, minimum stay 3 or 7 nights; ❄)

○ **Manzara Istanbul** (www.manzara-istanbul.com)

Sultanahmet & Around

This is the heart of Old İstanbul and the city's premier sightseeing area, so the hotels here and in the adjoining neighbourhoods (Cankurtaran, Küçük Aya Sofya, Binbirdirek, Çemberlitaş, Alemdar and Cağaloğlu) are supremely convenient. The main drawbacks are the carpet touts and the lack of decent bars and restaurants.

HOTEL IBRAHIM PASHA   Boutique Hotel €€
(Map p66; 📞212-518 0394; www.ibrahimpasha.com; Terzihane Sokak 7; r standard €99-195, deluxe €139-265; ❄@🛜; 🚇Sultanahmet) Exemplary designer hotel combining Ottoman style, contemporary decor and high levels of service. All rooms are gorgeous but some are small; opt for a deluxe one if possible. We love the comfortable lounge and the terrace bar with its knockout views of the Blue Mosque.

SIRKECI KONAK   Hotel €€
(Map p66; 📞212-528 4344; www.sirkecikonak.com; Taya Hatun Sokak 5, Sirkeci; d standard €155-185, superior & deluxe €170-270;

✳@🛜🚬; 🚪Gülhane) At this terrific hotel overlooking Gülhane Park, rooms are impeccably clean, well sized and loaded with amenities. There's a restaurant, roof terrace, indoor pool and hamam. Staff are incredibly helpful and the complimentary entertainment program includes cooking classes, walking tours and afternoon teas.

MARMARA GUESTHOUSE

Pension €

(Map p66; 📞212-638 3638; www.marmaraguest house.com; Terbıyık Sokak 15, Cankurtaran; s €30-65, d €40-70, f €60-100; ✳@; 🚪Sultan-ahmet) Manager Elif Aytekin and family really make guests feel welcome, offering plenty of advice, high levels of cleanliness and comfort, and a delicious breakfast on the vine-covered, sea-facing roof ter-race. Rooms have comfortable beds and double-glazed windows.

HOTEL
EMPRESS ZOE

Boutique Hotel €€

(Map p66; 📞212-518 2504; www.emzoe.com; Akbiyik Caddesi 4, Cankurtaran; s €70-90, d €105-160, ste €135-300; ✳🛜; 🚪Sultanahmet) This fabulous, constantly improving place is the prototype for most of Sultanahmet's boutique hotels. Its garden suites overlook a gorgeous flower-filled courtyard, where breakfast is served in warm weather. The terrace bar has great views.

SARI KONAK
HOTEL

Boutique Hotel €€

(Map p66; 📞212-638 6258; www.istanbulho telsari konak.com; Mimar Mehmet Ağa Caddesi 42-46, Cankurtaran; r €69-179, ste €129-279; ✳@🛜; 🚪Sultanahmet) Deluxe rooms are spa-cious and beautifully decorated, superior rooms are nearly as nice, and standard rooms, though small, are very attractive. Guests (mostly American) enjoy the roof terrace with its Sea of Marmara and Blue Mosque views, but can also use the com-fortable lounge and courtyard.

HANEDAN HOTEL

Hotel €

(Map p66; 📞212-516 4869; www.hanedanhotel. com; Adliye Sokak 3, Cankurtaran; s €30-50, d €45-65, f €75-100; ✳@🛜; 🚪Sultanahmet) The 11 rooms at this cheap, clean and comfortable choice feature lino floors, lace curtains and small white marble bath-rooms. One large and two interconnected rooms are perfect for families, and the roof terrace overlooks the sea and Aya Sofya.

Aya Sofya (p69) and the Bosphorus

Below: View from the Tomtom Suites hotel; **Right:** İstanbul Modern (p88)
(BELOW) HEMIS/ALAMY ©; (RIGHT) /GETTY IMAGES ©

HOTEL ALP   Hotel €€
(Map p66; ☏ 212-517 7067; www.alpguesthouse.
com; Adliye Sokak 4, Cankurtaran; s €35-60,
d €55-80, f €80-110; ✳ @ 🛜; 🚇 Sultanahmet)
In Sultanahmet's premier small-hotel enclave, the Alp offers attractive, well-priced
rooms. Bathrooms are small but clean,
and there are plenty of amenities. The
roof terrace is one of the best in this area,
with great sea views and comfortable
indoor and outdoor seating.

HOTEL ŞEBNEM   Hotel €€
(Map p66; ☏ 212-517 6623; www.sebnemhotel.
net; Adliye Sokak 1, Cankurtaran; s €40-70, d
€50-100, f €70-120; ✳ @ 🛜; 🚇 Sultanahmet)
Simplicity works a treat at the Şebnem.
Rooms have wooden floors, good bathrooms and comfortable beds with crisp
white linen. The large terrace has views
over the Sea of Marmara (as do the more
expensive double rooms), and two downstairs rooms have a private courtyard
garden.

AGORA LIFE
HOTEL   Hotel €€€
(Map p66; ☏ 212-526 1181; www.agora
lifehotel.com; Cağoloğlu Hamamı Sokak 6,
Cağoloğlu; s €69-129, d €79-209, ste €199-259;
✳ @ 🛜) In a quiet cul-de-sac, this hotel
offers good service and quiet elegance,
plenty of amenities in the rooms, and
a simply extraordinary view from the
rooftop terrace. Opt for a deluxe or suite
room if possible.

Beyoğlu & Around
Stay here to avoid the touts in the Old
City, and because buzzing, bohemian
Beyoğlu has the city's best wining, dining
and shopping. Most of the suite hotels
and apartment rentals are located here.

To reach Old İstanbul's historical sights
from Beyoğlu, walk across Galata Bridge
or catch the Taksim Meydanı–Kabataş
funicular followed by the tram.

BEŞ ODA   Boutique Hotel €€
(Map p80; ☏ 212-252 7501; www.5oda.com;
Şahkulu Bostan Sokak 16, Galata; ste €85-150;

✳ @ 🛜; 🚋 Karaköy, then funicular to Tünel)
The name means 'Five Rooms', and that's
exactly this stylish and friendly suite
hotel in bohemian Galata is offering. A
great deal of thought has gone into the
design: each suite has an equipped kitchenette, lounge area, custom-designed
furniture, large bed with good reading
lights, black-out curtains, and windows
that open to let in fresh air.

WITT ISTANBUL
HOTEL   Boutique Hotel €€€
(Map p80; 📞 212-293 1500; www.wittistanbul.
com; Defterdar Yokuşu 26; ste €160-390;
✳ @ 🛜; 🚋 Tophane) Showcasing nearly
as many designer features as an issue of *Monocle* magazine, this stylish
apartment hotel in the trendy suburb
of Cihangir has 18 suites with fully
equipped kitchenettes, seating areas,
CD/DVD players, iPod docks, Nespresso
machines, king-sized beds and huge
bathrooms. Penthouse and Sea View
suites have fabulous views.

TOMTOM SUITES   Boutique Hotel €€€
(Map p80; 📞 212-292 4949; www.tomtomsuites.
com; Tomtom Kaptan Sokak 18; ste €185-720;
🚋 Karaköy, then funicular to Tünel) We're more
than happy to beat the drum about this
suite hotel occupying a former Franciscan
nunnery off İstiklal. Its contemporary
decor is understated but elegant, with
particularly impressive bathrooms,
and each suite is beautifully appointed.
There's also a rooftop bar-restaurant with
fantastic views.

ANEMON GALATA   Hotel €€
(Map p80; 📞 212-293 2343; www.anemonhotels.
com; cnr Galata Kulesi Sokak & Büyük Hendek
Sokak, Galata; s US$140-210, d US$160-230, ste
US$225-270; ✳ @; 🚋 Karaköy) Located on
the attractive square surrounding Galata
Tower, this wooden building dates from
1842 but has been completely rebuilt
inside. Rooms are elegantly decorated
and well equipped; some have water
views. There's a rooftop bar-restaurant
with great views and the atmospheric

Sensus Wine Bar (Map p80; www.sensuswine. com; Büyük Hendek Sokak 5, Galata; ⊗10am-10pm; 🚇Karaköy, then funicular to Tünel) is in the basement.

WORLD HOUSE HOSTEL Hostel €
(Map p80; ☑212-293 5520; www.worldhouse istanbul.com; Galipdede Caddesi 85, Galata; d €45-55; @ 🛜; 🚇Karaköy, then funicular to Tünel) Some İstanbul hostels are impersonal hulks with junglelike atmospheres, but this is reasonably small and very friendly. Best of all is its location, close to Beyoğlu's entertainment strips but not too far from the sights in Sultanahmet.

 Eating

İstanbul is a food-lover's paradise, but Sultanahmet has the least impressive eating options. At night, we recommend crossing Galata Bridge and joining the locals in Beyoğlu. If we've included a telephone number in the review, it means you should book ahead.

Sultanahmet & Around

AHIRKAPI BALIKÇISI Seafood €€
(Map p66; ☑212-518 4988; Keresteci Hakkı Sokak 46, Cankurtaran; mezes ₺5-25, fish ₺15-70; ⊗4-11pm; 🚇Sultanahmet) This low-profile neighbourhood fish restaurant is tiny and relatively cheap. The food is so good and the eating alternatives in this area so bad that we've decided to share the locals' secret. Book ahead.

CIHANNÜMA Turkish €€€
(Map p66; ☑212-520 7676; www.cihannuma istanbul.com; And Hotel, Yerebatan Caddesi 18; mezes ₺5-19, mains ₺27-47; 🚇Sultanahmet) The view from the top-floor restaurant of this modest hotel is probably the Old City's best: you can see as far as the Dolmabahçe Palace and Bosphorus Bridge. Against this stunning backdrop, the menu showcases good kebaps (we recommend the the *kuzu şiş*), Ottoman-influenced stews and vegetarian dishes.

COOKING ALATURKA Turkish €€
(Map p66; ☑212-458 5919; www.cookingalatur ka.com; Akbıyık Caddesi 72a, Cankurtaran; set lunch or dinner ₺50; ⊗lunch Mon-Sat, dinner by reservation Mon-Sat; 🚇Sultanahmet) Dutch-born owner/chef Eveline Zoutendijk and her Turkish colleague Fehzi Yıldırım serve a set four-course menu of simple Anatolian dishes at this tranquil restaurant. The menu makes the most of the fresh seasonal produce. No children under six at dinner and no credit cards.

PAŞAZADE Turkish €€
(Map p66; ☑212-513 3750; www.pasazade.com; İbn-i Kemal Caddesi 5a, Sirkeci; mezes ₺7-18, mains ₺18-28; ⊗lunch & dinner; 🚇Gülhane) Advertising itself as an *Osmanlı mutfağı* (Ottoman kitchen), Paşazade has long garnered rave reviews. Well-priced dishes are served in the streetside restaurant

Kariye Museum (Chora Church)

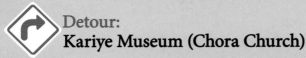

Detour:
Kariye Museum (Chora Church)

İstanbul has more than its fair share of Byzantine monuments, but few are as drop-dead gorgeous as the mosaic-laden church **Kariye Museum** (Chora Church; Kariye Müzesi; kariye.muze.gov.tr; Kariye Camii Sokak, Edirnekapı; admission ₺15; ⊙9am-7pm Thu-Tue Apr-Oct, to 4.30pm Nov-Mar; 🚌31E, 32, 36K & 38E from Eminönü, 87 from Taksim). Nestled in the shadow of Theodosius II's land walls, it receives a fraction of the Aya Sofya's visitors but offers an equally fascinating insight into Byzantine art.

Virtually all of the building's interior decoration – the famous mosaics and the equally striking frescoes – dates from 1312 and was funded by Theodore Metochites, a poet and man of letters. One of the most wonderful mosaics, above the door to the nave in the inner narthex, depicts Theodore offering the church to Christ. The building became a mosque under Beyazıt II (1481–1512) and a museum in 1945.

Most of the interior is covered with mosaics depicting Christ and the Virgin Mary. The frescoes, thought to have been painted by the same masters who created the mosaics, are reminiscent of those painted by the Italian master Giotto, the painter who ushered in the Italian Renaissance.

Next door, the elegant restaurant **Asitane** (📞212-635 7997; www.asitanerestaurant. com; Kariye Oteli, Kariye Camii Sokak 6, Edirnekapı; starters ₺12-18, mains ₺26-42; ⊙11am-midnight; 🌿; 🚌31E, 32, 36K & 38E from Eminönü, 87 from Taksim) serves Ottoman dishes devised for the palace kitchens. Its chefs have been tracking down historic recipes for years, and their versions will tempt most modern palates.

or on the rooftop terrace (summer only). Portions are large, the food is tasty and service is attentive. Top marks go to the traditional meze platter (₺17).

SEFA RESTAURANT
Turkish €

(Map p66; Nuruosmaniye Caddesi 17; portions ₺7-12, kebaps ₺12-18; ⊙7am-5pm; 🌿; 🚌Sultan-ahmet) Locals rate this place highly. It describes its cuisine as Ottoman, but what's really on offer here are *lokanta* (ready-made) dishes and kebaps at extremely reasonable prices. Order from an English menu or choose daily specials. Try to arrive earlyish for lunch because many of the dishes run out by 1.30pm. No alcohol.

HOCAPAŞA PIDECISI
Pide €

(Map p66; www.hocapasa.com.tr; Hocapaşa Sokak 19, Sirkeci; pides ₺8-14; ⊙10am-10pm Mon-Sat; 🚌Sirkeci) On this pedestrianised street lined with cheap eateries, *lokantas* serve *hazır yemek* (ready-made dishes), *köftecis* dish out flavoursome meatballs,

kebapçis grill meat to order and this much-loved *pideçisi* (opened in 1964) offers piping-hot pides accompanied by pickles.

Bazaar District

FATIH DAMAK PIDE
Pide €

(Büyük Karaman Caddesi 48, Zeyrek; pides ₺8-12; ⊙11am-11pm; 🚌Aksaray) It's worth making the trek to this unlicensed *pideçisi* overlooking the İtfaıye Yanı Park Karşısı (Fire Station Park) near the Aqueduct of Valens. It makes the best Karadeniz (Black Sea)–style pide on the Historic Peninsula, and free pots of tea are served with meals. Toppings are standard (the *sucuklu-peynirli* option with sausage and cheese is tasty), but there's also an unusual bafra pidesi (rolled-up pitta-style pizza). There's an organic open buffet brunch on weekends (₺12.50).

HAMDI RESTAURANT
Kebap €€

(Map p76; 📞212-528 8011; www.hamdirestorant. com.tr; Kalçın Sokak 17, Eminönü; mezes ₺7-15,

Detour:
Dolmabahçe Palace

Everyone from fans of the less-is-more aesthetic to enthusiasts of Ottoman architecture decry this final flourish of the imperial dynasty, finding that it has more in common with the Paris Opera than with traditional pavilion-style buildings such as Topkapı. But whatever the critics might say, the 19th-century imperial residence, **Dolmabahçe Palace** (Dolmabahçe Sarayı; www.millisaraylar.gov.tr; Dolmabahçe Caddesi, Beşiktaş; Selamlık ₺30, Harem ₺20, joint ticket ₺40; ⊙9am-6pm Tue-Wed & Fri-Sun Mar-Sep, to 4pm Oct-Feb; 🚊Kabataş then walk), with its opulent Selamlık (Ceremonial Suites) and slightly more restrained Harem is a clear crowd favourite.

Both the Selamlık and the Harem are visited on separate (and unfortunately rushed) guided tours. The **Selamlık**, with its huge chandeliers and crystal staircase made by Baccarat, is the most impressive of the two.

The tourist entrance is near the palace's ornate Clock Tower, built between 1890 and 1894. There's an **outdoor cafe** near here with premium Bosphorus views and cheap prices.

At the end of your tour, make sure that you visit the **Crystal Kiosk**, with its fairytale-like conservatory featuring etched glass windows and crystal fountain, piano and chair. It's next to the aviary on the street side of the palace.

Visitor numbers in the palace are limited to 3000 per day and this ceiling is often reached on weekends and holidays. Come midweek if possible, and even then be prepared to queue (often for a long period and in full sun).

kebaps ₺20-28, dessert ₺7-15; 🚊Eminönü) Hamdi Arpacı serves tasty kebaps made according to recipes from his hometown Şanlıurfa (Urfa). With phenomenal views from its top-floor terrace, the restaurant is always busy, so request a rooftop table when you book (or arrive early).

SIIRT FATIH BÜRYAN Turkish €
(Map p76; İtfaiye Caddesi 20a, Zeyrek; büryan ₺11, perde pilavi ₺10; 🚊Aksaray) This unlicensed eatery in the Kadın Pazarı (Women's Market), near the Aqueduct of Valens, specialises in two delicious dishes that are a speciality of the southeastern city of Siirt: büryan (lamb slow-cooked in a pit) and perde pilavi (chicken and rice cooked in pastry). Order either of these with a glass of frothy homemade ayran (salty yoghurt drink) and you'll be happy indeed.

BAHAR RESTAURANT Turkish €
(Map p76; Yağcı Han 13, off Nuruosmaniye Sokak, Nuruosmaniye; soup ₺4, dishes ₺9-15; ⊙11am-4pm Mon-Sat; 🖋; 🚊Çemberlitaş) Tiny (unlicensed) 'Spring' is popular with local shopkeepers; arrive early to score a table. Dishes change daily and with the season; try the delicious lentil soup, tasty hünkar beğendi (lamb stew) or creamy macaroni.

Beyoğlu & Around
A recent local-government ban on outdoor drinking in Beyoğlu has had a sorry impact on this neighbourhood's restaurant and bar scene. We, like many locals, can only hope that good sense prevails and the ban is rescinded in the near future.

The only enclave to escape the ban was Nevizade Sokak behind the Balık Pazarı, which continues to host boistrous crowds on weekend evenings.

ASMALI CAVIT Turkish €€
(Asmalı Meyhane; Map p80; 🕿212-292 4950; Asmalımescit Sokak 16, Asmalımescit; mezes ₺6-20, mains ₺18-24; 🚊Karaköy, then funicular to Tünel) Cavit Saatcı's place is quite pos-

sibly the best *meyhane* in the city. The old-fashioned interior gives no clue as to the excellence of the food on offer. Standout dishes include *yaprak ciğer* (liver fried with onions), *patlıcan salatası* (eggplant salad), *muska boreği* (phyllo stuffed with beef and onion) and *kalamar tava* (fried calamari). Bookings essential.

LOKANTA MAYA   Modern Turkish €€
(Map p80; ☎212-252 6884; www.lokantamaya. com; Kemankeş Caddesi 35a, Karaköy; mezes ₺11-28, mains ₺26-35; ⊙lunch Mon-Sat, dinner Tue-Sat, brunch Sun; ⎘; ⎇Karaköy) Critics and chowhounds alike are raving about the dishes created by chef Didem Şenol at her stylish restaurant near the Karaköy docks. The author of a successful cookbook on Aegean cuisine, Didem's food is light, flavoursome, occasionally quirky and always assured. Book for dinner; lunch is cheaper and more casual.

ZÜBEYIR OCAKBAŞI   Kebap €€
(Map p80; ☎212-293 3951; www.zubeyir ocakbasi.com; Bekar Sokak 28; mezes ₺4-6, kebaps ₺10-20; ⊙noon-1am; ⎇Kabataş, then funicular to Taksim) Every morning, the chefs at this popular *ocakbaşı* (grill house) prepare the fresh, top-quality meats to be grilled over their handsome copper-hooded barbecues that night: spicy chicken wings and Adana kebaps, flavoursome ribs, pungent liver kebaps and well-marinated lamb *şış* kebaps. Bookings essential.

MEZE BY LEMON TREE   Modern Turkish €€€
(Map p80; ☎212-252 8302; www.mezze.com. tr; Meşrutiyet Caddesi 83b, Tepebaşı; mezes ₺8-25, mains ₺26-36; ⎇Karaköy, then funicular to Tünel) Chef Gençay Üçok creates some of İstanbul's most interesting – and delicious – modern Turkish food. Come to his small restaurant to sample triumphs such as the monkfish casserole or grilled lamb sirloin with baked potatoes and red beets. Bookings essential.

KARAKÖY LOKANTASI   Turkish €€
(Map p80; ☎212-292 4455; Kemankeş Caddesi 37a, Karaköy; mezes ₺6-10, portions ₺7-12, grills ₺11-16; ⊙dinner daily, lunch Mon-Sat; ⎘; ⎇Karaköy) Known for its gorgeous tiled interior, genial owner and bustling vibe, Karaköy Lokantası serves tasty and well-priced food to its loyal local clientele. It functions as a *lokanta* during the day, but at night it morphs into a *meyhane*, with slightly

Entrance to Dolmabahçe Palace

KEN WELSH/GETTY IMAGES ©

higher prices. Bookings are essential for dinner.

ZENCEFIL   Vegetarian €
(Map p80; Kurabiye Sokak 8; soup ₺7-9, mains ₺9-17; ⏲10am-11pm Mon-Sat, noon-10pm Sun; ⚑; 🚃Kabataş, then funicular to Taksim) This vegetarian cafe's interior is comfortable and stylish, with a glassed courtyard and bright colour scheme, and its food is 100% homemade, fresh and varied. One chicken dish always features on the otherwise strictly vegetarian menu, and the cafe makes its own ginger beer and ginger ale as well as serving alcoholic drinks.

 ## Drinking

İstanbullus love a drink or three in the bars and rakı (aniseed brandy)–soaked meyhanes. The city's bohemian and student set gravitates to the bars in Beyoğlu's Cihangir, Asmalımescit and Nevizade enclaves. Alternatively, you can check out the alcohol-free, atmosphere-rich çay bahçesi or kahvehanes (coffeehouses) dotted around the Old City. These are great places to relax over

a nargile (₺15 to ₺25), accompanied by a Türk kahve (Turkish coffee) or çay.

Sultanahmet & Around
For hot drinks including (non-Turkish) coffee, head to **Denizen Coffee** (Map p66; Şehit Mehmet Paşa Yokuşu 8; ⏲8.30am-10pm Mon-Sat; 🚃Sultanahmet) and **Kahve Dünyası** (Map p76; Kızılhan Sokak 18, Eminönü; 🚃Eminönü).

HOTEL NOMADE TERRACE BAR   Bar
(Map p66; www.hotelnomade.com; Ticarethane Sokak 15, Alemdar; ⏲noon-11pm; 🚃Sultanahmet) This boutique hotel's intimate terrace overlooks the Aya Sofya and Blue Mosque. Settle down in a comfortable chair to enjoy a glass of wine, beer or freshly squeezed fruit juice.

YEŞİL EV   Bar, Cafe
(Map p66; Kabasakal Caddesi 5; ⏲noon-10.30pm; 🚃Sultanahmet) The elegant rear courtyard of this Ottoman-style hotel is an oasis for those wanting to enjoy a quiet drink. In spring, flowers and blossoms fill every corner; in summer, the fountain and trees keep the temperature down. You can order a sandwich, salad or cheese platter if you're peckish.

View from Mikla bar

İstanbul for Children

Children of all ages will enjoy the **Rahmi M Koç Museum** (Rahmi M Koç Müzesi; www.rmk-museum.org.tr; Hasköy Caddesi 5, Hasköy; adult/child ₺6/3; ☉10am-5pm Mon-Fri, to 6pm/8pm Sat & Sun winter/summer; 🚌47 from Eminönü, 54HT from Taksim, ⛴Hasköy), dedicated to the history of transport, industry and communications in Turkey, with numerous activities and gadgets. You can catch the İstanbul Şehir Hatları Haliç (Golden Horn) ferry there from Eminönü (₺2, 20 minutes). Get off at the second stop, Hasköy, and the museum is directly to the left of the ferry stop.

Haliç ferries leave Eminönü roughly every hour from 10.45am to 8pm; the last ferry returns from Hasköy at 8pm. Golden Horn (Haliç) İskelesi ferry dock is on the western side of the Galata Bridge, behind a car park next to the Storks building. Boats often also call at Karaköy, across the Golden Horn from Eminönü.

Older children will enjoy the ferry trip down the Bosphorus, particularly if it's combined with a visit to the fortress of Rumeli Hisarı (p85) – beware of the steep stairs here, which have no barriers.

In Sultanahmet, there are **playgrounds** in Kadırga Park, near Little Aya Sofya, and in Gülhane Park (p72). In Beyoğlu, there's one right at the water's edge, next to the Fındıklı tram stop and a *çay bahçesi;* it's very scenic, but be sure to watch your toddlers carefully!

See p338 for further suggestions.

Beyoğlu & Around

MIKLA
Bar

(Map p80; www.miklarestaurant.com; Marmara Pera Hotel, Meşrutiyet Caddesi 15, Tepebaşı; ☉from 6pm Mon-Sat summer only; 🚇Karaköy, then funicular to Tünel) It's worth overlooking the occasionally uppity service at this stylish rooftop bar to enjoy what could well be the best view in İstanbul. After a few drinks, consider moving downstairs to eat in the classy restaurant.

MANDA BATMAZ
Coffeehouse

(Map p80; Olivia Geçidi 1a, off İstiklal Caddesi; ☉9.30am-midnight; 🚇Karaköy, then funicular to Tünel) He's been working at this tiny coffeehouse for two decades, so Cemil Pilik really knows his stuff when it comes to making Turkish coffee. You'll find it behind the Barcelona Cafe & Patisserie.

MAVRA
Cafe

(Map p80; Serdar-ı Ekrem Caddesi 31a, Galata; ☉8am-midnight; 🚇Karaköy, then funicular to Tünel) Serdar-ı Ekrem Caddesi is one of Galata's most interesting streets, full of ornate 19th-century apartment blocks, avant-garde boutiques and laid-back cafes and bars. Mavra is the best of these, offering tasty cheap food and good tea and coffee amidst thrift-shop chic decor.

LEB-I DERYA
Bar

(Map p80; www.lebiderya.com; 6th fl, Kumbaracı Yokuşu 57, Galata; ☉4pm-2am Mon-Thu, to 3am Fri, 10am-3am Sat, to 2am Sun; 🚇Karaköy, then funicular to Tünel) On the top floor of a dishevelled building, Leb-i Derya has a small outdoor terrace and wonderful views. There's also food on offer.

LITERA
Bar

(Map p80; www.literarestaurant.com; 5th fl, Yeniçarşı Caddesi 32, Galatasaray; ☉11am-4am; 🚇Karaköy, then funicular to Tünel) Occupying the 5th floor of the handsome Goethe Institute building, Litera revels in its expansive views. It hosts plenty of cultural events.

360
Bar

(Map p80; www.360istanbul.com; 8th fl, İstiklal Caddesi 163; ☉noon-2am Mon-Thu & Sun, 3pm-4am Fri & Sat; 🚇Karaköy, then funicular to Tünel)

Street Eats

The most atmospheric place to try İstanbul's favourite fast-food treat, the *balık ekmek* (fish sandwich), is at the Eminönü end of the Galata Bridge. At the **stands (Map p76)** in front of fishing boats tied to the quay, mackerel fillets are grilled, crammed into fresh bread and served with salad; an optional squeeze of bottled lemon is recommended. A sandwich will set you back about ₺5, and can be accompanied by a glass of the *şalgam* (sour turnip juice) sold by nearby pickle vendors. Alternatively, **Fürreyya Galata Balıkçısı (Map p80)** serves an excellent version for ₺7.

Galatasaray's fish market, **Balık Pazarı** (Fish Market; Map p80; Şahne Sokak off İstiklal Caddesi, Galatasaray; 🚇), is full of small stands selling *midye tava* (skewered mussels fried in hot oil), *kokoreç* (grilled sheep's intestines stuffed with peppers, tomatoes, herbs and spices) and other snacks. You'll also find shops selling fish, caviar, fruit, vegetables and other produce; mostly on Duduodaları Sokak on the left (southern) side of the market.

İstanbul's most famous bar, and deservedly so. If you can score one of the bar stools on the terrace you'll be happy indeed: the view is truly magnificent. It morphs into a club after midnight on Friday and Saturday (cover charge around ₺40).

 Entertainment

For an overview of what's on, pick up a copy of *Time Out İstanbul* magazine when you hit town. Tickets for major events are available through **Biletix** (☎216-556 9800; www.biletix.com).

Nightclubs

The Beyoğlu clubs are cheaper than the sybaritic 'Golden Mile' (between Ortaköy and Kuruçeşme on the Bosphorus), more avant-garde and relatively attitude free. All venues are busiest on Friday and (especially) Saturday nights, and the action doesn't really kick off until 1am or 2am.

MINIMÜZIKHOL Club, Live Music
(MMH; Map p80; www.minimuzikhol.com; Soğancı Sokak 7, Cihangir; ☺Wed-Sat 10pm-late; 🚇Kabataş, then funicular to Taksim) The mothership for inner-city hipsters, MMH is a small, slightly grungy venue that hosts live

sets by local and international musicians midweek and the best dance party in town on weekends. It's best after 1am.

KIKI Club, Cafe
(Map p80; www.kiki.com.tr; Sıraselviler Caddesi 42, Cihangir; ☺closed Sun; 🚇Kabataş, then funicular to Taksim) Cool cafe by day and hip bar/club by night, Kiki has a loyal clientele who enjoy its pizzas, burgers, drinks and music (DJs and live sets). Regulars head to the rear courtyard and budget drinkers appreciate the happy hour (7pm to 9pm; Monday and Wednesday half-price drinks, Tuesday and Thursday free tapas).

LOVE DANCE POINT Gay
(www.lovedp.net; Cumhuriyet Caddesi 349, Harbiye; ☺11.30pm-5am Fri & Sat; 🚇Kabataş, then funicular to Taksim, then walk) Easily the most Europhile of the local gay venues, hosting gay musical icons and international circuit parties. Hard-cutting techno is thrown in with gay anthems and Turkish pop.

Live Music & Dance

HOCAPAŞA CULTURE CENTRE Performing Arts
(Hodjapasha Culture Centre; Map p66; ☎212-511 4626; www.hodjapasha.com; Hocapaşa Hamamı

Sokak 3b, Sirkeci; adult/child under 12yr whirling dervish show ₺50/30, Turkish dance show ₺60/40; 🚇Sirkeci) Occupying a beautifully converted 550-year-old hamam, the centre stages one-hour whirling-dervish performances for tourists (children under seven not admitted) on Friday, Saturday, Sunday, Monday and Wednesday at 7.30pm; and 1½-hour Turkish dance shows on Tuesday and Thursday (8pm), Saturday and Sunday (9pm).

BABYLON
Live Music, Club

(Map p80; www.babylon.com.tr; Şehbender Sokak 3, Asmalımescit; ⏰9.30pm-2am Tue-Thu, 10pm-3am Fri & Sat, club closed summer; 🚇Karaköy, then funicular to Tünel) İstanbul's pre-eminent live music venue offers an eclectic program featuring big-name international music acts, particularly during the festival season.

MUNZUR CAFE & BAR
Live Music

(Map p80; www.munzurcafebar.com; Hasnun Galip Sokak, Galatasaray; ⏰1pm-4am Tue-Sun, music from 9pm; 🚇Kabataş, then funicular to Taksim) Probably the best of Hasnun Galip Sokak's *Türkü evleri*, Kurdish-owned bars where musicians perform live *halk meziği* (folk music). Nearby **Toprak** (Map p80; ☎212-293 4037; www.toprakturkubar.tr.gg/ana-sayfa.htm; Hasnun Galip Sokak, Galatasaray; ⏰4pm-4am, show from 10pm) offers more of the same.

SALON
Live Music

(Map p80; ☎212-334 0700; www.saloniksv.com; İstanbul Foundation for Culture & Arts, Nejat Eczacıbaşı Bldg, Sadi Konuralp Caddesi 5, Şişhane; 🚇Karaköy, then funicular to Tünel) This intimate performance space hosts live contemporary music (mainly jazz), lectures and theatrical performances; check the website for program and booking details. Before or after the show, have a drink at **X Bar** (Map p80; www.xrestaurantbar.com; 7th fl, Sadı Konuralp Caddesi 5, Şişhane; ⏰9am-midnight Sun-Wed, to 4am Thu-Sat), on the top floor.

Shopping

Sultanahmet & Bazaar District

Many travellers are surprised to find that the highlight of their visit was searching and bartering for treasures in the city's atmospheric bazaars. The best of these are the Grand Bazaar and **Arasta Bazaar** (Map p66; 🚇Sultanahmet), which specialise in carpets, jewellery, textiles and ceramic goods.

COCOON
Carpets, Textiles

(Map p66; www.cocoontr.com; Küçük Aya Sofya Caddesi 13; ⏰8.30am-7.30pm; 🚇Sultanahmet) Felt hats, antique costumes and textiles from central Asia are artfully displayed in one store, while rugs from Persia, central Asia, the Caucasus and Anatolia adorn the other. Also has branches in the Arasta

Men cooking fish near the Galata Bridge
MARGIE POLITZER/GETTY IMAGES ©

Bazaar and **Grand Bazaar** (Map p76; www.
cocoontr.com; Halıcılar Çarşışı Sokak 38, Grand
Bazaar; 9am-7pm Mon-Sat; Beyazıt-Kapalı
Çarşı).

Beyoğlu & Around

For Turkish musical instruments, check
out the shops along Galipdede Caddesi,
which runs between Tünel Meydanı and
the Galata Tower; among them is **Lale
Plak** (Map p80; Galipdede Caddesi 1, Tünel;
9.30am-7.30pm Mon-Sat, 10.30am-7pm Sun;
Karaköy, then funicular to Tünel), with a fine
selection of Turkish classical, jazz and
folk music CDs.

For avant-garde fashion go to Serdar-ı
Ekrem Caddesi, also the home of
attractive hand-painted plates, platters,
bowls and tiles at the small atelier **SIR**
(Map p80; www.sircini.com; Serdar-i Ekrem
Sokak 66, Galata; closed Sun; Karaköy,
then funicular to Tünel). Camekan Sokak is
another good Galata street for shopping;
head to **Lâl** (Map p80; www.lalistanbul.com;
Camekan Sokak 4c, Galata; 10.30am-8pm;
Karaköy) where there are bags, scarves,

clothing and Anatolian lace and braid
jewellery, made by traditional artisans
but featuring a contemporary design
aesthetic; and **İroni** (Map p80; www.ironi.com.
tr; Camekan Sokak 4e, Galata; 10.30am-8pm;
Karaköy), with a range of silver-plated
Turkish-style homeware.

Curio hunters should wander through
the streets of Çukurcuma, where **A La
Turca** (Map p80; www.alaturcahouse.com;
Faikpaşa Sokak 4, Çukurcuma; 10.30am-
7.30pm Mon-Sat; Kabataş, then funicular
to Taksim) sells everything from antique
Anatolian kilims and textiles to top-
drawer Ottoman antiques.

DEAR EAST Arts & Crafts
(Map p80; www.deareast.com; Lüleci Hendek
Sokak 35, Tophane; 10.30am-7pm Mon-Sat;
Tophane) Interior designer Emel Güntaş
is one of İstanbul's style icons, and her
shop is a favourite destination for the
city's design mavens. The stock includes
cushions, carpets, kilims, silk scarves,
woollen shawls, porcelain, felt crafts,
paintings and photographs.

Left: Cağaloğlu Hamamı (p86);
Below: Spices for sale at the Spice Bazaar (p78)
(LEFT) IZZET KERIBAR/GETTY IMAGES ©; (BELOW) TRISTAN SAVATIER/GETTY IMAGES ©

ℹ️ Information

Dangers & Annoyances

İstanbul is no more nor less safe a city than any large metropolis, but there are a few dangers worth highlighting:

- Some İstanbullus drive like rally drivers, and there is no such thing as a generally acknowledged right of way for pedestrians.
- Bag-snatchings and muggings occasionally occur on Beyoğlu's side streets.
- There has been a recent police crackdown on gay venues in the city, especially hamams and saunas. Many have closed but those that remain open are in constant danger of being raided by police for 'morality' reasons.
- Males travelling alone or in pairs should be wary of being adopted by a friendly local who is keen to take them to a club for a few drinks. Many such encounters end up at *pavyons*, sleazy nightclubs run by the mafia where a drink or two with a female hostess will end up costing hundreds – sometimes thousands – of euros. If you don't pay up, the consequences can be violent.

Medical Services

Although they are expensive, it's probably best to visit a private hospital such as **Universal Taksim Alman Hastanesi** (Universal German Hospital; 📞212-293 2150; www.uhg.com.tr; Sıraselviler Caddesi 119; ⏱8.30am-6pm Mon-Fri, to 5pm Sat), which has English-speaking staff. It accepts credit-card payments and charges around ₺200 for a standard consultation.

Money

ATMs are everywhere. The *döviz bürosus* (exchange bureaux) in the arrivals hall at Atatürk International Airport offer rates comparable to those offered by city bureaux, which can be found on Divan Yolu (Sultanahmet), near the Grand Bazaar and around Sirkeci station (Eminönü).

101

Crazy about Keyif

The best setting to try out the magic combo of tea and nargile (water pipe) is the traditional *çay bahçesi* (tea garden), of which İstanbul has many. Locals come here to practice *keyif*, the Turkish art of quiet relaxation. To emulate them, follow the smell of apple tobacco to the following faves.

- **Tophane Nargile Cafes** (Map p80; off Necatibey Caddesi, Tophane; 🕙24hr; 🚊Tophane)
- **Erenler Çay Bahçesi** (Map p76; Yeniçeriler Caddesi 35, Beyazıt; 🕙7am-midnight; 🚊Beyazıt-Kapalı Çarşı)
- **Lale Bahçesi** (Map p76; Şifahane Caddesi, Süleymaniye; 🕙9am-11pm; 🚊Laleli-Üniversite)
- **Derviş Aile Çay Bahçesi** (Map p66; Mimar Mehmet Ağa Caddesi; 🕙9am-11pm Apr-Oct; 🚊Sultanahmet)
- **Set Üstü Çay Bahçesi** (Map p66; Gülhane Park, Sultanahmet; 🕙9am-10.30pm; 🚊Gülhane)
- **Yeni Marmara** (Map p66; Çayıroğlu Sokak, Küçük Ayasofya; 🕙10am-1am; 🚊Sultanahmet)
- **Cafe Meşale** (Map p66; Arasta Bazaar, Utangaç Sokak, Cankurtaran; 🕙24hr; 🚊Sultanahmet)
- **Türk Ocaği Kültür ve Sanat Merkezi İktisadi İşletmesi Çay Bahçesi** (Map p66; cnr Divan Yolu & Bab-ı Ali Caddesis; 🕙8am-midnight; 🚊Çemberlitaş)

❶ Getting There & Away

Air

Atatürk International Airport (IST, Atatürk Havalımanı; 📞212-463 3000; www.ataturk airport.com) 23km west of Sultanahmet. **Sabiha Gökçen International Airport** (SAW, Sabiha Gökçen Havalımanı; 📞216-588 8888; www.sgairport.com) 50km east of Sultanahmet.

Boat

Yenikapı is the dock for the **İstanbul Deniz Otobüsleri** (İDO; 📞212-444 4436; www.ido. com.tr) fast ferries across the Sea of Marmara to Bursa, Yalova and Bandırma (from where you can catch a train to İzmir). These carry both passengers and cars.

Bus

The Büyük İstanbul Otogarı is the city's main bus station for both intercity and international routes. Called simply the otogar (bus station), it's about 10km west of Sultanahmet.

The airport–Aksaray metro line stops here (otogar stop, ₺2, every 10 minutes or so from 5.40am until 1.40am). At Aksaray, you can connect with the tram to/from central İstanbul. A taxi will cost approximately ₺30/35 to Sultanahmet/Taksim.

There's a smaller bus station on the Asian shore of the Bosphorus at Harem. If you're arriving in İstanbul by bus from anywhere in Anatolian Turkey, it's much quicker to get out at Harem and take the car ferry to Sirkeci/Eminönü (₺2; every 30 minutes from 7am to 10.30pm). Leaving town, if your destination is serviced by frequent buses (eg Ankara or Antalya) you should have no trouble arriving at the Harem otogar and buying a ticket on the spot.

Bus services to/from İstanbul include Ankara (₺38 to ₺43, six hours), Bursa (₺25 to ₺30, four hours), Çanakkale (₺45, six hours), Denizli (for Pamukkale, ₺40 to ₺50, 10 hours), Edirne (₺25, 2½ hours), Göreme (₺65, 11 hours), İzmir (₺50, nine hours) and Selçuk (for Ephesus, ₺60, 11 hours).

Train

At the time of research, the Bosfor/Balkan Ekspresi ran to/from Bucharest, Sofia and Belgrade daily. Check **Turkish State Railways** (TCDD; 📞444 8233; www.tcdd.gov.tr) for details.

From 2014, high-speed trains to Ankara will depart from a new railway hub in Üsküdar, on the Asian shore.

❶ Getting Around

To/From the Airport

Atatürk International Airport

○ Many hotels will provide a free hotel shuttle pick-up if you stay with them for three nights or more. There are also cheap (but slow) shuttle-bus services from hotels to the airport. Check with your hotel.

○ Taxis cost around ₺40/50 to Sultanahmet/ Taksim Meydanı.

○ Havataş (Havaş) Airport Buses depart from outside the arrivals hall every 30 minutes between 4am and 1am (₺10, 40 minutes to one hour), stopping outside the Havaş ticket office on Cumhuriyet Caddesi, just off Taksim Meydanı.

○ There's an efficient metro service from the airport to Zeytinburnu (₺2, every 10 minutes or so from 5.40am until 1.40am), from where it's easy to connect with the tram to central İstanbul. From the international departures hall, follow the 'Metro/Subway' signs down the escalators and through the underground walkway. The entire trip takes around 60/70/95 minutes to Sultanahmet/Eminönü/Taksim.

Sabiha Gökçen International Airport

○ Taxis cost around ₺90/120 to Taksim/ Sultanahmet.

○ Havataş (Havaş) Airport Buses travel to the Havaş ticket office on Cumhuriyet Caddesi (₺12, 90 minutes), just off Taksim Meydanı, between 5am and midnight; after midnight there are shuttle services 30 minutes after every flight arrival.

Funicular Railway

The 19th-century Tünel climbs the steep hill from Karaköy to the foot of the İstiklal Caddesi (₺1.40). The three-minute service runs from 7am to 9pm Monday to Friday (from 7.30am on weekends), every five or 10 minutes.

A modern funicular railway climbs from Kabataş to Taksim Meydanı (₺2). The three-minute service runs around every three minutes.

Metro

A line connects Şişhane, near Tünel Meydanı in Beyoğlu, and Taksim Meydanı (₺2). Services run every five minutes or so from 6.15am until midnight.

Taxi

○ Rates are reasonable; Sultanahmet to Taksim Meydanı will cost around ₺15, with no evening surcharges.

○ If you take a taxi over either of the Bosphorus bridges it is your responsibility to cover the toll. The driver will add this to your fare.

Tram

An excellent *tramvay* (tramway) service runs past Zeytinburnu (where it connects with the metro to/from the airport) to Beyazıt-Kapalı Çarşı (for the Grand Bazaar), Sultanahmet, Eminönü, Karaköy (connecting with the Tünel) and Kabataş (connecting with the funicular to Taksim Meydanı). Services run every five minutes from 6am to midnight. The fare is ₺2; *jetons* are available from machines at tram stops.

Gallipoli & the North Aegean

Turkey's northern Aegean is a dramatic setting for some key historic sights. North of İzmir – a buzzing, Eurocentric metropolis with an attractive *kordon* (seafront) – the hilltop ruins of Bergama and Behramkale are breathtaking sites of antiquity. All around is wild countryside and refreshingly undeveloped coastline, with quiet Ege Deniz (Aegean Sea) beaches. Supplement sunbathing with diving in Ayvalık, windsurfing in Alaçatı and cruises to islands and bays.

The Greek influence in this region is inescapable. Many towns experienced the great population exchange of the 1920s, and in places like Ayvalık and Bozcaada island, the architecture, music and food seem like bittersweet echoes from across the horizon.

The beautiful, pine-strewn Gallipoli (Gelibolu) Peninsula, site of bloody WWI battles, is a hushed and poignant area. On the Anatolian side of the Dardanelles, Antipodean pilgrims and Turkish students give Çanakkale's nightspots a lively feel.

Bozcaada (p127)

Trojan Horse, Troy (p126)
DEMETRIO CARRASCO/GETTY IMAGES ©

Gallipoli & the North Aegean

BLACK SEA (KARADENİZ)

Pazarkule (Kastanies)
Edirne
Havsa
E80
Babaeski
Pınarhisar
Vize
Kıyıköy
Pythion
Lüleburgaz
Saray
Karacaköy
Karaburun
E87
Uzunköprü
Hamidiye
Hayrabolu
E80
Çerkezköy
Sinekli
İstanbul
Küplü
Muratlı
Çorlu
Çatalca
Silivri
Ferai
Kipi
İpsala
Malkara
E84
Tekirdağ
Marmara Ereğlisi
Keşan
Kumbağ
Erikli
Kadıköy
Mürefte
Marmara Island
İbrice (Saros)
Şarköy
GREECE

Bay of Saros
Bolayır
Sea of Marmara (Marmara Denızı)
İmralı Island
Gökçeada
Gelibolu
Karabiga
Erdek
1
Lapseki
Eceabat
Sinekçi
Edincik
Bandırma
Bayramdere
Gallipoli National Historic Park
Çanakkale
Bakacak
E90
Biga
Karacabey
Çalı
Kuşcenneti Milli Parkı
Kuş Gölü
E90
Aksakal
Gölü Ulubat
Bursa
Troy
Tevfikiye
Kirazlı
Çan
Gönen
Geyikli
Bayramiç
Hamdibey
Manyas
Ezine
Evciler
Pazarköy
Susurluk
Çaltılıbük
E87
Kalkım
Alexandria Troas
Etili
Yeniköy
6
Gülpınar
Biga Peninsula
Ayvacık
Güre İskelesi
Akçay
Edremit
Balıkesir
Babakale
7
Kadırga
Havran
İvrindi
Ören
Burhaniye
Bay of Edremit
Korucu
Kayapa
Konakpınar
Gömeç
Sarıbeyler
Savaştepe
Lesvos (GREECE)
3
Altınova
Kozak
Soma
Gelembe
Mytilini
AEGEAN SEA (EGE DENİZİ)
Dikili
Kınık
2
Zeytindağ
Palamut
Çandarlı
Yuntdağ
Demirci
Yeni Foça
Aliağa
Osmancalı
Saruhanlı
Akhisar
Foça
Muradiye
Gölmarmara
Karaburun
Menemen
Emiralem
Manisa
Marmara Gölü
Küçükbahçe
Mordoğan
Karaoğlanlı
Turgutlu
Ahmetli
Chios
E87
5
Sardis
Salihli
Çeşme
Buca
Kemalpaşa
E96
Alaçatı
Uzunkuyu
Menderes (Cumaovası)
Dağkızılca
Sığacık
Seferihisar
E87
Bayındır
Ödemiş
Birgi
Akkum
Teos
Torbalı

1 Gallipoli Peninsula
2 Bergama (Pergamum)
3 Ayvalık Old Town
4 Historic Kırkpınar Oil Wrestling Festival
5 İzmir
6 Bozcaada
7 Behramkale & Assos

50 km
30 miles

Gallipoli & the North Aegean's Highlights

Gallipoli Peninsula

This slender finger of land (p118) was İstanbul's first line of defence during the Ottoman Empire, and forces commanded by Winston Churchill and Mustafa Kemal (later Atatürk) clashed here in WWI. Today, memorials and cemeteries mark the beaches and ridges where 130,000 Allied and Turkish soldiers perished. Above: Lone Pine cemetery (p120); Top Right: Anzac Cove (p120); Bottom Right: Chunuk Bair (p120)

Need to Know

TOP TIP Visit on a tour for historical insights.

TRANSPORT From İstanbul, get there via the ferry to Bandırma and bus to Çanakkale. **For further coverage, see p118**

Gallipoli Peninsula Don't Miss List

BY BÜLENT 'BILL' YILMAZ KORKMAZ, GUIDE

1 ANZAC COVE

This is where the first Anzac soldiers landed on 25 April 1915, where the first shot was fired on that day and where the first Turkish soldier died. Eight months later, the Anzacs left from here as the campaign ended. It is where the Anzac legend was born, and where history was made.

2 W BEACH

Little-visited W Beach, 1.5km west of Seddülbahr, was one of the main British landing beaches – famous for the 'six VCs before breakfast'; ie six Victoria Crosses awarded to the Lancashire Fusiliers. It became the main British base, and remains of British-built piers; small boat wrecks, tunnels and trenches can be seen in the area.

3 CHUNUK BAIR

This hill was one of the Allies' main objectives in April 1915. You can see the Dardanelles (and the northern battlefields) from Chunuk Bair, so whoever held it could control the strait. The New Zealand Wellington Infantry Battalion captured and held it for 36 hours, losing over 90% of their men. Turkish soldiers under Mustafa Kemal finally defeated the British reinforcements and recaptured the hill, bringing victory to the Ottoman Empire.

4 THE NEW ZEALAND WALK

This walking trail starts from a fire trail 75m south of the Chunuk Bair New Zealand Memorial, and descends Rhododendron Ridge and the lower slopes of hills including the Tabletop to the New Zealand Number 2 Outpost. New Zealand soldiers took this route to Chunuk Bair, and later wounded troops retreated down here to the beach. It is sometimes steep and easier to go down than up.

5 ANAFARTALAR WAR MUSEUM

This museum, 6km north of Anzac Cove, displays relics from the battles, found by the Gündoğan family on their land.

Bergama (Pergamum)

At first glance, Bergama (p131) is simply a market town with an old Ottoman quarter. On the surrounding hills, however, stand the Acropolis, with classical ruins including the stunning theatre, and the Asclepion, Rome's pre-eminent medical centre. In town, the Red Basilica was a temple to Egyptian gods. Below: Acropolis library (p138); Top Right: Asclepion (p131); Bottom Right: Outside the Red Basilica (p132)

Need to Know

TOP TIP Take the cable car up to the Acropolis, and walk back down. **SHUTTLE** Until 7pm, free buses connect Bergama's otogar and town centre. **For further coverage, see p131**

JOHN ELK III/GETTY IMAGES ©

Bergama (Pergamum) Don't Miss List

BY ERSIN KIRMAZ, OWNER OF ODYSSEY GUESTHOUSE

1 ACROPOLIS

Remains discovered in the citadel (p138) date back millennia, but the first important buildings built here were the Temple of Athena and the 10,000-seat theatre. The city walls reached their largest size during the reign of Eumenes II (197–159 BC), who also built the Altar of Zeus, the library with 200,000 books and the Great Palace. In the Middle City were sacred areas dedicated to the goddesses Hera and Demeter, the Asclepius temple of healing, gymnasiums and the water supply. Another significant ruin is the Temple of Trajan, built by the Roman emperors Trajan and Hadrian.

2 ASCLEPION

With galleries, a 3500-seat theatre, a cult prayer room, a library and Asclepius temple, the Asclepion (p131) was an important health centre during the Roman period. The treatments here included psychotherapy, physical therapy, drinking sacred water, fasting, water and mud baths, oils and creams, and eating healthy vegetables.

3 RED BASILICA

Owing to the importance of Egyptian gods in the Roman Empire, Hadrian built this temple to Serapis and Isis. During the early Byzantine period, additions were made and the temple became one of Anatolia's first churches.

4 OLD TOWN

Hundreds of 160- to 180-year-old Ottoman and Greek stone houses stand on the narrow streets of Bergama old town (p131). Greek, Jewish, Muslim and Armenian communities lived side by side here during the Ottoman Empire, and there are old churches, mosques and a synagogue, as well as three old bridges.

5 ÇUKUR HAN

This 14th-century caravanserai (**Barbaros Mahallesi**) in the historic Ottoman bazaar is Bergama's only well-preserved caravanserai. Its 28 rooms provided accommodation for traders who came from other places with goods and animals. The lower floor was a depot, barn and workplace, while the traders ate and slept upstairs.

Ayvalık Old Town

Wandering between the wonderfully dilapidated stone houses and churches of the former Greek village (p129), winding along lanes where the shadows slowly lengthen, old men sip çay, dogs snooze and sunlight dapples cobbled squares, gives a glimpse of a vanishing way of life. Ayvalık's waterfront bars and fish restaurants seem far away: commercial development has yet to change the old town and the past is palpable.

Historic Kırkpınar Oil Wrestling Festival

The Turks produce colourful spectacles, but few sights are more memorable than Edirne's Tarihi Kırkpınar Yağlı Güreş Festivali (p126), one of the world's most bizarre sporting events. The 650-year-old contest sees muscular *pehlivan* (wrestlers), naked except for a pair of heavy leather shorts, coat themselves with olive oil and throw each other around. Dozens of matches are held simultaneously.

İzmir

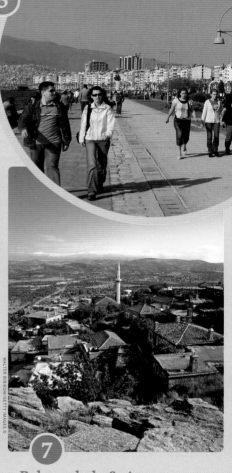

Once you clear İzmir's sprawling, traffic-clogged suburbs, Turkey's third-largest city (p135) is a relatively liberal place with a wonderful *kordon*. Just inland from the waterfront promenade, Alsancak's bars and clubs are good places to appreciate İzmir's alternative spirit. The port town had large Jewish and Levantine communities, which gave it a European ambience; Konak Pier was even designed by the same architect as the Eiffel Tower. İzmir's *kordon* (p135)

Bozcaada

One of Turkey's few inhabited Aegean islands, tiny Bozcaada (p127) has been one of the country's great wine-growing regions since ancient times. Vineyards still blanket its sunny slopes, and Bozcaada town is a fine place to try the local vino, with bars, restaurants and boutique hotels on its picturesque lanes. Between sips, explore the medieval fortress, wander the market, hit the beach and dine on fresh seafood. Men harvesting grapes for wine

Behramkale & Assos

Sandwiched between a blue bay and miles of undulating Aegean countryside, this hilltop village and harbour (p127) offer a combination of ruins and relaxation. Having admired the view from the 6th-century BC Greek temple, wander down Behramkale's cobbled streets and past the hillside ruins to Assos, where fish restaurants await. As Behramkale's statue of Aristotle suggests, the famous philosopher lived here in the 4th century BC. Behramkale

Gallipoli & the North Aegean's Best...

Old Towns

○ **Ayvalık** (p129) Narrow lanes wind through the sleepy former Greek village.

○ **Bozcaada town** (p127) Another picturesque old Greek village – this one on a viticultural Aegean island.

○ **Çanakkale** (p122) The Ottoman old quarter has hamams, mosques, a clock tower and lively nightspots.

○ **Bergama (Pergamum)** (p131) Ottoman district with atmospheric pensions and a hilltop restaurant with panoramic views.

Castles & Mosques

○ **Kilitbahir Fortress** (p120) Sturdy Ottoman edifice guarding the Dardanelles.

○ **Selimiye Camii** (p123) Masterful Ottoman architect's finest work.

○ **Konak Camii** (p134) Tile-covered 18th-century mosque.

○ **Bozcaada Fortress** (p127) Byzantine, with Venetian, Genoese and Ottoman additions.

Diving & Boat Trips

○ **Ayvalık** (p128) Dive to deep-sea red coral at sites such as Deli Mehmet and Kerbela.

○ **İzmir** (p141) Shimmy down the port city's glorious *kordon* on ferries between piers.

○ **Gallipoli Peninsula** (p119) Snorkel to a WWI shipwreck.

○ **Alibey Island** (p128) Cruise to the island, with its waterfront fish restaurants and old Greek town, from Ayvalık.

Need to Know

Ruined Temples

- **Temple of Athena** (p128) Behramkale's atmospheric 6th-century BC ruins.

- **Red Basilica** (p132) Originally a temple to Egyptian gods.

- **Temple of Telesphorus** (p131) Reached through an underground corridor in Pergamum's Asclepion.

- **Temple of Trajan** (p138) Still-standing marble columns; built by the clearly bashful Roman emperor Trajan.

RESOURCES

- **Çanakkale.com.tr** (www.canakkale.com.tr)

- **Gallipoli and the Anzacs** (www.anzacsite. gov.au)

- **Gallipoli Association** (www.gallipoli-association. org)

- **Gestaş ferries** (www. gestasdenizulasim.com.tr)

GETTING AROUND

- **Air** Flights to Çanakkale from İstanbul; to Edremit (near Ayvalık) from İstanbul and Ankara with Anadolu Jet and Bora Jet; and to İzmir from across Turkey.

- **Boat** Ferries to Bandırma from İstanbul; Bozcaada from Çanakkale and Yükyeri İskelesi; Alibey Island and Lesvos (Greece) from Ayvalık; and Chios (Greece) from Çeşme.

- **Bus** A good way to get between major spots such as Çanakkale, Ayvalık, Bergama and İzmir.

- **Car** Good roads; major hire companies in İzmir and İstanbul.

- **Dolmuş** Useful for rural spots such as Behramkale and Assos.

- **Tour** A good way to see the Gallipoli Peninsula and Troy.

BE FOREWARNED

- **Book ahead** If visiting the Gallipoli Peninsula and Çanakkale around Anzac Day (25 April) or the Turkish equivalent (18 March), or Edirne around the Historic Kırkpınar Oil Wrestling Festival (late June/early July).

- **Gallipoli tours** From Çanakkale, catch the ferry to Eceabat (₺2) and start the tour there; it's typically ₺30 cheaper than starting in Çanakkale.

- **Restaurants** Check the prices of fish and wine before ordering.

- **Driving** Avoid driving in the narrow lanes in old towns such as Ayvalık.

- **Tours** Check what you get, eg do cruises include lunch? How long will the driver wait at sights on a private taxi tour?

- **Hire car** A one-way journey (eg İzmir–İstanbul) is a convenient way to see the region, but will incur a relocation charge.

Left: İzmir (p135);
Above: Temple of Trajan (p138)
(LEFT) UCHAR/GETTY IMAGES ©;
(ABOVE) FILIPPO MARIA BIANCHI/GETTY IMAGES ©

Gallipoli & the North Aegean Itineraries

Enjoy a double-bill of classical ruins and old Greek villages in Bergama (Pergamum), Ayvalık, Behram-kale and Assos; then continue north via Bozcaada to the WWI sites around the Gallipoli Peninsula.

3 DAYS

BERGAMA (PERGAMUM) TO BEHRAMKALE & ASSOS

Aegean Cruise

Fly to İzmir from İstanbul (or elsewhere) and head north to **(1) Bergama (Pergamum)** for a look at some of the Aegean's finest classical ruins outside Ephesus (Efes). Make a beeline for the Acropolis, with its vertigo-inducing 10,000-seat theatre, and if time allows carry on to the Asclepion, a Roman medical centre where dream analysis and mud baths were employed. Then visit the Roman-Byzantine Red Basilica and Archaeology Museum.

If driving, take the scenic, inland route via Kozak to **(2) Ayvalık**, winding through idyllic pine-clad hills to the coastal town with its waterfront bars and old Greek

neighbourhood. Settle into an atmospheric pension, wander the lanes and markets, hop on a ferry or cruise to Alibey Island and dine on *balık* (fish) and rakı (aniseed brandy) at Balıkçı ('Fisherman') restaurant.

Next morning, take a day cruise across the Bay of Edremit to the twin villages of **(3) Behramkale and Assos**. Eat some meze in one of Assos' many harbourside restaurants and head uphill through Behramkale, where villagers set out stalls, to the ruined 6th-century BC Temple of Athena.

BEHRAMKALE & ASSOS TO THE GALLIPOLI PENINSULA
Coastal Meander

5 DAYS

Follow the previous itinerary to **(1) Behramkale and Assos** and, ferry schedules allowing, continue to tiny **(2) Bozcaada**, perfectly appointed in the Aegean, with winemakers, a medieval castle and a vine-draped old Greek neighbourhood. The mixed community of islanders and İstanbullu escapees offers stylish hotels and rustic pensions.

Catch a ferry to **(4) Çanakkale** (or to Yükyeri İskelesi, allowing you to stop en route to Çanakkale at the ruins of **(3) Troy**, of Trojan Horse fame). This friendly student town makes a great base, with an attractive old quarter and a military museum featuring

a replica minelayer. On the Çanakkale waterfront is the towering plywood horse that featured in the Brad Pitt movie *Troy*.

A short ferry ride across the Dardanelles leads to the **(5) Gallipoli Peninsula**, where memorials and cemeteries recall the 130,000 soldiers who died here in WWI. The northern peninsula has the significant Anzac sites of Lone Pine and Chunuk Bair.

To reach İstanbul, head east along the north shore of the Sea of Marmara; or, head along the south shore and take the ferry from Bandırma.

Assos (p127)

Discover Gallipoli & the North Aegean

Temple of Athena (p128), Behramkale
IZZET KERIBAR/GETTY IMAGES ©

Gallipoli (Gelibolu) Peninsula
✆0286

For a millennium, the slender peninsula that forms the northwestern side of the Dardanelles has been the key to İstanbul: any navy that could break through the strait had a good chance of capturing the capital of the Eastern European world. Many fleets have tried to force open the strait, but most, including the mighty Allied fleet mustered in WWI, have failed.

Today the Gallipoli battlefields are peaceful places, covered in brush and pine forests. But the battles fought here nearly a century ago are still alive in the memories of many, both Turkish and foreign, and especially among Australians and New Zealanders, who view the peninsula as a place of pilgrimage. The Turkish officer responsible for the defence of Gallipoli was Mustafa Kemal – the future Atatürk – and the Turkish victory is commemorated in Turkey on 18 March.

On Anzac Day (25 April), a dawn service marks the anniversary of the Allied landings, attracting thousands of travellers from Down Under and beyond. In recent years an increasing number of Turkish visitors are being bussed in by municipal councils to better understand the Turkish side of the story.

Tours

Unless you have some knowledge of the history, a guided tour is by far the best way to experience the peninsula. The

Gallipoli Peninsula

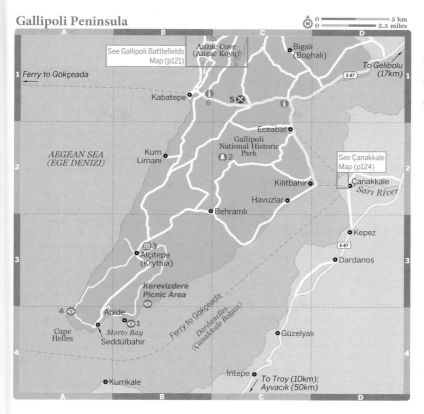

recommended tour providers generally offer five- or six-hour afternoon tours of the northern peninsula, including transport, guide and picnic lunch (typically ₺60/90 from Eceabat/Çanakkale). Condensed tours from İstanbul are often exhausting, as they involve visiting the battlefields straight after a five-hour bus ride.

CROWDED HOUSE TOURS   Tour
(☎ 814 1565; www.crowdedhousegallipoli.com;
Eceabat) Bülent 'Bill' Yılmaz Korkmaz's tours can be organised through Hotel Crowded House. Private tours and morning snorkelling to a WWI shipwreck at North Beach (₺35, including transportation and equipment) are also offered. One- and two-day packages involve a transfer from accommodation in İstanbul to the otogar (bus station), then a night in Eceabat before the tour.

Gallipoli Peninsula

HASSLE FREE TRAVEL AGENCY   Tour
(☎ 213 5969; www.anzachouse.com; Çanakkale)
Boat trips are also available.

If You Like...
Military History

The Gallipoli Peninsula's famous WWI sites are just a few of the much-contested area's military sights from across the centuries. Numerous museums also look at the experiences of soldiers in the WWI campaign.

1 KILYE BAY INFORMATION CENTRE
(Kilye Koyu Ana Tanıtım Merkezi; ⊙9am-noon & 1-5pm) Has an information centre with interactive displays, exhibition areas, a memorial, cinema and library.

2 KABATEPE INFORMATION CENTRE & MUSEUM
(Kabatepe Müzesi ve Tanıtma Merkezi; Map p119; admission ₺3; ⊙9am-1pm & 2-6pm) Reopened in 2012 with more interactive exhibits.

3 GALLIPOLI WAR MUSEUM
(Gelibolu Savaş Müzesi; ☎566 1272; Sahil Yolu; admission ₺3; ⊙9am-noon & 1-6pm Tue-Sun) On the main road into Gelibolu (at the top of the Gallipoli Peninsula), this museum evokes the battlefield experience, starting with the sandbags and barbed wire outside. Artefacts range from a letter home (on pink paper) to photos of recent excavations and dedications.

4 GALLERY OF THE GALLIPOLI CAMPAIGN
(Map p119; admission ₺3; ⊙8am-8pm) In Alçıtepe village (southern Gallipoli Peninsula), the museum has photos and artefacts enhanced by mock-ups, dioramas and sound effects.

5 SALIM MUTLU WAR MUSEUM
(Map p119; admission ₺1; ⊙8am-8pm) Also in Alçıtepe, this hodgepodge of rusty finds from the battlefields gives a sense of just how much artillery was fired.

6 FORTRESS
(admission ₺3; ⊙8am-5pm Tue-Sun winter, to 7.30pm summer) Kilitbahir's 15th-century Ottoman castle, with a grand seven-storey interior tower and a war museum in another tower, overlooks the Namazgah Tabyası, a mazelike series of 19th-century defensive bunkers.

Sights

Northern Peninsula

The **Gallipoli National Historic Park** (Gelibolu Yarımadası Tarihi Milli Parkı; Map p119) encompasses 33,500 hectares of the peninsula, all of the significant battle sites and over 50 war cemeteries (Allied and Turkish). The principal battles took place on its western shore, around Anzac Cove, 12km northwest of Ecebat, and in the hills east of the cove. The following are the most internationally famous of the numerous sites.

The ill-fated Allied landing began at **Anzac Cove**, beneath and just south of the steep cliffs of Arıburnu, on 25 April 1915. The **Anzac Commemorative Site** (Anzac Tören Alanı), where dawn services are held on Anzac Day, is nearby.

Lone Pine (Kanlısırt) is perhaps the most moving of the Anzac cemeteries. Australian forces captured the Turkish positions here on 6 August 1915, and 7000 men died, in an area the size of a soccer field, in four days. The trees that shaded the cemetery were swept away by a fire in 1994, leaving only one: a lone pine planted from the seed of the original solitary tree, which stood here at the beginning of the battle and gave the battlefield its name.

Continuing uphill, the road marks what was the thin strip of no-man's land between the two sides' trenches. The **Chunuk Bair New Zealand Cemetery and Memorial** (Conkbayırı Yeni Zelanda Mezarlığı ve Anıtı) is located at what was the first objective of the Allied landing in April 1915. As the Anzac troops made their way up the scrub-covered slopes, Mustafa Kemal brought up the 57th Infantry Regiment. The 57th was wiped out, but held the line and inflicted equally heavy casualties on Anzac forces below. Later, Chunuk Bair was at the heart of the struggle for the peninsula from 6 to 10 August 1915, when some 30,000 men died on this ridge.

Southern Peninsula

Fewer travellers visit the southern peninsula, where there are more British, French and Turkish memorials than Anzac sites. During low-season weeks, it's a good place to escape the traffic and tour groups, although the Çanakkale Şehitleri Anıtı in particular is becoming increasingly popular with Turkish groups.

In and around the villages of **Alçıtepe**, 12km south of Kabatepe, and **Seddülbahir** are several war museums, cemeteries and monuments. East of the latter, the **Çanakkale Şehitleri Anıtı** (Çanakkale Martyrs' Memorial; Map p119), also known as the Abide monument, is a gigantic four-legged, almost-42m-high stone table that commemorates the Turkish soldiers who fought and died at Gallipoli.

 Eating

DOYURANLAR GÖZLEME Turkish € (Map p119; ✆814 1652; mains ₺6) The village women in charge of this roadside restaurant serve *köfte* (meatballs), *menemen* (a type of omelette) and breakfast, but *gözleme* (savoury pancake) washed down with spicy peppers and *ayran* (salted yoghurt) is the smart order.

LIMAN RESTAURANT Seafood €€ (✆814 2755; İstiklal Caddesi 67, Eceabat; mains ₺12) 'Harbour' is a humble and extremely popular fish restaurant with a delightful covered terrace. Service is sharp and unobtrusive.

ⓘ Information

Kabatepe Information Centre & Museum (Kabatepe Müzesi ve Tanıtma Merkezi; Map p119; admission ₺3; ☉9am-1pm & 2-6pm) Roughly 1km east of the village of Kabatepe, and 750m southeast of the bottom of the road up to Lone Pine and Chunuk Bair.

Kilye Bay Information Centre (Kilye Koyu Ana Tanıtım Merkezi; ☉9am-noon & 1-5pm) About 3km north of Eceabat, some 200m off the İstanbul highway.

ⓘ Getting There & Around

With your own transport, you can easily tour the northern battlefields in a day. Covering both the northern and southern parts of the peninsula is

Gallipoli Battlefields

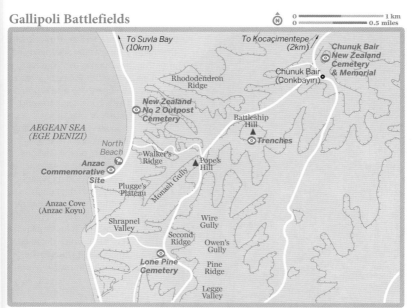

possible within one day, provided you get an early start. The most important group of monuments and cemeteries, from Lone Pine uphill to Chunuk Bair in the northern peninsula, can be toured on foot.

Bus & Dolmuş

Daily dolmuşes (minibuses; several in summer) connect Eceabat and Kabatepe (₺2.50, 15 minutes), and can drop you at the Kabatepe Information Centre & Museum.

Dolmuşes frequently run between Eceabat and Kilitbahir (₺1.50, 10 minutes).

Other services to/from Eceabat include Gelibolu (₺5, 50 minutes, hourly) and İstanbul (₺40, five hours, hourly).

Ferry

Eceabat–Çanakkale Ferries cross the Dardanelles (per person ₺2, car ₺23, 25 minutes) every hour on the hour between 7am and midnight, and roughly every two hours after that.

Kilitbahir–Çanakkale The small, privately run ferry (per person ₺2, car ₺18, 20 minutes) can carry only a few cars and waits until it is full before departing.

Taxi

Drivers in Eceabat will run you around the main sites for about ₺120, but they take only two to 2½ hours.

Çanakkale

📞 0286 / POP 104,321

With its student population, sweeping waterfront promenade and proximity to Gallipoli and Troy, Çanakkale has rightfully grown in stature as a travel destination. Its nightlife is raucous and international visitors often rate a night here as more intimate and friendly than some more famous Turkish party towns.

For a culture fix, the old town has original hamams and mosques.

During the summer, try to plan your visit for midweek to sidestep the hordes of holidaying Turks. Çanakkale is almost unbearably overcrowded around Anzac Day (25 April) and the Turkish equivalent, Çanakkale Deniz Zaferi (Çanakkale Naval Victory, 18 March).

◎ Sights & Activities

MILITARY MUSEUM   Museum
(📞 213 1730; Çimenlik Sokak; admission ₺4; ⏰ 9am-5pm Tue, Wed & Fri-Sun; 🅿) A park in the military zone at the southern end of the quay houses this museum. It's free to enter the park, which is open every day and is dotted with guns, cannons and military artefacts.

A late-Ottoman building contains informative exhibits on the Gallipoli battles and some war relics, including fused bullets that hit each other in midair. Nearby is a replica of the Nusrat minelayer (Nusrat Mayın Gemisi), which disabled three Allied ships in the Gallipoli campaign.

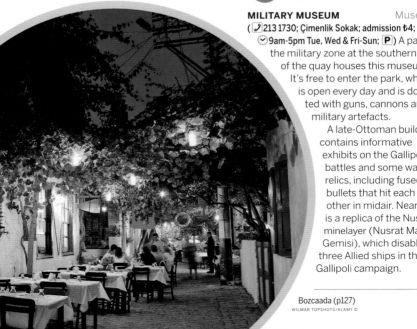

Bozcaada (p127)

Detour:
Edirne

Tucked away in the northwest corner of the country, Edirne is a small, dreamy city with magnificent Ottoman architecture and an old Roman district. The city is close to the Greek and Bulgarian borders, giving this 14th-century Ottoman capital a lively, frontier-town feel.

Ottoman mosques dot the centre, most notably the 16th-century **Selimiye Camii** (Selimiye Mosque; Mimar Sinan Caddesi), one of Turkey's finest mosques, designed by the great architect Mimar Sinan. The mosque is smaller but more elegant than Sinan's Süleymaniye Camii in İstanbul, and it is said that he considered this his finest work. Lit up at night, the complex is a spectacular sight with its two *medreses* (seminaries).

Most of Edirne's budget and midrange hotels are on Maarif Caddesi, including **Efe Hotel** (0284-213 6166; www.efehotel.com; Maarif Caddesi 13; s/d ₺100/150; ✳ @). Beyond its atmospheric, archival lobby with tartan carpets and polished wood, the small rooms have chaotic retro patterns, heavy furniture and soft lighting.

The city's dish of choice is Edirne *ciğeri* (thinly sliced deep-fried calf's liver, served with crispy fried red chillies and yoghurt) and the most interesting cafe is **Melek Anne** ('Angel' Anne's; 0284-213 3263; Maarif Caddesi 18; mains ₺7), popular with students and foodies. The 120-year-old house serves a rotating menu of homemade dishes, including unusual salads and hearty vegetarian choices.

Regular bus services to/from Edirne include Çanakkale (₺30, four hours) and İstanbul (₺12, 2½ hours). Demand for İstanbul is high so book ahead.

Mehmet the Conqueror built the impressive **Çimenlik Kalesi** (Meadow Castle) in 1452, and Süleyman the Magnificent repaired it in 1551. Inside are some paintings of the battles of Gallipoli.

CLOCK TOWER   Landmark

The five-storey Ottoman *saat kulesi* (clock tower) was built in 1897.

TROJAN HORSE   Monument

This much-larger-than-life model featured in the movie *Troy* (2004).

YALI HAMAM   Hamam

(Çarşı Caddesi 5; ⏰men 6am-11pm, women 8am-6pm) In this 17th-century hamam, the full works costs ₺30.

 **Sleeping**

If you intend to be in town around 25 April (Anzac Day), book well in advance and check prices carefully.

HOTEL LIMANI   Hotel €€

(217 4090; www.hotellimani.com; Yalı Caddesi 12; r ₺130-180; ✳ @) The 'Harbour' is the most popular option in Çannakale, its smallish rooms thoughtfully fitted with quality linens, pillows, drapery, wallpaper and polished floorboards. It's worth spending a little extra for a sea view. Don't miss a cocktail in the superb lobby restaurant.

HOTEL DES ETRANGERS   Boutique Hotel €€€

(214 2424; www.yabancilaroteli.com; Yali Caddesi 25-27; s/d ₺180/240; ✳ 🛜) An old French hotel has found new life thanks to a dedicated local couple who reopened its gilt-edged doors. The lobby is grand and the rooms are country-style Ottoman by the sea.

HOTEL KERVANSARAY   Boutique Hotel €€

(217 8192; www.otelkervansaray.com; Fetvane Sokak 13; s/d/tr ₺100/170/200; ✳ @) In an Ottoman house, the Kervansaray is the

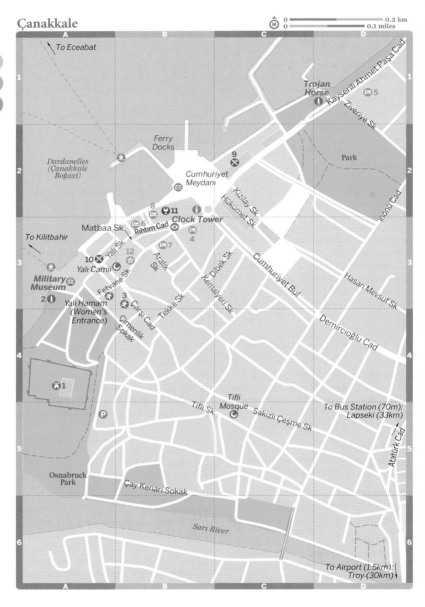

Çanakkale

0.2 km
0.1 miles

To Eceabat

Trojan Horse

Kayserili Ahmet Paşa Cad

Ziveriye Sk

Ferry Docks

Dardanelles (Çanakkale Boğazi)

Park

Inönü Cad

Cumhuriyet Meydanı

Kızılay Sk

Hükümet Sk

Matbaa Sk

Rıhtım Cad

Clock Tower

To Kilitbahir

Yalı Sk

Aralık Sk

Dibek Sk

Cumhuriyet Bul

Hasan Mevsuf Sk

Kemalyeri Sk

Military Museum

Yalı Camii

Fetvane Sk

Tekke Sk

Demircioğlu Cad

Yalı Hamam (Women's Entrance)

Çarşı Cad

Çimenlik Sokak

Tifli Mosque

Tifli Sk

Sakızlı Çeşme Sk

To Bus Station (70m); Lapseki (33km)

Atatürk Cad

Osnabruck Park

Çay Kenarı Sokak

Sarı River

To Airport (1.5km); Troy (30km)

To Bus Station (70m); Lapseki (33km)

only half-historic hotel in town. The smell of yesteryear may permeate the older rooms, but the dowdiness is kind of fun. The newer rooms have bathtubs instead of showers, but the garden is a little oasis.

ANZAC HOTEL   Hotel €

(☎ 217 7777; www.anzachotel.com; Saat Kulesi Meydanı 8; s/d/tr ₺75/90/120; ✳ @) The dependable Anzac has a mezzanine area for hanging out, and well-presented rooms with good-sized bathrooms.

Çanakkale

HOTEL AKOL Hotel €€€
(✆ 217 9456; www.hotelakol.com.tr; Kayserili Ahmet Paşa Caddesi; s/d/ste ₺150/200/370; ❄ ⊜) This old orange mare near the wooden horse is enormous and antiquated. Popular with tour groups, it's well serviced and ideal for anonymity. There's a roof bar that gets pretty loose on weekends.

Eating

The waterfront is lined with licensed restaurants and street stalls offering simple items.

YALOVA Seafood €€
(✆ 217 1045; www.yalovarestaurant.com; Gümrük Sokak 7; mains ₺15-20) This is a pure seafood restaurant that combines impeccable service with the best produce and preparation in Çanakkale. Ask for a tour of the 2nd floor where you can select your own fish. Wine is matched to order.

CAFE DU PORT Restaurant €€
(✆ 217 2908; Yalı Caddesi 12; ◷ 8am-11pm) Hotel Limani's popular restaurant is stylish and inviting, the chefs are the most versatile in Çanakkale and the service is brilliant for a regional city. The restaurant's specialities include steaks, salads and pastas, as well as some excellent cocktails.

ANAFARTALAR KEBAP Kebap €€
(✆ 214 9112; İskele Meydanı; mains ₺10; ◷ 8am-11.30pm) In a glass-walled hotel lobby, Anafartalar is the best place for an İskender kebap (döner kebap on fresh pide, with tomato sauce, browned butter and yoghurt).

Drinking & Entertainment

Most of Çanakkale's busiest bars and clubs cluster around Matbaa and Fetvane Sokaks.

BENZIN Bar, Cafe
(Eski Balıkhane Sokak 11; ☎) Friendly staff make this grungy waterfront bar-cafe, done out in 1960s decor, a relaxing spot for a drink and a bite (pizzas ₺8 to ₺12.50).

YALI HANI BAR Performance Space, Bar
(Fetvane Sokak 26) Upstairs in the 19th-century Yalı Han, this popular performance space opens and closes at whim. The outside gallery overlooks a courtyard tea garden.

ℹ Information

Çanakkale is centred on its harbour, with ATMs right by the docks, and hotels, restaurants, banks and bus offices all within a few hundred metres.
Tourist office (✆ 217 1187; Cumhuriyet Meydanı; ◷ 8am-7pm Jun-Sep, 8.30am-5.30pm Oct-May) Has brochures and bus timetables.

❶ Getting There & Away

Air

Turkish Airlines (www.thy.com) flies to/from İstanbul (55 minutes) three times a week. A Turkish Airlines shuttle bus (₺7) links central Çanakkale with the airport, 2km southeast; a taxi costs about ₺10.

Boat

Bozcaada (₺15/30 one way/return, 55 minutes, one daily Tuesday to Wednesday and Friday to Sunday)

Eceabat (₺3/25 per person/car, 15 minutes, several daily)

Kilitbahir (₺2/20 per person/car, 10 minutes, several daily)

Bus

Most buses pick up and drop off at the bus company offices near the harbour. Coming from İstanbul, hop on a ferry from Yenikapı to Bandırma, and take a bus from there to Çanakkale (₺20, 2½ hours, hourly). It's easier than trekking out to İstanbul's otogar.

Regular services to/from Çanakkale include Ankara (₺45, 10 hours), Ayvalık (₺25, 3½ hours), Bursa (₺30, 4½ hours), İstanbul (₺35, six hours) and İzmir (₺35, 5½ hours).

Troy (Truva)

🖉 0286

While not the most dramatic ancient site, Troy is testament to the importance of myth to the human experience. Some imagination is needed to reconstruct the city's former splendour but a decent guide will bring to life the scene of Homer's *Iliad*. **Troy** (🖉 283 0536; per person ₺15; ⏱ 8.30am-7pm May–mid-Sep, to 5pm mid-Sep–end Apr) is a popular destination for weekending school parties; try to visit midweek.

The first inhabitants lived here during the early Bronze Age. There were nine successive cities, Troy I to IX, dating from 3000 BC to AD 500. Most archaeologists believe the Trojan War happened during the existence of Troy VI (1700–1250 BC).

Slip-Sliding Away in Edirne

Edirne's **Tarihi Kırkpınar Yağlı Güreş Festivali** (Historic Kırkpınar Oil Wrestling Festival; www.kirkpinar.com) is one of the world's oldest and most bizarre sporting events, in which muscular men, naked except for a pair of heavy leather shorts, coat themselves with olive oil and throw each other around. The three-day contest takes place annually in late June/early July.

The oleaginous contest's origins go back six and a half centuries to the early Ottoman Empire, when 40 Ottoman soldiers conquered a Byzantine fortress. The soldiers, all keen wrestlers, celebrated by challenging each other to bouts. Two were so evenly matched that they fought for days without any clear result, until both of them finally dropped dead.

Wrestlers, classed by height, age and experience, compete in categories from *minik* (toddler) to *baş* (first class), with dozens of matches happening simultaneously in the Sarayiçi stadium. Bouts are capped at 30 or 40 minutes, after which they enter 'sudden death' one-fall-wins overtime. Prizes are awarded for gentlemanly conduct and technique, as well as the coveted and hotly contested *başpehlivan* (head wrestler) title.

Biletix (www.biletix.com) sells tickets to the wrestling for about ₺60. Transport and accommodation fill up fast around the festival. The stadium is by the Tunca River, about 1.5km north of the Üç Şerefeli Cami in central Edirne (take Hükümet Caddesi). A taxi from the centre costs about ₺7.

Detour:
Bozcaada

This stylish Aegean island is still relatively unknown outside the smart Turkish travel set. New wine bars and pensions seemingly open every summer, but Bozcaada town is still all charm, with a warren of picturesque, vine-draped old houses and cobbled streets beneath a medieval **fortress** (admission ₺2; ⊙10am-1pm & 2-6pm). The ferry docks next to the fortress.

Bozcaada is one of Turkey's great wine-growing regions, with vineyards blanketing its sunny slopes. You can taste their efforts in Bozcaada town.

Outside the school-holiday period (mid-June to mid-September) many businesses close; some eateries and bars open at weekends and on Wednesdays, when a market fills the main square.

The island is small, with lovely unspoilt sandy **beaches** along the southwest coast. Ayazma is the most popular and best equipped, boasting several cafes and a small, abandoned Greek monastery uphill.

The charming sleeping options in Bozcaada town's old Greek neighbourhood include boutique hotel **Dokuz Oda** (☏0532 427 0648; www.dokuzoda.com; Eylül Caddesi 43; s/d ₺130/190). Numerous restaurants serve the local seafood (check prices before ordering). In the old Greek quarter, **Sandal Restaurant** (☏0286-697 0278; Alsancak Sokak; mains ₺20-25; ⊙lunch & dinner; 🛜) serves meze and fish dishes.

Gestaş (☏0286-444 0752; www.gdu.com.tr) ferries sail to/from Çanakkale and Yükyeri İskelesi (Yükyeri harbour; return per person/car ₺5/45; 30 minutes, daily), 4km west of Geyikli, south of Troy.

Hourly dolmuşes (minibuses) connect Çanakkale otogar (bus stations) and Yükyeri İskelesi (₺10). In Bozcaada town, you can hire mountain bikes and pick up dolmuşes and taxis to Ayazma beach.

Turkey's new national archaeological and history museum has been commissioned to be built along the road to Troy.

 Tours

The travel agencies we've listed that offer afternoon Gallipoli tours also run morning trips to Troy (around ₺60 per person).

 Eating

TROIA PENSION   Pension €

(☏283 0571; www.troiapension.com; Truva Mola Noktası Tevfikiye; P ❄ 🛜) This newish guesthouse, a short walk from the entrance to the ruins, has a simple restaurant, run by an English-speaking guide.

HOTEL HISARLIK   Hotel €

(☏283 0026; www.thetroyguide.com) Some 500m from the ruins, this hotel restaurant, run by a local guide's family, serves Turkish home cooking.

Behramkale & Assos
☏0286

The former Greek settlement of Behramkale, also known as Assos *köyü* (village), spreads out around the ancient temple to Athena. At the bottom of the steep hill dotted with ruins and medieval city walls, Assos, also known as Assos *liman* (harbour), is a former working harbour with a small pebble beach. Its old stone buildings and warehouses have been transformed into hotels and fish restaurants.

On weekends and public holidays from the beginning of April to the end

127

Dives, Cruises & Day Trips

The waters around Ayvalık are famed among divers for their deep-sea red coral, with marine life including moray eels, grouper, octopus and sea horses. There's even a wrecked jet to check out. One of the best local dive companies is the **Korfez Diving Center** (☑312 4996, 0532 266 3589; www.korfezdiving.com; Atatürk Bulvari Özaral Pasaji 61; ☺Mar-Nov), which moors its boat by the fish market. A day's diving costs ₺90 and courses are ₺500.

Lying just off Ayvalık, Alibey Island (known locally as Cunda) makes a perfect day trip with its waterfront fish restaurants and old Greek town. Boats (₺4, 15 minutes, every 15 minutes) run from June to early September; dolmuşes (₺2) and taxis (₺25) also run over the causeway.

Cruises head around the bay's islands, including Alibey, and stop here and there for swimming, sunbathing and walking (around ₺50 per person, including lunch). They generally depart at 11am and return by 6.30pm. **Jale Tour** (☑331 3170; www.jaletour.com; Yeni Liman Karsisi) also cruises to Assos (₺60), leaving at 10.30am and returning by 7.30pm.

---

of August, tourists pour in by the coach load. There are few facilities other than an ATM and pharmacy in Behramkale.

 Sights

TEMPLE OF ATHENA   Ruin
(☑217 6740; admission ₺8; ☺8am-7.30pm) Right on top of the hill in Behramkale village is this 6th-century BC Ionic temple. The short tapered columns with plain capitals are hardly elegant, and the concrete reconstruction hurts more than helps, but the site and the view out to Lesvos are spectacular and well worth the admission fee.

Villagers set up stalls all the way up the hill to the temple, touting local products from bags of dried herbs or mushrooms to linen and silverware.

 Eating

Proximity to the sea accounts for the higher prices at the harbour. Be sure to check the cost of fish and wine before ordering.

EHL-I KEYF   Turkish €
(☑721 7106; www.assosehlikeyf.com.tr; gözleme ₺5; ☎) This multilevel restaurant in Behramkale combines excellent, fresh food with attentive service and a very pleasant outlook. Choose from a long menu of *izgara* (grills) and *gözleme*, cocktails, coffee and ice cream.

UZUNEV   Seafood €€
(☑721 7007; mains ₺15-20; ☺lunch & dinner) Uzunev is the pick of Assos's nonhotel restaurants, with blue wooden chairs lining the terrace. Try the speciality, sea bass à l'Aristotle (steamed in a special stock), or the seafood meze (₺10).

ⓘ Getting There & Around

In summer, there's a shuttle service throughout the day between Behramkale and Assos (₺1, every 30 minutes); in winter, there are occasional dolmuşes (₺8). Regular buses run from Çanakkale (₺12, 1½ hours) to Ayvacık, where you can pick up a dolmuş/taxi to Behramkale (₺30, 20 minutes).

Ayvalık
☑0266 / POP 37,182

Ayvalık is an attractive, work-a-day fishing town with a secret. The palm-tree-lined waterfront, nearby beaches and smattering of fish restaurants are much like elsewhere on the Aegean, but wander a few streets back to find an old Greek village in spirited abandon. Colourful, shuttered doors conceal cafes and craft stores, time lapses in the afternoon sun and visitors slow down in the languid atmosphere.

Olive-oil production is the traditional business around here, and is still thriving, with lots of shops selling the end product. Ayvalık was affected by the population exchange in the early 1920s (see p335).

 Sights & Activities

There are few specific sights but Ayvalık's old town is a joy to wander around, with its maze of cobbled streets lined with wonderfully worn-looking Greek houses. You can pick up a map with information about sights, including the former Greek Orthodox churches, at Tarlakusu Gurmeko (p130) and **Çöp Madam** (312 6095; Alibey Cami Caddesi 2; 9am-5pm) craft shop.

MARKETS   Market

Thursday sees one of the region's largest and most vibrant markets. Seek out the *köy pazarı* (village market) next to the main *pazar yeri* (bazaar). A daily *balık pazarı* (fish market) also takes place on the front.

Sleeping

ISTANBUL PANSIYON   Pension €

(312 4001; www.istanbul pansiyonayvalik.com; Neşe Sokak Aralığı 4; s/d ₺35/70; P ❄ 🛜) This lovely pension on the edge of the bazaar opens onto a quiet public square. Breakfast is a delight in the lush garden, among flowers and ceramic jugs or under a green canopy.

KELEBEK PENSION   Pension €€

(312 3908; www.kelebek-pension.com; Mareşal Çakmak Caddesi 108; s/d/tr ₺60/100/135; ❄) In this colourful seven-room pension, you can see the sea from your bedroom. The white-and-blue building also has a terrace for breakfast. Bikes are available to rent.

TAKSIYARHIS PENSION   Pension €€

(312 1494; www.taksiyarhispension.com; Mareşal Çakmak Caddesi 71; per person without bathroom ₺45; ❄) This 120-year-old Greek house, behind the eponymous church, has a vine-shaded terrace with sweeping views, period chic rooms with exposed wooden beams, and areas that beckon for an afternoon nap. Breakfast costs ₺10 extra.

BONJOUR PANSIYON   Pension €€

(312 8085; www.bonjourpansiyon.com; Fevzi Çakmak Caddesi, Çeşme Sokak 5; s/d without bathroom ₺60/100; ❄) This 300-year-old mansion exudes an overwhelming sense of sentimentality in the ageing furniture and 1st floor, bathroomless rooms.

The coast at Bozcaada (p127)
SALVATOR BARKI/GETTY IMAGES ©

Ayvalık

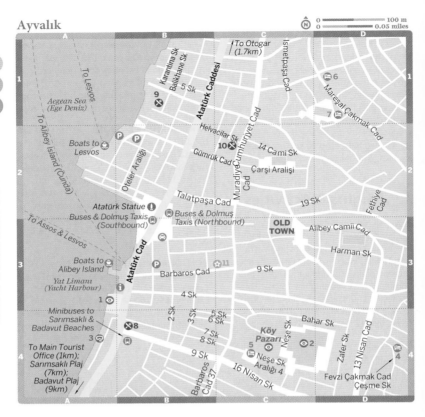

Eating & Drinking

BALIKÇI
Seafood €€

(☏ 312 9099; Balıkhane Sokak 7; mains ₺17; ⊙ dinner) Run by a local association of fishermen and marine environmentalists, this is a fine place to sample sea fare and settle into the tiled terrace or, from 8.30pm onwards, sit inside for a better view of the Turkish troubadours who get a singalong going.

TARLAKUSU GURMEKO
Cafe €€

(☏ 312 3312; Cumhuriyet Caddesi 53; ⊙ 8.30am-8.30pm; ☏) This artsy coffeehouse is surprisingly urbane and the brew is top notch. Nibbles include cookies, brownies, soup, salads, cheese plates and börek (filled pastry; ₺4.50).

AVŞAR BÜFE
Fast Food €

(Atatürk Caddesi; ⊙ 24hr high season, 7am-3am low season) Ayvalık *tost* ('toast'), essentially a toasted sandwich, is famous throughout Turkey – and this is the place to get it. The greasy delicacy typically costs just ₺4 (or ₺3 for just cheese).

SANAT FABRIKASI
Bar

(☏ 312 3045; www.sanatfabrikasi.com.tr; Barbaros Caddesi 4, Sokak 1-3) The 'arts factory' is a newly opened hub for live performance that attracts an appreciative, youthful crowd to its cosy theatre and attached bar.

ℹ Information

In high season you can get tourist information from the **kiosk** (Yat Limanı; ⊙ Jun-Sep) on the waterfront south of the main square.

Ayvalık

ℹ Getting There & Around

Boat

From May to September, boats sail daily except Sunday to/from Lesvos, Greece. From October to May, boats sail on Tuesday, Thursday and Saturday. For information and reservations (at least 24 hours before departure), contact Jale Tour (see p128).

Bus

It is possible to make a day trip to Bergama by bus (₺7, 1¾ hours). Hourly buses leave the otogar between 8am and 7pm and drive slowly south through town, so you can jump on at the main square.

   Coming from Çanakkale (₺15, 3¼ hours, five a day), larger companies, such as Ulusoy, provide *servises* (free shuttles) to their offices in Ayvalık centre (or a taxi costs ₺7). Smaller companies may drop you on the main highway.

   There are hourly buses to/from İzmir (₺16, three hours).

Car

Car parks along the waterfront (a better option than driving in Ayvalık old town's fiendishly narrow lanes) generally cost ₺8/12 per day/night.

Bergama (Pergamum)

📞 0232 / POP 60,559

Bergama, a laid-back market town, is the modern successor to the once-powerful ancient city of Pergamum. Unlike busy Ephesus, Pergamum is a site of quiet, classical splendour, offering uncrowded access to the Asclepion, ancient Rome's pre-eminent medical centre, and the mountainside Acropolis.

Sights & Activities

Bergama's attractions open from 8.30am to 6.30pm daily between June and September and 8.30am to 5.30pm in low season (except the museum, which is closed on Monday). The two main archaeological sites – the Acropolis (p138) and the Asclepion – are on top of steep hills, several kilometres out of town.

ASCLEPION   Ruin
(Temple of Asclepios; admission/parking ₺15/3)
This renowned ancient medical centre was founded by Archias, a local who had been cured at the Asclepion of Epidaurus (Greece). Treatments included mud baths, the use of herbs and ointments, enemas and sunbathing. Diagnosis was often by dream analysis.

   Pergamum's centre came to the fore under Galen (AD 131–210), the physician to Pergamum's gladiators, who was recognised as perhaps the greatest early physician. Under Galen's influence, the medical school here became renowned. His work was the basis for Western medicine well into the 16th century.

   The Asclepion is 2km uphill from the town centre as the crow flies (but it's a winding road), signposted from Cumhuriyet Caddesi north of the tourist office. Soft drinks are available from the stalls by the car park, albeit at a premium.

Bergama

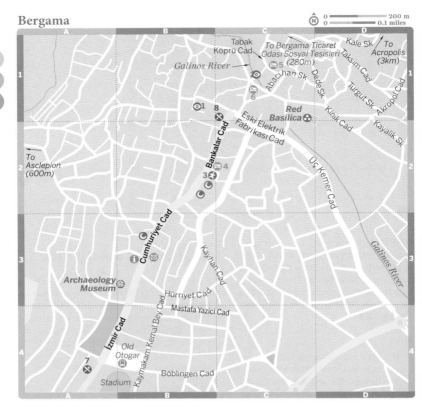

A Roman bazaar street, once lined with shops, leads from the entrance to the centre, where you'll see the base of a column carved with snakes, the symbol of Asclepios (Aesculapius), god of medicine. Just as the snake sheds its skin and gains a 'new life', so the patients at the Asclepion were supposed to 'shed' their illnesses. Signs mark a circular **Temple of Asclepios**, a **library** and, beyond it, a **Roman theatre**.

You can take a drink from the **sacred well**, although the plastic tube out of which the water flows doesn't look particularly inviting, and pass along the vaulted underground corridor to the **Temple of Telesphorus**, another god of medicine. Patients slept in the temple hoping that Telesphorus would send a cure or diagnosis in a dream.

RED BASILICA Ruin

(Kınık Caddesi; admission ₺5) The cathedral-sized Red Basilica was originally a giant temple to the Egyptian gods Serapis, Isis and Harpocrates, built in the 2nd century AD. It's still an imposing place, though rather scattered and battered-looking these days. Be careful as you make your way around.

In his Revelation, St John the Divine wrote that this was one of the seven churches of the Apocalypse, singling it out as the throne of the devil. Look for a hole in the podium in the centre, which allowed a priest to hide and appear to speak through the 10m-high cult statue. The building is so big that the Christians didn't convert it into a church but built a basilica inside it. The most intact section, the southern rotunda, was used for religious and cult rituals.

ARCHAEOLOGY MUSEUM Museum
(Arkeoloji Müzesi; ☑631 2884; Cumhuriyet Caddesi; admission ₺5) The museum boasts a small but substantial collection of artefacts, including Greek, Roman and Byzantine gravestones, busts and pillars. Look out for the scale replica of the Altar of Zeus (the original is in Berlin) and, in the main hall, finds from the nearby, and now underwater, site of Allianoi.

HACI HEKIM HAMAMI Hamam
(Cumhuriyet Caddesi; ◷6am-11pm) This 16th-century hamam charges ₺40 for the full works.

 **Sleeping**

The northern end of Cumhuriyet Caddesi, in the old town, is the best area to stay.

HERA BOUTIQUE HOTEL Boutique Hotel €€€
(☑631 0634; www.hotelhera.com; Tabrak Körpü Caddesi 21; d from ₺200; P ❄ ☏) A pair of 200-year-old Greek houses are home to Bergama's most sophisticated accommodation. The 10 rooms, named after mythological Greek deities, feature timber ceilings, parquetry floorboards and curios handpicked by the erudite couple in charge. The breakfast spread comes highly recommended.

ODYSSEY GUESTHOUSE Pension €
(☑631 3501; www.odysseyguesthouse.com; Abacıhan Sokak 13; s/d from ₺45/50, without bathroom from ₺35/45) This grand old house is a good choice, with superb views of the Red Basilica from the upstairs

terrace. The main building has some basic doubles, with excellent showers. Self-caterers enjoy the small kitchenette and there's a copy of Homer's *Odyssey* in every room.

CITI HOSTEL Hostel €
(☑830 0668; Bankalar Caddesi 10; s/d/tr ₺35/60/80; ❄☏) This great new, old-school hostel is run by the friendly İmdat (translation: *help*), a Turkish-Australian chap with decades of travel experience. Basic, spotless rooms on two levels encircle a spacious courtyard filled with fake grass, orange furniture and two large trees.

 Eating

The **Monday market** (◷8am-6pm), stretching from the old otogar past the Red Basilica, is great for fresh fruit and veg.

KERVAN Turkish €€
(☑633 2632; İzmir Caddesi; mains ₺12; ❄) Popular among locals for its large outdoor terrace and excellent food, including a good range of kebaps, pide, *çorba* (soup) and *künefe* dessert (syrup-soaked dough and sweet cheese sprinkled with pistachios).

BERGAMA TICARET ODASI SOSYAL TESISLERI Restaurant €€
(☑632 9641; Ulucamii Mahallesi; mains ₺15; ◷9am-midnight) Run by the municipality, this is the best restaurant serving alcohol. The outdoor terrace and school-cafeteria-style interior have panoramic views and

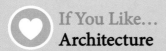

If You Like...
Architecture

İzmir has a cosmopolitan past, with Jewish and Levantine communities still living here, and its buildings display the mix of influences that created the city formerly known as Smyrna. Look out for the following around Konak Meydanı and Kemeraltı Bazaar.

1 KONAK CLOCK TOWER
(Saat Kulesi; Konak Meydanı) This late-Ottoman clock tower, designed by the Levantine French architect Raymond Charles Père, was built in 1901 to mark the 25th anniversary of Sultan Abdül Hamit II's coronation. Its ornate Orientalist style may have been meant to atone for Smyrna's European ambience.

2 KONAK CAMII
(Konak Meydanı) Beside the clock tower, this attractive mosque (1755) is covered in Kütahya tiles.

3 KONAK PIER
(Atatürk Caddesi) Gustave Eiffel, who designed Paris' famous tower, also designed the site of today's shopping centre in 1890.

4 KIZLARAĞASI HAN
(Kemeraltı Bazaar; ⏰8am-5pm) This glorious caravanserai is a much smaller, calmer version of İstanbul's famous Grand Bazaar. It's touristy, with many items from the far end of the Silk Road (China), but good for a wander. There's a cafe in the courtyard, where merchants once tethered their camels.

5 HISAR CAMII
(Kemeraltı Bazaar) The interior of the city's largest mosque is quintessentially İzmiri: the blue-and-gold motifs on the domed ceiling are simpler and less Oriental than classic Ottoman designs. Also look out for the roses and grapes carved along the bottom of the women's gallery and the designs on the stone staircase.

reasonable food. It's located in a park 300m up the hill behind the main street. You should avoid walking alone in the area at night.

SARMAŞIK LOKANTASI   Turkish €
(📞632 2741; Istiklal Meydani 6; mains ₺8) One of the more dependable local restaurants on the main street, with a heavy rotation of village stews, soups and rice dishes.

❶ Information

Modern Bergama lies spread out on either side of one long main street, along which almost everything you'll need can be found.

Tourist office (📞631 2851; İzmir Caddesi 54; ⏰8.30am-noon & 1-5.30pm) Just north of the museum; the board outside has useful information such as bus and minibus times.

❶ Getting There & Away

Services to/from Bergama's *yeni* (new) otogar include Ankara (₺55, eight to nine hours, nightly), Ayvalık (₺8, 1¼ hours, hourly), İstanbul (₺50, 11 hours, at least nightly) via Bursa, and İzmir (₺10, two hours, hourly).

The *yeni* otogar lies 7km from the centre, just off the İzmir–Çanakkale highway. Between 6am and 7pm, *servises* run between there and the central *eski* (old) otogar. A taxi costs about ₺25. Some buses from Çanakkale drop you at the junction near the *yeni* otogar, walking distance from the station.

❶ Getting Around

Bergama's sights are so spread out that it's hard to walk round them all in one day. The Red Basilica is over 1km from the tourist office, the Asclepion is 2km away and the Acropolis is over 5km away.

Bus

Between 6am and 7pm, half-hourly buses run through town between the old otogar and the market area (₺2), 200m past the Red Basilica at the foot of the road (and the cable car) up to the Acropolis.

Taxi

A convenient option is to book a 'city tour'. From the centre to the Asclepion, Red Basilica and Acropolis, with 30 minutes at the first two sights and an hour at the latter, should cost around ₺50. Individual fares from the tourist office area are about ₺8 to the Asclepion, and ₺15 to the Acropolis.

İzmir

♪ 0232 / POP 2.8 MILLION

The grand port city of İzmir, Turkey's third-largest, is a proudly liberal, long-time centre of commerce that has emerged as a smart alternative base for travel in the west of the country. Formerly the famed Greek city of Smyrna, İzmir lives by its *kordon* (seafront) which, especially around leafy Alsancak, is as fetching and lively as any large seaside city in the world.

With its Levantine and Jewish heritage, İzmir feels distinct from the rest of Turkey. That's certainly not to say there aren't Turkish flags aplenty between the palms, but the city does have a relatively liberal, laid-back atmosphere. İzmir is also developing a reputation for its cultural and civic foresight, turning formerly decrepit industrial buildings such as the **Old Gas Factory** into communal and creative spaces.

Sights & Activities

KORDON & ALSANCAK
Seafront, Neighbourhood

It's difficult to imagine life in İzmir without its iconic boulevard. A triumph of urban renewal, the *kordon*'s pedestrianised confines are home to a great selection of bars and restaurants that attract droves of people at the end of the day to watch the picture-perfect sunsets. Inland, the Alsancak district is now the focus of the city's nightlife and fashion.

KONAK MEYDANI
Square

On a pedestrianised stretch of Cumhuriyet Bulvarı, this wide plaza, named after the Ottoman *hükümet konağı* (government mansion), pretty much marks the heart of the city; signs pointing to the centre simply say 'Konak'.

AGORA
Ruin

(Agora Caddesi; admission ₺8; ⏰ 8.30am-7pm, to 5.30pm Sat; P) The ancient agora, built for Alexander the Great, was ruined in an earthquake in AD 178, but rebuilt soon after by the Roman emperor Marcus Aurelius. Colonnades of reconstructed Corinthian columns, vaulted chambers and arches give you a good idea of what a Roman bazaar must have looked like. Later, a Muslim cemetery was built on the site and many of the old tombstones can be seen around the perimeter of the agora. The site is entered on the south side, just off Gazi Osman Paşa Bulvarı.

KEMERALTI BAZAAR
Bazaar

(⏰ 8am-5pm) İzmir's Kemeraltı Bazaar is the city's heart and soul, and a great place to get lost for a few hours. There are bargains galore, especially leather goods, clothing and jewellery. Seek out the flower and bead markets, then stop

Kemeralti Bazaar, İzmir
/GETTY IMAGES ©

İzmir

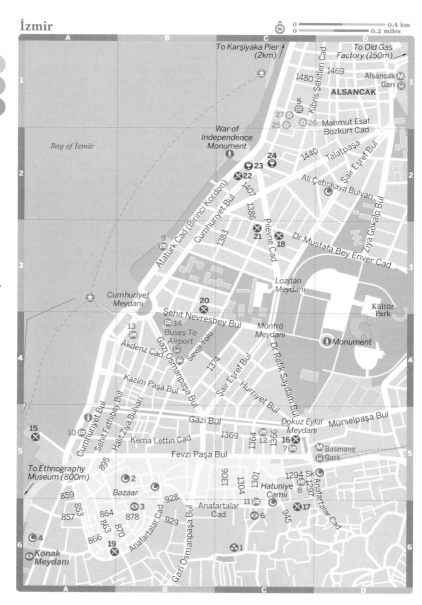

for a reviving shot of Turkish coffee in one of the delightful cafes at its core.

Anafartalar Caddesi rings the main bazaar area and is its principal thoroughfare.

ŞIFALI LUX HAMAM Hamam

(445 2209; Anafartalar Caddesi 660; bath & massage from ₺30; men 8am-10pm, women 7am-6pm) This clean hamam has a lovely domed and marble interior.

İzmir

MASK MUSEUM Museum

(☑ 465 3107; www.izmirmaskmuzesi.com; Cumbalı Sokak 22; admission ₺5; ☉ 10.30am-7pm) Tucked away in an old house on a street filled with bars, this new museum has an interesting collection of ceremonial and decorative masks from around the world.

 Sleeping

İzmir's waterfront is dominated by large high-end business hotels, while inland are more budget and midrange options, particularly around Kemeraltı Bazaar and Basmane train station.

Bazaar & Basmane

If you want a budget hotel, we recommend heading to 1368 Sokak, west of Basmane train station. Southwest of the station is an insalubrious area after dark.

MET BOUTIQUE
HOTEL Boutique Hotel €€€

(☑ 483 0111; www.metotel.com; Gazi Bulvari 124; d from ₺180; P ❄ 🛜) Met is indicative of the increased popularity of İzmir for both travel and business. The new boutique

hotel in the CBD has sleek rooms with soothing colour schemes and streamlined furniture, but could do with standalone desks or a little extra space. Still, the lobby cafe area is genuinely funky and the service is worthy of the world's great cities.

HOTEL BAYLAN BASMANE Hotel €€

(☑ 483 1426; www.hotelbaylan.com; 1299 Sokak 8; s/d ₺80/140) The newer Baylan is Basmane's best option. The entrance via the huge car park is a little disconcerting, but inside is a spacious and attractive hotel with a welcoming terrace out the back. All rooms have polished floorboards and large bathrooms. Management speak little English.

KONAK SARAY
HOTEL Boutique Hotel €€

(☑ 483 7755; www.konaksarayhotel.com; Anafartalar Caddesi 635; s/d ₺70/120; ❄ @) Visitors should treat the Konak Saray Hotel as the best opportunity to stay in a beautifully restored old Ottoman house in İzmir. It's located in a less touristy part of the bazaar and the inward-facing small rooms are modern (minibars, plasma screens) and well priced. There's also a great top-floor restaurant. A more-expensive

137

KEVIN LANG/ALAMY ©

Don't Miss **Acropolis**

These stunning hilltop ruins are most easily reached on a five-minute **cable car** (one way ₺4) ride from Bergama. The road up here winds 5km from the Red Basilica to a car park (₺3) at the top, with souvenir and refreshment stands nearby. A short cut shaves a couple of kilometres from the walk up; opposite the Red Basilica, take Mahmut Şevket Paşa Sokak, the narrow lane between Aklar Gıda groceries and a carpet shop, which leads to the Lower Agora.

The ruins include the **library**, one of the ancient world's greatest repositories of knowledge, and the marble-columned **Temple of Trajan** (pictured). Built during the reigns of Trajan and Hadrian, and used to worship them as well as Zeus, the temple is the only Roman structure surviving here.

Descend through a tunnel to the vertigo-inducing, 10,000-seat **theatre**. Its builders took advantage of the spectacular view, and conserved precious space on the hilltop, by building the impressive and unusual theatre into the hillside. Hellenistic theatres are usually wider and rounder; Pergamum's hillside location made rounding impossible, so its height was increased instead.

Above the stage is the ruined **Temple of Dionysus**; below the theatre is the base of the **Altar of Zeus**, which was originally covered with friezes depicting Olympian gods battling their subterranean foes.

To escape the crowds and get good views, walk downhill behind the Altar of Zeus, or turn left at the bottom of the theatre steps, and follow the sign to the *antik yol* (antique street). Ruins sprawl downhill to a building on the site of the **Middle City**, protecting some fantastic **mosaic floors**; look for the grotesque faces at the far end. With sights beyond including the **Lower Agora**, from here you could ruin-hop back down to the Red Basilica. For transport details, see p134.

NEED TO KNOW
Akropol; admission ₺20

second branch, popular with tour groups, occupies a renovated Ottoman home high above the Agora.

GÜZEL İZMİR OTELI
Hotel €

(📞483 5069; www.guzelizmirhotel.com; 1368 Sokak 8; s/d ₺40/70) One of Basmane's better choices, the Good İzmir is friendly, safe and terribly convenient for bus and train access. The rooms are nothing special – avoid the small and damp few – but it's good value for money at the low end.

Alsancak & Seafront
North of Gazi Bulvarı is safer and more pleasant, with hotels firmly in midrange and top-end territory.

KEY HOTEL
Boutique Hotel €€€

(📞482 1111; www.keyhotel.com; Mimar Kemalettin Caddesi 1; d €270; P ✳ 🛜) Key Hotel is a black, gold and brown masterpiece down by Konak Pier. Located in a former bank building, the original vault is now a glass-topped atrium while the hotel includes glass elevators, a superb ground-floor restaurant and concierge service. The rooms have hi-tech touches, rain showers and king-size beds to lie for. The owner is a local soft drink magnate who plans to replicate the hotel elsewhere in Turkey.

MYHOTEL
Boutique Hotel €€€

(📞445 5241; www.myhotel.com.tr; Cumhuriyet Bulvarı 132; s/d ₺160/220; ✳ 🛜) In a brilliant location just a street back from the sea, MyHotel is a low-key alternative to the fancier chain hotels nearby. The lobby bar and restaurant are super cool and the spacious rooms are still in decent shape since their decade-old imagining.

SWISSÔTEL GRAND EFES
Hotel €€€

(📞414 0000; www.swissotel.com.tr; Gazi Osman Paşa Bulvarı 1; s/d €140/160; P ✳ @ 🏊) Swissotel has adapted well to the Turkish market, and this İzmir branch is no exception. Occupying a prime location overlooking Cumhuriyet Meydanı and the bay, the Grand Efes is the choice location for business and glamour travel. The underwater restaurant is excellent, while the day spa (open to nonguests) was recently voted the best in the world.

İZMIR PALAS OTELI
Hotel €€

(📞465 0030; www.izmirpalas.com.tr; Atatürk Caddesi; s/d from ₺120/165; P ✳) Established in 1927 and rebuilt in '72, the 138-room Palas is a storied beast, but it's popular and quite comfortable, and the location is tremendous overlooking the bay, with fine fish restaurants on the doorstep.

 Eating

The *kordon* restaurants have outside tables with views of the bay – some serve excellent food. On and around Kıbrıs Şehitleri Caddesi in Alsancak, you'll lose the sunset views but gain on atmosphere; in particular try 1453 Sokak.

For fresh fruit and veg, freshly baked bread and delicious savoury pastries, head for the **canopied market**, just off Anafartalar Caddesi.

SAKIZ
Modern Turkish €€

(📞484 1103; Şehıt Nevresbey Bulvarı 9a; mains ₺12-25; ⏱noon-2pm & 7.30-10pm Mon-Sat) With a wooden terrace and red-and-white tablecloths, Sakız is informal and fabulous. Its fresh meze includes recommended sardines, octopus and *köz patlıcan* (smoked eggplant with tomatoes and peppers); the unusual mains include sea bass with asparagus and stir-fried fish with artichoke. Live traditional guitar music sets the scene on weekends.

REYHAN
Patisserie €

(📞444 7946; Dr Mustafa Bey Enver Caddesi 24; cheesecake ₺6.75) This institution is serious about sweet stuff, with a professional taster and headset-wearing waiters. Decadent delights like strawberry cheesecake and almond-cream cake with pineapple and almonds sit alongside favourites like carrot cake and a yummy Turkish breakfast.

VELI USTA BALIK PIŞIRICISI
Seafood €€€

(📞464 2705; Atatürk Caddesi 212; mains ₺20; ⏱noon-10.30pm) This relaxed, quality seafood restaurant outstrips the strip thanks to the maroon-sweater-clad staff, and dishes like fresh, good-value *dil şiş* (grilled sole). The crowd is abundant and friendly.

DENIZ RESTAURANT — Seafood €€€

(☎464 4499; Atatürk Caddesi 188; mains from ₺17; ⏱11am-11pm) This old favourite on the *kordon* trades a little on its reputation – and it's far from good value – but the mezes like octopus in oregano and baked sardines are worth the snobby service. The house speciality is *tuzda balık* (fish baked in a block of salt that's broken at your table; suitable for three or four people).

ANKARA LOKANTASI — Turkish €

(☎445 3607; Anafartalar Caddesi 779; dishes ₺6-12) Near the Basmane train station is this humble eatery that fills with local workers during the week and a relaxed drop-in crowd on weekends. It's a traditional 'point-and-pick' joint with loads of meat, rice and vegetable dishes.

SIR WINSTON TEA HOUSE — Cafe €

(☎421 8861; Dr Mustafa Bey Enver Caddesi 20; sandwiches ₺13, tea ₺4-8) On a street known for its cafes, this is one of the best, serving dozens of teas, hot and cold coffees, good salads and pastas. There's shady seating outside. There's a second branch behind the Swissotel.

%100 — Restaurant, Cafe €€€

(☎441 5593; Konak Pier, Atatürk Caddesi; mains ₺22) Down the end of Konak Pier, %100 has a huge menu, with steak, sushi and pizza highly recommended by our table. It's a great place for a lazy cocktail (₺20) or midshop coffee by the water's edge. Service is excellent.

MENNAN — Bakery €

(899 Sokak 30; cornet ₺3.50) This cafe in the bazaar is known for its excellent homemade ice cream.

RIZA AKSÜT — Patisserie €

(863 Sokak 66; cake ₺3; ❄) In the Baş Durak area of the bazaar, try the *peynir tatlısı* (sponge dessert made with cheese), preferably *kaymaklı* (with cream), at this dessert shop.

🍷 Drinking & Entertainment

On the *kordon*, the row of bars around Balık Pişiricisi Restaurant is particularly popular. Alsancak plays host to the city's hottest nightlife, particularly in the clubs and bars on side streets such as Sokak 1482.

SUNSET CAFE — Bar

(☎463 6549; Ali Çetinkaya Bulvarı 2a) On the edge of the boulevard, Sunset Cafe makes a great sunset drinking hole, with colourful booths on the street and a relaxed, youthful crowd. The cheap beer flows freely, but the one-toilet bathroom gets a little tight.

TYNA — Bar

(Ali Çetinkaya Bulvarı 5; beer ₺4) The outside tables are hot property at this pizzeria on a small square. Most just come for a beer; pizzas cost ₺6.

AKSAK LOUNGE — Bar

(1452 Sokak 10) In a typical İzmir mansion with high ceilings, balconies and a courtyard garden, Aksak attracts a cultured crowd to its jazz nights on Tuesday and Sunday.

BEYAZ CAFE — Live Music

(White Cafe; ☎422 6645; www.beyazcbr.com; 1452 Sokak 4) Near the plaque to poet Can Yücel, the White Cafe is a folk music haunt with excellent Turkish cuisine. Perfect for a good, honest night on the tiles.

1888 — Nightclub

(☎421 6690; www.1888.com.tr; Cumhuriyet Bulvarı 248) This newish nightclub around an old Ottoman courtyard hosts everything from film and cultural festivals to frantic disco parties.

ℹ Information

Banks and ATMS are found all over the centre.

İzmir Döviz (☎441 8882; Fevzi Paşa Bulvarı 75; ⏱8am-7pm Mon-Sat) Money changer where no commission is charged.

Tourist office (☎483 5117; 1344 Sokak 2) Inside the ornately stuccoed İl Kültür ve Turizm

Müdürlüğü building just off Atatürk Caddesi.
Has English-, German- and French-speaking
staff.

Dangers & Annoyances

Like any big city, İzmir has its fair share of crime.
However, the main tourist routes are fairly safe,
with the notable exceptions of the Kadifekale
neighbourhood and the area around Basmane
train station, which is something of a red-light
district – lone women should take special care. Do
not enter Kemeraltı Bazaar after dark, and be alert
to pickpockets and thieves there during the day.

Getting There & Away

Air

There are many flights to İzmir's **Adnan
Menderes Airport** (☎ 455 0000; www.
adnanmenderesairport.com) from European
destinations.

Turkish Airlines (☎ 484 1220; www.thy.com;
Halit Ziya Bulvarı 65) offers direct flights from
Turkish cities, including İstanbul (both airports),
and Europe. Other airlines serving İzmir:

Atlasjet (www.atlastjet.com)

Izair (www.izair.com.tr)

Onur Air (www.onurair.com.tr)

Pegasus Airlines (www.flypgs.com)

Sun Express (www.sunexpress.com.tr)

Bus

İzmir's otogar lies 6.5km northeast of the city
centre. For travel on Friday or Saturday to coastal
towns to the north of İzmir, buy your ticket at least
a day in advance. The bus companies' city-centre
offices are mostly found at Dokuz Eylül Meydanı.
Servises shuttle passengers between these offices
and the otogar.

Services, generally hourly, include Ankara (₺40,
eight hours), Antalya (₺45, seven hours), Bergama
(₺10, two hours), Bodrum (₺25, 3¼ hours), Bursa
(₺25, five hours), Çanakkale (₺35, six hours),
Denizli (for Pamukkale, ₺25, 3¼ hours), İstanbul
(₺45, nine hours), Kuşadası (₺15, 1¼ hours),
Marmaris (for Datça and Bozburun Peninsulas,
₺38, four hours) and Selçuk (₺9, one hour).

Train

Most intercity services arrive at Basmane Garı.
There are daily trains to/from Selçuk (₺4.75, 1½
hours), Bandırma (coordinating with ferry to/
from İstanbul, ₺18, six hours) and Ankara (₺27, 15
hours) via Eskişehir.

Getting Around

To/From the Airport

The airport is 18km south of the city on the way to
Ephesus and Kuşadası.

Hourly Havaş buses (₺10, 30 minutes) leave
from Gazi Osman Paşa Bulvarı near the Swissôtel
between 3.30am and 11.30pm, and run to the
Swissôtel from domestic arrivals, leaving 25
minutes after flights arrive.

Boat

The most pleasant way to cross İzmir is by **ferry**
(☉6.40am-11.40pm). Roughly half-hourly
timetabled services, with more at the beginning
and end of the working day, link the piers at
Karşiyaka, Bayraklı, Alsancak, Pasaport, Konak
and Göztepe. *Jetons* (transport tokens) cost ₺3
each.

Car

Large international car-hire franchises, including
Budget, Europcar, Hertz, National Alamo and Avis,
and smaller companies are at the airport; some
also in town. **Green Car** (☎0232-446 9060;
www.greenautorent.com; Mithatpaşa Caddesi 57,
Karataş, İzmir) is one of the largest local car-hire
companies.

Taxi

You can either hail a taxi, or pick one up from a
taxi stand or outside one of the big hotels. Fares
start at ₺3.75 then cost ₺0.30 per 100m. Make
sure the meter is switched on.

Ephesus, Bodrum & the South Aegean

Turkey's sparkling Aegean coast boasts 4000 years of civilisation – and it's got the ruins to prove it. The most famous of these are ancient sites such as Ephesus, Priene, Miletus and Didyma, where excavations continue to yield astonishing new treasures.

In summer, the coast's population swells as millions of tourists descend on Kuşadası, Marmaris and, especially, Bodrum, the most glamorous of all Anatolia's seaside getaways. Yet despite the nonstop partying, this whitewashed town somehow preserves an air of refinement, while new boutique hotels and elegant eateries keep springing up, both here and in the exclusive (but easily visited) coastal villages of the Bodrum Peninsula.

All of the commotion aside, it's still possible to experience the elemental pleasures of rugged terrain, village life and spectacular Aegean views on the more remote Datça and Bozburun Peninsulas. The coast is most peaceful in spring or fall (when prices drop, too).

Ephesus' Great Theatre (p147)

Îçmeler on the Bozburun Peninsula (p180)

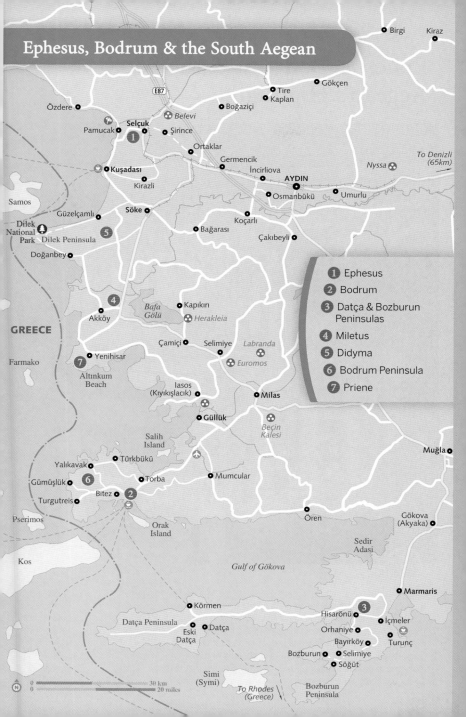

Ephesus, Bodrum & the South Aegean

Birgi
Kiraz
Gökçen
Tire
Kaplan
Özdere
E87
Belevi
Boğaziçi
Selçuk
Pamucak
Şirince
Ortaklar
Germencik
Nyssa
To Denizli (65km)
İncirliova
Kuşadası
AYDIN
Kirazli
Osmanbükü
Umurlu
Samos
Güzelçamlı
Söke
Koçarlı
Dilek National Park
Dilek Peninsula
Bağarası
Çakıbeyli
Doğanbey

1 Ephesus
2 Bodrum
3 Datça & Bozburun Peninsulas
4 Miletus
5 Didyma
6 Bodrum Peninsula
7 Priene

GREECE
Farmako
Bafa Gölü
Kapıkırı
Herakleia
Akköy
Çamiçi
Selimiye
Labranda
Yenihisar
Euromos
Altınkum Beach
Iasos (Kıyıkışlacık)
Milas
Güllük
Beçin Kalesi
Salih Island
Muğla
Yalıkavak
Türkbükü
Gümüşlük
Torba
Mumcular
Turgutreis
Bitez
Ören
Gökova (Akyaka)
Pserimos
Orak Island
Sedir Adası
Kos
Gulf of Gökova
Marmaris
Körmen
Hisarönü
İçmeler
Datça Peninsula
Orhaniye
Turunç
Eski Datça
Datça
Bayırköy
Bozburun
Selimiye
Söğüt
Simi (Symi)
To Rhodes (Greece)
Bozburun Peninsula

0   30 km
0   20 miles

Ephesus, Bodrum & the South Aegean's Highlights

① Ephesus

Its pillars and facades glinting in the Aegean sun, the capital of the Roman province of Asia Minor is Europe's most complete classical metropolis (p156). Walking down the Curetes Way, it's easy to imagine that the camera-clicking tourists flowing over the street's well-worn marble blocks are toga-clad ancient Ephesians. Above: Curetes Way (p160); Top & Bottom Right: Ephesian sculpture and mosaics

Need to Know

TOP TIP Visit in the morning or late afternoon to avoid crowds and midday sun. **PHOTOGRAPHY** Sunny mornings provide ideal photo opportunities. **For further coverage, see p156**

Ephesus Don't Miss List

BY MEHMET ESENKAYA, OWNER OF NO-FRILLS EPHESUS TOURS

1 LIBRARY OF CELSUS

This library is both a cultural building and a funerary monument. After the death of Celsus Polemaeanus, who had been appointed governor of Ephesus, his son erected the magnificent reading room over his tomb. The facade has a converse curve, which increases its monumental appearance – an effect that was previously thought to have existed only in Greek architecture.

2 TERRACED HOUSES

This affluent district (p161) enjoyed its peak between the 2nd and 4th centuries AD. Wealthy citizens and priests of noble lineage occupied the one-storey houses, which had spacious rooms grouped around an open-air courtyard. The Ephesus Museum in Selçuk has a collection of murals, furniture and utensils from the houses.

3 GREAT THEATRE

This theatre (p161), built against the slope of Mt Panayır, was one of the Aegean's largest, measuring 60m from the stage to the top of the galleries. The auditorium held 24,000 spectators, with another thousand in the vaulted galleries, and the stage facade was adorned with niches, columns, reliefs and statues.

4 ROMAN BOURSE

The Byzantine Church of the Virgin Mary, previously a Roman commercial building, housed the Third Ecumenical Council, where Nestorius, founder of the school of Antioch and the Patriarchate of Istanbul, put forward a view opposing the divine nature of Christ and regarding Mary as the mother of a human being. The Alexandrian school supported the traditional view that Mary was the mother of God, and Nestorius was exiled. Reverence for the Virgin Mary increased in Ephesus, which became a Christian centre.

5 TEMPLE OF SERAPIS

This 2nd-century temple, dedicated to the Egyptian god Serapis, is evidence of the atmosphere of religious tolerance in cosmopolitan Ephesus. The marble Corinthian temple is remarkable for the size of its monolithic columns. Some of the huge blocks weigh over 50 tonnes.

Bodrum

The Aegean's most beautiful tourist town is dominated by the 15th-century Castle of St Peter, built by the Knights Hospitaller and captured by Süleyman the Magnificent. In the 20th century, Bodrum (p171) was the stomping ground of dissidents, intellectuals and writers, and its arty sophistication has endured. Below: Castle of St Peter (p173); Top Right: Windmill; Bottom Right: Ancient Theatre

Need to Know

TOP TIP For upcoming events at the castle and ancient theatre, visit www.biletix.com. **DRIVING** Most roads follow a clockwise one-way system. **For further coverage, see p171**

Bodrum Don't Miss List

BY ZAFER KUSTU, MANAGER OF SU OTEL

1 CASTLE OF ST PETER

Pride of Bodrum, the castle (p173) was completed by the Crusaders and additions made in the 15th century. It survives in good condition, overlooking modern Bodrum, and now includes the Museum of Underwater Archaeology (a world first) and some wonderful cafes. The best views of Bodrum are from the top of the castle. The annual International Bodrum Ballet Festival, which takes place here in late August and early September, is a cultural highlight.

2 ANCIENT THEATRE

Overlooking Bodrum, this antique Roman theatre (Kıbrıs Şehitler Caddesi) is just a few hundred metres from the town centre. It sports great views at sunset. In the summer, various arts, music and dance performances take place here.

3 MARINA YACHT CLUB

This venue (Neyzen Tevfik Caddesi 5; ☎316 1228) has become one of Bodrum's favourite nightspots. Beautifully fitted out, it boasts three restaurants: one serving international cuisine; the Italian bistro, a welcome addition to the Bodrum scene; and upstairs – the best of the lot – outstanding views of the harbour are coupled with superbly presented food. It's a five-star location and, after 10.30pm, the excellent music ranges from jazz to Cuban dance and lounge lizard. Don't forget to book ahead in peak season.

4 WINDMILLS

Near Bodrum centre, these four hilltop windmills have great views of Bodrum town and harbour. They are owned by local people and haven't been restored.

5 MYNDOS KAPISI (MYNDOS GATE)

Alexander the Great conquered Bodrum after destroying the town's 4th-century 7km-long walls. Named Myndos Gate (Turgutreis Caddesi) because of its western position on the road to Myndos (modern-day Gümüşlük), this is the only surviving gate in the town. Its excavation and restoration were completed fairly recently. The nearby tombs, mosaics and other ruins are also interesting.

Datça & Bozburun Peninsulas

Travellers have been slow to discover these rugged peninsulas (p180), perhaps put off by their proximity to tacky Marmaris. This has left two sinuous fingers of quiet countryside, where the ruined Dorian port city Knidos is the main sight. Simply pottering between the rustic beach villages, blue bays and forested hinterland is immensely pleasurable. Knidos (p180), on the Datça Peninsula

3

4

Miletus

Before its harbour silted up, Miletus (p174) was a great port city and a centre of Greek thought and culture. The Milesian School of philosophers were essentially history's first scientists, favouring observation of nature and rational discourse. The mixed Hellenistic-Roman architecture includes the 15,000-seat Great Theatre and the Baths of Faustina, constructed for Marcus Aurelius' wife. Miletus Museum exhibits exquisite gold pendants, necklaces and rings from ancient tombs. Great Theatre walkway (p174)

Priene

Priene (p174) was a significant port city in ancient times (between 300 and 45 BC to be exact). The League of Ionian Cities held congresses here, and Priene was famed for shipbuilding and sailing until its harbours silted up. Today, its ruins, including the Temple of Athena and a 6500-seat theatre – one of the best-preserved Hellenistic theatres anywhere – are strewn romantically across Mt Mykale. Temple of Athena (p174)

Bodrum Peninsula

Running west of Bodrum town, this chichi peninsula (p177) is a summer playground for Turkey's glitterati. Unpopulated hills with the occasional ruin run along the middle, while the coastline is riddled with bays and villages where exclusive resorts and stylish restaurants mix with open-air vegetable markets and sandy beaches. Head past the neon-lit party town of Gümbet to find sweet spots such as Gümüşlük. Bodrum town (p171)

Didyma

Didyma's Temple of Apollo (p174), once the ancient world's second-largest temple (with 122 columns), helps visitors to visualise the lost grandeur of Selçuk's desiccated Temple of Artemis, which was the largest (with 127 columns). Thick, towering columns still stand here, as they did when this Oracle of Apollo had an importance second only to the Oracle of Delphi. Covered ramps lead to the *cella* (inner room) where the oracle prophesied. Temple of Apollo (p174)

Ephesus, Bodrum & the South Aegean's Best…

Peninsulas

⊙ **Bozburun** (p180) Deeply indented coastline, and farming and fishing villages.

⊙ **Bodrum** (p177) Cool summer retreat for Turkey's beautiful people, with village markets and seafood restaurants.

⊙ **Datça** (p180) Rugged landscape with a ruined 5th-centry BC Dorian port city at its tip.

⊙ **Dilek** (p176) Mountainous reserve with quiet beaches and walking trails, overlooking the Greek island of Samos.

Architecture

⊙ **Ephesus** (p156) The former Roman capital's thoroughfares and theatres are a triumph of marble and stone.

⊙ **Bodrum** (p171) A Crusader castle overlooks whitewashed houses with bright-blue trim.

⊙ **Şirince** (p179) The hill village has stone-and-stucco houses on cobbled lanes.

⊙ **Priene** (p174) The Romans made few modifications to this former port city's Hellenistic buildings, preserving its uniquely 'Greek' look.

Museums

⊙ **Ephesus Museum** (p165) Artefacts from Ephesus' Terraced Houses and the phallic god Priapus.

⊙ **Museum of Underwater Archaeology** (p173) Displays antiquities found while renovating its home, Bodrum's Castle of St Peter.

⊙ **Miletus Museum** (p174) Artefacts and information about life before the region's ancient harbours silted up.

⊙ **Dibek Sofrası** (p178) Ottoman antiques including jewelled daggers, fountain pens and ornate coffee cups.

Eating

◦ **Bodrum fish market**
(p172) Choose at the
fishmongers' tables and
get it cooked at adjoining
restaurants.

◦ **Bitez** (p177) Weekend
buffet brunches are a local
ritual in the beach village.

◦ **Olive Farm** (p181) Olive-
grove tours, tastings and a
shop on the Datça Peninsula.

◦ **Ejder Restaurant** (p164)
Opposite Selçuk's Byzantine
aqueduct, the Anatolian
cuisine has attracted celebs
including the Clinton clan.

Need to Know

◦ **Bodrum Express
Lines** (www.
bodrumexpresslines.com)

◦ **Bodrum Ferryboat
Association** (www.
bodrumferryboat.com)

◦ **EphesusSelcuk.com**
(www.ephesusselcuk.com)

◦ **Hidden Datça** (www.
hiddendatca.com)

◦ **Meander Travel** (www.
meandertravel.com)

◦ **Neyzen Travel &
Yachting** (www.neyzen.
com.tr)

GETTING AROUND

◦ **Air** Flights to İzmir (near
Ephesus), Bodrum and
Dalaman (near Marmaris)
from across Turkey and
Europe.

◦ **Boat** Ferries from
Kuşadası to Samos
(Greece); Bodrum to
Datça, Turgutreis, Kos
(Greece) and Rhodes
(Greece); Turgutreis to Kos
and Kalymnos (Greece);
Datça to Rhodes and
Symi (Greece).

◦ **Bus** A good way to get
between major towns.

◦ **Car** Good roads;
major hire companies
at the abovementioned
airports.

◦ **Dolmuş** Useful for rural
spots such as Ephesus,
Şirince and the Bodrum,
Datça and Bozburun
Peninsulas.

◦ **Tour** A good way to
see the ruins of Ephesus,
Priene, Miletus, Didyma
and Knidos.

BE FOREWARNED

◦ **Bodrum** In high summer,
accommodation fills up
fast; marina-area hotels
get noise from nightspots.

◦ **Restaurants** Check the
prices of fish and wine
before ordering.

◦ **Ephesus** Book guides
in advance, rather than
picking up a guide or
audioguide at the gate.

◦ **Terraced Houses**
Entrance costs ₺15, on
top of the ₺25 Ephesus
admission fee.

◦ **Tours** Check what you
get: is Miletus Museum
included in a tour of Priene,
Miletus and Didyma? Do
cruises include lunch?

◦ **Visa** If paying a return
visit to Greece, check your
Turkish visa is multi-entry.

◦ **Antiquities** People at
historical sights may try to
sell you 'ancient coins' and
other claimed artefacts;
they are often fakes, and
buying antiquities is illegal.

eft: Museum of Underwater Archaeology (p173),
Bodrum; **Above:** Şirince (p179)

Ephesus, Bodrum & the South Aegean Itineraries

Take in stunning peninsulas, ancient ruins and wild Aegean hills, or marvel at Ephesus' enduring splendour and see coast and ruins around Kuşadası.

3 DAYS

BODRUM TO BOZBURUN PENINSULA

Peninsula Perambulator

Get off to a stylish start in blue-and-white **(1) Bodrum**, where the Crusader castle overlooks twin bays and a well-oiled holiday machine. The former haven for dissidents, intellectuals, writers and artists offers highbrow attractions, such as boutique hotels and slick bars. Between the beaches, cruises and seafood in the fish market, try to fit in a day trip west to the **(2) Bodrum Peninsula's** beaches and villages.

Next, head east along the Gulf of Gökova, or board a ferry in Bodrum and set sail across the gulf to the mountainous back country, secluded coves and hidden archipelagos of the **(3) Datça Peninsula**. Eski Datça is an ideal base, its cobbled streets and stone Ottoman houses close to Knidos, the ruined 5th-century BC Dorian port city. From Datça town, you can go on diving trips and *gület* (traditional wooden yacht) cruises to the Greek island of Symi.

If time allows, detour down the adjoining, and similarly rugged, **(4) Bozburun Peninsula**. Bozburun town has idyllic bays and brilliantly blue waters for swimming.

Top Left: Castle of St Peter (p172), Bodrum; **Top Right:** Dilek National Park (p176), Dilek Peninsula

5 DAYS

EPHESUS TO DILEK PENINSULA

Beaches & Ruins

Stroll down the Curetes Way, following in Anthony and Cleopatra's footsteps, through Europe's greatest ruined classical city: **(1) Ephesus**, once the capital of the Roman province of Asia Minor. Relax after touring the ruins in low-key **(2) Selçuk**, where you can power up on Selçuk *köfte* (meatballs) and poke around more ancient relics. These include the Byzantine Basilica of St John, built to honour John's visits to Ephesus, and Ayasuluk Fortress.

Detour into the hills and spend a night in **(3) Şirince**, a beautifully preserved stone-and-stucco Greek village with boutique hotels for appreciating the country quiet. Next, the coastal holiday town of **(4) Kuşadası** makes an unrefined but handy base for a range of activities. Splash into the Aegean waters on a scuba-diving trip or, if children are in tow, at beaches and water parks. Next, take another look at the region's classical ruins on a 'PMD' day trip (also run from Selçuk) to **(5) Priene**, **(6) Miletus** and **(7) Didyma**, respectively former port cities and a temple to Apollo.

Finish with a day trip along the **(8) Dilek Peninsula**, where you can mix mountain walks with swimming in azure coves, all with views of the Greek island of Samos.

Ephesus, Bodrum & the South Aegean

Grotto of the Seven Sleepers, Ephesus
DE AGOSTINI/GETTY IMAGES ©

Ephesus (Efes)

More than anywhere else, the Greco-Roman world comes alive at **Ephesus** (☏892 6010; admission/parking ₺25/7.50; ⊙8am-6.30pm May-Oct, to 4.30pm Nov-Apr). After almost 150 years of excavation, the city's recovered and renovated structures have made Ephesus Europe's most complete classical metropolis – and that's with 82% of the city still to be unearthed.

As capital of Roman Asia Minor, Ephesus was a vibrant city of over 250,000 inhabitants. Counting traders, sailors and pilgrims to the Temple of Artemis, these numbers were even higher, meaning that in Ephesus one could encounter the full diversity of the Mediterranean world and its peoples. So important and wealthy was Ephesus that its Temple of Artemis (in present-day Selçuk) was the biggest on earth, and one of the Seven Wonders of the Ancient World.

 Tours

Always try to ascertain that your guide is licensed and well informed, and understand exactly how much time you'll get on-site (as opposed to local shops).

Half-/full-day tours (₺79/99) with **No-Frills Ephesus Tours** (☏892 8838; www.nofrillsephesustours.com; Sen Jean Caddesi 3a, Selçuk; ⊙8am-8pm summer, 9am-5pm winter) include transport and well-informed guides, and forgo annoying side trips to souvenir shops. Tours run daily from 1 April to 31 October. Look for the 'Sea Spirit Travel' sign in Selçuk.

Other tours may be cheaper, but this is often because their prices are being subsidised by expected commission on carpet-shop sales after the tour.

See Ephesus and the surrounding area from above with **Selcuk Ephesus SkyDiving** (☏892 2262; www.selcukephesus.com/skydiving; flights ₺120-400) in a two-seater microlight out of Selçuk Airport, just east of Ephesus.

Sights

Ephesus takes 1½ to two hours (add 30 minutes if visiting the Terraced Houses). Take a hat, sunglasses, sunscreen and water; overpriced shops at the top entrance sell some of these. The site lacks restrooms. Most individual ruins have English-language signage.

The following itinerary starts from the Magnesia (Upper) Gate and proceeds down the Curetes Way to the Lower Gate.

UPPER EPHESUS   Ruin

First you'll encounter the **Varius Baths**, situated at the main entrances so that visitors could wash before entering.

Next comes the **Upper Agora**, a large square used for legislation and local political talk. The structure was originally flanked by grand columns and filled with polished marble. In the middle was a small **Temple of Isis**; a testament to the cultural and trade connections between Ephesus and Alexandria (Egypt).

The **Odeon**, a 5000-seat theatre, was primarily used for municipal meetings. The once-lavish building boasts marble seats and carved ornamentation.

Two of six original Doric columns mark the entrance to the ruined **Prytaneum** (town hall) and city treasury.

The Prytaneum also hosted the **Temple of Hestia Boulaea**, where the city's eternal flame was tended to by vestal virgins, and was fronted by a giant Artemis statue. The fertility goddess was carved with huge breasts and welcoming arms.

A side street called the Sacred Street led to Ephesus' **Asclepion** (hospital).

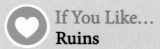

If You Like...
Ruins

Ephesus was once a major city and the classical ruins spill well beyond the boundaries of today's archaeological site. Indeed, it's worth looking out for new surprises outside the Lower Gate, where archaeologists continue to dig; in 2007 a gladiator's cemetery was discovered near the Stadium. A little further from Ephesus are two intriguing sites, visited by most Ephesus tours (though check in advance).

1 MARY'S HOUSE
(Meryemana; ☏894 1012; admission per person/car ₺12.50/5; ⏰8am-7pm May-Oct, to 4.30pm Nov-Apr) Legend has long attested that St John brought the Virgin Mary to Ephesus and, in 1881, a French priest claimed this was her house. Atop these ruined, mostly 6th-century AD house foundations, a chapel has been built; everything beneath the pale red line on its exterior is from the original foundation. The site is 7km from Ephesus' Upper Gate (8.5km from the Lower Gate). Taxis cost ₺50 return from Selçuk's otogar (bus station).

2 GROTTO OF THE SEVEN SLEEPERS
The road from Mary's House to Ephesus passes a turn-off to this cave, where seven persecuted Christians legendarily slumbered for centuries, awaking to find churches in previously pagan Ephesus. The area became a Byzantine pilgrimage site, and the necropolis has many rock-carved graves. Walk 200m from the car park (1.5km from Ephesus) to see the tombs, following the hill path. Although the grotto itself is fenced off, a large hole in the fence allows entry.

Protected by the god Asclepius and his daughter Hygieia, doctors used the Asclepian snake symbol, often etched into the stone.

The ruined **Temple of Domitian** was built when the unpopular ruler, who persecuted Christians, demanded a temple in his honour. It was demolished when he died.

The **Pollio Fountain** and **Memius Monument** hint at the lavish nature of

Ephesus

A Day in the life of the Ancient City

Visiting Ephesus might seem disorienting, but meandering through the city that was once second only to Rome is a highlight of any trip to Turkey. The illustration shows Ephesus in its heyday – but since barely 18% of Ephesus has been excavated, there's much more lurking underfoot than is possible to depict here. Keep an eye out for archaeologists digging away — exciting new discoveries continue to be made every year.

A typical Ephesian day might begin with a municipal debate at the **Odeon** ❶ . These deliberations could then be pondered further while strolling the **Curetes Way** ❷ to the **Latrines** ❸ , perhaps marvelling on the way at imperial greatness in the sculpted form of Emperor Trajan standing atop a globe, by the Trajan fountain. The Ephesian might then have a look at the merchandise on offer down at the Lower Agora, before heading back to the **Terraced Houses** ❹ for a leisurely lunch at home. Afterwards, they might read the classics at the **Library of Celsus** ❺ , or engage in other sorts of activities at the **Brothel** ❻ . The good citizen might then supplicate the gods at the **Temple of Hadrian** ❼ , before settling in for a dramatic performance at Ephesus' magnificent **Great Theatre** ❽ .

FACT FILE

○ Ephesus was famous for its female artists, such as Timarata, who painted images of the city's patron goddess, Artemis.

○ The Great Theatre could hold up to 25,000 spectators.

○ According to ancient Greek legend, Ephesus was founded by Amazons, the mythical female warriors.

○ Among Ephesus' 'native sons' was the great pre-Socratic philosopher, Heraclitus.

Brothel
As in other places in the ancient Mediterranean, a visit to the brothel was considered rather normal for men. Visitors would undertake progressive stages of cleansing after entering, and finally arrive in the marble interior, which was decorated with statues of Venus, the goddess of love. A foot imprint on the pavement outside the rubble indicates the way in.

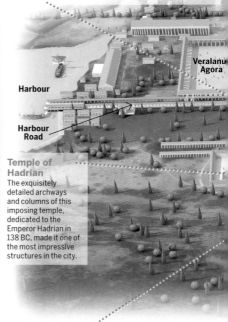

Harbour

Veralanu Agora

Harbour Road

Temple of Hadrian
The exquisitely detailed archways and columns of this imposing temple, dedicated to the Emperor Hadrian in 138 BC, made it one of the most impressive structures in the city.

Library of Celsus
Generations of great thinkers studied at this architecturally advanced library, built in the 2nd century AD. The third-largest library in the ancient world (after Alexandria and Pergamum), it was designed to guard its 12,000 scrolls from extremes of temperature and moisture.

CHRIS DELISO

Latrines
A fixture of any ancient Greco-Roman city, the latrines employed a complex drainage system. Some wealthier Ephesians possessed a 'membership', which allowed them to reserve their own seat.

Great Theatre
Built into what is today known as Mt Panayır, the Great Theatre was where Ephesians went to enjoy works of classical drama and comedy. Its three storeys of seating, decorated with ornate sculpture, were often packed with crowds.

Odeon
The 5000-seat Odeon, with its great acoustics, was used for municipal meetings. Here, debates and deliberations were carried out by masters of oratory – a skill much prized by ancient Greeks and Romans.

Lower Agora

Trajan Fountain

Hercules Gate

Upper Agora

Terraced Houses
These homes of wealthy locals provide the most intimate glimpse into the lives of ancient Ephesians. Hewn of marble and adorned with mosaics and frescoes, they were places of luxury and comfort.

Curetes Way
Ephesus' grandest street, the long marble length of the Curetes Way, was once lined with buzzing shops and statues of local luminaries, emperors and deities.

KEN WELSH/GETTY IMAGES ©

Don't Miss **Library of Celsus**

This magnificent library in Ephesus commemorates the early-2nd-century-AD governor of Asia Minor, Celsus Polemaeanus.

Capable of holding 12,000 scrolls in its wall niches, this was the largest ancient library after Alexandria and Pergamum. The valuable texts were protected from temperature and humidity extremes by a 1m gap between the inner and outer walls.

Facade niches hold replica statues of the Greek Virtues: Arete (Goodness), Ennoia (Thought), Episteme (Knowledge) and Sophia (Wisdom).

ancient Ephesus' fountains, which filled the city with the relaxing sound of rushing water.

CURETES WAY   Ruin
This was Ephesus' main thoroughfare, ringed by statuary, great buildings, and rows of shops selling incense, silk and other goods.

Halfway down, the honorary **Trajan Fountain (Curetes Way)** was originally fronted by a huge statue of the great emperor, grasping a pennant and standing on a globe.

The **men's latrines**, a square structure, has toilet 'seats' along the back walls. Although wealthy men would have had

private home bathrooms, they'd also use the public toilets; some even paid a membership fee to claim a specific seat.

Further down are the **brothel** ruins. Some experts believe that visiting sailors and merchants simply used it as a guesthouse and bath, which of course would not necessarily exclude prostitution services.

The ornate, Corinthian-style **Temple of Hadrian** honours Trajan's successor. One of Ephesus' most famous attractions, it originally had a wooden roof and doors. Note its main arch; supported by a central keystone, this architectural marvel remains perfectly balanced, with no need for cement or mortar.

TERRACED HOUSES
Ruin

(Yamaç Evleri; admission ₺15) The Terraced Houses are well worth the additional ₺15. The roofed complex contains (at present) seven well-preserved Roman homes. In dwelling 2, keep an eye out for wall graffiti: these hand-scrawled images include everything from pictures of gladiators and animals to names and love poems. The colourful mosaics, painted frescoes and marbles provide breathtaking insight into the lost world of Ephesus and its aristocracy.

MARBLE STREET
Ruin

Ephesus' third-largest street is currently closed due to excavations. Instead, you'll cross the **Lower Agora**, a 110-sq-metre former textile and food market that once had a massive colonnade.

After exiting, you'll see the **Great Theatre**. Originally built under Hellenistic King Lysimachus, it was reconstructed by the Romans. Seating rows are pitched slightly steeper as they ascend, meaning that upper-row spectators still enjoyed good views and acoustics. The theatre could hold about 25,000 people.

HARBOUR STREET
Ruin

Formally the Arcadian Way, Harbour St was built by Byzantine Emperor Arcadius (r AD 395–408) in an attempt to revive the fading city. It greeted visitors after they patronised the **Harbour Baths**. Look for the high column at the arcade's end to see how far inward the sea reached in those days.

After exiting the Lower Gate, the ruined **Gymnasium of Vedius** (2nd century AD) had exercise fields, baths, toilets, covered exercise rooms, a swimming pool and a ceremonial hall. Further along is the contemporaneous **Stadium**.

Getting There & Away

Selçuk is 3km away, and Kuşadası 19km away. Technically, hotels cannot take you to Ephesus, so take a taxi, car or tour. Ephesus' two entry points are 3km apart.

Minibuses between Selçuk, Pamucak and Kuşadası pass the Ephesus turn-off (₺4, five minutes from Selçuk), a 20-minute walk to the Lower Gate's ticket office. A taxi from Selçuk runs ₺20.

Selçuk
☑ 0232 / POP 28,158

Were it not for nearby Ephesus, Selçuk might be just another provincial Turkish town; that said, it does have more than the usual number of attractions, from graceful **Roman aqueduct** ruins to one of the Seven Wonders of the Ancient World.

Like all small places catering to short-term visitors, there's plenty of competition, which can result in both good deals and less-welcome pressure. Yet all in all, Selçuk remains a likeable, down-to-earth town, and a good base for regional adventures.

Sights

TEMPLE OF ARTEMIS
Ruin

(Artemis Tapınağı; ⏲8.30am-5.30pm) Just beyond Selçuk's western extremities, in an empty field, stands a solitary reconstructed pillar: all that remains of the massive Temple of Artemis, one of the Seven Wonders of the Ancient World.

A sign of the great love and attachment Ephesians felt for their fertility avatar, the structure had 127 columns at its height. You can get a sense of this grandeur by visiting Didyma's better-preserved Temple of Apollo (p174), which had 122 columns.

BASILICA OF ST JOHN
Ruin

(St Jean Caddesi; admission ₺5; ⏲8.30am-6.30pm summer, to 4.30pm winter) Even after a century of restoration, this once-great basilica of Byzantine Emperor Justinian (r 527–65) remains a skeleton of its former self. Nevertheless, it makes for a pleasant stroll, with excellent hilltop views.

The church was inspired by the local connection with St John, who reportedly visited Ephesus twice and wrote his gospel on this hill. These legends, and the existence of a 4th-century tomb

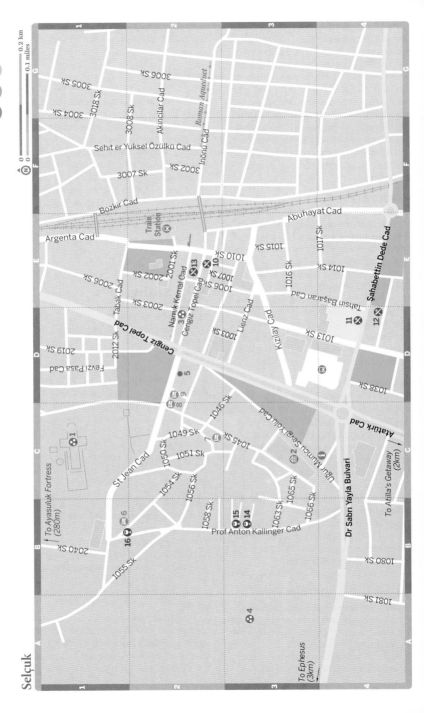

supposedly housing John's relics, inspired Justinian to build the basilica here. In Byzantine times, the site drew thousands of pilgrims.

AYASULUK FORTRESS   Castle
(St Jean Caddesi; admission €8; ⊙8.30am-6.30pm summer, to 4.30pm winter;) Selçuk's crowning achievement is accessed via the Basilica of St John – and on the same ticket. The partially restored fortress's remains date from Byzantine and Ottoman times.

 Sleeping

Selçuk specialises in good-value, family-run pensions, though more upscale hotels exist, too. Alongside the attentive service, free extras and bus station pick-ups, there can be pressure to buy (carpets, tours etc). You should be OK at the following.

ATILLA'S GETAWAY   Hostel €
(☎892 3847; www.atillasgetaway.com; Acarlar Köyü; s/d incl breakfast & dinner €24/40; ❄️ 🛜 ☀️) This friendly 'backpacker's resort' is located 2.5km south of town, but linked to the otogar (bus station) by regular free shuttles. Basic rooms are spread around an outdoor pool, itself flanked by a billiards table, 'chill-out area' of floor pillows and low wood tables, plus an outdoor bar and dining area.

AKAY HOTEL   Hotel €€
(☎892 3172; www.hotelakay.com; 1054 Sokak 7; s/d/tr from €30/50/80; ❄️ @ 🛜 ☀️) The quality of this smart, Swiss-run hotel near İsa Bey Camii shows in the impeccable service and attention to detail. Enclosed from the outside street, Akay preserves a quiet elegance with its stone foundations, white walls, inviting turquoise pool and patio. Dinners (mains ₺12 to ₺15) are on the relaxing roof terrace.

HOMEROS PENSION   Pension €€
(☎892 3995; www.homerospension.com; 1048 Sokak 3; s/d/tr ₺50/80/110; ❄️ 🛜) A longtime favourite on the pension scene, friendly Homeros offers a dozen rooms, unique for their colourful hanging textiles and handcrafted furniture. Enjoy good views, coffee and dinners (₺15) from the roof terraces.

HOTEL BELLA   Hotel €€€
(☎892 3944; www.hotelbella.com; St Jean Caddesi 7; s/d from €80/120; ❄️ @ 🛜) Well situated near St John's Hill, this posh little hotel comes with a pricey carpet and jewellery shop, catering primarily to older Americans and Brits. The well-designed rooms have Ottoman flourishes, and the relaxing roof terrace offers dinners (₺25).

NAZ HAN   Pension €€
(☎892 8731; www.nazhan.net; 1044 Sokak 2; r €60-80; ❄️ @) A hotel with boutique aspirations by St John's Hill, Naz Han

occupies a century-old Greek house, where the rooms and relaxing courtyard are decorated with artefacts and antiques. There's also a small roof terrace.

Eating

Selçuk offers dependable and reasonably priced Turkish fare. Pensions and hotels also offer good meals.

EJDER RESTAURANT
Anatolian €€
(Cengiz Topel Caddesi 9e; mains ₺7-17; ⏰breakfast, lunch & dinner) Roughly opposite the Byzantine aqueduct, this tiny, time-tested local favourite serves delicious Turkish dishes. If you can't decide, take the whole sizzling Anatolian meat platter.

WALLABIES AQUADUCT RESTAURANT
Turkish €€
(☎892 3204; Cengiz Topel Caddesi 2; mains ₺10-16) Beneath the hotel of the same name, Wallabies spills out onto the square beneath the Byzantine aqueduct, guaranteeing atmospheric summer dining. International offerings complement traditional Anatolian fare (try the house speciality, chicken dish *krep tavuk sarması*).

SELÇUK KÖFTECISI
Köfte €
(Şahabettin Dede Caddesi; mains ₺6-9; ⏰breakfast, lunch & dinner) This classic *köfte* (meatball) joint, family-run since 1959, offers great but small meat portions and tasty side salads.

MARKET
Market €
(Şahabettin Dede Caddesi; ⏰9am-5pm Sat winter, 8am-7pm Sat summer) Self-caterers (and sightseers) will enjoy Selçuk's Saturday market, behind the bus station. This and the Wednesday market (behind the train station) offer fruits, veg and cheeses from village farms.

Drinking

Drinking with fellow travellers and your hosts at your pension is generally more worthwhile than Selçuk's desultory bar/cafe scene.

If you do go out, you'll find the action concentrated along Prof Anton Kallinger

Mary's house (p157), Ephesus

SVETLANA KUZNETSOVA/ALAMY ©

CONNIE COLEMAN/GETTY IMAGES ©

Don't Miss **Ephesus Museum**

This museum holds artefacts from Ephesus' Terraced Houses, including jewellery and cosmetic boxes, plus coins, funerary goods and ancient statuary. The famous effigy of phallic god Priapus, visible by pressing a button, draws giggles. Look out for the multi-breasted, egg-holding marble Artemis statue, a very fine work indeed.

Visit the museum after touring Ephesus. After midday, it gets busy with cruise crowds being rushed through.

NEED TO KNOW

892 6010; Uğur Mumcu Sevgi Yolu Caddesi; admission ₺5; 8.30am-6.30pm summer, to 4.30pm winter

Caddesi and Siegburg Caddesi, including **Destina** (Prof Anton Kallinger Caddesi 24; 10am-3am) and **Amazon** (Prof Anton Kallinger Caddesi 22;). There are also a few scattered cafes near İsa Bey Camii; opposite, **Odeon Beer Garden** (1054 Sokak 1; 6am-midnight) is one of a few laid-back places for a drink on Selçuk's northern side.

ℹ Information

Banks with ATMs and exchange offices line Cengiz Topel and Namık Kemal Caddesis.
Selçuk Hospital (892 7036; Dr Sabri Yayla Bulvarı)

Tourist office (www.selcuk.gov.tr; Agora Caddesi 35; 8am-noon & 1-5pm daily summer, Mon-Fri winter)

ℹ Getting There & Around

Bus

Buses include İzmir (₺9, one hour, every 40 minutes in summer), Bodrum (₺25, 3¼ hours, three daily), İstanbul (₺45 to ₺50, 10 hours, three night-time and one daytime) via Bursa; and Denizli (₺25, 4½ hours, two daily) for the Med and Pamukkale, which is also served by a direct bus (goes at 9.30am and returns at 5pm).

Below: Bazaar area, Bodrum (p171);
Right: Güvercin Ada (Pigeon Island), Kuşadası
(BELOW) MICHELE FALZONE/GETTY IMAGES ©; (RIGHT) FIRECREST/ROBERT HARDING/GETTY IMAGES ©

Dolmuş

For Kuşadası (₺5, 30 minutes), dolmuşes (minibuses) run every 20 to 30 minutes from 6.55am to 10pm during summer, fewer in winter.

Taxi

Taxis to İzmir's Adnan Menderes Airport cost about ₺130.

Train

There's a direct train to İzmir's Adnan Menderes Airport (₺4.50, 55 minutes). Services start at 6.25am and finish at 7.30pm. From the train's airport stop, it's a 15- to 20-minute stroll to the departures terminal. The train continues into İzmir, and there are also daily services to Denizli.

Kuşadası

📞 0256 / POP 68,225

Kuşadası is a popular package-tour destination for Northern Europeans and, as the coastal gateway to Ephesus, the Med's fourth-busiest cruise port. It could be better than it is, but lacking Bodrum's sights and ambience, it remains a distant runner-up in the Aegean party scene, though the many Irish pubs and discos do make an effort.

If you want nightlife, or simply like being near the sea, Kuşadası is a good base, though Selçuk offers better value.

👁 Sights & Activities

Local travel agencies offer trips to Ephesus (full day with lunch for €45), Priene, Miletus and Didyma (€50), or more distant places such as Pamukkale (€45).

KUŞADASI FORTRESS   Fortress
Kuşadası's minor stone fortress on causeway-connected **Güvercin Ada** (Pigeon Island) exhibits handicrafts and features pigeon coops on stilts.

 ## Sleeping

Kuşadası centre has pensions and business hotels, none terribly atmospheric, while package-tour resorts cover the outlying coasts.

LIMAN HOTEL Pension €€
(Mr Happy's; ☎614 7770; www.limanhotel.com; Kıbrıs Caddesi, Buyral Sokak 4; s/d €25/38; ❄@🛜) From owner Hasan ('Mr Happy') to the cooks and the cleaners, everyone at Liman is friendly and helpful. It's not particularly fancy, but the rooms are clean and spacious enough, while the rooftop terrace/bar has great views – perfect for the buffet breakfast. Local information and help arranging trips are on hand.

HOTEL ILAYDA Business Hotel €€
(☎614 3807; www.hotelilayda.com; Atatürk Bulvarı 46; s/d ₺80/140; ❄@🛜) This shiny,

renovated seaside option has nice design touches and a good restaurant. It has all mod cons, and great views from some rooms, and from the rooftop terrace.

**SEZGIN HOTEL
GUEST HOUSE** Hostel €
(☎614 4225; www.sezginhotel.com; Arslanlar Caddesi 68; s/d/tr/f €25/35/50/60; ❄@🛜🏊) Sezgin offers clean rooms with big, comfortable beds and small balconies overlooking a garden and pool. There's a self-catering family room (though note the pension is near loud bars). Call for free port or bus-station pick-up.

**CLUB
CARAVANSERAIL** Historic Hotel €€
(☎614 4115; www.kusadasihotelcaravanserail. com; Atatürk Bulvarı 2; s/d/ste €80/100/150; ❄🛜) A grand 17th-century stone caravanserai, this photogenic structure is lit at night, and accessed by giant stairs

167

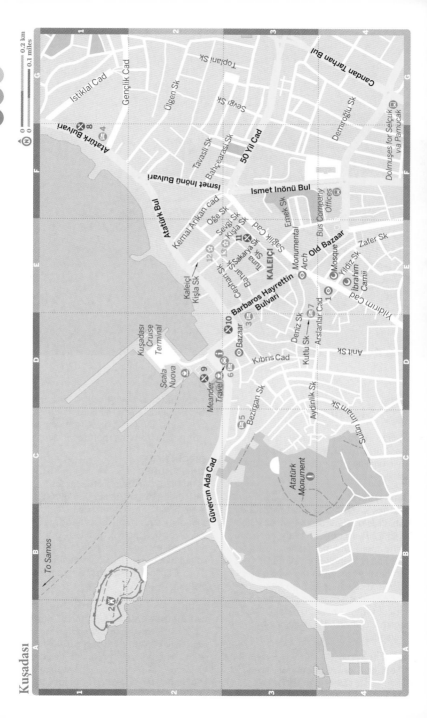

Kuşadası

EPHESUS, BODRUM & THE SOUTH AEGEAN KUŞADASI

Kuşadası

leading to a secluded inner courtyard. The rooms' Ottoman decor is authentic, the kitschy 'Turkish nights' less so.

HOTEL STELLA   Pension €
(📞 614 1632; www.hotelstellakusadasi.com; Bezirgan Sokak 44; s/d ₺40/70; ❄ @ ≋) Central Hotel Stella, on a hilly street, makes a good budget fallback, with tidy rooms offering sea-and-city views.

Eating

Waterfront dining is atmospheric but can be expensive – be sure to verify seafood prices before ordering. Kaleiçi, Kuşadası's old quarter, offers characterful backstreet eats and some fun, more Turkish cafes.

FERAH   Seafood €€€
(📞 614 1281; İskele Yanı Güvercin Parkı İçi; mains ₺15-25; ⏰ lunch & dinner) This waterfront restaurant is one of the classier options, with great sunset sea views and good-quality mezes and seafood.

SARAY   International €€€
(📞 0544 921 6224; Bozkurt Sokak 25; mains ₺15-35; ⏰ breakfast, lunch & dinner; 📶) Saray

does international fare and some decent Turkish choices, plus good vegetarian options. It can get kitschy during evening singalongs and on Wednesday's 'Turkish Night', though.

CIMINO   Italian €€
(Atatürk Bulvarı 56b; mains ₺5-19; ⏰ lunch & dinner) Opposite the seafront and featuring jazz music, Cimino is the best local option for Italian food and coffees.

**KAZIM USTA
RESTAURANT**   Seafood €€€
(📞 614 1226; Liman Caddesi 4; mezes ₺5-12, mains ₺15-30; ⏰ breakfast, lunch & dinner) Opposite the tourist office by the water, Kazim Usta opened in 1950 and since then has become known as Kuşadası's top fish restaurant. Salad, and fish soup or calamari for an appetiser, followed by sea bream and a drink, will run about ₺55 per person. Waterfront tables require advance booking in summer.

 Drinking & Entertainment

Kuşadası's nightlife scene comprises **Barlar Sokak** (Bar St), a cacophonous central zone patronised by tourists and fronted by touts; the more laid-back old cafes of **Kaleiçi**; and **Cape Yılancı** on the southern coast, with its giant bar/club/concert complexes.

ORIENT BAR   Live Music
(www.orientbar.com; Kaleiçl Kişla Sokak 14 & 17) On a side street, this perennial favourite in an atmospheric old stone house has trellises across the lattice roof. Mellow sounds, such as live acoustic guitar, feature.

BIZIM MEYHANE   Meyhane
(Kişla Sokak) This characterful and slightly eccentric place, with low beams, stone walls and hung instruments, is popular with Turks and tourists. It does good live Turkish music.

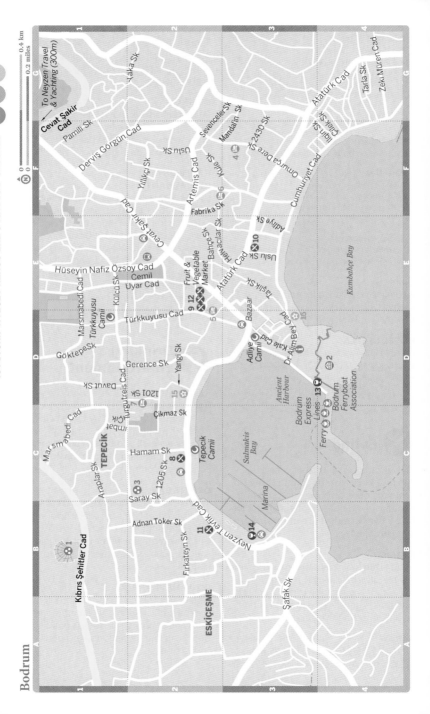

Bodrum

170

ℹ️ Information

ATM-equipped banks are on Barbaros Hayrettin Bulvarı.

Özel Kuşadası Hastanesi (📞613 1616; Anıt Sokak) Excellent, English-speaking private hospital 3km north of the centre of town (Selçuk road).

Tourist office (Liman Caddesi, İskele Meydanı; ⏱️8am-noon & 1-5pm Mon-Fri) Near the cruise-ship dock, and under the walls.

ℹ️ Getting There & Around

Meander Travel (www.meandertravel.com; Kıbrıs Caddesi 1; ⏱️9am-9pm) operates ferries to Samos (Greece; single/same-day return €35/40; daily departures April to October) and, like most Kuşadası travel agencies, sells tickets.

Kuşadası's otogar is at Kahramanlar Caddesi's southern end, on the bypass highway. Bus companies on İsmet İnönü Bulvarı sell tickets and offer free *servis* (shuttle minibuses) to it.

Buses include Bodrum (₺25, 2½ hours, three daily in summer); in winter you can take a dolmuş to Söke (₺5, at least every 30 minutes year-round).

For İzmir Adnan Menderes Airport, make the short trip to Selçuk (p165) and catch the train; or take a bus to İzmir otogar and switch to the local bus. A taxi costs around ₺160.

Şehiriçi minibuses (₺1.50) run every few minutes in summer (every 15 to 20 in winter) from Kuşadası otogar to the centre, and along the coast.

Bodrum
📞0252 / POP 34,866

Although more than one million tourists flock to its beaches, boutique hotels and clubs each summer, Bodrum (Halicarnassus in ancient times) never loses its cool. More than any other Turkish seaside get-away, it has an enigmatic elegance, from the town's grand crowning castle and glittering marina to its flower-filled cafes and white-plastered backstreets. Even in the most hectic days of high summer, you can still find little corners of serenity, in the town and especially in its outlying coastal villages.

◎ Sights

MAUSOLEUM Ruin
(Map p170; Turgutreis Caddesi; admission ₺8; ⏱️8.30am-5.30pm Tue-Sun) One of the Seven Wonders of the Ancient World, the Mausoleum was the greatest achievement of Carian King Mausolus (r 376–353 BC). Before his death, the king had planned his own tomb, to be designed by Pythius (architect of Priene's Temple of Athena). When he died, his wife (and sister), Artemisia, oversaw the completion of this enormous, white-marble tomb topped by stepped pyramids.

A few ancient elements survive, including the entry to Mausolus' tomb chamber. The site has relaxing gardens, and models, drawings and documents indicate the grand dimensions of the original Mausoleum.

Activities

BLUE CRUISES
Boat Tour

Countless excursion boats are moored along Neyzen Tevfik Caddesi; a 'blue cruise' on board one of these is a fun day trip. Like the ferry companies, some even access peninsula bays, saving you a sweaty minibus ride. **Karaada** (Black Island), with hot-spring waters gushing from a cave, is a popular destination where you can swim and loll in supposedly healthful orange mud.

Book cruises at your hotel, or on the moored excursion boats, ideally a day ahead. Group tours start from €12.

NEYZEN TRAVEL & YACHTING
Boat Tour

(316 7204; www.neyzen.com.tr; Kibris Sehitleri Caddesi 34) *Gület* trips, including a nice circular tour of the Gulf of Gokova, down to Knidos and hugging the coast all the way back to Bodrum.

Sleeping

It's more expensive than other coastal resorts, but many hotels offer discounted rates for advance bookings.

SU OTEL
Boutique Hotel €€€

(Map p170; 316 6906; www.bodrumsuhotel. com; Turgutreis Caddesi, 1201 Sokak; s/d/ste from €70/95/115; ❄ ? ☎) Epitomising Bodrum's traditional white-and-bright-blue decor, the Su has sun-filled bedrooms, some with balconies overlooking the terraced gardens and inviting pool. The friendly management helps with all local activities; out of high season, it even runs a cooking class.

KAYA PENSION
Pension €€

(Map p170; 316 5745; www.kayapansiyon.com. tr; Eski Hükümet Sokak 14; s/d/tr ₺100/120/140; ❄ ?) One of Bodrum's better pensions, with clean, simple rooms and a beautiful

flowering courtyard for breakfast or drinks. The helpful staff can arrange activities.

OTEL ATRIUM
Hotel €€

(Map p170; 316 2181; www.atriumbodrum. com; Fabrika Sokak 21; s/d incl half board from ₺100/120; ❄ ? ☎) This mid-size hotel amid tangerine trees has bright and fairly spacious rooms. It's good value for families, and has a pool (with separate kids' section), poolside bar, two restaurants and free parking. It's a five- to 10-minute walk to both centre and beach.

ANFORA
Pension €

(Map p170; 316 5530; www.anforapansiyon. com; Omurça Dere Sokak 23; s/d from ₺45/70; ❄ ?) Rooms are well kept and clean (though can be cramped) at this friendly pension, a worthy budget contender. Although Bar St's a few blocks away, it's not too loud at night.

Eating

Bodrum's waterfront has pricey, big-menu restaurants (not all bad), but also discreet backstreet contenders, fast-food stalls and a famous fish market/seafood-restaurant scene on Cevat Şakir Caddesi, which is also the site of the fruit and veg market.

Generally, Bodrum's western bay eateries are more upscale, while the eastern bay has more informal fare.

LA PASIÓN
Spanish €€

(Restaurante Español; Map p170; www.lapasion -bodrum.com; cnr Atatürk Caddesi & Uslu Sokak; set menus ₺18-35; ⏰lunch & dinner) At this refined Spanish restaurant, the lunch menus change weekly and, given the intricacy of the starters and desserts, are surprisingly good value (₺18 per person). It occupies an old stone home with a flowering courtyard and Spanish music wafting on the breeze.

FISH MARKET
Seafood €€

(Map p170; Cevat Şakir Caddesi; mezes from ₺4, fish ₺20; ⏰dinner Mon-Sat) Bodrum's fish market (sometimes called *'manavlar'* for the fruit stands at the entrance to this small network of back alleys) offers a

LOUIS-LAURENT GRANDADAM/GETTY IMAGES ©

Don't Miss **Castle of St Peter**

The Knights Hospitaller, based in Rhodes, built this Bodrum castle using marble and stones from the famed Mausoleum, completing it in 1437. When Süleyman the Magnificent captured Rhodes in 1522, the Knights were forced to cede the castle, and the Ottomans promptly built a mosque in it.

The **Museum of Underwater Archaeology** has antiquities, reconstructions and multimedia displays, and the battlements offer splendid views. Heading in, you'll pass a carved marble **Crusader coats of arms**. Next is the castle's main court, an **amphorae collection** and **glass-blowing workshop**.

A reconstruction of a late-Roman ship's stern discovered off Yassıada is displayed in the chapel. Left of here and up the towers is the **Glass Wreck Hall**, housing a ship that sank in 1025, while carrying three tonnes of glass. The **French Tower** has finds from the world's only fully excavated Classical Greek shipwreck.

The **Carian Princess Hall** exhibits a gold crown and other jewellery, popularly associated with a 4th-century BC Carian queen.

The **English Tower**, built during the reign of King Henry IV of England (1399–1413), was a show of solidarity with the Byzantines against the Muslim Turks.

The **Uluburun Wreck Hall** contains **Bronze Age shipwrecks**, including the world's oldest excavated wreck, the 14th-century BC *Uluburun*. Full-size replicas of the interior and the wreck site exist. The **Treasure Room** displays pieces including an Egyptian queen's golden scarab.

Enter the dungeons at **Gatineau Tower**, where the Knights imprisoned their enemies.

NEED TO KNOW

Map p170; ☎ 316 2516; www.bodrum-museum.com; admission ₺10, Glass Wreck Hall ₺5, Carian Princess Hall ₺5; ⏲ 9am-noon & 1-7pm Tue-Sun summer, 8am-noon & 1-5pm winter, Glass Wreck Hall 10am-noon & 2-4pm Tue-Fri, Carian Princess Hall 10am-noon & 2-4pm Tue-Sun

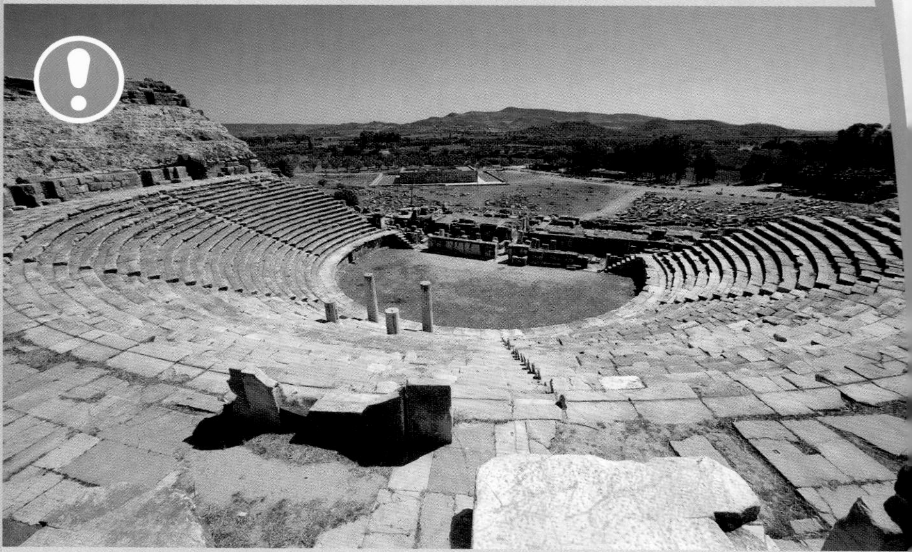

SAMUEL MAGAL/GETTY IMAGES ©

Don't Miss Priene, Miletus & Didyma

These ancient settlements run in a line south of Kuşadası. Visiting all three in one day is easily done by car or on a 'PMD' tour (typically minimum four people, around €50 for transport, lunch and an hour at each) with Kuşadası and Selçuk travel agencies.

Like Ephesus, **Priene** (☎547 1165; admission ₺5; ⏰8.30am-7.30pm mid-May–mid-Sep, to 5.30pm mid-Sep–mid-May) was a sophisticated port city. Although it leaves more to the imagination, Priene enjoys a commanding mountainside position, shady trees and less crowds. The Romans made few modifications of its Hellenistic buildings, which has preserved its uniquely 'Greek' look.

On a high bluff, five re-erected columns evoke the ruined Classical Ionian **Temple of Athena's** original appearance. The 6500-seat **theatre** is among the best-preserved Hellenistic theatres anywhere.

Miletus (Milet; ☎875 5562; admission ₺3; ⏰8.30am-7.30pm mid-May–mid-Sep, to 5.30pm mid-Sep–mid-May), once a great port city, has impressive mixed Hellenistic-Roman architecture and **Miletus Museum** (admission ₺3; ⏰8.30am-4.30pm), which illustrates the original relationship between the three sites – before river silt deformed the Anatolian coast, filling Miletus' and Priene's harbours. The city was a leading centre of Greek thought and culture. Rome later took over, and a Christian congregation developed following St Paul's visits. Look out for the 15,000-seat Hellenistic **Great Theatre** (pictured), reconstructed by the Romans, the ruined **Temple of Apollo** and vast **Baths of Faustina**.

Didyma's (Didim) astonishing 122-column **Temple of Apollo** (☎811 0035; admission ₺3; ⏰9am-7.30pm mid-May–mid-Sep, to 5.30pm mid-Sep–mid-May) was the ancient world's largest after Ephesus' Temple of Artemis. Thick and towering columns still stand here. Didyma's Oracle of Apollo had an importance second only to the Oracle of Delphi.

unique sort of direct dining: you choose between myriad fresh catches on ice at fishmongers' tables and have them cooked (about ₺6 extra) at any adjoining restaurant. Options run from top-end fish to farm fish; waiters can help you decide.

The plain restaurants spill across the small streets, which get incredibly crowded. Book ahead for evening dining. **Meyhane Deniz Feneri** (Map p170; ☎316 3534; Belediye Gıda Çarşısı 12; fish ₺18-35) is a local tip. Dinner for two with a few mezes, drinks and fish will run at least ₺100 here.

MARINA KÖFTECISI
Köfte €€
(Map p170; ☎313 5593; Neyzen Tevfik Caddesi 158; mains ₺10-17) With a waterfront view, this is an excellent spot for traditional *köfte*. Try the *kaşarlı köfte* (meatballs with cheese from sheep's milk), served with pitta bread drizzled with tomato sauce and yoghurt.

DÖNER TEPECIK
Kebap €
(Map p170; Neyzen Tevfik Caddesi; kebaps from ₺6; ☺breakfast, lunch & dinner) Across from the eponymous mosque, this local favourite does tasty kebaps on homemade bread.

HADIGARI
Bar
(Map p170; www.hadigari.com.tr; 1025 Sokak 2; ☺7pm-5am) Bodrum's oldest bar rocks on from its auspicious location under the Castle of St Peter.

KÜBA BAR
Club
(Map p170; Neyzen Tevfik Caddesi 62; ☺7pm-4am) Bodrum's poshest and most popular address for Turkish clubbers, Küba has all the plasma screens, disaffected DJs, shiny poles and laser beams one would expect. It does good international fare by evening.

MARINE CLUB CATAMARAN
Club
(Map p170; www.clubcatamaran.com; Dr Alim Bey Caddesi; admission weekday/weekend ₺35/40; ☺10pm-4am mid-May–Sep) Bodrum's party boat, this floating nightclub sails at 1.30am, keeping the licentiousness offshore for a good three hours. Free shuttles run every 15 minutes to the eastern bay.

Drinking & Entertainment

The Turkish jet set fills the western-bay clubs, while the foreign masses frequent the loud waterfront bars and clubs of Bar St (Dr Alim Bey Caddesi and Cumhuriyet Caddesi). The Marina Yacht Club (p149) is a local favourite.

The castle and Ancient Theatre (p149) host opera, ballet and rock performances.

The site of Bodrum's Mausoleum (p171)
ALI KABAS/ALAMY ©

Detour:
Dilek Peninsula

About 26km south of Kuşadası, the Dilek Peninsula juts westwards into the Aegean, almost touching Samos. West of Güzelçamlı, **Dilek National Park** (Dilek Milli Parkı; www.dilekyarimadasi.com; admission per person/car ₺4/10; ⏰7am-7.30pm Jun-Sep, 8am-5pm Oct-May) is a mountainous reserve with walking trails, stunning vistas and azure coves for swimming.

A brown sign outside the entrance points to **Zeus Mağarası** (the 'Cave of Zeus'), where the water's refreshingly cold in summer and warm in winter.

After the Dilek National Park entry gate, four rounded bays with pebble beaches lie below. The road then tapers off at a high-security military compound covering the peninsula's end.

Accessing the first cove, **İçmeler Köyü** (1km past the entrance), involves a steep walk down to the sandy but somewhat dirty beach. The road above has great views from designated pullover points.

About 3km beyond İçmeler Köyü, an unpaved turn-off heads 1km downhill to **Aydınlık Beach**. This 800m-long pebble-and-sand strand is backed by pines.

Dilek's third bay, **Kavaklı Burun**, has a sand-and-pebble surf beach. As at Aydınlık, there's a second entrance 1km further down. The final visitable beach, **Karasu Köyü**, is the most placid, and enjoys revelatory views of mountainous Samos. You might even see a dolphin.

Each bay has a **restaurant shack** (mains ₺8-25), serving everything from steak to sea bass. In summer, dolmuşes run from Kuşadası every 15 minutes for Dilek (third/fourth bay ₺5/7, 40 minutes).

ℹ Information

ATMs line Cevat Şakir Caddesi and harbour-front streets.

Tourist office (Kale Meydanı; ⏰8am-6pm Mon-Fri, daily summer)

ℹ Getting There & Away

Air

Bodrum International Airport (BJV), 36km from Bodrum town, is served by almost 50 airlines, mostly charters and budget airlines working in summer. AtlasJet (www.atlasjet.com) offers direct İstanbul flights; Pegasus Airlines (www.flypgs.com) often has good deals.

Take Turkish Airlines' Havaş bus (₺19) from Bodrum otogar two hours before departure (if flying with them). It also meets flights and drops passengers in central Bodrum. Taxis cost ₺90 from the city centre and ₺100 from the airport, although other airlines may start their own shuttle buses.

Boat

Contact the Bodrum Ferryboat Association (☎316 0882; www.bodrumferryboat.com; Kale Caddesi Cümrük Alanı 22; ⏰8am-8pm) for information on departures (its website departure info isn't always reliable).

Datça Ferries (single/return/car ₺25/40/70, two hours) leave Bodrum at 9am daily from June to mid-September; at 9.30am on Tuesday, Thursday, Saturday and Sunday in April, May, early June and October. Same-day returns aren't possible.

Kos (Greece) Ferries (one hour; one way or same-day return €32, open return €60) leave Bodrum daily year-round (weather permitting) at 9.30am, returning at 4.30pm. A cheaper Kos ferry (one way €12, return €20) is operated by Bodrum Express Lines (☎316 1087; www.bodrumexpresslines.com; Kale Caddesi 18; ⏰8am-6pm). Usually, a Monday to Saturday hydrofoil departs at 9.30am, returning at 5pm.

Rhodes (Greece) Hydrofoils (one way and same-day return €60, open-day return €120, 2¼ hours) leave Bodrum from June to September at 8.30am on Monday and Saturday, returning at 5pm.

Bus

Daily and nightly services include Ankara (₺55, 11 hours), Antalya (₺42, 7½ hours), Denizli (₺25, 4½ hours), Fethiye (₺30, five hours), İstanbul (₺68, 12 hours), İzmir (₺25, 3½ hours), Kuşadası (₺20, 2½ hours) and Marmaris (₺15, three hours).

Car & Motorcycle

Car-rental agencies, mostly on Neyzen Tevfik Caddesi, include Avis (☎316 2333; www.avis.com; Neyzen Tevfik Caddesi 92a) and Neyzen Travel & Yachting (☎316 7204; www.neyzen.com.tr; Kibris Sehitleri Caddesi 34). Cars are typically €45 to €65 per day, motorcycles and scooters €15 to €30 per day.

Bodrum Peninsula

The Bodrum Peninsula makes a beautiful day trip from Bodrum town, with exclusive resorts and laid-back coastal villages where you can enjoy good swimming and stylish eats. Despite the visible inroads of modern tourism, tradition and tranquillity are partially preserved by local open-air vegetable markets and the rugged coastline, overlooked by almost unpopulated hills in the peninsula's centre.

The ruins of **Pedasa**, on the main peninsula road near the Bitez turn-off, are a relic of the lost Lelegian civilisation that predated the Carians. The small site features defensive wall foundations and a ruined temple.

Bitez is a summer nightlife centre, but it remains an actual village, framed by lovely orchards. The fine sandy beach is good for swimming, packed with umbrellas and loungers, satellites of the restaurants and cafes behind them (some open year-round). On weekends, seafront restaurants' brunch buffets have become quite the local tradition.

Ortakent's 3km sand beach is mostly the domain of packed lounge chairs by summer, but the water here is nevertheless among the peninsula's cleanest (and coldest), due to wave action. The eastern **Scala Beach** (www.scalabeach.net) is quieter.

The peninsula's second-largest village, **Turgutreis**, is a workaday place, but has

Bodrum Peninsula

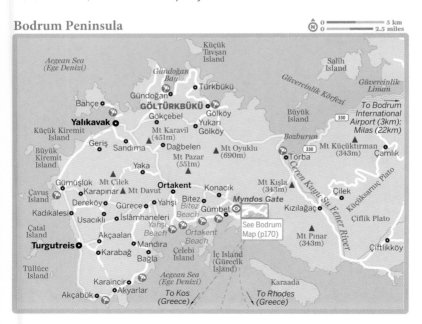

5km of sandy beaches and over a dozen tiny islets. Its new marina offers ferries for Bodrum town and Kos (Greece). Bodrum Ferryboat Association sails to/from Kos (30 minutes, €15/20 one way/same-day return) daily.

Gümüşlük has been preserved from the worst tourist developments because it lies around the ruins of ancient Carian Myndos, making it a protected archaeological zone. The ruins disappear into the sea, continuing out to the facing Rabbit Island, which can be reached by foot when the tide's low. Accessible from the main coastal road down a dirt track, Gümüşlük has an escapist feel, and it's good for a swim and drink or fresh fish meal at simple yet stylish eateries on the beach.

Near the upmarket village of **Yalıkavak**, the **Dibek Sofrası** (www.dibeklihan.com; Yakaköy Çilek Caddesi; ☾May-Oct) complex contains a restaurant, art gallery, museum and vineyard. It exhibits Ottoman antiques such as jewelled daggers, antique fountain pens and ornate coffee cups collected by the owners.

Placid **Gündoğan**, surrounded on both sides by hills glistening with wealthy villas, offers good swimming right in the centre.

Türkbükü's reputation as Turkey's poshest beach getaway is kept alive by the Turkish celebrities, politicians and business moguls who flock here each summer. Better beaches exist elsewhere on the peninsula, but visiting this privileged cove is an interesting sociocultural experience.

Despite being a short ride from Bodrum, **Torba** has stayed quieter and more family-oriented. It has a slightly escapist touch and a nice beach, though it lacks the seclusion of the peninsula's more distant corners.

 Eating

The following are reviewed in the same order as the villages above.

LEMON TREE   International €€€
(☎363 9543; Sahil Yolu 28, Bitez; mains ₺18-30; ☾8am-late) Right at Bitez beach, this popular place with breezy white-and-

Şirince

Detour:
Şirince

Once a Greek-populated mountain village, Şirince's 19th-century stone-and-stucco homes, bucolic wooded setting and long winemaking tradition have made it popular with tourists. While the deluge has affected its original charms, Şirince ('Pleasantness') remains a beautiful place. Crowds dissipate by evening (1pm to 3pm is busiest).

In the population exchange of the 1920s (see p335), Şirince was repopulated by Turks from northern Greece, who retained the local alcohol trade. You can sample their wines (made from raspberry, peach, black mulberry and pomegranate) in local restaurants and cafes. If ordering expensive wine, ask for it to be poured in front of you. Local miscreants have been known to give refills of cheap house wine, presuming (correctly) that tourists will never know the difference.

Accommodation includes the boutique hotels **Terrace Houses** (✆0532 263 7942; www.ephesushousessirince.com; r from ₺215, cottage ₺275; ❄ 🛜) and **Kırkınca Pansiyon** (✆898 3133; www.kirkinca.com; s/d ₺130/250; ❄). At the village entrance, **Artemis Şirince Şarap Evi Restaurant** (✆898 3240; www.artemisrestaurant.com; mains ₺9.50-28; ☉breakfast, lunch & dinner) occupies the former Greek schoolhouse and has great views from its outside terrace and garden. Minibuses (₺3) run from Şelçuk every 30 minutes in summer, hourly in winter.

green decor lets you eat and drink at shaded tables or loungers on the sand. There's an appetising blend of Turkish and international fare. Even locals come for the massive buffet brunch (₺17.50, from 10am to 2pm on weekends).

PALAVRA   Seafood €€€
(✆358 6290; www.palavrabalik.com; Yahşi Beldesi, Ortakent; mezes ₺5-15, fish ₺20; ☉8am-midnight) Ortakent's popular fish restaurant follows the peninsula custom of dining right on the sand, with a delicious range of home-cooked mezes and fish dishes to complement the local wine.

LIMON   Seafood €€
(✆394 4044; www.limongumusluk.com; Gümüşlük; mezes ₺14-28; ☉lunch & dinner mid-Jun–mid-Sep; ⚲) Above Gümüşlük on the old Myndos Rd to Yalıkavak, Limon sprawls around Roman and Byzantine ruins. The unique mezes include seaweed slathered in olive oil and garlic, and stuffed zucchini flowers.

TERZI MUSTAFA   Seafood €€
(✆387 7089; www.terzimustafaninyeri.com; Atatürk Caddesi 10, Gündoğan; fish ₺16-24) Right on the sand at Gündoğan's central waterfront, this local favourite serves marine delicacies from shrimp to sea bream, cooked to perfection and sprinkled with herbs and olive oil.

SHIP AHOY   Bar, Restaurant
(✆377 5070; Yalı Mevkii, Türkbükü; mains ₺17-16; ☉May-Aug) Nothing says power like Türkbükü's understated Ship Ahoy: essentially just a wide dock extending over the water, it's the first port of call for Türkbükü's glamorous summer guests. While the average traveller could not even approach a Western beach bar frequented by glitterati and politicos, in Turkey you can even reserve a table.

DA VITTORIO   Italian €€
(✆346 7002; Manastır Mevkii, Hoşgörü Sokak 5, Torba; mains ₺10-20; ☉lunch & dinner) Housed on the Marmara Bodrum's private beach in Torba, this excellent Italian eatery is open to the public.

Olive orchard, Datça Peninsula

ZACH HOLMES/ALAMY ©

ℹ️ Getting Around

From Bodrum, turquoise dolmuşes serve peninsula coastal spots (₺4 to ₺9). The terminus name is printed or painted on the minibus. From the otogar, two main lines traverse the peninsula. The first (west) serves Bitez, Ortakent, Turgutreis, Gümüşlük and Yalıkavak. The second (north) serves Torba and Yalıkavak.

Turgutreis, Gümüşlük and Yalıkavak also get a separate dolmuş. From Yalıkavak to Bodrum takes one hour or so; estimate 15 minutes between each bay.

Dolmuşes run between at least 7am and 11pm year-round. You can often solicit a passing dolmuş and go 'indi bindi' (₺2.50) to the next bay, although some bays aren't connected, requiring a change in Bodrum town.

Datça & Bozburun Peninsulas

An elemental and tranquil experience awaits on the adjoining peninsulas of Datça (occasionally called Reşadiye) and Bozburun (or Hisarönü). Unwinding wonderfully for over 100km into the Aegean Sea, they feature stunning azure coves, hidden archipelagos and craggy, thickly forested peaks.

◎ Sights & Activities

The mountainous, deeply indented Bozburun Peninsula is the perfect place to kick-start a scooter and roll down the winding country roads, discovering villages that modernity forgot. Scooter rentals from nearby Marmaris average ₺45 per day in season; ask your accommodation about organising one.

Marmaris offers a range of diving and boat trips; again, ask your accommodation about organising an outing.

KNIDOS   Ruin
(admission ₺8; ⏰ 8.30am-7pm May-Oct, 9am-6pm Nov-Apr) Knidos, a once-prosperous Dorian port city dating to 400 BC, lies in scattered ruins covering 3km of the Datça Peninsula's tip. Here, dramatic and steep hillsides, terraced and planted with groves of olive, almond and fruit trees, rise above two idyllic bays where yachts drop anchor.

The round **temple of Aphrodite** once contained the world's first freestanding female statue. Also here are the 5000-seat Hellenistic **lower theatre**, a 4th-century-BC **sundial** and some fine carvings from an erstwhile Byzantine church.

An on-site restaurant offers great views.

Datça's **Karnea Turizm** (📞712 8842; Iskele Mahallesi Atatürk Caddesi 54b) offers a half-day Knidos tour (₺60 per person). Knidos Taxi, near Cumhuriyet Meydanı, will take up to three people for ₺100 (including two hours of waiting). Datça harbour excursion boats serve Knidos, at around 9am, returning in the early evening (₺30 per person).

KNIDOS
YACHTING Ferry
(📞712 9464; Yat Limanı 4a, Datça) Organises diving trips (₺80/110 for one/two dives).

OLIVE
FARM Food & Drink, Homewares
(📞712 8377; Güller Dağı Çiftliği 30, Eski Datça; ⏰8am-7pm) Olive-grove tours, tastings and a shop will placate lovers of liquid gold. It's 600m before the main road's Datça turn-off.

 Sleeping & Eating

Popular bases on the two peninsulas are Eski (Old) Datça, the capital of an Ottoman district stretching into today's Greece, with cobbled streets and old stone houses; and Bozburun, a rustic farming-and-fishing village on Sömbeki Körfezi (Sömbeki Bay), an agreeable spot where only a little tourism has arrived.

Eski Datça

YAĞHANE PANSIYON Pension €€
(📞712 2287; www.suryaturkey.com; Karaca Sokak 42; s/d ₺70/130) In the Surya Yoga Centre, this seven-room pension is ideal for chilling out, with yoga and ayurvedic

If You Like...
Getting Wet

Kuşadası and the surrounding Aegean coast are prime territory for wetting your toes, offering activities from scuba dives to water-park slides.

1 ADALAND
(📞618 1252; www.adaland.com; Çamlimanı Mevkii; adult/child ₺50/40; ⏰10am-6pm May-Oct) Just north of Kuşadası near Pamucak, Adaland calls itself one of the world's top 10 water parks. Free entry for children aged under three.

2 AQUA FANTASY
(📞893 1111; www.aquafantasy.com; Kuşadası beach; adult/child €22/13; ⏰10am-6pm) Declaring itself Europe's largest, this 18-hectare water park by Kuşadası beach also has a hotel/spa centre. Free entry for kids under three.

3 AQUAVENTURE DIVING CENTER
(📞612 7845; www.aquaventure.com.tr; Miracle Beach Club; ⏰8am-6pm) Offers PADI open-water courses (€250) and reef dives (from €30). Call for free pick-up from most Kuşadası hotels.

4 BELEDIYE HAMAMI
(📞614 1219; Yıldırım Caddesi 2; admission €14; ⏰9am-7pm Apr-Oct) Kuşadası's emancipated hamams offer mixed bathing (with towels). The 600-year-old Belediye is a restored, clean and atmospheric bath.

5 KADINLAR DENIZI
(Ladies Beach) Kadınlar Denizi eclipses Kuşadası town's small artificial beach, although it gets very crowded with package tourists from the big nearby hotels. It's 2.5km south of town, served by regular dolmuşes. Further south are several small beaches, again backed by big hotels.

massage also available. The compact rooms have nonallergenic wooden floors and fans; two share facilities.

MEHMET ALI AĞA KONAĞI
Historic Hotel €€€

(☎ 712 9257; www.kocaev.com; stone house r €180-300, stone house ste €350-420, mansion r €385-425, mansion ste €625-700; ❀ @ ☒) Just north of Eski Datça, in Reşadiye (formerly Elaki), this opulent boutique hotel's historically furnished rooms sprawl across four buildings, amid rose and citrus gardens. The hamam has been restored to its original spa function, and celebrated restaurant Elaki cooks creative Med flavours (mains €25 to €40).

DEDE GARDEN HOTEL
Hotel €€€

(☎ 712 3951; Can Yücel Sokak; s/d ₺180/230; ❀ ☒) This 150-year-old stone manor, tucked within a walled garden, has a relaxed bar and seven individually designed rooms with kitchens.

DATÇA SOFRASI
Turkish €

(☎ 712 4188; Hurma Sokak 16; mains ₺6-10) This stylish bistro beneath a vine-clad pergola specialises in one of the vegetables Turks do best: eggplant. It also serves good grilled fish and meat.

Bozburun

YILMAZ PANSIYON
Pension €

(☎ 456 2167; www.yilmazpansion.com; İskele Mahallesi 391; s/d ₺60/90; ❀) Around 100m east of the marina, this friendly little pension is great value: 10 simple but cheerful rooms, a modern shared kitchen, and a vine-covered terrace just metres from the sea. It arranges local cruises.

PEMBE YUNUS
Pension €€

(Pink Dolphin; ☎ 456 2154; www.bozburun pembeyunus.com; Kargı Mahallesi 37; s/d with half board ₺80/160; ❀) Located 700m from the marina, the 'Pink Dolphin' is a friendly, rustic place, with some rooms enjoying huge terraces with vast sea views. The home-cooked three-course set dinners cost ₺25. The hotel uses its private boat for Symi trips.

SABRINAS HAUS
Luxury Hotel €€€

(☎ 456 2045; www.sabrinashaus.com; d/ ste from €375/750) Reachable by boat or a half-hour walk, Sabrinas Haus is the ultimate, pamperific escape. Tastefully designed rooms occupy three buildings in a beautiful mature garden. The infinity pool and seafront deck and bar are super, and the spa offers massages and treatments. Partial credit card prebooking payment is required, and kids under 14 aren't allowed.

FISHERMAN HOUSE
Seafood €€

(☎ 456 2730; İskele Mahallesi 391; mezes ₺4, seafood mezes ₺12-15, fish per 500g ₺20-30) Fresh fish at honest prices is served at this place run by the fisherman who owns Yilmaz Pansiyon.

KANDIL RESTAURANT
Seafood €€

(☎ 456 2227; İskele Mahallesi 3; mains ₺10-12) This square-side local favourite serves cheap mezes, and varied fish and grills.

MARIN CAFE BAR
Cafe, Bar

(☎ 456 2181; Atatürk Caddesi 56; beer ₺5) Very chilled-out cafe-bar, near the Pembe Yunus.

ⓘ Getting There & Away

Dalaman Airport, 92km southeast of nearby Marmaris, gets many summer charters; Turkish carriers such as Pegasus Airlines sometimes have great deals. Turkish Airlines runs the Havaş shuttle bus (₺25) to Dalaman Airport from Marmaris otogar, departing three hours before each Turkish Airlines flight. Otherwise, buses serve Dalaman (₺15, 1½ hours, hourly); from there, it's a short, expensive taxi ride to the airport (₺42).

Regular services to/from Marmaris otogar include Bodrum (₺15, three hours) and Fethiye (₺20, three hours).

Boat

From May to September, hydrofoils connect Datça with the Greek islands of Rhodes (single/return ₺90/180, 45 minutes) and Symi (single/return ₺60/120, 15 minutes) on Saturday; check locally. A *gület* cruise to Symi runs two to three times weekly (₺140, 70 minutes). It requires at least eight people; you can reserve by phone.

Knidos Yachting (p181) sells hydrofoil, ferry and *gület* tickets.

From May to mid-September, daily ferries serve Bodrum (passenger single/return ₺25/40, car and driver ₺70, extra passengers ₺10 each, two hours) from Körmen harbour at Karaköy (5km northwest of Datça). In April and October they run on Monday, Wednesday and Friday.

Tickets are sold at the **Bodrum Ferryboat Association** (📞712 2143; fax 712 4239; www. bodrumferryboat.com; Turgut Özal Meydanı), by Datça mosque. Confirm details there or phone them beforehand (the website may be out of date). Tickets are also sold at the **Ulusoy bus office** (📞712 9598; **Atatürk Caddesi 25;** ⊙**8am-10pm)**, near Datça main square. A free shuttle takes you from Datça (or Eski Datça, with prior notice) to Karaköy harbour.

Bus & Dolmuş

Hourly Eski Datça–Datça minibuses (₺2.50) depart, wait 30 minutes, and return (May to October). In low season, it's every two hours.

Hourly summer dolmuşes run from Datça's main square Cumhuriyet Meydanı to Marmaris (₺13, 1¾ hours, less frequently in low season) for onward bus connections. Buses from Marmaris drop you on Datça's main street, 500m before the square.

Six daily summer minibuses from Bozburun serve Marmaris (₺10, 1½ hours, 55km), with onward bus connections.

EPHESUS, BODRUM & THE SOUTH AEGEAN DATÇA & BOZBURUN PENINSULAS

Antalya & the Mediterranean Coast

Turkey's western Mediterranean coast, known as the Turquoise Coast or Turkish Riviera, is a region of endless azure sea, sandy beaches and mountains rising up to almost 3000m. Add to that a surfeit of ancient ruins strewn through the aromatic scrub, pine forests, and plenty of sports and activities, and you've hit Mediterranean pay dirt.

Dramatic ways to see this stretch of coastline include skimming through the crystal waters on a boat trip or a *gület* (traditional wooden yacht) cruise; and walking a section of the Lycian Way, high above what the Turks call the Akdeniz (literally, 'White Sea').

Beyond Antalya, the eastern Mediterranean coast offers a less razzle-dazzle glimpse of 'real' Turkey. Enormous vegetable farms and fruit orchards are worked overtime between the mountains and coastline, and here you'll meet modern, secular and friendly locals, and see historic sights from castles to caves.

Kaputaş cove and beach (p206), near Kaş
IZZET KERIBAR/GETTY IMAGES ©

Beachside restaurants, Ölüdeniz (p203)

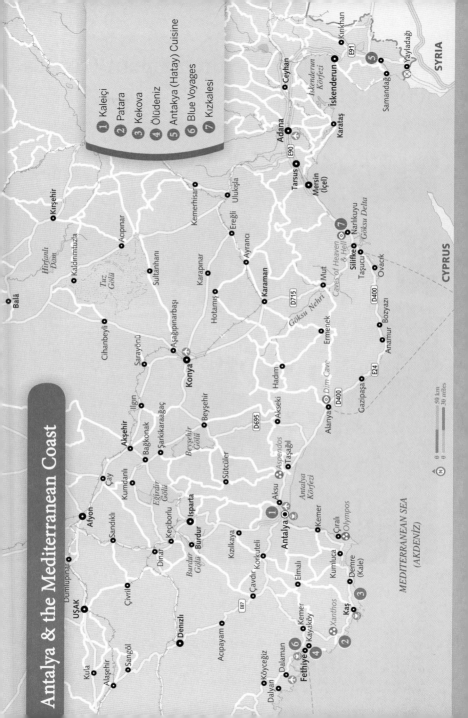

Antalya & the Mediterranean Coast

1 Kaleiçi
2 Patara
3 Kekova
4 Ölüdeniz
5 Antakya (Hatay) Cuisine
6 Blue Voyages
7 Kızkalesi

MEDITERRANEAN SEA
(AKDENİZ)

SYRIA

CYPRUS

Antalya & the Mediterranean Coast's Highlights

Kaleiçi

Kaleiçi (p213) climbs the hill from its Roman harbour to ancient walls; the name of Antalya's old town literally means 'within the castle'. The winding streets of Ottoman houses witnessed early-20th-century upheaval: Antalya was ceded to Italy after WWI, before Atatürk's army liberated the city in 1921. Above: Roman harbour (p213); Top Right: Suna & İnan Kıraç Kaleiçi Museum; Bottom Right: Hadrian's Gate

Need to Know

TOP TIP Kale Bar has Kaleiçi's best harbour and sea view. **NAVIGATION** Signs on Kaleiçi's street corners point the way to most pensions. **For further coverage, see p213**

Kaleiçi Don't Miss List

BY METIN BOZADA, OWNER OF WHITE GARDEN PANSIYON

1 WANDERING THE LANES

Antalya's old quarter (p213) is a sloping nest of interwoven streets, studded with ancient monuments, lovely small hotels, boutiques, bars and restaurants. These eventually disgorge into the exquisite little restored Roman harbour, now a modern marina with boat trips on offer. In the 17th century, about 3000 houses were jammed into this area within the old city walls. Today, fine examples of Ottoman architecture remain in the maze of narrow passages, and many of the houses have been restored, allowing you to stay in an Ottoman mansion.

2 HADRIYANÜS KAPISI

At the top of Hesapçi Sokak, the monumental Hadrian's Gate, also known as Üçkapılar or the 'Three Gates', was built for the Roman emperor's visit to Antalya. Attalus III, nephew of the city's founder Attalus II, ceded Attelia (as Antalya was then called) to Rome in 133 BC. When Hadrian visited in AD 130, he entered through this triumphal arch.

3 SUNA & İNAN KIRAÇ KALEIÇI MUSEUM

This small ethnography museum (www.kaleicimuzesi. org; Kocatepe Sokak 25; admission ₺2; 9am-noon & 1-6pm Thu-Tue) is found in a lovingly restored Kaleiçi mansion. The 2nd floor has a series of dioramas depicting some important rituals and customs of Ottoman Antalya. Most impressive is the collection of Çanakkale and Kütahya ceramics in the exhibition hall behind it, in the former Greek Orthodox church of Aya Yorgi (St George), which has been restored.

4 BALIK PAZARI HAMAMI

Kaleiçi is an atmospheric place to experience a traditional Turkish hamam, especially in the 700-year-old **Balık Pazarı Hamamı** (Fish Market Bath; ☎0242-243 6175; Balık Pazarı Sokak; bath ₺15, package ₺40; 8am-11pm). You can have a bath and scrub, or the full package of a bath, a peeling, and a soap and oil massage.

5 MEVLEVI TEKKE

This whirling dervish lodge in the Yivli Minare complex probably dates from the 13th century and has been restored.

Patara

Patara (p204) boasts Turkey's longest sand beach, a chunk of the Lycian Way footpath and some of the region's most extensive ruins. The Mediterranean getaway was ancient Lycia's principal port, and the birthplace of St Nicholas, the 4th-century Byzantine bishop who later passed into legend as Santa Claus.

Below: Patara beach; Top Right: Lycian ruins; Bottom Right: Xanthos River

2

Need to Know

TOP TIP The beach is a nesting ground for sea turtles; parts are sometimes off limits. **RUINS** Climb to the top of the theatre for views. **For further coverage,** see p204

Patara Don't Miss List

BY UFUK GÜVEN, CO-OWNER OF BOUGAINVILLE TRAVEL

1 TRIUMPHAL ARCH

Patara has some of the area's finest Lycian ruins; it was Lycia's major port and, according to the Bible, Sts Paul and Luke changed boats here while on their third mission from Rhodes to Phoenicia. You pass through this 2nd-century triple-arched triumphal arch (p204) at the entrance to the ruins, with a necropolis containing some Lycian tombs nearby.

2 BOULEUTERION

Just north of the 5000-seat theatre is the *bouleuterion*, ancient Patara's 'parliament' where it is believed members of the Lycian League met. The league was perhaps history's first proto-democratic union, and this was maybe the world's first parliament. The *bouleuterion* recently reopened after a two-year, ₺8.5 million reconstruction.

3 LYCIAN WAY

This beautiful 509km waymarked footpath runs along the coast of ancient Lycia, from Fethiye to Antalya. From Patara you can walk a circle in a day, which takes you past the 2000-year-old Delikkemer water siphon and Patara Aqueduct, both built by the Romans; and Tava village, with olive, eucalyptus and pine trees along the way.

4 CANOEING

On the Xanthos River (p205) you can glide past junglelike riverbanks and discover the rich ecosystem, with river turtles, birds and crabs. On the way, stop for a rejuvenating mud bath, and end your journey on Patara Beach (p204), Turkey's longest beach.

5 HORSE RIDING

Patara Beach is very wide: even when the turtles are nesting (July to September) and you cannot get too close to the waves for fear of damaging their eggs, you can ride on the beach (p205). Look out for the tracks left by the turtles coming to lay eggs. Horse rides lead through Patara Forest's olive- and pine-tree-lined paths, then cross the dunes to the beach and carry on through farmland. You can also ride to other places such as the ruins and Xanthos River.

191

Kekova

One of the Turquoise Coast's most stunning areas is this watery paradise (see boxed text, p210), its rippling shallows and vertiginous slopes dotted with Lycian tombs. Most easily visited on a boat trip from Kaş, Kekova island was once part of the Lycian city of Simena. Due to 2nd-century AD earthquakes, it is now the famous Sunken City (Batık Şehir); the water's smooth surface glitters and fish dart above the ancient ruins.

Antakya (Hatay) Cuisine

Originating from a slither of Turkish territory between Syria and the eastern Mediterranean, Antakya's cuisine (p230) reflects the city's Arab characteristics. Local specialities include the zingy *kekik salatasası* (thyme salad with spring onions and tomatoes); *muhammara* (a meze dip of crushed walnuts, red pepper and olive oil; also called *cevizli biber,* or walnutty peppers); and *sürk* (tangy soft cheese flavoured with dried red pepper). *Muhammara* and other Middle Eastern foods

YVETTE CARDOZO/GETTY IMAGES ©

Kızkalesi

Seemingly floating in the eastern Mediterranean, 300m from the town of the same name, Kızkalesi (p226) – Maiden's Castle – is reached by boat, swimming or dolphin-themed pedalo. It's an extraordinary optical illusion, and inside the island castle there are mosaics, a vaulted courtyard and towers to explore. A causeway once connected Kızkalesi to the town's other fortress, Corycus Castle.

Blue Voyages

A cruise (p202) along the Turquoise Coast on a *gület* (traditional wooden yacht), between Fethiye and Olympos or Marmaris, is a few days of paradise. Requiring less organisation, a day trip by boat is also a wonderful way to get out on the Med, visiting beaches, islands, swimming spots and ruins. In summer, Turkish sea dogs tout day cruises from Fethiye, Ölüdeniz, Kaş, Olympos, Antalya, Alanya and beyond. *A gület at Kaleköy harbour (p210)*

Ölüdeniz

Daniel Craig jumps off Baba Dağ (Mt Baba) in the Bond film *Skyfall* – and so can you. A tandem paraglide (p203) from the 1960m-high peak, from where you can see Rhodes (Greece) on a clear day, can take up to 40 minutes. Parasailing is also offered on Ölüdeniz' distinctive beach, a spit of sand backed by a blue lagoon. Lazing on the beach beneath soaring mountains is unforgettable.

Antalya & the Mediterranean Coast's Best...

Museums

○ **Antalya Museum** (p216) Lycian artefacts and statues of Olympian gods.

○ **Hatay Archaeology Museum** (p227) One of the finest collections of Roman and Byzantine mosaics.

○ **Anamur Museum** (p223) Frescoes and mosaics from the city of Anemurium.

○ **Fethiye Museum** (p199) Lycian pottery, jewellery, statuary, votive stones and sarcophagi.

○ **Mosaic Museum** (p223) A mosaic of Zeus' daughters, the Three Graces.

Historical Sites

○ **Caves of Heaven & Hell** (p223) Where Zeus is said to have held the monster Typhon captive.

○ **Anemurium** (p221) Anamur's sprawling, eerily quiet mountainside Byzantine city.

○ **Kayaköy** (p205) A ghost town of 4000 Greek stone houses, deserted during post-WWI upheavals.

○ **Xanthos** (p208) The capital of ancient Lycia, one of the Teke peninsula's countless Lycian ruins.

Beaches

○ **Kaputaş** (p206) Idyllic sandy cove between Kaş and Kalkan.

○ **Patara** (p204) Turkey's longest uninterrupted beach, a nesting ground for sea turtles.

○ **Ölüdeniz** (p203) Lagoon-backed spit of white sand.

○ **Olympos** (p211) Accessed via the ruined Lycian city.

○ **Cleopatra's Beach** (p219) With fine views of Alanya Castle.

○ **Kızkalesi** (p224) One of the region's loveliest beaches, with two castles.

Need to Know

Sundowner Spots

o **Gület deck** (p202) Boats stop at spots such as Kekova island, with flawless sunset views.

o **Kale Bar** (p216) Cocktails and harbour and sea views in Kaleiçi, Antalya.

o **Kismet** (p201) Bar and cabaret near Fethiye seafront.

o **Giorgio's Bar** (p209) Cocktails and live music facing Kaş main square.

o **Red Tower Brewery Restaurant** (p221) Alanya's multistorey pleasure palace with harbour views.

RESOURCES

o **Alanya Guide** (www. alanya.tv)

o **Antalya Guide** (www. antalyaguide.org)

o **Kirca Travel** (www. kircatravel.com)

o **Lycian Way** (www. lycianway.com)

o **Ölüdeniz Guide** (www. oludeniz.com.tr)

GETTING AROUND

o **Air** Dalaman to İstanbul and Europe; Antalya to İstanbul, Ankara and Europe; Antakya (Hatay) to İstanbul, Ankara and İzmir.

o **Boat** Ferries from Fethiye to Rhodes (Greece), Kaş to Meis/Kastellorizo (Greece), Alanya and Taşucu to Girne/Kyrenia (Northern Cyprus).

o **Bus** A good way to get between major towns.

o **Car** A great region for a road trip; car-hire companies at the airports and Fethiye.

o **Dolmuş** Useful for coastal spots off the D400 highway.

o **Transfers** Havaş shuttles (www.havas. net/en) from Fethiye to Dalaman airport (₺20).

BE FOREWARNED

o **Gület** Most boats use their diesel engine more than their sails.

o **Alanya** Has some of Turkey's most bawdy, bright and banging nightclubs – all good fun, so long as your accommodation isn't next door.

o **Ruins** Tour some crumbling sites with caution, eg Mamure Castle's towers.

o **Fethiye–Antalya** The inland route is about three hours quicker (and ₺8 cheaper on the bus) than the coastal route.

o **Boat trips** Check what you're getting: is lunch included and how long will you have at the various stops?

o **Summer** Reserve accommodation and activities such as *gület* cruises well in advance during the high season (July to August).

o **Winter** The western Mediterranean is very seasonal; pensions close and boat trips do not operate from roughly October to April.

Left: View from Alanya Castle (p217);
Above: Antalya Museum (p216)

Antalya & the Mediterranean Coast Itineraries

Home of the Lycian Way and coastal ruins, the area's seductive scenery and beach towns are easily accessible.

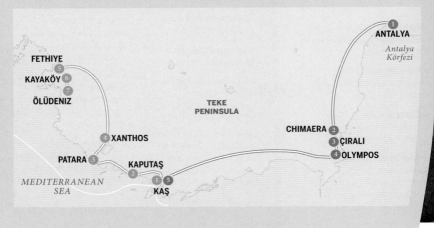

ANTALYA TO KAŞ

3 DAYS
Turkish Riviera

This Mediterranean cruise covers some of Turkey's most stunning coastline, starting in the classically beautiful and stylishly modern city of **(1) Antalya**. Stay in a boutique hotel in the gorgeous old town, Kaleiçi, where streets of Ottoman houses tumble downhill to the Roman harbour. Beyond here, the Antalya Museum's ancient exhibits illustrate the area's Lycian past. Tours and boat trips explore the coast and, in June and September, the Aspendos Opera & Ballet Festival takes place in the nearby Roman amphitheatre.

Next, head southwest to the **(2) Chimaera**, a mystical cluster of naturally occurring flames on Mt Olympos.

Stay at a beachside pension in nearby **(3) Çıralı**, a haven for nature lovers and post-backpackers, and visit the ruins of a fire-worshipping city in neighbouring **(4) Olympos**.

There are more ancient ruins across the Teke peninsula in **(5) Kaş**, a laid-back harbourside town where one of the Lycians' distinctive tombs stands between whitewashed fish restaurants in the pretty backstreets. Surrounded by beaches, Kaş is an excellent base for activities including wreck diving, sea kayaking and boat trips to Kekova island, where you can see the underwater ruins of a Lycian city.

KAŞ TO ÖLÜDENIZ
Turquoise Coast

5 DAYS

Even by Mediterranean standards, **(1) Kaş** is a supercharged activity centre. Come to this deceptively mellow seaside spot for everything from walking the Lycian Way to PADI open-water diving courses, canyoning and mountain biking.

Next, beach-hop up the Teke peninsula, stopping at exquisite **(2) Kaputaş**, with its dazzling turquoise shallows, and **(3) Patara**, Turkey's longest beach. Patara's 18km of sands are backed by ancient ruins including the *bouleuterion,* the 'parliament' where the Lycian League met. You can learn more about the league at **(4) Xanthos**, the evocative remains of Lycia's grandest city.

Next, follow in James Bond's footsteps to **(5) Fethiye**, nestling in an island-dotted bay that featured in the movie *Skyfall*. Overlooked by a Roman theatre and rock-cut tombs, Fethiye's natural harbour is a springboard for *gület* cruises and boat trips.

A land-based day trip leads to the ghost town **(6) Kayaköy**, whose stone houses and churches were abandoned in the early 1920s. From there, a pretty 8km walking trail winds to stunning **(7) Ölüdeniz**, where you can paraglide from Baba Dağ (Mt Baba) down to the beach and lagoon.

Interior of a church in the abandoned village Kayaköy (p205)
JULIAN KAESLER/GETTY IMAGES ©

Discover Antalya & the Mediterranean Coast

Antalya's Roman harbour (p213)
IZZET KERIBAR/GETTY IMAGES ©

Fethiye

☎0252 / POP 81,500

In 1958 an earthquake levelled Fethiye, sparing only the remains of the ancient city of Telmessos. Today, this seaside city is once again a prosperous, growing Mediterranean hub, although low-key for its size, due mostly to the restrictions on high-rise buildings.

Fethiye's natural harbour is perhaps the region's finest, tucked away in the southern reaches of a broad bay scattered with pretty islands, in particular Şövalye Adası, glimpsed briefly in the James Bond film *Skyfall*. The nearby coast offers many beautiful day trips, including Ölüdeniz and the lush, butterfly-flecked gorge and beach at **Butterfly Valley**.

 Sights

TELMESSOS Ruin

Fethiye's most recognisable sight is the **Tomb of Amyntas** (admission ₺8; ☉8am-7pm May-Oct, to 5pm Nov-Apr), an Ionic temple facade carved into the rock face in 350 BC. Located south of the centre, it is best visited at sunset. Other, smaller rock tombs lie about 500m to the east.

Behind the harbour in the town centre is a partially excavated 2nd-century BC Roman **theatre**. In town you'll see curious **Lycian stone sarcophagi** (circa 450 BC), including one north of the **belediye** (city hall).

On the hillside above town (along the Kayaköy road), you can't miss the ruined tower of a **Crusader fortress**, built by the Knights of St John at the start of the 15th century on earlier (perhaps Lycian, Greek and Roman) foundations.

FETHIYE MUSEUM — Museum

(www.lycianturkey.com/fethiye-museum.htm; 505 Sokak; admission ₺3; ⊙8am-5pm) Focusing on Lycian finds from Telmessos as well as the ancient settlements of Tlos and Kaunos, this museum exhibits pottery, jewellery, small statuary and votive stones. Its most prized possession is the 358 BC Trilingual Stele, which has helped to decipher the Lycian language.

Activities

OCEAN YACHTING
TRAVEL AGENCY — Adventure Sports

(☏612 4807; www.oceantravelagency.com; İskele Meydanı 1; ⊙9am-9pm Apr-Oct) Parasailing (₺180 for 45 minutes), half-day horse-riding excursions (₺50), day-long rafting trips (₺85), other water sports, 'blue voyages' and boat tickets.

EUROPEAN DIVING CENTRE — Diving

(☏614 9771; www.europeandivingcentre.com; Fevzi Çakmak Caddesi 133) Diving trips (per person ₺100 for beginners; two dives, all equipment and lunch per person ₺125 for advanced divers) and three-day PADI courses (₺700).

SEVEN CAPES — Kayaking

(☏0537 403 3779; www.sevencapes.com) Daily sea-kayak tours (€40), including a four-hour tour between Ölüdeniz and the secluded beach getaway at Kabak via Butterfly Valley (€50), and 'night paddling' (€45).

OLD TURKISH BATH — Hamam

(Tarihi Fethiye Hamamı; ☏614 9318; www.oldturkishbath.com; Hamam Sokak 2-4, Paspatur; bath & scrub ₺35, massage ₺20-50; ⊙7am-midnight) Low-key and small, this 16th-century hammam is in the oldest section of Fethiye. Open to men and women.

Tours

The popular (and often crowded) 12-Island Tour (per person incl lunch ₺30-35, on sailboat ₺50; ⊙10.30am-6pm mid-Apr–Oct) is a boat trip around Fethiye Bay (Fethiye Körfezi), cruising between islands and usually stopping at five or six for swimming, snorkelling, beaches, mud baths, ruins and lunch. Buy tickets from travel agencies or from the boat companies at the marina.

Excellent boat tours of the same length go to or include **Butterfly Valley** (per person ₺25) via Ölüdeniz, allowing you to walk, swim and visit ruins. The **Saklıkent Gorge Tour** (per person ₺45) to the rugged 18km-long gorge includes the hilltop ruins of the Lycian city at **Tlos** and a trout lunch; and the **Dalyan Tour** (per person ₺50; ⊙ 9am-6.30pm) includes a shuttle to the peaceful former farming town, a tour of **Köyceğiz Gölü** (Lake Köyceğiz), the **Sultaniye** mud baths, the ruins of the Carian city **Kaunos** and **İztuzu Beach**, a loggerhead turtle nesting site.

Sleeping

Most accommodation is up the hill behind the marina in Karagözler or further west. Many pensions will organise transport from the otogar (bus station).

YILDIRIM
GUEST HOUSE — Pension, Hostel €

(☏614 4627, 0543 779 4732; www.yildirim guesthouse.com; Fevzi Çakmak Caddesi 21; d/tr ₺80/90; ❄@🛜) Shipshape Yildirim has a half-dozen spotless rooms, some facing the harbour. Host Omer offers excursions, pick-ups, laundry, evening meals (₺15), Saturday hikes on the Lycian Way walking trail (₺10) and free bikes for guests.

VILLA DAFFODIL — Guest House €€

(☏614 9595; www.villadaffodil.com; Fevzi Çakmak Caddesi 115; s/d ₺85/120; ❄🛜♨) This large Ottoman-styled and flower-bedecked guesthouse is one of the few older buildings to survive the earthquake and development. Rooms have stylish furnishings and a homely feel; the best (including 204, 502 and 602) have balconies and sea views.

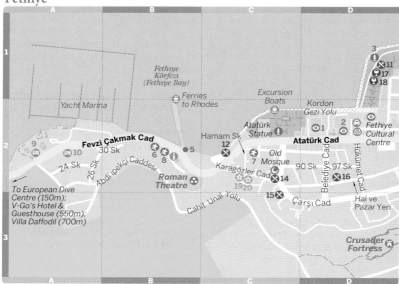

YACHT CLASSIC HOTEL
Boutique Hotel €€€

(☎612 5067; www.yachtclassichotel.com; Fevzi Çakmak Caddesi 1; s/d/ste ₺150/250/350; ❄ 🛜 🏊) This efficient and friendly hotel is a symphony in white, with just about the most stylish hotel hamam on the Med coast and a large pool terrace overlooking the harbour. Shoot for a 3rd- or 4th-floor room with huge terrace above the sea, complete with jacuzzi.

V-GO'S HOTEL & GUESTHOUSE
Pension, Hostel €€

(☎612 5409, 614 4004; www.v-gohotel.com; Fevzi Çakmak Caddesi 109; r per person €20, f €60; ❄ @ 🛜 🏊) This super-modern hostel-cum-guesthouse has rooms in two buildings, most looking out to the sea or pool. There's a great terrace with chill-out chairs and a bar with self-service music and DVDs.

Eating

Fethiye's enormous canal-side **market** takes place on Tuesday.

REIS
Seafood €€

(☎0532 472 5989, 612 5368; www.reis restaurant.com; Hal ve Pazar Yeri 62; mains ₺12-20; ⏰10am-midnight) To taste Fethiye's fish, buy your own (per kilo ₺18 to ₺25) from the fishmongers in the central covered market, then take it to one of the restaurants opposite. Reis charges ₺5 per head for cooking the fish, plus a sauce, green salad, bread with garlic butter and fruit. It also does meze and meat dishes. Book ahead.

İSKELE OCAKBAŞI
Barbecue €€

(☎614 9423; Şehit Feti Bey Parkı; mezes ₺6-19, grills ₺12-26; ⏰9am-1am) Overlooking the water and a small park (outside seating), İskele serves excellent meat dishes from its *ocakbaşı* (barbecue). Non-Turkish dishes (₺18 to ₺40) are available.

MEĞRI LOKANTASI
Turkish €€

(☎614 4047; www.megrirestaurant.com; Çarşı Caddesi 26; mains ₺7-13, mixed plates ₺17-25; ⏰8am-11.30pm low season, to 1am high season) Packed at lunchtime with locals who spill onto the streets, the Meğri offers hearty home-style cooking. Choose from the

Fethiye

◎ Top Sights

◎ Sights

⬡ Activities, Courses & Tours

⬢ Sleeping

⊗ Eating

⊖ Drinking

⊕ Entertainment

⬒ Shopping

huge display of meze and mains or try *güveç* (casserole; ₺20 to ₺25).

DENIZ RESTAURANT Seafood €€
(✆612 0212; Uğur Mumcu Parkı Yanı 10/1; mains ₺15-30) One of Fethiye's best seafood restaurants, the 'Sea' exhibits everything alive and swimming in tanks (the grouper is best) and excels in unusual meze.

PAŞA KEBAB Kebap €
(✆614 9807; Çarşı Caddesi 42; mezes ₺4-7, pides ₺6-10, kebaps ₺11.50-22.50; ◷9am-1am) Has a well-priced menu with useful photos of dishes. Try the gigantic beef, tomato and cheese Paşa Special (₺16). There's also pizza (₺12.50 to ₺16.50).

🍷 Drinking & Entertainment

Most of Fethiye's bars and nightclubs are along Hamam Sokak in the old town, including the recommended **Car Cemetery** (✆612 7872; Haman Sokak 25; ◷10am-4am) and **Kum Saati Bar** (Haman Sokak 31), and

Dispanser Caddesi, south of the Martyrs' Monument.

KISMET Bar, Cabaret
(✆0545 922 2301; Uğur Mumcu Parkı Yanı) This welcoming bar and cabaret (shows most Friday nights in season; phone for an update) is good for a sundowner.

VAL'S COCKTAIL BAR Bar
(✆612 2363; Uğur Mumcu Parkı Yanı; ◷9am-1am) Englishwoman Val's little bar has a mean selection of poison, strong coffee, and a resident grey parrot.

On the Deep Blue Sea

A four-day, three-night cruise on a *gület* (traditional wooden yacht) along the Turquoise Coast – known locally as a 'blue voyage' *(mavi yolculuk)* – is a trip highlight for many people. On the usual Fethiye–Olympos route, the Demre–Olympos leg of the journey is by bus (1¼ hours). From Fethiye, boats usually call in at Ölüdeniz and Butterfly Valley and stop at Kaş, Kalkan and/or Kekova, with the final night at Gökkaya Bay opposite the eastern end of Kekova. A less common (but some say prettier) route is Marmaris–Fethiye.

Food is usually included; you sometimes have to pay for water and soft drinks. Boats usually have between six and eight smallish but comfortable double and triple cabins. Most people sleep on mattresses on deck as the boats are not air-conditioned.

Boats depart at least daily between late April and October. The price is usually between €165 and €195 (up to €275 in midsummer). Take the usual precautions to avoid being fleeced: shop around, get recommendations, avoid touts, only deal with local agencies, don't necessarily pick the cheapest option (the crew may skimp on food and services), check out your boat and ask to see the guest list, ignore gimmicks such as free water sports, and book well ahead year-round.

Recommended operators:

○ **Before Lunch Cruises** (☎ 0535 636 0076; www.beforelunch.com; Fethiye)

○ **Ocean Yachting** (☎ 0252-612 4807; www.bluecruise.com; Fethiye)

○ **Olympos Yachting** (☎ 0242-892 1145; www.olymposyachting.com; Olympos)

○ **V-Go Yachting & Travel Agency** (☎ 0252-612 2113; www.bluecruisesturkey.com; Fethiye and Olympos)

🛍 Shopping

**OLD ORIENT CARPET &
KILIM BAZAAR** Carpets
(☎ 0532 510 6108; c.c_since.1993@hotmail.com; Çarşı Caddesi 5) The discerning buy their carpets and kilims here.

ℹ Information

Tourist office (☎ 614 1527; İskele Meydanı; ⏱ 8am-7pm Mon-Fri, 10am-5pm Sat & Sun May-Sep, 8am-noon & 1-5pm Mon-Fri Oct-Apr) Helpful information centre.

ℹ Getting There & Away

Buses from the otogar, 2.5km east of the town centre, head east along the coast at least every hour in high season, stopping at Kaş (₺13, two hours) and Olympos (₺35, 4¾ hours). For Antalya, take the quicker inland route (₺20, 3½ hours).

Minibuses to places in the vicinity depart from the stops near the mosque.

Catamarans sail to Rhodes, Greece (one way/same-day return/open return €50/60/75, 1½ hours) from late April to October. Ocean Yachting Travel Agency (p199) and **Yeşil Dalyan** (☎ 612 4015; www.yesildalyantravel.com; Fevzi Çakmak Caddesi 35b) sell tickets.

ℹ Getting Around

A taxi from the otogar to the pensions west of the centre costs about ₺5, to Dalaman airport between ₺80 and ₺100.

Agencies including **Levent Rent a Car** (☎ 614 8096; www.leventrentacar.net; Fevzi Çakmak Caddesi 37b) hire out scooters (₺30 per day).

Ölüdeniz

📞 0252 / POP 4595

With its sheltered (and protected) lagoon beside a lush national park, a long spit of sandy beach and Baba Dağ (Mt Baba) casting its shadow across the sea, Ölüdeniz, 15km south of Fethiye, is a tourist association's dream come true. Accordingly, many people think package tourism has turned the motionless charms of the 'Dead Sea' into a Paradise Lost, but Ölüdeniz' allure is undeniable.

Activities

ÖLÜDENIZ BEACH & LAGOON   Beach
Opposite the post office, look out for the guarded entrance to **Ölüdeniz Tabiat Parkı** (Ölüdeniz Nature Park; Ölüdeniz Caddesi; adult/student ₺4.50/2; ⏱8am-8pm), a lovely place with mountains soaring above its beach and lagoon. There are showers, toilets and cafes here.

BOAT EXCURSIONS   Cruise
Throughout summer, boats explore the coast, charging ₺15 to ₺25 for a day trip (including lunch), and typically taking in Gemile Bay, the Blue Cave, Butterfly Valley and St Nicholas Island, with time for swimming. Ask the tourist office for more information.

PARAGLIDING   Paragliding
(tandem flight ₺120-150) The descent from 1960m-high Baba Dağ can take up to 40 minutes, with views over the Blue Lagoon, Butterfly Valley and, on clear days, Rhodes. Reliable companies include **Easy Riders** (📞617 0114; www.easyriders paragliding.com; Han Camp Ölüdeniz) and **Pegas Paragliding** (📞617 051; Çetin Motel Ölüdeniz). Parasailing (₺100) on the beach is also possible.

Eating

BUZZ BEACH BAR GRILL   International €€€
(📞617 0526; www.buzzbeachbar.com; Belcekız 1 Sokak; mains ₺18.50-35.50; ⏱restaurant 8am-midnight, bar noon-2am) This two-level waterfront place offers a wide menu from pasta and pizza (₺11.50 to ₺17.50) to steak and seafood.

Butterfly Valley

KEVEN OSBORNE/FOX FOTOS/GETTY IMAGES ©

OBA MOTEL
RESTAURANT International €€

(✆617 0158; www.obamotel.com.tr/Erestaurant.asp; Mimar Sinan Caddesi; mains ₺15-25; ⏱8am-midnight) Partly housed in a wooden cabin, the leafy Oba's restaurant dishes up home-style food. The menu offers everything from snacks to mains, including a half-dozen vegie options.

 Information

Tourist office (✆617 0438; www.oludeniz.com.tr; Ölüdeniz Caddesi 32; ⏱8.30am-11pm Jun-Aug, to 7pm May, Sep & Oct, to 5pm Nov-Apr) Central information booth and booking service.

 Getting There & Away

Minibuses leave Fethiye (₺5, 25 minutes) roughly every five to 20 minutes. A taxi costs ₺40 to ₺45.

Patata

✆0242 / POP 950

Patara can claim Turkey's longest uninterrupted beach as well as some of Lycia's finest ruins. Traditional life goes on in the adjoining village, laid-back little Gelemiş, the perfect spot to mix ruin-rambling with some dedicated sun worship.

Patara was celebrated for its temple and Oracle of Apollo, of which little remains, and was Lycia's major port.

 Sights & Activities

ANCIENT PATARA Ruin

(admission ₺5; ⏱9am-7pm May-Oct, 8am-5pm Nov-Apr) From the highway turn-off, Gelemiş is 2km to the south and it's another 1.5km to the ruins, which includes admission to the beach. You'll pass under a 2nd-century **triumphal arch** at the entrance to the site. Next is a **Harbour Baths complex** and the remains of a **Byzantine basilica**.

You can climb to the top of the 5000-seat **theatre** for a view of the site. Just north of the theatre is the recently restored *bouleuterion*, ancient Patara's 'parliament' where it is believed members of the Lycian League met. Nearby is the **colonnaded agora**, which leads to a dirt track and a **lighthouse** built by Emperor Nero. Across the ancient harbour (now a reedy wetland) is the enormous **Granary of Hadrian** and a Corinthian-style **temple-tomb**.

PATARA BEACH Beach

Backed by large sand dunes, this 18km-long sandy beach is unique for the region. You can get here by following the road for a kilometre past the ruins, or by turning right at the Golden Pension and following the track waymarked with blue arrows, which heads for the sand dunes along the western side of the archaeological section. In the summer, wagons pulled by tractors (₺2) trundle down from the village.

Street scene, Kaş
BORUT FURLAN/GETTY IMAGES ©

Detour:
Kayaköy

About nine kilometres south of Fethiye is **Kayaköy** (admission ₺5, free after closing; ⏱8.30am-6.30pm May-Oct, 8am-5pm Nov-Apr), ancient Karmylassos, an eerie ghost town of 4000-odd abandoned stone houses. They once made up the Greek town of Levissi, and today form a memorial to cross-Aegean peace and cooperation.

Levissi was deserted during the population exchange (p335), and damaged by an earthquake in 1957. It was the inspiration for Eskibahçe, the setting of Louis de Bernières' novel, *Birds Without Wings*.

The timeless village is set in a lush valley with some fine vineyards nearby. The Kataponagia and Taxiarkis churches retain some of their painted decoration and black-and-white pebble mosaic floors.

From Ölüdeniz/Hisarönü, Kayaköy is a pretty 8km/one-hour walk.

You can get a good lunch at **Cin Bal** (📞618 0066; www.cinbal.com; mains ₺15-20), the region's most celebrated grill restaurant; or **İstanbul Restaurant** (📞618 0148; mains ₺15-25; ⏱8am-midnight), serving grills and meze made from the produce of the surrounding vegetable gardens and orchards.

Minibuses link Kayaköy with Fethiye (₺4, 20 minutes) and Hisarönü (for Ölüdeniz; ₺2, 15 minutes). A taxi to Fethiye/Hisarönü costs ₺35/18.

On the beach, you can rent umbrellas and sunbeds, and there is a refreshment stand.

KIRCA TRAVEL Canoeing, Horse Riding
(📞843 5298; www.kircatravel.com) Based at the **Flower Pension** (📞0530 511 0206, 843 5164; www.pataraflowerpension.com; s/d ₺45/60, 4-/6-person apt ₺100/150; ❄@🛜), Kirca offers six-hour canoeing trips (₺50) on the Xanthos River and three-hour horse-riding trips (₺70) through the Patara dunes.

PATARA JEEP SAFARI Driving Tour
(📞0554 393 2699; www.patarajeepsafari.com; tours ₺60) Tour the Patara dunes, Xanthos and Saklıkent Gorge on four wheels.

Eating

TLOS RESTAURANT Turkish €€
(📞843 5135; mezes ₺3-6, pides ₺6-15, mains ₺12-20; ⏱8am-midnight; 🐾) Run by the moustached Osman, the Tlos has an open kitchen by the centre under a large plane tree.

LAZY FROG International €€
(📞843 5160; mains ₺15-25; ⏱8am-1am) With its very own kitchen garden, this central, popular place offers steaks, vegetarian options and *gözleme* (savoury pancakes) on its relaxing terrace.

ⓘ Getting There & Away

Buses on the Fethiye–Kaş route drop you on the highway 4km from the village. From here dolmuşes (minibuses) run to the village every 30 to 40 minutes.

In season, minibuses depart from the beach via Gelemiş to Fethiye (₺12, 1½ hours) and Kaş (₺10, 45 minutes).

Kaş
📞0242 / POP 7200

Kaş may not sport the region's finest beaches, but it's a yachties' haven and the town's atmosphere is wonderfully mellow. The surrounding areas are ideal for day trips by sea or scooter, and a plethora of adventure sports are on offer, including some excellent wreck diving.

Extending to the west of the old town is the 6km-long Çukurbağ Peninsula. At the start of it you'll find a well-preserved

Kaş

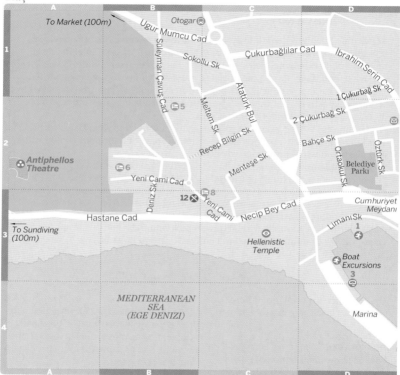

ancient theatre, about all that's left of ancient Antiphellos, the original Lycian town here.

Sights & Activities

ANTIPHELLOS RUINS Ruin

Walk up hilly Uzun Çarşı Sokak, the Roman-era road that locals call Slippery Street, to reach the **King's Tomb**. This 4th-century BC Lycian sarcophagus is mounted on a high base with two lions' heads on the lid.

Antiphellos was a small settlement and the port for Phellos, the larger Lycian town further north in the hills. The small Hellenistic **theatre** could seat some 4000 spectators and is in good condition. You can also walk to the **rock tombs** cut into

the sheer cliffs above town, which are illuminated at night. The walk is strenuous so go at a cool time of day.

BEACHES Beach

Büyük Çakıl (Big Pebble) is a relatively clean beach about a kilometre from the town centre, while **Akçagerme Plajı** is a public beach opposite the exit to Gökseki, along the main road west to Kalkan. **İnceboğaz** is a shingle beach at the start of the peninsula. But the best idea is to hop on one of the water taxis (₺10) in the harbour and head for one of three beaches on the peninsula opposite at **Liman Ağzı**.

If you are heading west on the main coast road, about 7km before Kalkan look out for **Kaputaş**, a perfect little sandy cove with a beach.

DIVING

Diving

Kaş is the regional centre for diving in the Mediterranean, with wrecks and a lot more underwater life than you'd expect below the surface. Diving companies include **Subaqua Diving Centre** (☎ 0532 221 0129; www.subaquadive.com) and **Sundiving** (☎ 0532 254 0710, 836 2637; www.sundiving. com; Hastane Caddesi 3). An introductory dive costs around €35, it's €50 for two dives and lunch for experienced divers, and three-day open-water PADI courses start at €285.

Tours

Among the stalwart tours on offer, the three-hour **bus and boat trip** (₺40 to ₺50) to Üçağız and Kekova (p210) is a fine day out and includes great swimming opportunities.

Other standard tours go to the **Mavi Mağara** (Blue Cave), Patara and the chichi harbourside town of **Kalkan**, or to **Longos** and several small nearby islands. There are also overland excursions to Saklıkent Gorge.

A great idea is to charter a boat from the marina. A whole day spent around the islands of Kaş should cost from ₺200 to ₺250, accommodating up to eight people.

BOUGAINVILLE TRAVEL

Outdoor Activities

(☎ 836 3737; www.bougainville-turkey.com; İbrahim Serin Sokak 10) English-Turkish tour operator with much experience in organising activities lasting a full day, including: canyoning (₺110); mountain biking (₺90); paragliding (₺210 for flights lasting 20 to 30 minutes); scuba diving (₺55 per dive including all equipment, ₺80 for a first dive); and sea kayaking (₺70). Also an expert on Lycian Way trekking.

Detour:
Xanthos

The Teke peninsula is the former Lycia, home of the ancient civilisation that, after gaining independence from Rome in 168 BC, established the Lycian League. This loose confederation of 23 city-states is often cited as history's first proto-democratic union.

Of the many Lycian ruins scattering the area's hillsides and shorelines, **Xanthos** (admission ₺5; ☉9am-7pm May-Oct, 8am-5pm Nov-Apr) is one of the most notable, featuring on Unesco's World Heritage List.

Up on a rock outcrop at Kınık, 63km southeast of Fethiye, Xanthos was the capital and grandest city of Lycia, with a fine **Roman theatre** and pillar **tombs**.

You'll see the Roman theatre with the **agora** opposite the car park, but the **acropolis** is badly ruined. Follow the path in front of the ticket office to the east along the colonnaded street to find excellent **mosaics**, the attractive **Dancers' Sarcophagus** and **Lion Sarcophagus,** as well as some excellent **rock tombs**.

Minibuses run roughly hourly from Fethiye (₺8, one hour), and buses may stop along the nearby highway if you ask.

OLYMPICA TRAVEL AGENCY
Travel Agency

(☏0532 498 8228, 836 2049; www.olympica travel.com; Cumhuriyet Meydanı, Necip Bey Caddesi 14) Specialises in 'build your own activity packages' according to clients' requirements.

XANTHOS TRAVEL
Outdoor Activities

(☏0533 561 0710, 836 3292; www.xanthostravel. com; İbrahim Serin Caddesi 5a) Activities include sea kayaking in Kekova (₺60 to ₺70; ₺90 including Aperlae).

🛏 Sleeping

HIDEAWAY HOTEL
Hotel €€

(☏0532 261 0170, 836 1887; www.hotelhide away.com; Eski Kilise Arkası Sokak 7; s ₺40-60, d ₺60-120; ❄@🛜🏊) Located on a quiet street, the Hideaway's comfortable rooms have balcony and (mostly) sea views. The white-on-white rooms with rain showers and ceiling fans are positively luxurious. There's a roof terrace with terminals, DVD player, honour-system bar, and views over the water and amphitheatre. Full meals are available, as is real coffee!

WHITE HOUSE PENSION
Pension €€

(☏0532 550 2663, 836 1513; www.orcholiday. com; Yeni Cami Caddesi 10; s ₺60-85, d ₺100-140; ❄🛜) Decked out in wood, wrought iron, marble and terracotta paint, this stylish and welcoming little gem has eight attractive rooms and a pretty terrace.

ANI PENSION & GUESTHOUSE
Pension €

(☏0533 326 4201, 836 1791; www.motelani.com; Süleyman Çavuş Caddesi 12; s ₺30-50, d ₺50-60; ❄@🛜) Host Ömer offers 15 smallish but spotless rooms with balconies and new bathrooms. There's a relaxing roof terrace with DVD player, köşk (lounge area) with cushions and water pipes, and a bar.

NARR HOTEL
Boutique Hotel €€

(☏836 2024; www.narrhotelcom; Hükümet Caddesi; s ₺60-100, d ₺85-140; ❄🛜🏊) This narrow 15-room hotel, opposite Little Pebble Beach's bathing platforms, is good value for its location and style. Seven rooms look at the sea and the Greek island of Meis.

🍴 Eating

You'll find some excellent restaurants to the southeast of the main square, especially around Sandıkçı Sokak. There's also a big outdoor Friday market along the old Kalkan road.

İKBAL Modern Turkish €€€
(☎836 3193; Sandıkçı Sokak 6; mains ₺20-34; 9am-midnight) This Turkish-German eatery serves excellent prepared fish dishes and the house speciality, slow-cooked leg of lamb, from a small but well-chosen menu. There's a good selection of Turkish wines.

ŞARAPHANE Turkish €
(☎0532 520 3262, 836 2715; Yeni Cami Caddesi 3; mains ₺12-25) In the old part of Kaş, the 'Wine House' emphasises the fruit of the vine amid cosy surrounds with an open kitchen, bleached timber floors and a roaring fire in the cooler months. It has a great atmosphere and service, with nice touches like complimentary homemade mezes.

KÖŞK Meze €€
(☎836 3857; Gürsoy Sokak 13; mains ₺14-25) In a lovely little square off a cobbled street just up from the water, Köşk occupies a rustic, 150-year-old house with two terraces and seating in the open courtyard. It serves good grills and gorgeous mezes (₺6 to ₺7).

BLUE HOUSE Meze €€
(☎836 1320; Sandıkçı Sokak 8; mains ₺20-34) This family-run restaurant has a great ambience, lovely views and excellent meze. The ladies work from the kitchen of their own house, which you pass through to reach the terrace.

Drinking

GIORGIO'S BAR Bar
(☎0544 608 8687; Cumhuriyet Meydanı) Facing the main square, Georgio's has great music (played live several times a week) and service. Prices are not bad (cocktails from ₺18) given the location.

MOON RIVER Bar
(☎836 4423; İbrahim Serin Sokak 1/D; beer ₺5; 8am-3am;) This lounge has live music frequently throughout the week, as well as good coffee and reasonably priced drinks.

Information

Tourist office (☎836 1238; Cumhuriyet Meydanı; 8am-5pm daily May-Oct, 8am-noon & 1-5pm Mon-Fri Nov-Apr) Has town plans and a few brochures.

Ampitheatre at Xanthos

DEDE BURLANNI/GETTY IMAGES ©

Don't Miss **Kekova**

Along the northern shore of the long island of Kekova are ruins, partly submerged 6m below the sea and referred to as the Batık Şehir (Sunken City). These famous underwater ruins are the result of a series of severe earthquakes in the 2nd century AD; most of what you can still see is a residential part of the ancient city of Simena. Foundations of buildings, staircases and moorings are also visible.

It is forbidden to anchor or swim around or near the Sunken City. The closest you'll get is on a sea-kayaking tour (₺60 per person including transfers and lunch, or ₺90 with **Aperlae**, an isolated ancient Lycian city on the Sıçak Peninsula) run by a Kaş travel agency.

The easiest way to visit is on a boat tour from Kaş or Kalkan, starting with a bus ride to **Üçağız**, where you'll board the boat. Declared off-limits to development, Üçağız is a fishing and farming village in an idyllic setting on a bay. It was ancient Teimiussa, with its own Lycian necropolis.

After visiting Kekova, you'll have lunch on the boat and continue to **Kaleköy** (called Kale locally), a protected village on the site of Simena, with a couple of submerged Lycian tombs just offshore. There's usually about an hour to explore Kaleköy, and climb to the hilltop Crusader **fortress** (admission ₺8). Inside, the ancient world's tiniest theatre is cut into the rock, and nearby are ruins of several temples and public baths. From the top you can look down upon a field of Lycian tombs, and the old city walls are visible on the outskirts.

Tours from Kaş (₺50 per person) generally leave at 10am and return around 6pm.

ⓘ Getting There & Away

The otogar is along Atatürk Bulvarı, 350m north of the centre. Daily services include İstanbul (₺65, 15 hours), İzmir (₺40, 8½ hours) and dolmuşes at least hourly to Olympos (₺18, 2½ hours), Antalya (₺23, 3½ hours), Fethiye (₺15, 2½ hours) and Patara (₺7.50, 45 minutes).

Olympos & Çıralı

📋 0242

Between Kumluca and Kemer, a road leads southeast from the main highway (veer to the right then follow the signs for 11km) to Olympos, site of an ancient city. On the other side of the mountain is Çıralı, a holiday hamlet that contains that most enigmatic of classical icons: the eternal flame of the Chimaera.

Olympos

An important Lycian city, Olympos worshipped Hephaestus (Vulcan), the god of fire, which may have been inspired by the Chimaera. It later declined, before its fortunes improved with the arrival of the Romans. Set inside a deep shaded valley that runs directly to the sea, the **ruins** (admission ₺3, 10 entries to ruins & beach ₺7.50; 🕘 9am-7.30pm May-Oct, 8am-6pm Nov-Apr) of ancient Olympos appear 'undiscovered' among the vines and flowering trees. Ramble along the Ulupınar Stream that trickles down a rocky gorge to the beach.

You can swim at the beach or engage in the numerous activities available locally. The **Adventure Centre** (☎ 892 1316; Kadır's Tree Houses; 🕘 8.30am-10pm) can organise boat cruises, canyoning, mountain biking, diving, sea kayaking, trekking and rock climbing.

Eating

VARUNA PANSIYON   Restaurant €€
(☎ 0532 602 7839, 892 1347; www.olympovaruna. com; mains ₺10-15; 🕘 8am-11pm) Serves a range of snacks and mains including pides (₺7 to ₺9), trout and şiş kebaps (roast skewered meat) in an attractive open dining room.

Çıralı

This relaxed, family-friendly hamlet of upscale pensions and hotels leads down to and along a beach lined with a dozen restaurants, including **Orange Home Restaurant** (☎ 825 7293; mezes ₺6-7, mains ₺12-25).

🛏 Sleeping

Çıralı is a delightful beach community for nature lovers and post-backpackers.

Driving in, you cross a small bridge where taxis wait to run people back up to the main road. Continue across the bridge and you'll come to a junction in the road with innumerable signboards.

From the junction after the bridge, go straight on for the pensions nearest to the path up to the Chimaera. Turn right for those closer to the beach and the Olympos ruins.

MYLAND NATURE   Pension €€€
(☎ 0532 407 9656, 825 7044; www.myland nature.com; s ₺113-167, d ₺168-225, tr ₺205-279; ❄ 🛜) This artsy, holistic place offers massage, free yoga and meditation workshops. The spotless and spacious wooden bungalows are set around a pretty garden, and the food (vegetarian set meal ₺20) garners high praise.

HOTEL CANADA   Hotel €€
(☎ 0532 431 3414, 825 7233; www.canada hotel.net; d €55-60, 4-person bungalow €85-90; ❄ @ 🛜 ☒) A beautiful place to stay. The garden is filled with hammocks, citrus trees, a pool and 11 bungalows (some ideal for families), and the comfortable main building has 26 rooms. The Turkish-Canadian hosts serve excellent set meals (€10).

SIMA PEACE PENSION   Pension €€
(☎ 0532 238 1177, 825 7245; www.simapeace. com; s/d/tr ₺80/120/140; ❄ @) A comfortable '60s throwback, this stalwart just down from the beach has five rooms and two bungalows hidden in an orange grove. Host Aynur cooks like a dream (evening buffet ₺15 to ₺20).

OLYMPOS LODGE   Resort €€€
(☎ 825 7171; www.olymposlodge.com.tr; s €140-160, d €175-195; ❄ @ 🛜) Situated right on the beach, Olympos boasts cool citrus orchards, manicured gardens and strutting peacocks. The rooms in five separate villas are peaceful and luxurious, and the breakfasts are legendary.

ℹ Getting There & Away

Buses along the Fethiye–Antalya coastal road will generally drop off/pick up at the stops near

RON WATTS/GETTY IMAGES ©

Don't Miss **Chimaera**

Known in Turkish as Yanartaş or 'Burning Rock', the Chimaera is a cluster of flames that blaze spontaneously from crevices on the rocky slopes of Mt Olympos. At night, it's easy to see why ancient peoples attributed these extraordinary flames to the breath of a monster.

Gas (thought to contain methane) seeps from the earth and bursts into flame upon contact with the air. Although a flame can be extinguished by covering it, it will reignite nearby. At night the 20 or 30 flames in the main area are clearly visible at sea.

The best time to visit is after dinner. From Çıralı, follow the road along the hillside marked for the Chimaera until you reach a valley and walk up to a car park. From there it's a 20- to 30-minute climb up a stepped path to the site; bring or rent a torch (flashlight). It's a 7km walk from Olympos; most pensions will run you there (₺5). Three-hour 'Chimaera Flame Tours' (₺15) depart at 8pm from Olympos and 9pm from Çıralı.

NEED TO KNOW
admission ₺4, torch rental ₺3

the Olympos and Çıralı junctions. From there, accommodation options will generally pick you up (₺20 to ₺25) if you book in advance. Minibuses (₺5) also run to both Olympos and Çıralı.

Antalya
☎ 0242 / POP 964,000
Situated directly on the Gulf of Antalya (Antalya Körfezi), the largest Turkish city on the western Mediterranean coast is both classically beautiful and stylishly modern.

It boasts the wonderfully preserved ancient Kaleiçi district, a splendid Roman-era harbour and one of Turkey's finest museums.

Good-value boutique hotels have mushroomed in Antalya, the gateway to the Turkish Riviera. There are some excellent bars and clubs, and the opera and ballet season at the **Aspendos** (Aspendos Opera ve Bale Festivalı; www. aspendosfestival.gov.tr) amphitheatre attracts critical attention.

⊙ Sights & Activities

Antalya is an excellent base for excursions to several ancient ruins: the Lycian-Roman-Byzantine port of Phaselis; the ancient Pisidian mountain city of Termessos; Perge, the Pamphylian town; Aspendos, with its well-preserved Roman theatre; and Selge, another ancient mountaintop settlement.

Travel agencies in Kaleiçi offer tours, including **Nirvana Travel Service** (Map p214; ☏ 0532 521 6053, 244 3893; www.nirvanatour.com; 4th fl, İskele Caddesi 38). A full-day Termessos tour, with a stop at the Düden Şelalesi (Düden Falls), costs ₺100 including lunch. Tours to Perge and Aspendos with a side-trip to Manavgat Waterfall cost ₺115. There are plenty of car-rental agencies, including **Gaye Rent a Car** (☏ 247 1000; www.gayerentacar.com; İmaret Sokak 1), hiring out cars for ₺50 to ₺90 (scooters ₺30 to ₺40) per day.

YIVLI MINARE — Landmark
(Fluted Minaret; Map p214) This handsome and distinctive minaret, erected by the Seljuks in the early 13th century, is Antalya's symbol. The adjacent mosque (1373) is still in use. Nearby to the west are two 14th- and 16th-century **türbe** (tombs; Map p214).

KALEIÇI — Historic Area
(Map p214) Antalya's historical district begins at the main square, **Kale Kapısı** (Fortress Gate; Map p214), which is marked by an old stone **clock tower** (saat kalesi; Map p214) and a **statue of Attalus II**, the city's founder. To the north is the **İki Kapılar Hanı**, a sprawling 15th-century covered bazaar.

Walk south from the clock tower along Uzun Çarşi Sokak and wander further into this protected zone; many of the gracious old **Ottoman houses** have been restored and converted.

The restored **Roman harbour**, now a marina for yachts and excursion boats, was Antalya's lifeline from the 2nd century BC until the late 20th century, when a new port was constructed about 12km west.

BOAT EXCURSIONS — Cruise
(Map p214) Excursion yachts offer one-/two-hour trips (₺20/35) from Kaleiçi's Roman harbour; or a six-hour voyage (₺80 with lunch) to the seaside town of Kemer, Phaselis, the Gulf of Antalya islands and some beaches such as Konyaaltı Plajı. Some trips go as far as Olympos, Demre (once the Lycian and Roman city of Myra) and even Kaş.

Sleeping

The old town of Kaleiçi is virtually vehicle-free and has everything you need. Kaleiçi's winding streets can be confusing, but signposts abound.

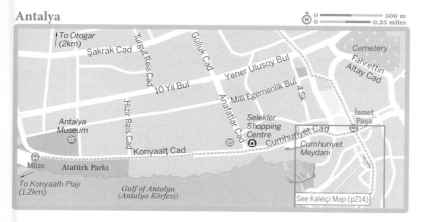

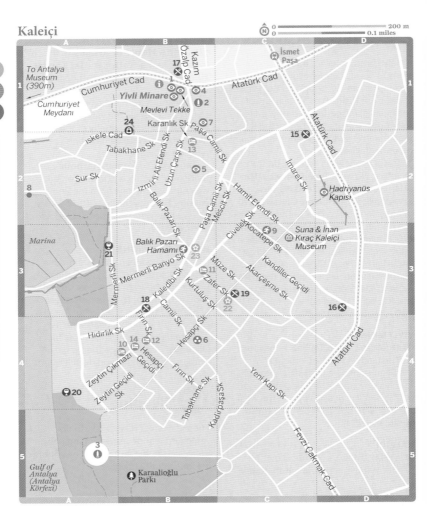

Kaleiçi

TUVANA HOTEL Boutique Hotel €€€
(Map p214; ☎247 6015; www.tuvanahotel.com;
Karanlık Sokak 18; s & d €140-300; ❄ 🛜 ⛱)
Among the Mediterranean coast's most
beautiful and intimate hotels, this discreet
compound of six Ottoman houses has
been converted into a refined city hotel.
Rooms are suitably plush, with kilims,
linen and brass light fittings as well as
mod cons. Main restaurant Seraser is
world-class.

WHITE GARDEN PANSIYON Pension €
(Map p214; ☎241 9115; www.whitegardenpan
sion.com; Hesapçı Geçidi 9; s/d ₺40/60, 4-person
apt ₺120; @ ⛱) Rooms combine tidiness
and class beyond their price level, with
impeccable service from Metin and staff.
The building is a fine restoration and
guests can use the pool at the **Secret Palace** (Map p214; ☎244 1060; www.secretpalace
pansion.com; Fırın Sokak 10; s/d ₺50/70;
❄ @ ⛱) pension, an 11-room Ottoman
conversion behind the White Garden.

Kaleiçi

HOTEL HADRIANUS   Hotel €€
(Map p214; ☑ 244 0030; www.hadrianushotel.
com; Zeytin Çıkmazı 4; s ₺65-80, d ₺80-120;
❄ �) This 10-room 'almost boutique'
hotel is set in 750 sq metres of garden,
a veritable oasis in Kaleiçi. Rooms at the
top are larger and contain faux antique
and Ottoman-style furnishings. Good
value.

**MEDITERRA ART
HOTEL**   Boutique Hotel €€
(Map p214; ☑ 244 8624; www.mediterraart.com;
Zafer Sokak 5; s €50-80, d €70-120; ❄ @ ≋)
This upscale masterpiece of wood and
stone once housed a Greek tavern
(19th-century frescoes and graffiti adorn
the restaurant). It offers sanctuary by a
cutting-edge pool, a marvellous winter
dining room and small, modestly luxurious rooms in four buildings.

 Eating

Numerous cafes and eateries are tucked
in and around the harbour area. For cheap
eating, walk east to the **Dönerciler Çarşısı**
(Market of Döner Makers; Map p214; Atatürk

Caddesi) along Atatürk Caddesi, or north
to the rooftop kebap places around Kale
Kapısı (p213).

VANILLA   International €€
(Map p214; ☑ 247 6013; www.vanillaantalya.
com; Zafer Sokak 13; mains ₺22-40) This
ultra-modern, British-Turkish restaurant's banquettes, glass surfaces and
cheery orange bucket chairs provide a
streamlined and unfussy atmosphere,
allowing you to concentrate on the menu
of Mediterranean-inspired international
dishes. Slick cafe-bar **The Lounge** (Map
p214; ice cream ₺3.50, cakes ₺10; ⏱ 9am-1am;
î) is next door.

SERASER   Mediterranean,
Modern Turkish €€€
(Map p214; ☑ 247 6015; www.seraserrestaurant.
com; Karanlık Sokak 18, Tuvana Hotel; mains
₺29-50; ⏱ 1pm-midnight) Tuvana Hotel's restaurant is among Antalya's best, offering
international dishes with a Mediterranean
twist in fine Ottoman surrounds. Try the
sea bass wrapped in vine leaves or the
quail with mustard honey glaze and the
Turkish coffee *crème brûlée*.

Detour:
Antalya Museum

The comprehensive **Antalya Museum** (📞236 5688; www.antalya-ws.com/english/museum; Konyaaltı Caddesi 1; admission ₺15; ⏰9am-7pm Tue-Sun mid-Apr–Oct, 8am-5pm Tue-Sun Nov–mid-Apr) is about 2km west of the centre of Antalya, accessible on the *tramvay* (tram). The big halls cover everything from the Stone and Bronze Ages to Byzantium, including finds from ancient Lycian cities and the Roman/Byzantine province of Pamphylia, marble busts, statues of Olympian gods and gold artefacts.

SIM RESTAURANT　　Meze €€
(Map p214; 📞248 0107; Kaledibi Sokak 7; mains ₺12.50-20) A choice of seating makes this simple but charming restaurant a unique experience: underneath the canopy in the narrow passageway at the front, wedged against ancient Byzantine walls; on the ground floor, with global graffiti to read; and upstairs, where eclectic antiques complement *köfte*, mezes and glorious *çorbalar* (soups).

PARLAK RESTAURANT　　Anatolian €€
(Map p214; 📞241 6553; www.parlakrestaurant.com; Kazım Özlap Caddesi 7; mains ₺10-24) Opposite the jewellery bazaar is this sprawling open-air patio restaurant in an old caravanserai favoured by locals. It's famous for its charcoal-grilled chicken and excellent mezes.

GÜL RESTORAN　　Meze €€
(Map p214; 📞243 2284; Kocatepe Sokak 1; mains ₺9-24) This intimate garden restaurant is shaded by a grove of Antalya's famous orange trees. The meze buffets (₺8) are well known.

🍷 Drinking & Entertainment

Kaleiçi offers buzzy beer gardens with million-dollar views, live music venues with everything from rock to *türkü* (Turkish folk music), and raunchy, pricey clubs.

CASTLE CAFÉ　　Bar
(Map p214; 📞248 6594; 1st fl, Hıdırlık Sokak 48; beer ₺7.50; ⏰8am-11pm) Our favourite place along the cliff's edge just opposite the Hıdırlık Kalesi, the appropriately named Castle is buzzy, affordable and a good place to meet a younger crowd of Turks.

KALE BAR　　Bar
(Map p214; 📞248 6591; Mermerli Sokak 2; beer ₺9, cocktails from ₺21; ⏰11am-midnight) This patio bar attached to the CH Hotels Türkevi may very well command Antalya's most spectacular harbour and sea view.

DEM-LIK　　Live Music
(Map p214; 📞247 1930; Zafer Sokak 6; beer ₺5, coffee ₺4; ⏰noon-midnight) Located (mostly) in a large garden behind high stone walls, where Antalya's university crowd downs ice-cold beers and listens to (mostly) jazz, reggae and blues (live at the weekend).

KRALIN BAHÇESİ　　Live Music
(Map p214; 📞0535 480 6834; Paşa Camii Sokak 33; ⏰9am-3am) A cafe offering nargiles (water pipes) by day and live-act *türku* venue by night. Music starts at 9pm.

ℹ Information

Tourist office (📞241 1747; Cumhuriyet Meydanı; ⏰8am-6pm May-Oct, 8.30am-5.30pm Nov-Apr) Tiny but relatively helpful office.

ℹ Getting There & Away

Air

Antalya's airport is 10km east of the city centre on the D400 highway. There's a tourist information desk and car-hire counters here. Turkish Airlines and AnadoluJet have several daily flights year-round to/from İstanbul (₺75 to ₺120 one way) and Ankara (₺50 to ₺170).

Bus

Antalya's otogar is about 4km north of the city centre on highway D650. Services (at least daily) include Ankara (₺50, eight hours), Çanakkale (₺65, 12 hours), Eğirdir (₺25, 3½ hours), Fethiye (coastal/inland route, ₺25/18, 7½/four hours), Göreme (₺40, nine hours), İstanbul (₺65, 11½ hours) and İzmir (₺40, eight hours).

ⓘ Getting Around

Antalya's single-track old-style *tramvay* (₺1.25) runs every half-hour between 7.30am and 9pm. The tram runs from the Antalya Museum (Müze stop) along Konyaaltı Caddesi, Cumhuriyet Caddesi, Atatürk Caddesi and Isıklar Caddesi. You pay as you board.

To/From the Airport

A taxi will cost you about ₺35.

To/From the Bus Station

The AntRay tram has a stop called Otogar at the bus station that is eight stops from the central İsmet Paşa stop just outside Kaleiçi. It takes 20 minutes and costs ₺1.50. A taxi between the otogar and Kaleiçi should cost ₺25.

Alanya

☎ 0242 / POP 103,700

Alanya has mushroomed from a sparsely populated highway town fronting a sandy beach to a tourist machine. At night, the city can resemble 'Vegas by the Sea' with laser-shooting nightclubs, and aside from taking a boat cruise or stroll along the waterfront, many visitors stay by their hotel's pool. However, Alanya has something up its ancient sleeve: its impressive fortress complex, with the remains of a fine Seljuk castle, some atmospheric ruins, and even something of a small traditional village.

◉ Sights

ALANYA CASTLE   Fortress
(Alanya Kalesı; admission ₺10; ⏱ 9am-7pm Apr-Oct, 8am-5pm Nov-Mar) This awesome Seljuk-era castle overlooks the city, Pamphylian plain and Cilician mountains.

Before reaching the entrance, the road passes a turn-off for the village of

View over Alanya Castle and town

View over Alanya Castle and town

HUGH SITTON/GETTY IMAGES ©

217

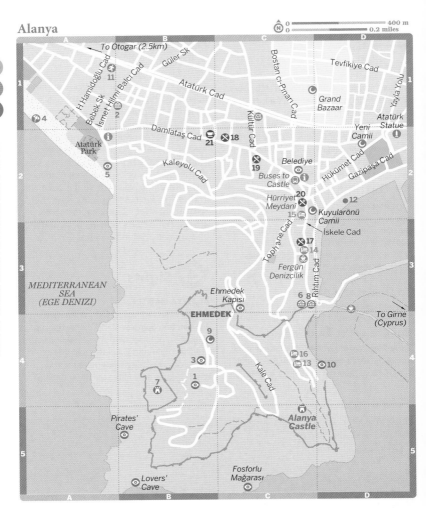

Ehmedek, which was the Turkish quarter during Ottoman and Seljuk times. Old wooden houses cluster around the fine 16th-century **Süleymaniye Camii**, Alanya's oldest mosque. Also here is a former Ottoman **bedesten** (vaulted covered market) and the **Akşebe Türbesi**, a distinctive 13th-century mausoleum.

At the end of the road is the entrance to the **İç Kale** (Inner Fortress), with mostly poorly preserved ruins.

The road to the fortress, Kaleyolu Caddesi, winds 3.5km uphill. Catch a

bus opposite the tourist office (₺1.25, 15 minutes past the hour and, in summer, also 15 minutes before the hour). Taxis are around ₺15 each way.

KIZILKULE Historic Building
(Red Tower; admission ₺4; ⏰9am-7pm Apr-Oct, 8am-5pm Nov-Mar) This five-storey octagonal defence tower, with a central cistern within for water storage, looms over the harbour. Constructed in 1226 by the Seljuks (who also built the fortress), it was the first structure erected after the Armenian-controlled

Alanya

town surrendered to the sultan. There's a small **ethnographic museum** here and steps lead to a roof terrace with harbour views. To the south is Turkey's only remaining Seljuk-built **tersane** (shipyard).

ALANYA MUSEUM Museum
(İsmet Hilmi Balcı Caddesi; admission ₺3; 🕓9am-7pm Tue-Sun Apr-Oct, 8am-5pm Tue-Sun Nov-Mar) Alanya's small museum houses artefacts including tools, jugs and jewellery from local Pamphylian sites.

CLEOPATRA'S BEACH Beach
(Kleopatra Plajı) Sandy and quite secluded in low season, and with fine views of the fortress, Cleopatra's Beach is the city's best.

DRIPSTONE CAVE Cave
(Damlataş Mağarası; adult/child ₺4.50/2.25; 🕓10am-7pm) This stalactite-studded cave has humidity levels of 95% and is said to produce a certain kind of air that, if breathed long enough, has the ability to relieve asthma sufferers.

 **Activities**

ALANYA AQUA CENTRE Amusement Park
(www.alanyaaquacenter.com; İsmet Hilmi Balcı Caddesi 62; adult/child ₺25/12; 🕓9am-6pm) An impressive water park.

 Tours

Many local operators organise tours to the ruins along the coast west of Alanya and to Anamur. A typical tour to Aspendos, Side's glorious Roman and Hellenistic ruins and Manavgat costs around ₺75 per person, while a 4WD safari visiting villages in the Taurus Mountains is about ₺60 per person. Some tours also take in the beautiful Sapadere Canyon.

EXCURSION BOATS Boat Tour
(per person incl lunch ₺35) Every day at around 10.30am, boats leave for a six-hour voyage around the promontory, visiting several caves, as well as Cleopatra's Beach. Other cruises include sunset jaunts around the harbour (from ₺20).

 Sleeping

Alanya has hundreds of hotels and pensions, most designed for groups and those in search of *apart oteller* (self-catering flats). A few independent places can be found along İskele Caddesi.

CENTAUERA Boutique Hotel €€€
(📞519 0016; www.centauera.com; Andızlı Camii Sokak 4, Tophane; r €110-140; ⓟ❄️📶) The romantic Centauera fills a restored Ottoman

219

house in the quiet Tophane heritage neighbourhood under Alanya castle, overlooking the elegant sweep of Alanya bay. Dinner is also available on request and for outside guests. A 10-minute stroll from the harbour.

VILLA TURKA
Boutique Hotel €€€

(☏513 7990; www.hotelvillaturka.com; Kargı Sokak 7, Tophane; r €84-130; ❄ @ 🛜) Like nearby Centauera, Villa Turka showcases a restored Ottoman house in Tophane. Rooms feature quality bed linen, honeytoned cedar decor and antique furniture. Views take in the Taurus Mountains and the nearby Red Tower. Breakfast often incorporates organic goodies from local farms, and dinner is available.

SEAPORT HOTEL
Business Hotel €€

(☏513 6487; www.hotelseaport.com; İskele Caddesi 82; s/d ₺120/200; ❄) The last hotel on the İskele hotel strip and just steps from the Red Tower, the Seaport offers efficient service and brilliant sea views from half of its well-appointed rooms. Rates include a dinner buffet, but the food can be disappointing.

TEMIZ OTEL
Hotel €€

(☏513 1016; http://temizotel.com.tr; İskele Caddesi 12; s/d ₺65/120; ❄) 'Clean Hotel' is nothing short of that. Its 32 rooms on five floors are spacious; those facing the sea with balconies offer a bird's-eye view of the club and bar action below.

Eating

Most of the following will pick you up from and bring you back to your accommodation.

İSKELE SOFRASI
Seafood €€

(Tophane Caddesi 2b; mezes ₺6-8, mains ₺15-30) Run by the friendly Öz family, this intimate place serves more than 70 meze, including *girit ezmesi* (mash of feta, walnuts and olive oil). The terrace with harbour views is perfect with a cold beer and the shrimp *güveç* (seafood casserole).

OTTOMAN HOUSE
Turkish €€€

(☏511 1421; www.ottomanhousealanya.com; Damlataş Caddesi 31; mains ₺20-32) Alanya's most atmospheric eatery occupies a 100-year-old stone villa surrounded by lush gardens. The *beğendili taş kebabı* (traditional Ottoman combination of sautéed lamb and eggplant purée) and grilled seafood dishes are all good. Visit on Thursday or Sunday night for all-you-can-eat barbecue; on Tuesdays there's a meze buffet and Turkish dancing.

LOKANTA SU
Mediterranean €€€

(☏512 1500; www.lokantasualanya.com; Damlataş Caddesi 14a; mains ₺20-35) From Italy to the Middle East, Lokanta Su's pricey menu covers the best of the Mediterranean. The restored Ottoman house's beautiful courtyard is also a lovely spot to come for a drink from one of Alanya's best wine lists. The pizza menu showcases some innovative touches.

SOFRA
Anatolian €€

(İskele Caddesi 8a; mains ₺8-16) A modern spin on the traditional Turkish eatery, with tasty kebaps, *mantı* (Turkish ravioli) and eastern Anatolian *içli köfte* (ground lamb and onion in a bulgur wheat shell). The healthy complimentary self-serve salad bar is good value.

Drinking & Entertainment

Alanya features some of the most bawdy, bright and banging nightclubs in all of Turkey. More restrained entertainment options also feature.

EHL-I-KEYF
Nargile Cafe

(Damlataş Caddesi 32) The shaded garden of this restored Ottoman residence is a trendy hang-out for Alanya's bright young things, and a great antidote to the more touristy bars and cafes around town. Enjoy a tea or freshly squeezed juice with nargile and backgammon. Only alcohol-free beer is available.

PETER HORREE/ALAMY ©

Don't Miss **Anemurium**

Although founded by the Phoenicians in the 4th century BC, most of the ruins visible at Anemurium date from the late Roman, Byzantine and medieval eras. The site is both sprawling and eerily quiet, with ruins stretching 500m to the pebble beach, and massive city walls scaling the mountainside.

From the car park and sprawling **necropolis**, walk southeast past a 4th-century **basilica**; look behind it for a pathway of mosaic tiles leading to the sea. Above the church is one of two **aqueducts**. Opposite the 2nd-century **theatre** is the more-complete **odeion**, with 900 seats and a tile floor. The best-preserved structure in Anemurium is the **baths complex**; look for the coloured mosaic tiles that still decorate portions of the floor.

Approaching Anamur from the west or from the Cilician mountains, a sign points south towards 'Anemurium Antik Kenti'. The road then bumps along for 2km to the *gişe* (ticket kiosk); it's another 500m to the car park.

NEED TO KNOW

Anemurium Ancient City; admission ₺3; ⊗8am-7pm Apr-Oct, to 5pm Nov-Mar

---

RED TOWER BREWERY RESTAURANT   Brewery

(www.redtowerbrewery.com; İskele Caddesi 80) This multistorey pleasure palace offers harbour views, two decent beers in the ground-floor brew pub, 1st- and 3rd-floor restaurants, and sushi and live music in the 6th-floor Sky Lounge. Enjoy a pint of the hoppy Pilsner on the alfresco deck.

ℹ Information

Tourist office (✆513 1240; Damlataş Caddesi 1; ⊗8am-5pm May-Oct, closed Sat & Sun Nov-Apr) Main branch.

Tourist office (Damlataş Caddesi; ⊗9am-6pm Mon-Fri) Smaller branch.

If You Like...
History

While exploring Kaleiçi's winding lanes, look out for the following venerable relics, in addition to the area's many other mosques, towers, hamams and historic sights.

1 TEKELI MEHMET PAŞA CAMII
(Map p214; Uzun Çarşı Sokak) This 18th-century mosque, repaired extensively in 1886 and 1926, has beautiful calligraphy in the coloured tiles above the windows.

2 KESIK MINARE
(Truncated Minaret; Map p214) This stump of a tower marks the ruins of a substantial building that played many roles: a 2nd-century Roman temple, the 6th-century Byzantine Church of the Virgin Mary, a mosque three centuries later and a church again in 1361. Fire destroyed most of it in the 19th century, but you can see bits of Roman and Byzantine marble from the outside.

3 SEFA HAMAMI
(Map p214; 0532 526 9407, 241 2321; www.sefahamam.com; Kocatepe Sokak 32; bath ₺18, package ₺40; 9.30am-10pm) This atmospheric hamam retains much of its 13th-century Seljuk architecture.

4 HIDIRLIK KALESI
(Map p214; Kaleiçi) This 14m-high tower may once have served as a lighthouse in the 2nd century AD.

ⓘ Getting There & Away

Boat
Fergün Denizcilik (511 5565, 511 5358; www.fergun.net; İskele Caddesi 84) operates twice-weekly summer services to Girne (Kyrenia), Northern Cyprus (₺77/127 one way/return plus harbour tax). Buy a ticket and present your passport at least a day before departure for immigration formalities.

Bus
The otogar is on the coastal highway (Atatürk Caddesi), 3km west of the centre (₺12 by taxi). Most services are less frequent off-season, but buses generally leave hourly for Antalya (₺15, two hours) and regularly head east along the coast.

Anamur
0324 / POP 35,100

Close to both the massive Byzantine city of Anemurium and Mamure Castle, and with a pretty good beach, Anamur is a great place to relax. It's the centre of Turkey's banana-growing industry, and you'll see local *muzler* (bananas; shorter and sweeter than imported ones) on sale.

Between May and September, the beach here is one of a dozen nesting sites of the loggerhead turtle (*Caretta caretta*) along Turkey's Mediterranean coast (along with Fethiye and Patara). The loggerhead (Turkish: *deniz kaplumbağası*) is a large, flat-headed turtle coloured reddish brown on top and yellow-orange below that spends most of its life in the water. An adult can weigh up to 200kg.

◉ Sights

Anamur lies north of highway D400. About 2.5km southeast of the main roundabout is İskele, a popular waterfront district with hotels and restaurants. Anemurium is 8.5km west while Mamure Castle is 7km east.

MAMURE CASTLE   Fortress
(Mamure Kalesi; admission ₺3; 8am-7.30pm Apr-Oct, to 5pm Nov-Mar) This tremendous castle, with crenellated walls, 39 towers and part of its original moat still intact, is the biggest and best-preserved fortification on the Turkish Mediterranean coast. The rear sits directly on the beach, where sea turtles come in summer to lay their eggs; the castle's front end almost reaches the highway.

Detour:
Narlıkuyu and Caves of Heaven & Hell

On a cove 5km southwest of Kızkalesi is the village of Narlıkuyu. Inside its **Mosaic Museum** (Mozaik Müzesi), in a compact 4th-century Roman bath, is a wonderful mosaic of the Three Graces: Aglaia, Thalia and Euphrosyne, the daughters of Zeus.

Absolute waterfront restaurants include the **Kerim** (mains ₺15-25) near the museum, and the **Narlıkuyu** (mains ₺15-25) on the opposite side of the cove.

Near Narlıkuyu, a road winds north for 3km to several **caves** (admission ₺5; ☺8am-7pm) – sinkholes carved out by a subterranean river and places of great mythological significance.

The **Chasm of Heaven** (Cennet Mağarası) – an underground cavern 200m long, 90m wide and 70m deep – is reached via 450-odd steps to the left of the car park. Near a landing not far from the cave mouth is the 5th-century Byzantine **Chapel of the Virgin Mary**, used for a short time in the 19th century as a mosque.

Running off this large cavern is the **Cave of Typhon** (Tayfun Mağarası), a damp, jagged-edged, devilish theatre. Locals believe this to be a gateway to the eternal furnace and Strabo mentions it in his *Geography*. According to legend, the cave's underground river connects with the hellish River Styx.

Up the hill from the Chasm of Heaven is the **Cave-Gorge of Hell** (Cehennem Mağarası), with almost vertical walls and a heart-stopping viewing platform extending over a 120m-deep pit. This charred hole is supposedly where Zeus imprisoned the 100-headed, fire-breathing monster Typhon after defeating him in battle.

Around 600m west is **Asthma Cave** (Astim Mağarası), which supposedly relieves sufferers of the affliction.

The 13th-century castle was constructed by the rulers of the Armenian kingdom of Cilicia on the site of a 3rd-century Roman fortress. Karamanoğlu Mehmet Bey took Mamure in 1308 and alterations began, including the addition of a **mosque** in the eastern courtyard. Here you'll also see remnants of an **aqueduct** that brought water from the mountains 5km away, a **stable**, and the holes in the walls that served as the **guards' barracks**. To the west is the **Kaleiçi** (castle interior), where the top brass lived.

Climbing the castle's **towers**, especially the one with a dungeon, is an adventure; some stairs are pretty crumbled. Your reward is a view of the sea and the ruins of **Softa Castle** (Softa Kalesi), also built by the Armenian rulers of Cilicia (near Bozyazı, some 18km to the east).

FREE **ANAMUR MUSEUM**　　　Museum
(Anamur Müzesi; Adnan Menderes Caddesi 3; ☺8.30am-5pm) Highlights here are archaeological finds from Anemurium, including frescoes from private houses, bathhouse mosaics and an unusual clay sarcophagus. Look for the iron scales in the shape of a woman.

Eating

İSKELE SOFRASI　　　Turkish €€
(Sokak 1909; mains ₺8-12) Just one block back from the beach, this popular family eatery turns out top-notch mezes and heaving grills – order the *patlıcan* (eggplant) kebap. Good fish dishes, Anamur's best pide and cold beer are also available.

MARE VISTA
RESTAURANT   International, Italian €€
(814 2001; İnönü Caddesi 28; mains ₺10-15) Reasonably priced, considering its location opposite the beach, the 'Sea View' has international and some Italian-themed dishes (including the ubiquitous pizza), as well as salads and sandwiches. Service can be slow, so count on ordering a second beer.

ℹ Information

Tourist office (814 5058; 8am-noon & 1-5pm Mon-Fri) In the otogar complex behind the police station.

ℹ Getting There & Away

Several buses run daily to Alanya (₺25, three hours), and east along the coast.

ℹ Getting Around

Anamur's otogar is on the intersection of the D400 highway and 19 Mayıs Caddesi. A taxi between here and İskele costs ₺12. Expect to pay ₺60 for a taxi to Anemurium and back, with an hour's waiting time.

Half-hourly dolmuşes from next to the mosque, over the road from the otogar, can drop you off at the Anemurium turn-off on the main highway (₺2), from where it's a 2.5km walk. Frequent dolmuşes heading east along the D400 will drop you outside Mamure Castle (₺2).

Kızkalesi
 0324 / POP 1750

Kızkalesi boasts one of the region's loveliest beaches, but also two castles, one of which seems to be floating at sea. It's also a springboard for one of Turkey's richest archaeological areas, the **Olba Plateau**, a virtual open-air museum of ruins, located to the west and southwest en route to Silifke.

The scene here is more inclusive than you'd expect of a typical Turkish coastal village, due to the easygoing locals and the prevalence of foreign archaeology buffs strolling the foreshore.

Left: Tombs carved into the rock face at Telmessos (p198);
Below: Street scene in Fethiye's old town (p198)

(LEFT) IMAGES & STORIES/ALAMY ©; (BELOW) IAN DAGNALL/ALAMY ©

 Sights

CORYCUS CASTLE
Fortress

(Korykos Kalesı; admission ₺3; ☺8am-8pm Apr-Oct, to 5pm Nov-Mar) At the northern end of the beach, Corycus Castle was either built or rebuilt by the Byzantines, briefly occupied by the Armenian kingdom of Cilicia and once connected to Kızkalesi by a causeway. Walk to the east, where a ruined tower affords a fine view of the 'sea castle'.

NECROPOLIS
Ruin

Across the highway from Corycus Castle is a necropolis, once the burial ground for tradespeople. Tombs and rock carvings include a 5th-century relief of a warrior with a raised sword.

Sleeping

RAIN HOTEL
Hotel €€

(☏523 2782; www.rainhotel.com; per person €40-70; ❄ @) With a friendly vibe set by manager Mehmet, the Rain is a popular choice. Affiliated with Cafe Rain (p226) and its attached travel agency, it has a similar anything-is-possible ethos, including day trips and scuba-diving excursions. The spotless and spacious rooms are sparingly decorated and, with fridges, conducive to long stays.

YAKA HOTEL
Hotel €€

(☏0542 432 1996, 523 2444; www.yakahotel.com.tr; s/d/tr ₺70/110/130; ❄ @ 🛜) Yakup Kahveci, the Yaka's multilingual and quick-witted owner, runs Kızkalesi's most welcoming hostelry. The 17 rooms are impeccably tidy, breakfast (or specially ordered dinner) is eaten in the attractive garden, and there's nothing Yakup doesn't know and/or can't organise locally. The Yaka is also a great place to meet travellers, especially those interested in archaeology.

225

IMAGES & STORIES/ALAMY ©

Don't Miss **Kızkalesi Castle**

Lying 300m from the shore, Kızkalesi Castle is like a suspended dream. Check out the **mosaics** in the central courtyard and the vaulted **gallery**, and climb one of the four **towers** (the one at the southeast corner has the best views). It's possible to swim to the castle or rent a pedalo (around ₺10), but most people catch the boat (₺5) from in front of Albatross restaurant.

NEED TO KNOW

Maiden's Castle; admission ₺3; ⏱to 5pm May-Oct

HOTEL HANTUR — Hotel €
(☎523 2367; www.hotelhantur.com; s ₺60/80;
❄ @ 🛜) The Hantur has a front-row seat on the sea and cool, comfortable rooms. All have balconies, but try to grab one facing the sea. There's a breezy front garden and helpful, friendly management.

🍴 **Eating & Drinking**

Another option is the seafood restaurants at Narlıkuyu.

CAFE RAIN — International €€
(☎523 2234; mains ₺15-25) Rain's rainbow decor complements the cheery menu of tasty, good-value international favourites and what might be the eastern Mediterranean's finest *börek* (pastry filled with cheese or meat). In the evenings, travellers transform it into a companionable cocktail bar.

PAŞA RESTAURANT — Kebap €€
(☎523 2230; Plaj Yolu 5; mains ₺8-16) Just off central Cumhuriyet Meydanı, this large open spot has grills and meze sat better prices than the beachfront restaurants. Keeping things super-competitive is the adjacent and equally good value **Tanem** ('Sweetheart') restaurant.

VILLA NUR
Cafe €€

(☎ 523 2340; mains ₺10-18) Readers have written raving letters about the meals served at this seafront pension owned by a Turkish-German couple. The European-style cakes are exceptional.

TURKISH TURTLES CLUB
Bar

Exposed bricks and giant beer cans make this the funkiest place in town. You may be keeping company with Turkish teenagers from Adana or Mersin, proudly showing off their newly inked tattoos.

❶ Getting There & Around

Frequent buses link Kızkalesi with Silifke (₺4, 30 minutes) and Mersin (₺7, 1½ hours).

Frequent Kızkalesi–Silifke buses/dolmuşes stop in Narlıkuyu (₺2, 10 minutes).

Antakya (Hatay)
☎ 0326 / POP 213,300

Built on the site of ancient Antiocheia ad Orontem, Antakya, officially known as Hatay, is a prosperous and modern city near the Syrian border. Under the Romans, Antioch's Christian community developed out of the already large Jewish population that was at one time led by St Paul.

Today Antakya is home to a mixture of faiths – Sunni, Alevi and Orthodox Christian – and has a cosmopolitan and civilised air. Locals call their hometown Barış Şehri (City of Peace), and that's just what it is.

The Arab influence permeates local life, food and language; indeed, the city only became part of Turkey in 1939 after centuries conjoined in some form or another to Syria. Take time to stroll along the Orontes (Asi) River and through the bazaars and back lanes of this underrated jewel of the Turkish Mediterranean.

Antioch figures in Christian history. Both Peter and Paul lived here for a few years, and almost certainly preached in the Church of St Peter, which St Luke the Evangelist, who was born in Antioch, had donated to the city's Christian congregation.

Sights

HATAY ARCHAEOLOGY MUSEUM
Museum

(Hatay Arkeoloji Müzesi; Gündüz Caddesi 1; admission ₺8; ⊙9am-6.30pm Tue-Sun Apr-Oct,

Antakya Sarcophagus (p229), displayed at the Hatay Archaeology Museum

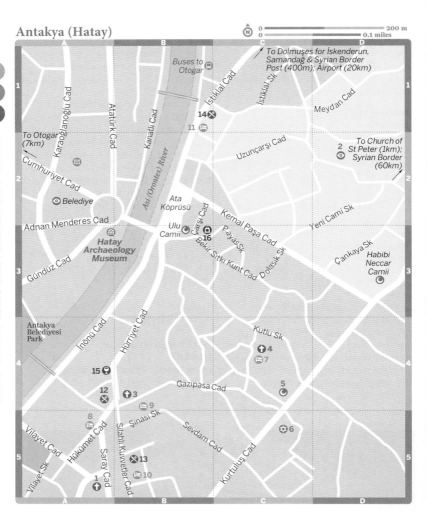

8.30am-noon & 12.30-4.30pm Nov-Mar) This museum contains one of the world's finest collections of Roman and Byzantine mosaics, covering a period from the 1st century AD to the 5th century. Many were recovered almost intact from Tarsus (St Paul's birthplace) or Harbiye, what was Daphne in ancient times, 9km to the south.

The tiles forming the mosaics are so tiny that at first glance you may mistake them for paintings. Be sure to see the full-body mosaic of **Oceanus & Thetis** (2nd century; Salon 4); the **Buffet Mosaic** (3rd century; Salon 2) with dishes of chicken, fish and eggs; the standard scenes of hunting and fishing (eg **Thalassa & the Nude Fishermen**, with kids riding whales and dolphins, in Salon 4); the stories from mythology, including the fabulous 3rd-century mosaics of **Narcissus** (Salon 2) and **Orpheus** (Salon 4); and the quirky subjects, including the happy hunchback with an oversized phallus, the black fisherman and the mysterious portrayal of a raven, a scorpion, a dog and

Antakya (Hatay)

a pitchfork attacking an 'evil eye' (all in Salon 3).

Also on display are artefacts recovered from various local mounds and tumuli (burial mounds), including the so-called **Antakya Sarcophagus** (Antakya Lahdı), an impossibly ornate tomb with an unfinished reclining figure on the lid.

BAZAAR
Bazaar

A sprawling market fills the backstreets north of Ulus Alanı and Kemal Paşa Caddesi. The easier way to see it is to follow Uzunçarşı Caddesi, the main shopping street.

Around the 7th-century **Habib Neccar Camii** (Kurtuluş Caddesi) you'll find most of Antakya's remaining **old houses**, with carved stone lintels or wooden overhangs, and courtyards within the compounds. St Peter probably lived in this area, then the Jewish neighbourhood, between AD 42 and 48.

 Sleeping

BELKIS KONUK EVI VE PANSIYON
Pension €€

(☏212 1511; www.belkisev.com; Gazipasa Caddesi, Güllübahçe Sokak; s/d ₺60/120; ✳) Rooms in this cute family pension frame a whitewashed inner courtyard dotted with leafy trees. Expect decor merging rustic with chintzy, and a warm welcome.

Bathrooms are on the compact side, but breakfast in the shaded and dappled courtyard is a great start to the day.

LIWAN HOTEL
Boutique Hotel €€€

(☏215 7777; www.theliwanhotel.com; Silahlı Kuvvetler Caddesi 5; s/d ₺130/200; ✳ 🌐) This 1920s Eclectic-style building, once owned by the president of Syria, contains two dozen tastefully furnished rooms across four floors. There's a courtyard restaurant and an atmospheric stone bar, which features live music from 11pm to 2.30am most weekends. Not all rooms have windows, so check when you book.

ANTAKYA CATHOLIC CHURCH GUESTHOUSE
Guest House €

(☏215 6703; www.anadolukatolikkilisesi.org/ antakya; Kutlu Sokak 6; per person ₺30; ✳) A delightful place to stay (if you can get in), this church-run guesthouse has eight tidy double rooms wrapped around a leafy (and suitably reflective) courtyard. Guests are invited (though not required) to attend daily mass in the church opposite.

MOZAIK OTEL
Hotel €€

(☏215 5020; www.mozaikotel.com; İstiklal Caddesi 18; s/d ₺85/130; ✳ 🌐) This 'almost boutique' hotel is an excellent choice near the bazaar. The two dozen rooms are decorated with folksy bedspreads and mosaic reproductions. One of the most central and quiet options.

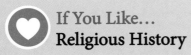

If You Like...
Religious History

In this ecumenical city you'll find at least five different religions and sects represented within a couple of blocks of one another.

1 CHURCH OF ST PETER
(St Pierre Kilisesi; admission ₺8; ⏰9am-noon & 1-6pm Apr-Oct, 8am-noon & 1-5pm Nov-Mar) This early Christian church cut into the slopes of Mt Staurin (Mountain of the Cross) is thought to be the earliest place where the newly converted met and prayed secretly.

2 ORTHODOX CHURCH
(Hürriyet Caddesi 53; ⏰divine liturgy 8.30am & 6pm) Most of Antakya's 1200-strong Christians worship at this fine church, rebuilt with Russian assistance after a devastating earthquake in 1900. It has a lovely courtyard, some beautiful icons, an ancient stone lectern and a valuable church plate.

3 ROMAN CATHOLIC CHURCH
(Kutlu Sokak 6; ⏰10am-noon & 3-5pm, mass 8.30am daily & 6pm Sun) This Italian-ministered church (1852) occupies two old-quarter houses, with the chapel in a former living room.

4 SERMAYE CAMII
(Capital Mosque; Kurtuluş Caddesi 56) Has an ornate şerefe (balcony) on its minaret.

5 SYNAGOGUE
(Kurtuluş Caddesi 56) Just south of the Sermaye Camii.

6 ANTIOCH PROTESTANT CHURCH
(Saray Caddesi; ⏰9am-6pm) Relatively new Korean-ministered Methodist church.

ANTIK BEYAZIT HOTEL
Boutique Hotel €€
(✆216 2900; www.antikbeyazitoteli.com; Hükümet Caddesi 4; s/d ₺100/130; ❄ 🎱) Housed in a pretty French Levantine colonial house (1903), Antakya's first boutique hotel is looking a bit frayed, though the antique furnishings, Oriental carpets and ornate chandelier in the lobby evoke an elegant past. Rooms are fairly basic; those in the rear have loft-style bedrooms and access to a back studio.

 Eating & Drinking

There are many restaurants on or just off Hürriyet Caddesi. Good places to relax over a drink and snack are the tea gardens in the riverside **Antakya Belediyesi Parkı**.

Arab (particularly Syrian) influences permeate Hatay cuisine. Handfuls of mint and wedges of lemon accompany kebaps, hummus is readily available, and the many local specialities include *oruk* (torpedo-shaped croquette of spicy minced beef encased in bulgur wheat flour and fried; not unlike Lebanese *kibbeh*).

ANTAKYA EVI
Turkish €€
(Silahlı Kuvvetler Caddesi 3; mains ₺7-12) This old villa, decorated with photos and antique furniture, serves spicy Hatay specialities, local mezes (₺6 to ₺8) and robust grills. There's live Turkish folk music on Friday and Saturday night.

HATAY SULTAN SOFRASI
Turkish €€
(www.sultansofrasi.com; İstiklal Caddesi 20a; mains ₺10-16) Antakya's premier spot for affordable local meals, this place turns out dishes at a rapid pace. The manager happily guides diners through the menu, and it's a top spot for mezes, spicy local kebaps and *künefe* (cake of fine shredded wheat laid over a dollop of fresh mild cheese, on a layer of sugar syrup topped with chopped walnuts).

ANADOLU RESTAURANT
Turkish €€
(Hürriyet Caddesi 30a; mains ₺8-35) Popular with families, the local glitterati and businesspeople, Antakya's culinary hot spot

serves a long list of fine mezes (₺6 to ₺12) on gold-coloured tablecloths in a splendid alfresco garden. Meat dishes include Anadolu kebap and the special *kağıt,* or 'paper' kebap.

CABARET Bar, Cafe

(Hürriyet Caddesi) This local student hang-out with brick walls and shuttered windows is an atmospheric spot for a tea, coffee or something stronger. There's occasional live music, cheap snacks and a cosy private courtyard.

 Shopping

DOĞAL DEFNE DÜNYASI Homewares, Textiles

(Çarşı Caddesi 16) Sells high-quality soaps from Harbiye, and gorgeous silk scarves woven and block-printed by hand.

 Getting There & Around

Air

Hatay airport is 20km north of the city. A taxi is around ₺30, and Havaş run a regular bus (₺10) into central Antakya.

Pegasus Airlines (www.flypgs.com) Regular flights to/from İstanbul (from ₺60) and İzmir (from ₺70).

Turkish Airlines (www.turkishairlines.com) Regular flights to/from İstanbul (from ₺75) and Ankara (from ₺65).

Bus

Antakya's intercity otogar is 7km northwest of the centre. A taxi to/from the centre will cost ₺15. Ask about *servis* transfers from central Antakya.

Direct buses go to destinations including Ankara, Antalya, İstanbul, İzmir and Şanlıurfa (₺30, seven hours).

Cappadocia & Central Anatolia

This vast swath of Anatolia is Turkey's historical heartland. Many pivotal events have occurred on these plains and mountains: Atatürk founded the Turkish capital, Ankara, as the Ottoman Empire was crumbling, and Julius Caesar famously boasted *'Veni, vidi, vici'* (I came, I saw, I conquered) after a victory near Amasya. Today, Amasya and Safranbolu alike have restored their Ottoman old quarters, offering the chance to stay in atmospheric half-timbered mansions.

Central Anatolia's dusty roads also lead to one of Turkey's most distinctive sights, the winding valleys of fairy chimneys (rock formations) in Cappadocia. Here, you can start the day with a hot-air balloon flight, return to terra firma – and keep descending – in the underground cities, tour Byzantine cave monasteries with biblical frescoes, and sample troglodyte living in a rock-cut hotel.

The Pamukkale and Eğirdir areas complete this region's bounty of rock formations, ruins and ethereal scenery.

Hot-air balloons over Cappadocia

APROTT/GETTY IMAGES ©

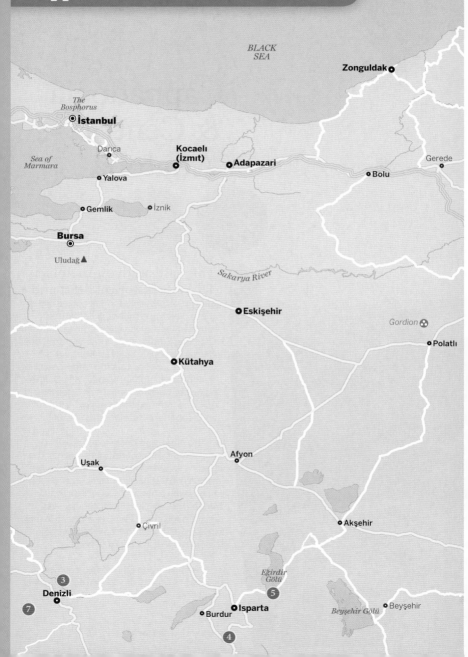

Cappadocia & Central Anatolia

Sinop

Cide

İnebolu

Amasra

Kastamonu

Samsun

Bafra

Karabük

Tosya

Osmancık

Kurşunlu

Ilgaz

Çankırı

Çorum

ANKARA

Kırıkkale

Sungurlu

Hattuşa

Yozgat

1 Cappadocia
2 Safranbolu
3 Pamukkale
4 Sagalassos
5 Eğirdir
6 Amasya
7 Afrodisias

Kırşehir

Tuz Gölü
(Salt
Lake)

Kayseri

Nevşehir

Göreme

Derinkuyu

Aksaray

Ihlara Vadisi
Turistik Tesisleri

Ala Dağlar
National Park

Yahyalı

Niğde

Konya

N

0   100 km
0   50 miles

Cappadocia & Central Anatolia's Highlights

1
Cappadocia

Cappadocia's (p246) moonscape of curvy valleys and fairy chimneys initially steals the show, but its history is also remarkable. Over the centuries, folk including Byzantine monks, farmers and winemakers have carved cave churches, cottages, pigeon houses and underground cities in the soft rock. Above: Derinkuyu underground city (p256); Top Right: Güllüdere (Rose Valley); Bottom Right: Karanlık Kilise (p253)

Need to Know

TOP TIP Don't make any bookings at Nevşehir otogar. **TRANSPORT** Mix tours with exploring the valleys on foot or scooter. **For further coverage, see p246**

Local Knowledge

Cappadocia Don't Miss List

BY MUSTAFA DEMIRCI, OWNER OF
AYDINLI CAVE HOUSE, GÖREME

1 GÖREME OPEN-AIR MUSEUM

Cappadocia's rocky valleys were an important site for early Christianity. Because it was easy to carve churches and houses in the soft rock by hand, Christians chose this area to live and teach safely. Göreme Open-Air Museum (p253) was the heart of the religious community, and you can still see the rock-carved monastery complex's many small chapels and beautiful churches, their frescoes painted with natural dye 1000 years ago. Especially in Karanlık Kilise (Dark Church), it's possible to see the frescoes as they must have looked centuries ago.

2 HOT-AIR BALLOONING

Millions of years ago, Mt Erciyes and Mt Hasan were active volcanoes and their lava formed tuff, creating Cappadocia's beautiful rock formations. It is really amazing to see it all spread out beneath a hot-air balloon basket (p251) early in the morning.

3 UNDERGROUND CITIES

From about the 7th to the 12th century, Christian people in Cappadocia were unsafe because of armies from abroad mounting military attacks. They built hundreds of underground cities (p256) here to hide from their enemies. In some of the cities, you can go seven or eight levels underground, and they all have churches, kitchens, wineries, food storage, living rooms and natural air ventilation.

4 HIKING IN GÜLLÜDERE (ROSE VALLEY)

In the late afternoon, walking in this valley of pink rock near Göreme is beautiful, because its colour intensifies at sunset. Güllüdere (p247) also has churches and panoramic viewpoints, and the trailheads are at Çavuşin and Kızılçukur viewpoint (opposite the Ortahisar turn-off).

5 WINE TASTING

Cappadocia's climate is perfect for growing grapes, and wine has been made here for thousands of years. Şıra Hotel runs lovely tastings of Cappadocian and central Anatolian wines, including the famous reds Kalecik Karası, Öküzgözü, Boğazkere, and the famous whites Emir and Narince.

237

Safranbolu

Shattering the image of central Anatolia as a dry and dusty place, Safranbolu's gorgeous Ottoman old town (p277) is a warren of boutique hotels, museums and quaint little cafes. Hotels organise day trips to local forests, villages, canyons and caves. Top Right: Cinci Hamam; Bottom Right: Exhibits in the Kaymakamlar Müze Evi Ottoman house (p277)

Need to Know

TOP TIP Safrantat is a good shop to try Safranbolu's beloved candy. **BUS TICKETS** The tourist office can help book them. **For further coverage, see p277**

Safranbolu Don't Miss List

BY İBRAHIM CANBULAT, ARCHITECT AND OWNER OF GÜLEVI SAFRANBOLU

1 CITADEL

From here one can see all the geography of the settlement in and on the canyons. Also visit the Kent Tarıhı Müzesi here – it gives a good introduction to local life – and look out for the clock tower (1797). Built by grand vizier (prime minister) İzzet Mehmet Paşa, it is the oldest clock tower in Turkey.

2 ÇARŞI

This is the old Ottoman town, with an organic street pattern and public buildings such as mosques and hamams right on the creeks, deep in the valley, and houses on the slopes. Each street is named after the local artisans' specialities and their functions: Semerciler (saddle makers), Yemeniciler (shoe makers), Demirciler (ironsmiths), Arasta (row of shops beside a mosque), Çarşısı (market) and so on. The small cafes were official meeting places for the artisans' guild. Climb onto the roof of the Cinci Hanı, Safranbolu's famous 17th-century caravanserai, for views across Çarşı's red-tiled roofs.

3 OTTOMAN MANSIONS

Some of Çarşı's finest mansions have been opened as museum houses (p277), such as Kaymakamlar Müze Evi, which was owned by a lieutenant colonel and has typical Ottoman features including wooden ceiling decorations and cupboard bathrooms; Kileciler Evi (1884), its 99 cupboards symbolising the 99 names of God; and Hakki Asmaz Evi (Beybağı Sokak) with its pool.

4 CINCI HAMAM

Cinci Hamam is one of the best bathhouses in Anatolia, right in Çarşı with separate baths for men and women. Go for the full works and have a Turkish coffee afterwards.

5 LOCAL TASTES

Discover Çarşı's many local tastes and ingredients: saffron (only with the red stigmas), *sahlep* (orchid bulb powder; a great thickener for desserts), *kaplica* (wild wheat) bulgur, and the Byzantine candy *yaprak helva* (white sesame-seed *helva* spotted with ground walnuts).

Pamukkale

Pamukkale's (p263) name, 'Cotton Castle', is a reference to its glistening white mountain of calcite travertines, brimming with mineral-rich water. Look beyond the famous formations, however, and you'll see the ruined baths, theatres and temples of Hierapolis, a Roman and Byzantine spa city established around 190 BC. Its ruins include the Martyrium of St Philip the Apostle, an intricate octagonal structure on terrain where St Philip was supposedly martyred.

Pamukkale's travertines (p265)

Sagalassos

Ancient Sagalassos (p269) is the quintessential romantic ruin, its fountains, baths, monuments and 7000-seat theatre strewn among the peaks of Ak Dağ (White Mountain). One of the Mediterranean region's largest archaeological projects, the city thrived under the Romans and became a Christian Byzantine outpost before declining during the Ottoman Empire. Today, it's the very antithesis of the busy 'Ephesus experience', with panoramic views over the mountains and plains.

Eğirdir

5 Occupying a peninsula in the lake of the same name, Eğirdir (p267) is a tranquil base for exploring the forested hills and mountains of the surrounding Lake District. Come here for hiking, climbing, beaches, remote ruins and boat trips, where you can try some fishing and bliss out amid the lake's breezy blue waters and verdant lagoons. Eğirdir's family-run pensions are perfect for relaxing among mountain and lake views. Lake Eğirdir (p267)

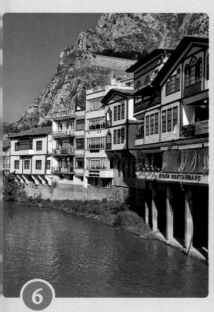

6

Amasya

As well as a fairy-tale collection of Ottoman mansions, history has given Amasya (p280) a set of Pontic rock tombs, carved into the wrinkly cliffs overlooking town. Above it all, Harşena Castle surveys the narrow river valley, completing the perfect setting for Turkey's own Romeo and Juliet–style fable about doomed lovers, Ferhat and Sirin. Amasya was a centre of Islamic study, and numerous Ottoman mosques and *medreses* (seminaries) remain. Ottoman houses in Amasya

7

Afrodisias

Out in the Anatolian boondocks, its 1000-year-old ruins battling with thickets and brambles, Afrodisias (p266) was once the capital of the Roman province of Caria. The 270m-long stadium is one of the biggest and best-preserved classical stadiums, with 30,000 seats; from its tunnel, you can imagine the fated exhilaration of gladiators. The on-site museum exhibits reliefs from the Sebasteion, once a temple to Roman emperors.

Cappadocia & Central Anatolia's Best...

Restaurants

● **Kebapçı İskender** (p261) Try Bursa's famous İskender kebap.

● **Zenger Paşa Konağı** (p273) Ottoman ephemera and Ankara views.

● **Taşev** (p279) Contemporary dining in Ottoman Safranbolu.

● **Strabon Restaurant** (p283) *Balık* (fish) on a riverside deck in Amasya.

● **Köy Evi** (p254) Village food served in cave rooms.

● **Seten Restaurant** (p254) Modern mezes and Anatolian classics in Göreme.

Ruins

● **Hattuşa** (p276) The Hittite capital, from where the ancient empire was run.

● **Sagalassos** (p269) Roman outpost in a rousing mountaintop setting.

● **Hierapolis** (p263) Atop Pamukkale's travertines, a classical spa city.

● **Afrodisias** (p266) Overgrown Roman provincial capital, abandoned in the 12th century.

● **Göreme Open-Air Museum** (p253) Karanlık Kilise's (Dark Church) colourful Byzantine frescoes look freshly painted.

Activities

● **Eğirdir** (p267) Hiking, climbing, beaches, boat trips, swimming, fishing and, of course, lazing.

● **Ihlara Valley** (p255) Hike the gorge's full length for cave churches and serene countryside.

● **Göreme** (p248) Hot-air ballooning, horse riding, hiking, biking, cooking classes and hamams.

● **Pamukkale** (p263) Scale the travertines, sample their mineral-rich waters and wallow among submerged columns in Hierapolis' balmy Antique Pool.

Architecture

◦ **Çarşı** (p277) Safranbolu's lovingly restored Ottoman old town; many of its houses contain historic hotels.

◦ **Ulu Camii** (p259) Bursa's 20-domed, 14th-century mosque overlooks the first Ottoman capital.

◦ **Hatuniye Mahallesi** (p280) Amasya's heritage Ottoman neighbourhood, with balconies bulging over the river.

◦ **Anıt Kabir** (p270) The mausoleum of modern Turkey's founder, Atatürk, is the last word in monumental tributes.

RESOURCES

◦ **Safranbolu.gov.tr** (www.safranbolu.gov.tr)

◦ **EğirdirTurkey.com** (egirdirturkey.com)

◦ **İDO** (www.ido.com. tr/en)

◦ **Havaş** (www.havas. net/en)

◦ **Göreme Tourism Society** (www.goreme. org)

GETTING AROUND

◦ **Air** Flights to Ankara Esenboğa from Turkish and foreign airports; from İstanbul to Nevşehir, Kayseri (both Cappadocia) and Denizli (near Pamukkale).

◦ **Boat** İDO ferries cross the Sea of Marmara between İstanbul and Bursa.

◦ **Bus** A good way to get between major towns; shuttles link Cappadocia with its two airports.

◦ **Car** Good roads; major hire companies in Ankara and small companies in Göreme.

◦ **Dolmuş** Useful for small journeys in Cappadocia.

◦ **Tour** A good way to see Cappadocia's remoter sights and Afrodisias, Sagalassos and Hattuşa.

◦ **Train** High-speed trains from Ankara to Konya and Eskişehir, and long-distance trains to eastern Anatolia.

BE FOREWARNED

◦ **Distances** Anatolia is vast; don't try to cover too much.

◦ **Ankara Esenboğa** İstanbul's airports offer more choice; even flying domestically, it may save you time and money to travel via İstanbul.

◦ **Accommodation** Splashing out is virtually compulsory in Safranbolu, and worth budgeting for in Cappadocia with its cave hotels.

◦ **Eğirdir** Ensure your bedroom windows have screens: harmless but irritating lake bugs fly towards lit areas.

◦ **Bus** Between Bursa and İstanbul, *karayolu ile* (by road) buses wind around the Bay of İzmit, taking one to two hours longer than *feribot ile* (by ferry) services.

◦ **Ruins** Visiting rugged sites such as Afrodisias, Sagalassos and Soğanlı, go prepared with water, sunscreen, sturdy shoes, long trousers and so on.

Left: Ruins at Hattuşa (p276), the ancient Hittite capital; **Above:** Ihlara Valley (p255)

Cappadocia & Central Anatolia Itineraries

Anatolia is a huge landmass, accounting for 97% of Turkey, but by focusing on a few key areas, you can cover the major sights – not least Cappadocia's fairy chimneys – in a reasonable amount of time.

5 DAYS
PAMUKKALE TO CAPPADOCIA
Ruins & Rock Formations

Start this Anatolian voyage at **(1) Afrodisias**, a Roman provincial capital and a stunning example of Turkey's less-visited classical ruins. Next, take your first look at Anatolia's spectacular rock forma-tions in **(2) Pamukkale**, with its powder-white mountain of calcite travertines. You can swim among sunken pillars in the classical spa city Hierapolis.

Refreshed, head across the Anatolian plains to **(3) Sagalassos**, a ruined mountaintop city that the Seljuks and Byzantines fought over. Relax after this rocky site in lakeside **(4) Eğirdir**, which

offers hearty pensions and outdoor activities beneath Davraz Dağı (2635m).

There is more beautiful scenery in **(5) Cappadocia**. Göreme is the best base for exploring the region's fairy chimneys, Byzantine cave churches and underground cities, its troglodytic accommodation and village lanes surrounded by sinuous valleys.

It's possible to see the best of Cappadocia in a couple of days: start the day with a dawn hot-air balloon ride over the fantastical landscape, take a tour to remoter spots such as Soğanlı, and see in the sunset on a valley walk or panoramic restaurant terrace.

CAPPADOCIA TO SAFRANBOLU
Historical Journey

Get off to a stunning start in **(1) Cappadocia**, where you can acclimatise to the surreal rocky moonscape by wandering around Göreme village and making numerous çay stops. To explore the region's fascinating Byzantine history, mix tours to Ilhara Valley's cave churches with shorter missions on foot and scooter.

After you wave goodbye to the fairy chimneys, it's worth spending a night in Turkey's oft-overlooked capital, **(2) Ankara**. Here you can visit the Museum of Anatolian Civilisations and the Citadel, to join the nationalistic pilgrims at the mausoleum of Turkey's founding father, Atatürk, and experience a modern Anatolian city. Next, return to the countryside at the ruins of **(3) Hattuşa**, which was the Hittites' mountain capital over 3000 years ago.

Fast-forwarding a few millennia, an Ottoman double-bill awaits in riverside **(4) Amasya**, its half-timbered houses overlooked by cliffs riddled with Pontic rock tombs, and **(5) Safranbolu**. Alleys lined with candy stores, cobblers and Turkey's finest collection of restored Ottoman mansions give Safranbolu storybook charm.

Anıt Kabir mausoleum (p270), Ankara

Discover Cappadocia & Central Anatolia

Whirling dervishes at the Sarıhan caravanserai (p249)
BLAINE HARRINGTON III/ALAMY ©

CAPPADOCIA

As if plucked from a whimsical fairy tale and set down upon the stark Anatolian plains, Cappadocia is a geological oddity of honeycombed hills and towering phallic boulders of otherworldly beauty. Fashioned through lashings of volcanic ash, moulded by millennia of rain and river flow, this fantastical topography is equally matched by the human history here. People have long utilised the region's soft stone, seeking shelter underground, leaving the countryside scattered with the fresco-adorned rock-cut churches of early Christians, cavernous subterranean refuges, and villages half-burrowed into the earth itself.

Cappadocia woos both outdoor enthusiasts who revel in the lunarscape and the cultured set, more likely to enjoy the panoramas from the balcony of their boutique cave-hotel with fine local wine in hand. Whatever your tastes, this region's accordion-ridged valleys, shaded in a palette of dusky orange and cream, are an epiphany of a landscape – the stuff of psychedelic daydreams.

Dangers & Annoyances

Most buses arriving in Cappadocia terminate in Nevşehir, from where a free *servis* (shuttle bus) will ferry you to your final destination. Make sure that your ticket states that it is for Göreme, not just 'Cappadocia'. Avoid any dealings with the infamous tour companies at Nevşehir otogar (bus station) and do not get onto their private shuttle buses. The official bus company *servis* buses usually meet your bus as it arrives and are clearly marked with the bus company logo. If you find yourself without a *servis* or taxi and you have booked a hotel, phone it for assistance.

Walking in central Cappadocia's valleys is a wonderful experience and should not be missed, but solo travellers who do not want to hire a guide to explore should buddy-up before venturing into the more isolated areas. It's also advised to avoid the valleys and unlit roads between villages during the evenings.

 Tours

Travel agents abound. Prices are usually determined by all operators at the beginning of each season. Make your decision based on the quality of the guide and the extent of the itinerary.

Most tour companies offer both full-day tours (to destinations such as the Ihlara Valley, the underground cities and Soğanlı) and guided day hikes in the Cappadocian valleys.

Guided day hikes are usually in the Güllüdere (Rose), Kızılçuker (Red) or Meskendir Valleys. Costs vary according to the destination, difficulty and length.

The full-day Ihlara Valley trip usually includes a short guided hike in the gorge, lunch and a trip to an underground city; most operators charge about ₺90.

Most itineraries finish at a carpet shop, onyx factory or pottery workshop, but it is still worth taking a tour. It is interesting to see a traditional Cappadocian artisan at work, but make it clear before the trip begins if you are not interested.

Book tours directly from agents in Cappadocia rather than buying an expensive tour package upon arrival in İstanbul.

❶ Getting There & Away

Air

Kayseri Airport (Erkilet Airport; ☎0352-337 5494; Kayseri Caddesi) and Nevşehir Airport (Kapadokya Airport; ☎0384-421 4451; Nevşehir Kapadokya Havaalanı Yolu, Gülşehir) serve central Cappadocia. The main operators are Turkish Airlines (www.thy.com), Pegasus Airlines (www.flypgs.com) and Sun Express (www.sunexpress.com).

Bus

Buses from İstanbul to Cappadocia travel overnight (in high summer there may also be day buses) and bring you to Nevşehir, where (if the bus is terminating there) a bus company *servis* will take you on to Göreme. From Ankara you can travel more comfortably during the day.

❶ Getting Around

To/From the Airport

Ask your accommodation in Cappadocia to book an airport shuttle bus for you, or book directly; Cappadocia Express (☎0384-271 3070; www.cappadociatransport.com; Iceridere Sokak 3, Göreme; per passenger ₺20) operates for all flights to/from both airports. It picks up from and drops off to hotels throughout Göreme and central Cappadocia.

Car & Motorcycle

Cappadocia is great for self-drive visits. Roads are often empty and their condition is reasonable.

Public Transport

Belediye Bus Corp dolmuşes (minibuses; ₺2.50 to ₺3) travel between Ürgüp and Avanos via Ortahisar, the Göreme Open-Air Museum, Göreme, Çavuşin and (on request) Paşabağı and Zelve. The services leave Ürgüp at 10am, noon, 4pm and 6pm, and Avanos (going the opposite way) at 9am, 11am, 1pm, 3pm and 5pm. You can hop on and off anywhere along the route.

There's also an hourly *belediye* (municipal council) bus running between Avanos and Nevşehir (₺4) via Çavuşin (10 minutes), Göreme (15 minutes) and Uçhisar (30 minutes). It leaves Avanos from 7am to 7pm.

The Ihlara Valley can be visited on a day tour from Göreme.

Taxi

Taxis are a good option for moving from town to town. Meters operate but a negotiated price is also welcome.

A taxi from Nevşehir to Göreme should cost around ₺35.

Göreme

☎ 0384 / POP 2138

Surrounded by epic sweeps of lunarscape valleys, this remarkable honey-coloured village, hollowed out of the hills, may have long since grown out of its farming hamlet roots but its charm has not diminished. In the back alleys new boutique cave hotels are constantly popping up but tourists still have to stop for tractors which trundle up narrow winding roads where elderly ladies dally for hours on sunny street-side stoops doing their knitting. Nearby, the Göreme Open-Air Museum is an all-in-one testament to Byzantine life, while if you wander out of town into the golden-hued valleys you'll find storybook landscapes and little-visited rock-cut churches at every turn. With its easygoing allure and stunning setting, it's no wonder Göreme continues to send travellers giddy.

Activities

TOPDECK CAVE RESTAURANT COOKING CLASSES   Cooking Course
(☎ 271 2474; Hafız Abdullah Efendi Sokak 15; €40; ⊙ classes 9am-11am) Mustafa Ciftçi runs recommended Turkish cooking classes (reservation-only) from his family home and restaurant. All the fiddly chopping and sweating over the stove is worth it for the slap-up lunch afterwards when you get to eat your creations.

DALTON BROTHERS   Horse Riding
(☎ 0532 275 6869; Müze Caddesi; 1/2hr ₺45/90) Horse riding in the valleys on Anatolian horses with Göreme's 'horse whisperer' Ekrem Ilhan.

CEMAL RANCH   Horse Riding
(☎ 0532 291 0211; cemalhome50@hotmail.com; İsak Kale, Ortahisar; 1/2hr ₺40/75, half-day ₺150) Ranch with stunning valley views, offering riding excursions in the surrounding countryside.

Left: Hot-air balloons (p251) over a valley near Göreme; **Below:** Sagalassos ruins (p269)

KIRKIT
VOYAGE Guided Tours
(☏ 511 3148; www.kirkit.com; Atatürk
Caddesi 50, Avanos) Walking, biking, canoeing, horse-riding and snowshoe trips
(as well as guided tours and airport
transfers).

OLD GÖREME
RESTORATION FUND Charity
(www.goremecharity.com) The charity's twice-
yearly 'Open House' events offer a rare
chance to see some of Göreme's privately
owned cave homes.

WHIRLING DERVISH
CEREMONY Religious
(Sema; ☏ 511 3795; admission €25; ⊙9.30pm
Apr-Oct, 9pm Nov-Mar) The restored 1249
Seljuk caravanserai **Sarıhan** (Yellow Caravanserai; admission ₺3; ⊙9am-midnight), 6km
east of Avanos, is the atmospheric setting
for 45-minute whirling dervish ceremonies. You must book ahead; most hotels
in Cappadocia will arrange it for you. The
price may vary according to how much
commission your tour agent or hotel is
skimming off the top.

Walking

Göreme village is surrounded by the
magnificent **Göreme National Park**. The
valleys are easily explored on foot; each
needs about one to three hours. Most are
interconnected, so you could easily combine several in a day, especially with the
help of the area's many dolmuşes. Don't
forget a bottle of water and sunscreen.
Pensions have basic maps and can recommend good routes.

Although many of the valleys now have
trailhead signposts and signage has been
put up at strategic points along the paths
of Güllüdere and Kızılçukur Valleys, many
of the trails remain only basically marked
and there's no detailed map of the area
available. It's quite easy to get lost if you
don't stick to the trails.

249

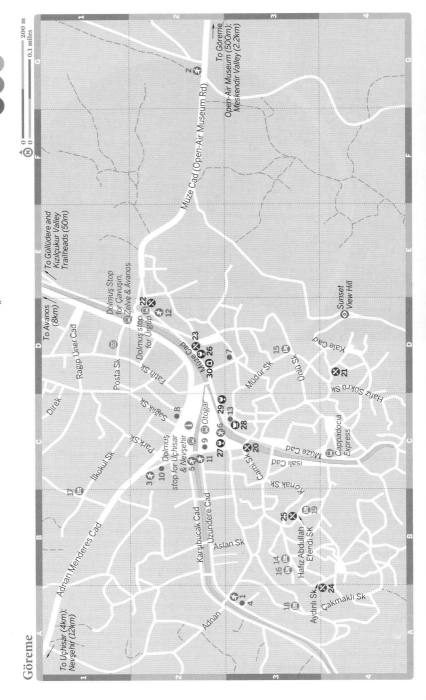

Göreme

To Uçhisar (4km);
Nevşehir (12km)

To Avanos
(8km)

To Güllüdere and
Kızılçukur Valley
Trailheads (50m)

To Göreme
Open-Air Museum (500m);
Meşkendir Valley (2.2km)

Open-Air Museum Rd

Muze Cad (Open-Air Museum Rd)

Adnan Menderes Cad

Ragıp Üner Cad

Posta Sk

Direk

İlkokul Sk

Park Sk

Sağlık Sk

Fatih Sk

Muze Cad

Karşıbucak Cad

Uzundere Cad

Aslan Sk

Adnan

Çamlık Sk

Konak Sk

İsali Cad

Muze Cad

Müdür Sk

Ünlü Sk

Kale Cad

Hafız Şükrü Sk

Cappadocia
Express

Hafız Abdullah
Efendi SK

Aydınlı Sk

Çakmaklı Sk

Sunset
View Hill

Dolmuş Stop
for Çavuşin,
Zelve & Avanos

Dolmuş stop
for Ürgüp

Dolmuş
stop for Uçhisar
& Nevşehir

Otogar

200 m
0.1 miles

Göreme

MEHMET GÜNGÖR   Walking
(📞 0532 382 2069; www.walkingmehmet.com;
Noriyon Cafe, Müze Caddesi; 4hr/full day €60/80)
Göreme's most-experienced local walking
guide has an encyclopaedic knowledge of
the surrounding valley trails and can put
together itineraries to suit all interests
and levels of fitness.

Hot-Air Ballooning
Cappadocia is one of the best places in
the world for hot-air balloon flights. Flight
conditions are favourable, with balloons
operating most mornings throughout the
year. It's a truly magical experience and
many travellers judge it to be the highlight
of their trip.

Book a dawn flight; on later-morning
flights, winds can become unreliable and
potentially dangerous. Transport between
your hotel and the balloon launch site
is included in the hefty price, as is a
champagne toast.

There's a fair amount of hot air
between the operators about who is and
isn't inexperienced, ill-equipped,
underinsured and unlicensed, but be
aware that hot-air ballooning can be
dangerous. Check your chosen tour
operator's credentials and make sure

your pilot is experienced and savvy; even
if it means asking to see their licences
and logbooks. Don't pick the cheapest
operator if it means they might be taking
short cuts with safety or overfilling
balloon baskets.

Balloons travel with the wind, so
companies can't ensure a particular
flight path on a particular day. All
companies try to fly over the fairy
chimneys, but sometimes (albeit rarely)
the wind doesn't allow this. Occasionally,
unfavourable weather conditions mean
that the pilot will cancel the flight for
safety reasons; you'll be offered a refund
or a flight on the next day. Take a warm
jumper or jacket; women should wear flat
shoes and trousers. Most companies will
not take up children aged under seven.

The following agencies have good
credentials:

○ **Butterfly Balloons** (📞 271 3010; www.
butterflyballoons.com; Uzundere Caddesi 29,
Göreme) With superlative pilots Mustafa,
the first Turkish citizen to gain a US pilot's
licence, and Englishman Mike, a fellowship
member of the Royal Meteorological
Society, standard flights (one hour, up to 16
passengers) cost €175.

○ **Royal Balloon** (271 3300; www. royalballoon.com; Dutlu Sokak 9) Seasoned pilot Suat Ulusoy heads up this team of local and international pilots. Standard flights (one hour, up to 20 passengers) cost €175.

○ **Voyager Balloons** (271 3030; www. voyagerballoons.com; Müze Caddesi 36/1, Göreme) Recommended for their multilingual pilots. Standard flights cost €160.

Hamams

ELIS KAPADOKYA HAMAM   Hamam
(271 2974; Adnan Menderes Caddesi; soak, scrub & massage €25; ⏱10am-midnight) Unwind after the chimney-spotting and treat yourself to a thorough massage at the beautiful Elis Kapadokya Hamam, which has mixed and women-only areas.

KELEBEK TURKISH BATH SPA   Hamam
(271 2531; Kelebek Hotel, Yavuz Sokak; soak & scrub €30) Cappadocia's most luxurious hamam experience with a full-range of spa-style added extras.

 Tours

MIDDLE EARTH TRAVEL   Adventure Tour
(271 2559; www.middleearthtravel.com; Cevizler Sokak 20) The adventure-travel specialist offers climbing and treks ranging from local, one-day expeditions (€35 to €60 per person) to one-week missions through Ala Dağlar National Park, along the Lycian Way or St Paul's Trail, through the Kaçkar Mountains or up Mt Ararat.

HERITAGE TRAVEL   Guided Tour
(271 2687; www.turkishheritagetravel.com; Uzundere Caddesi) Local tours with the knowledgeable Mustafa are highly recommended (group tours €45 per person, or €100 per person for a private tour). The company also offers more offbeat tours such as photography jeep safaris (€125 per person) plus tailor-made packages.

YAMA TOURS   Guided Tour
(271 2508; www.yamatours.com; Müze Caddesi 2) A range of one-day Cappadocia group tours, and three-day trips to Nemrut Dağı (Mt Nemrut).

NEŞE TOUR   Guided Tour
(271 2525; www.nesetour.com; Avanos Yolu 54) Offers Cappadocian day tours and longer trips to Nemrut Dağı.

NOMAD TRAVEL   Guided Tour
(271 2767; www.nomadtravel.com.tr; Belediye Caddesi) Offers an excellent Soğanlı tour.

NEW GÖREME TOURS   Guided Tour
(271 2166; www.newgoreme.com) Fun and friendly private tours.

 Sleeping

If you're visiting between October and May, pack warm clothes as it gets cold at night and pension owners may delay putting the heating on. Ring ahead, too, to check that your choice is open. This is only a sample of the numerous rock-cut retreats in this fairy-chimney-punctured village.

KELEBEK HOTEL & CAVE PENSION   Hotel €€
(271 2531; www.kelebekhotel.com; Yavuz Sokak 31; fairy chimney s/d €40/50, deluxe s/d €52/65, ste s €64-144, ste d 80-180; 🛜🏊) Local guru Ali Yavuz leads a charming team at one of Göreme's original boutique hotels. Spread over two gorgeous stone houses, each with fairy chimney protruding skyward, rooms exude Anatolian inspiration. Kelebek continues to innovate, and now offers complimentary village garden breakfast visits to every guest.

KOZA CAVE HOTEL   Hotel €€
(271 2466; www.kozacavehotel.com; Cakmaklı Sokak 49; s/d €75/90, ste €115-140; 🛜) Bringing a whole new level of eco-inspired chic to Göreme, Koza is a masterclass in stylish sustainable tourism. Owner Derviş lived in Holland and has incorporated Dutch eco-sensibility into every cave crevice. Grey water is reused, and recycled materials and local handcrafted furniture are utilised in abundance to create sophisticated, elegant spaces.

AYDINLI CAVE HOUSE   Hotel €€
(271 2263; www.thecavehotel.com; Aydınlı Sokak 12; r from €70-140; 🛜) Proprietor Mus-

JOHN SONES SINGING BOWL MEDIA/GETTY IMAGES ©

Don't Miss **Göreme Open-Air Museum**

First an important Byzantine monastic settlement, then a pilgrimage site from the 17th century, this cluster of fresco-filled rock-cut churches, chapels and monasteries is an easy 1km walk uphill from the centre of Göreme.

Avoid weekends if possible, and arrive early in the morning, at midday or near closing to bypass tour groups. Your ticket is valid all day if you want to leave and return.

The museum's most famous church, the stunning, fresco-filled **Karanlık Kilise** (Dark Church), is one of Turkey's finest surviving churches and well worth the extra outlay.

Also look out for the 13th-century **Çarıklı Kilise** (Sandal Church). The footprints marked in the floor represent the last imprints left by Jesus before he ascended to heaven.

Across the road from the museum, 50m downhill, the 10th-century **Tokalı Kilise** (Buckle Church) is one of Göreme's biggest and finest churches, with an underground chapel and fabulous frescoes.

NEED TO KNOW

Göreme Açık Hava Müzesi; ☏271 2167; admission ₺15, Karanlık Kilise admission ₺8; ⏲8am-5pm

tafa has masterfully converted his family home into a haven for honeymooners and those requiring a little rock-cut style with their solitude. Guests rave about the warm service and immaculate, spacious cave rooms, formerly used for drying fruits, storing wheat and making wine. The family suite has an active tandoor oven and antique kitchen utensils.

THE DORM CAVE   Hostel €
(☏271 2770; www.travellerscave.com; Hafız Abdullah Efendi Sokak 4; d/tr €30/45; 🛜) This superb new hostel shuns the boutique craze in favour of backpacker-friendly-priced beds. Upstairs a couple of snug, private rooms offer brilliant value.

KISMET CAVE HOUSE   Hotel €€

(☏271 2416; www.kismetcavehouse.com; Kağnı Yolu 9; d €75; ☏) Guests consistently hail the intimate experience created by the unobtrusive Faruk and his family at this cave house. The rooms host local antiques, colourful rugs and quirky artwork while communal areas are home to cosy cushion-scattered nooks.

CAPPADOCIA CAVE SUITES   Luxury Hotel €€€

(☏271 2800; www.cappadociacavesuites.com; Ünlü Sokak 19; r €135-275; ❄ ☏) Uncomplicated service, spacious, modern-meets-megalithic suite rooms and cool, converted stables. Fairy Chimney 1 is our pick for its cosy living room, ideal for balloon viewing.

🍴 Eating

KÖY EVI   Anatolian €€€

(☏271 2008; Aydınkıragı Sokak 40; set menu ₺25; 🍴) The simple, wholesome, tasty flavours of village food are the main act at this brilliant set-menu restaurant, which serves up a taste-bud tour of Göreme while the lady chefs shovel out more steaming hot bread from the *tandır* (oven). Inside, the warren of cave rooms have been kept authentically basic, which adds to the homespun appeal.

SETEN RESTAURANT   Modern Turkish €€€

(☏271 3025; www.setenrestaurant.com; Aydınlı Sokak; mains ₺16-40) Brimming with an artful Anatolian aesthetic, Seten is a feast for the eye as well as for the stomach. The restaurant is an education for newcomers to Turkish cuisine and a treat for well-travelled tongues. Signature chefs and attentive service complement classic dishes done right and a dazzling array of mezes done differently enough to keep you coming back.

TOPDECK CAVE RESTAURANT   Anatolian €€€

(☏271 2474; Hafız Abdullah Efendi Sokak 15; mains ₺15-20; ⏱dinner only; 🍴) Chef Mustafa and his gracious family have transformed an atmospheric cave room in their house into a cosy restaurant where the kids pitch in with the serving and diners dig into hearty helpings of Anatolian favourites with a spicy twist. Choose the mixed meze plate for a flavour-packed blowout.

NAZAR BÖREK   Börekçisi €

(☏271 2441; Müze Caddesi; gözleme & börek ₺6-9; ☏) Head here for supremely tasty traditional Turkish staples served up by friendly Rafik and his team. Nazar remains our long-standing favourite for its hearty plates of *gözleme* (savory pancakes) and *sosyete böregi* (stuffed spiral pastries served with yoghurt and tomato sauce), while the convivial atmosphere encourages diners to linger long after their meal has finished.

Ihlara Valley

Detour:
Ihlara Valley (Ihlara Vadisi)

Ihlara Valley (admission ₺8, parking ₺2; 🕐8am-6.30pm), 60km southwest of Göreme, was a favourite retreat of Byzantine monks, who cut churches into the base of its towering cliffs. Following the river, as it snakes between painted churches, jagged cliffs, piles of boulders and a sea of greenery, is an unforgettable experience.

Good, quiet times to visit are midweek in May or September. To walk the short stretch with most churches, take the steep steps leading down from the **Ihlara Vadisi Turistik Tesisleri** (Ihlara Valley Tourist Facility), 2km from Ihlara village. Alternatively, there are entrances in Ihlara village – signposted after the *belediye* (local council) building – at Belisırma and at Selime.

As most visitors only walk the short, 90-minute stretch between the Ihlara Vadisi Turistik Tesisleri and Belisırma, walking the full route between Ihlara village and Selime is blissfully serene.

Belisırma to Selime takes about two hours; the full route is around five to six hours, stopping in Belisırma for lunch. Start early in the day, particularly in summer, when you'll need to shelter from the sun.

Midway along the gorge, below Belisırma village, four low-key licensed riverside restaurants serve basic meals. There are also restaurants in Ihlara village and Selime.

Travel agencies in Göreme and elsewhere offer full-day tours to Ihlara for about ₺90, including lunch. On weekdays, six dolmuşes run between Aksaray and Ihlara village via Selime and Belisırma (₺4, 45 minutes). At weekends there are fewer services.

DIBEK   Anatolian €€
(📞271 2209; Hakkı Paşa Meydanı 1; mains ₺10-22; 📷) Diners sprawl on cushions and feast on traditional dishes and home-made wine at this family restaurant, set inside a 475-year-old building. Many book ahead (at least three hours) for the slow-cooked *testi kebap* meal ('pottery kebap', with meat or mushrooms and vegetables cooked in a sealed terracotta pot, which is broken at the table; ₺28).

**LOCAL
RESTAURANT**   Modern Turkish €€
(📞271 2629; Müze Caddesi 38; mains ₺11-32) New owners have brought in a creative chef and enthusiastic staff to give this old-timer a fresh lease of life. The steak dishes are scrumptious by themselves but don't forget to order the *patlican*

(eggplant) salad which is gloriously smoky perfection on a plate.

Drinking

FAT BOYS   Bar, Restaurant
(📞0535 386 4484; Belediye Caddesi; beer ₺7, mains ₺8-16; 🕐noon-late; 🛜) This lounge-style bar is a winner. The hungry can order from a global pub-grub menu which stars Aussie-style pies, as well as burgers, nachos and Vegemite on toast. While the pool table and board games are tempting diversions, it's the friendly staff and well-stocked bar which make this place so popular.

CAFE ŞAFAK   Cafe
(Müze Caddesi; coffee ₺5-7, mains ₺7-18; 🛜)
Hands down the best coffee in Göreme.

Underground Cities

During the 6th and 7th centuries, Byzantine Christians extended and enlarged Cappadocia's network of underground cities, thought to have first been carved out by the Hittites. When Persian or Arab armies marauded through, Cappadocia's Christians would hide in these subterranean vaults for months at a time.

Many tours visit an underground city as part of a day trip. Touring the cities is rather like tackling an assault course: narrow walkways lead into the depths of the earth, through stables with handles used to tether animals, churches with altars and baptism pools, walls with air-circulation holes, granaries with grindstones, and blackened kitchens with ovens. Be prepared for unpleasantly crowded and sometimes claustrophobic passages. Avoid visiting on weekends, which are generally busy. It's worth having a guide: they can conjure up the details of life below ground.

The cities' air shafts, which were disguised as wells, descend almost 100m in some cities. As new rooms were constructed, debris would be excavated into the shafts, which would then be cleared and deepened so work could begin on the next floor.

Around 37 underground cities have been opened and there are at least 100 more. It is thought that Derinkuyu and Kaymaklı housed about 10,000 and 3000 people respectively.

Kaymaklı underground city (admission ₺15; ⊙8am-5pm, last admission 4.30pm), a maze of tunnels and rooms carved eight levels deep (four are open), is the most convenient and popular underground city. Get here early in July and August to beat the tour groups, or from about 12.30pm to 1.30pm when they break for lunch.

Derinkuyu underground city (Deep Well; admission ₺15; ⊙8am-5pm, last admission 4.30pm), 10km south of Kaymaklı, has larger rooms on seven levels. When you reach the bottom, look up the ventilation shaft to see just how far down you are.

With an exposed-brick interior, displaying quirky art, Şafak is a little slice of New York cafe-cool which delivers in the caffeine-hit stakes. There's a good menu as well if you're feeling peckish.

MYDONOS CAFE   Cafe
(Müze Caddesi 18; drinks ₺3-8) Subdued jazzy background music and wall displays of old vinyl dust jackets fill the interior with subtle bohemian flair while the balcony is the perfect pit stop for sunny Cappadocian afternoons. We love the decadent hot chocolate and French-press coffee.

RED RED WINE HOUSE   Bar
(☎271 2183; Müze Caddesi; glass of wine ₺10) In a former stable with arched ceilings, this seductive local feels like an ancient bootlegger's secret mixing den decorated by lovers of adult contemporary. A steady chain of guests smoke fruity pipes and sip increasingly palatable Cappadocian wines.

 **Shopping**

TRIBAL COLLECTIONS   Carpets
(☎271 2400; Müze Caddesi 24; ⊙9am-8pm) As well as being home to some mighty-fine rugs, owners Ruth and Faruk are known for their highly recommended educationals (a kind of carpets 101) which explain the history and artistry of these coveted textiles.

Information

Money

There are standalone ATM booths in, and around, the otogar. Some of the town's travel agencies will exchange money, although you're probably better off going to the **post office** (PTT; Posta Sokak) or **Deniz Bank** (Müze Caddesi 3).

Tourist Information

There's an information booth at the otogar that is open when most long-distance buses arrive, but it's run by the **Göreme Turizmciler Derneği** (Göreme Tourism Society; ☑271 2558; www.goreme.org), a coalition of hotel and restaurant owners, and staff can't supply much meaningful information. They give out and sell maps.

 ## Getting There & Away

There are daily long-distance buses from Göreme's otogar to destinations including Ankara (₺30, 4½ hours), Antalya (₺45, nine hours), İstanbul (₺40 to ₺50, 11 to 12 hours) and Selçuk (₺50, 11½ hours). Normally you're ferried to Nevşehir's otogar to pick up the main service (which can add nearly an hour to your travelling time).

Getting Around

There are several places to hire mountain bikes (about ₺25 for a day), mopeds and scooters (₺45 to ₺55), cars (₺90 to ₺130) and quads, including **Hitchhiker** (☑271 2169; www.cappadociahitchhiker.com; Uzundere Caddesi) and **Oz Cappadocia** (☑271 2159; www.ozcappadocia.com; Uzundere Caddesi). It pays to shop around.

Refill your tank in Nevşehir, Avanos, Ürgüp or one of the garages on the main road near Ortahisar and İbrahimpaşa.

Soğanlı

☑0352 / POP 400

Let's get one thing straight: despite the science-fiction setting, no scene in *Star Wars* was ever filmed near Soğanlı, or anywhere else in Turkey. But don't despair, Chewbacca fans, there's still ample reason to travel to this tiny village 36km south of Mustafapaşa, namely a reverential series of rock-cut churches hidden in two dramatic, secluded valleys.

To reach Soğanlı, turn off the main road from Mustafapaşa to Yeşilhisar and proceed 4km to the village. Buy your ticket for the **churches** (adult/child ₺5/free;

One of Soğanlı's churches

GKISAKIS/GETTY IMAGES ©

If You Like...
Fairy Chimneys

Göreme's neighbouring villages are dotted with cave churches and castles, easily reached on a scooter or by walking along the valleys of fantastic rock formations.

As well as the sights listed below, the **Devrent Valley** (2km [1.2mi] from Aktepe) has some of Cappadocia's best-formed and most thickly clustered cones, offering anthropomorphic fun. Also known as Imagination Valley, it's south of Aktepe (near Zelve) on the Avanos–Ürgüp road.

1 UÇHISAR CASTLE
(Uçhisar Kalesi; admission ₺3; ☉8am-8.15pm) This tall, volcanic-rock outcrop riddled with tunnels and windows is visible for miles around. Watching the sun set over the Rose and Pigeon Valleys from here is a popular activity.

2 ÇAVUŞIN CHURCH
(Big Pigeon House Church; admission ₺8; ☉8am-5pm) Just off the highway on Çavuşin's northern edge, a rickety iron stairway climbs to Cappadocia's first post-iconoclastic church, with some fine frescoes.

3 ÇAVUŞIN OLD VILLAGE RUINS
Above Çavuşin's main square, this steep and labyrinthine complex of abandoned houses is cut into a rock face. The **Church of John the Baptist**, one of Cappadocia's oldest churches, is at the top of the cliff path.

4 ZELVE OPEN-AIR MUSEUM
(admission ₺8, parking ₺2; ☉8am-7pm Apr-Oct, to 5pm Nov-Mar) The Çavuşin–Avanos road passes a turn-off to these three valleys of abandoned homes and churches, a 9th- to 13th-century monastic retreat that was inhabited until 1952. En route to Zelve from the turn-off, **Paşabağı** is a formerly monastic valley with mushroom-shaped fairy chimneys and a three-headed formation.

5 ORTAHISAR CASTLE
(☉9am-6pm) Overlooking the farming village of Ortahisar, this 18m-high rock was used as a fortress in Byzantine times.

☉8am-8.30pm, to 5pm in winter) near the Kapadokya Restaurant.

The valleys of **Aşağı Soğanlı** and **Yukarı Soğanlı** were first used by the Romans as necropolises and later by the Byzantines for monastic purposes, with ancient rock-cut churches.

Most of the interesting churches are in the right-hand valley (to the north), easily circuited on foot in about two hours. All are signposted, but be careful as many are in a state of disrepair.

Furthest up the right-hand valley is the **Yılanlı Kilise** (Church of St George or Snake Church). Turn left here, cross the valley floor and climb the far hillside to find more churches and return to the village.

Eating

SOĞANLI RESTAURANT Turkish €€
(📞653 1016; mains ₺10-15; 🍴) This popular lunch pit stop for Soğanlı day tours rustles up a mean *menemen* (scrambled eggs) as well as decent *çorbas* (soups), *gözleme* and tasty casseroles. The very basic pension rooms (₺35 per person) at the back are small but serviceable.

ℹ Getting There & Away

It's easiest to rent a car or sign up for a day tour in Göreme.

CENTRAL & WESTERN ANATOLIA
Bursa
📞0224 / POP 1,704,441

Modern, industrial Bursa is built around the mosques, mausoleums and other sites from its incarnation as the first Ottoman capital. Despite being built-up and somewhat chaotic, its durable Ottoman core and abundant parks keep it remarkably placid in places. The soaring peaks of Mt Uludağ (one of Turkey's premier ski resort) are 22km away.

Bursa's historic contributions to Islamic development has given it an austere reputation; you'll see many headscarved women and devout prayer in overflowing mosques. Yet locals are welcoming, and the city's culture and traditions include Karagöz shadow puppets.

Sights

Central Cumhuriyet Alanı (Republic Sq) is also called Heykel (statue), after its large **Atatürk statue**.

There are a number of ancient markets (p266) around Ulu Camii.

BURSA CITY MUSEUM   Museum
(Bursa Kent Müzesi; ☑220 2486; www.bursakent muzesi.gov.tr; 8 Atatürk Caddesi; admission ₺1.50; ☺9.30am-5.30pm Tue-Sat) This multimedia museum chronicles Bursa's history, culture and ethnography from the earliest sultans onwards. Films show old-fashioned artisans at work.

ULU CAMII   Mosque
(Atatürk Caddesi) This enormous Seljuk-style shrine (1396) is Bursa's most dominant and durable mosque. Having pledged to build 20 mosques after defeating the Crusaders, Sultan Beyazıt I settled for one mosque, with 20 small domes.

BURSA CITADEL   Castle
(Osman Gazi ve Orhan Gazi Türbeleri; admission by donation) Some ramparts and walls still survive on the steep cliff, the site of Bursa's citadel and oldest neighbourhood. Walk up Orhan Gazi (Yiğitler) Caddesi, to reach the Hisar (Fortress) or Tophane. On the summit, a park contains the **Tombs of Sultans Osman and Orhan** (Osman Gazi ve Orhan Gazi Türbeleri; Timurtaş Paşa Park; admission by donation), the Ottoman Empire's founders, rebuilt in baroque style in 1868. Remove shoes before entering. There's a **tea garden** with views over the valley.

Tours

KARAGÖZ TRAVEL AGENCY   Tour
(☑221 8727; www.karagoztravel.com; cnr Kapalıçarşı & Eski Aynalı Çarşı 4) Offers interesting local tours, including city excursions.

Ulu Camii, Bursa

MURAT TANER/GETTY IMAGES ©

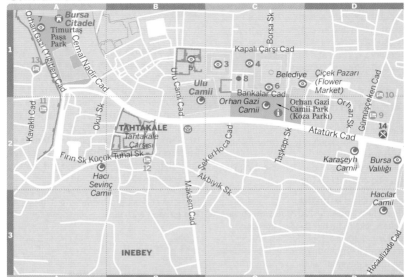

 Sleeping

Bursa is primarily a business tourist destination and hotels are priced accordingly. If sensitive to smoke, check the room first.

KITAP EVI Boutique Hotel €€

(Book House; ☎225 4160; www.kitapevi.com.tr; cnr Kavaklı Mahallesi & Burç Üstü 21; s/d/ste €100/140/230; ❄ @) The 'Book House', a former Ottoman house and bookstore, draws an artistically inclined clientele with its eclectic decor. Well-polished wood fixtures, and little touches like artwork and stained glass, complement the rows of bookshelves and empty leather suitcases. The restaurant is excellent.

SAFRAN OTEL Pension €€

(☎224 7216; www.safranotel.com; Orta Pazar Caddesi; s/d ₺90/150; ❄ ☎) Occupies an elegant restored Ottoman house near the Osman and Orhan tombs, in a historic district. Although the exterior partly includes a Byzantine wall, rooms are thoroughly modern (with a hint of the Ottoman retained in its distinctive carpets).

HOTEL ÇEŞMELI Hotel €€

(☎224 1511; Gümüşçeken Caddesi 6; s/d ₺80/120; ❄) Run by two sisters (and employing only women), this is a good spot for female travellers, close to the market. Although the rooms are a bit dated, they're spacious enough and the Çeşmeli remains a friendly central spot.

HOTEL EFEHAN Business Hotel €€

(☎225 2260; www.efehan.com.tr; Gümüşçeken Caddesi 34; s/d ₺110/140; ❄ @) The central Efehan offers good value, good service and fresh standard rooms (and family-sized rooms). The top-floor breakfast hall offers good views of the city. Avoid the south-facing suite, which gets blasted by the neighbouring mosque's call to prayer.

OTEL GÜNEŞ Hostel €

(☎222 1404; İnebey Caddesi 75; s/d ₺35/50) The Güneş has seen better days but remains the only true budget accommodation in Bursa's centre, run by a kind family. Rooms are small but clean (choose between those with regular and 'Turkish traditional' toilets).

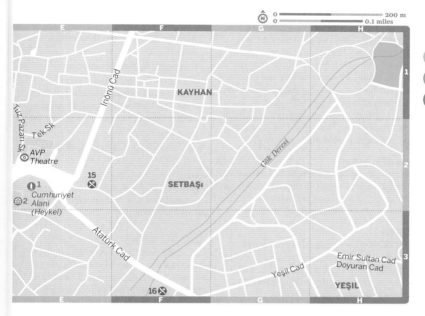

Central Bursa

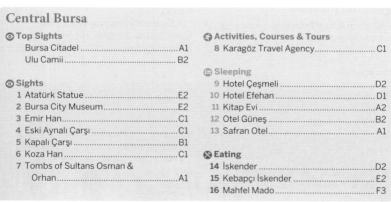

✦ Eating & Drinking

Bursa's famous for its rich İskender kebap, and its candied chestnut dessert (*kestane şekeri*; also called *maron glacé*).

KEBAPÇI İSKENDER　　　　Kebap €€
(Ünlü Caddesi 7; İskender kebap ₺18; ☺lunch & dinner) This refuge for serious carnivores is known nationwide: it's where the legen-

dary İskender kebap was created in 1867. This is the main branch of approximately 12 other eponymous eateries around Bursa.

İSKENDER　　　　　　　Kebap €€
(Atatürk Caddesi 60; mains ₺16; ☺lunch & dinner) This central spot (which also claims to have created the İskender kebap) does hearty versions of the local favourite, at slightly cheaper prices.

ARAP ŞÜKRÜ
Seafood €€

(Sakarya Caddesi; mezes ₺7-20; ⏲lunch & dinner) Situated in a cobblestoned lane in the former Jewish quarter, about a 10-minute walk from Ulu Cami, this historic restaurant serves fresh and excellent seafood and mezes. Try the *karides güveç* (shrimp casserole), grilled octopus, and rakı (aniseed brandy) with melon. Similar restaurants line the same street, regaled by accordion-wielding Roma bands.

MAHFEL MADO
Restaurant, Bar €

(Namazgah Caddesi 2; mains ₺5-10; ⏲breakfast, lunch & dinner) Bursa's oldest cafe is known for its *dondurma* (ice cream), and has a nice shady ravine setting.

GREN
Bar, Cafe

(☎223 6064; www.grencafe.com; Sakarya Caddesi 46) Bursa's hip 'photography cafe' has regular exhibitions, workshops and events, matching its antique-camera decor and arty young clientele.

ℹ Information

ATMs are on Atatürk Caddesi; for exchange offices visit the Covered Market.

Tourist office (⏲9am-5pm Mon-Fri, to 6pm Sat) Beneath Atatürk Caddesi, in the shop row at Orhan Gazi Alt Geçidi's northern entrance.

Dangers & Annoyances

Cross Atatürk Caddesi by the *alt geçidi* (pedestrian underpasses). Disabled people can use the lift at Atatürk Alt Geçidi (the underpass nearest to Heykel); the nearby florist's has the key.

ℹ Getting There & Away

Air

Flights from Yenişehir Airport (www.yenisehir. dhmi.gov.tr) are scarce. Check with Turkish Airlines (www.thy.com).

Bus & Ferry

Bursa's otogar is 10km north of the centre on the Yalova road. Destinations include Ankara (₺35, six hours, hourly), Bandırma (₺15, two hours, regular), Çanakkale (₺40, five hours, regular), İstanbul (₺24, three hours, frequent), İzmir (₺30, 5½ hours, hourly) and Yalova (₺9, 1¼ hours, half-hourly).

Otogar-centre taxis run ₺25 to ₺30.

For İstanbul, the metro-bus-ferry combo – metro to the final stop (₺2) and then a bus (₺3) to

Ruins at Hierapolis

the Mudanya İDO fast ferry (☎444 4436; www.ido.com.tr) terminal – is quickest. Ferries also link İstanbul to Yalova nearby.

Car

Car hire is available through Economy Car Rentals (www.economycarrentals.com).

Pamukkale
☎0258 / POP 2630

The village of Pamukkale has long been famous for its mountain of gleaming white calcite shelves overrunning with warm, mineral-rich waters – the so-called 'Cotton Castle' (*pamuk* means 'cotton' in Turkish).

While many visitors are content to laze in the travertines, just above them lies Hierapolis, once a Roman and Byzantine spa city. Unesco World Heritage status has brought more extensive measures to protect the glistening bluffs, and bathing has been restricted.

◉ Sights & Activities

The travertines/terraces and Hierapolis, both located on a hill right above Pamukkale village, are accessed on the same ticket (₺30).

The site's southern entrance is just over 2km from Pamukkale, on the hill at the entrance to Hierapolis, so you can see both attractions while walking downwards, finishing up back in the village.

The northern entrance, at the edge of Pamukkale itself, is at the base of the terraced mountain, meaning you walk uphill over the travertines before reaching Hierapolis. If you're just after a little R&R in the pools, this is a quick and easy option.

Pensions often provide free lifts to the south gate. You can stay inside as long as you like (the park is open during daylight hours).

HIERAPOLIS   Ruin
Hierapolis' paved pathways, well-trimmed hedges, flower-filled expanses and park benches are far more genteel than most Turkish archaeological sites. To see an ancient site on flat and well-maintained terrain, this is the place.

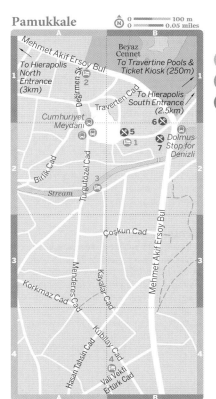

Pamukkale

🛏 **Sleeping**
1 Artemis Yoruk Hotel..............................B2
2 Hotel Hal-Tur A1
3 Kervansaray Pension A2
4 Melrose Hotel.......................................B4

❌ **Eating**
5 Kayaş...B2
6 Mehmet's Heaven.................................B1
7 Mustafa's...B2

The curvaceous mountaintop means that the city's ruins are relatively compact, with the main sites easily accessible. The ruins evoke life in a bygone era, in which Greeks and Romans, Jews, pagans and Christians, and spa tourists peacefully coexisted.

Hierapolis became a curative centre when founded around 190 BC by Eumenes II of Pergamum. It prospered under the Romans and Byzantines, but recurrent earthquakes eventually brought disaster, and Hierapolis was abandoned after a 1334 tremor.

HIERAPOLIS ARCHAEOLOGY MUSEUM
Museum

(admission ₺3; ⊙9am-12.30pm & 1.30-7pm Tue-Sun) Housed in former Roman baths, this excellent museum displays spectacular sarcophagi and small finds from Hierapolis and Afrodisias, including friezes and Roman-era statuary from Afrodisias' famous school.

ANTIQUE POOL
Swimming

(admission ₺25, public pool admission ₺7.50; ⊙9am-7pm, public pool 9am-8pm) The sacred pool – nowadays, the separate-ticket swimming pool in the Antique Pool spa's courtyard – has submerged sections of original fluted marble columns to lounge against. The mineral-rich water, which is more-than-balmy at 36°C, was thought to have restorative powers in antiquity, and

may well still do. In summer, it's busiest from 11am to 4pm.

 ## Sleeping

Pamukkale's numerous pensions and small hotels offer good value. Many places have pools (with water from the travertines or other springs).

If you have a preference, and especially in high summer, book ahead. This often scores you a free lift from Denizli's otogar or train station.

Don't be surprised if you're blasted from your bed at 5am by the mosque's call to prayer.

ARTEMIS YORUK HOTEL
Hostel €

(☎272 2073; www.artemisyorukhotel.com; Atatürk Caddesi; s/d from ₺40/50; ❄@🛜⛱) This centrally located Turkish-Australian operation offers simple rooms with balconies set around a palm-lined outdoor pool, flanked by cushioned nooks and overlooked by an open terrace/bar. The indoor pool is heated by Pamukkale's mineral-rich waters. There's a sauna and Turkish bath, where massages are available.

MELROSE HOTEL
Pension €€

(☎272 2250; www.melrosehousehotel.com; Vali Vekfi Ertürk Caddesi 8; s/d/tr €31/37/43; ❄@🛜⛱) A step above the average Pamukkale pension (but pricier, too), the Melrose has an array of sumptuously decorated big modern rooms with wood floors, including suites, family rooms and the deluxe room (€60), with a jacuzzi and bar. There's a good restaurant and pool.

HOTEL HAL-TUR
Hotel €€

(☎272 2723; www.haltur.net; Mehmet Akif Ersoy Bulvarı 71; s/d/tr from €40/60/85; ❄@⛱) The Hal-Tur has fantastic travertine views, and clean and well-kept (if dated) rooms. The excellent pools (with separate kids' section) and ping-pong table make it great for families.

KERVANSARAY PENSION
Pension €

(☎272 2209; www.kervansaraypension.com; İnönü Caddesi; s/d ₺45/60; ❄@⛱) The

Hierapolis

0 ——— 200 m
0 ——— 0.1 miles

Travertines

Frontinus St

Antique Pool

Hierapolis Archaeology Museum

Sacred Pool

Travertines

Southern Entrance

Beyaz Cennet

To Pamukkale Village (500m)

KEVEN OSBORNE/FOX FOTOS/GETTY IMAGES ©

Don't Miss **Travertines**

Pamukkale's saucer-shaped travertines (also known as terraces) wind sideways down the powder-white mountain. To protect the unique calcite surface, guards oblige you to go barefoot. Although the ridges look rough, the constant water flow keeps the ground mostly soft, even gooey in places, and the risk of slipping is greater than that of cutting your feet. (If still concerned, just leave your socks on.) To walk straight down without stops takes 30 to 45 minutes. The constant downward motion can be hard on the knees.

Although the terrace pools aren't particularly deep, you can get fully submerged if you try. If you don't wish to get too wet, there are plenty of dry sections leading down. Going at midday means crowds and sunlight reflecting off the dazzling white surface; later afternoon is better.

rooms are not as impressive as other midrange places, but some have balcony views of the travertines, and there's a relaxing pool. It's also a very short walk to the park's north (lower) gate.

 Eating

KAYAŞ Restaurant, Bar €
(Atatürk Caddesi 3; mains ₺5-14; ☺lunch & dinner) This central place has a long bar and opposing big TV (for football matches, generally). It's probably the friendliest

spot for drinks, but it also has decent Turkish food at better prices than other places.

MUSTAFA'S International €€
(Atatürk Caddesi 22; mains ₺8-15; ☺breakfast, lunch & dinner) This streetside place doesn't have views, but does have good pizzas, wraps and salads.

MEHMET'S HEAVEN Turkish €€
(Atatürk Caddesi 25; mains ₺12-20; ☺breakfast, lunch & dinner) Mehmet's has an interior with wide cushions and a back terrace with travertine views. The Turkish fare is decent.

If You Like...
Markets

The ancient markets around Bursa's Ulu Camii are rich in Ottoman history and architecture, and are good places to pick up traditional items such as Karagöz shadow puppets and silk.

1 KAPALI ÇARŞI
(Covered Market; Kapalı Çarşı Caddesi) This sprawling market contains the 14th-century *bedesten* (warehouse), reconstructed after the 1855 earthquake.

2 ESKI AYNALI ÇARŞI
(Old Mirrored Market; Kapalı Çarşı Caddesi) Originally a hamam, the 14th-century Eski Aynalı Çarşı features a domed ceiling with skylights. Karagöz shadow puppets and other traditional items are sold here. Found in the Kapalı Çarşı.

3 KOZA HAN
(Cocoon Caravanserai; ⏰8.30am-8pm Mon-Sat, 10.30am-6pm Sun) This 15th-century market has a small courtyard mosque (1491) and expensive *ipek* (silk) shops. Bursa's ancient silk tradition remains the prime local handicraft and some villagers still cultivate silkworms; come in June or September to see them haggling over sacks of cocoons.

4 EMIR HAN
(Kapalı Çarşı Caddesi) Bursa was on the Silk Road, and camel caravans stored their precious cargo in the ground-floor rooms while drovers and merchants slept and did business upstairs. Silk purveyors still sell here.

ℹ Information

As with any small tourist town, most pensions have a favourite travel provider and disparage everyone else, so compare offers. The **tourist office** (⏰8am-7pm Mon-Sat) is by the upper Hierapolis gate.

ATMs exist; Denizli has banks.

ℹ Getting There & Away

Most Pamukkale bus services involve changing in Denizli. In summer direct buses serve Selçuk (₺27) and Kuşadası (₺30).

Buses and dolmuşes run frequently between Denizli and Pamukkale (₺5, 40 minutes). Most people choose advance hotel booking to get the free lift from Denizli (and often, back again). Taxis from Denizli centre/airport cost ₺60/85.

Regular services to/from Denizli include Ankara (₺35, seven hours), Antalya (₺25, five hours), Bodrum (₺25, 4½ hours), Bursa (₺42, nine hours), Fethiye (₺25, five hours), İstanbul (₺40 to ₺65, 12 hours), İzmir (₺21, four hours) and Nevşehir (Cappadocia, ₺40, 11 hours).

Afrodisias

Afrodisias' (admission incl museum ₺8; ⏰9am-7pm May-Sep, to 5pm Oct-Apr) relative remoteness amidst Roman poplars, green fields and warbling birds safeguards its serenity from the masses. Afrodisias outdoes Ephesus for sheer scale, and its on-site museum is more impressive. The city had several incarnations – including as capital of Roman Caria and a Byzantine Orthodox city – before being abandoned in the 12th century.

Afrodisias is largely overgrown, with many side paths passing through thickets and bramble. While this lends a certain exotic feel, it's sensible to wear long pants and good shoes. Some Afrodisian ruins are also surrounded by brackish pools of black water, and unexpected soft patches may lurk underfoot. Try to keep upwind of the occasional tractors, from which workmen spray chemicals at the weeds.

The cafe, shop, toilets and museum are inside the entrance. Take the circular site tour first, saving the (cooler) indoor museum for last. The counter-clockwise route around the site is less affected by the occasional midmorning package-tour groups.

ℹ Getting There & Away

Afrodisias is 55km southeast of Nazilli and 101km from Denizli. Tours from Pamukkale usually run ₺70 per person (depending on the operator and number of participants). Generally, a four-person minimum is required. You'll have around 2½ hours on-site. Otherwise, car rental (₺80 per day, plus ₺70 for petrol) or taxis are options for small groups.

Eğirdir

☎ 0246 / POP 19,417

Enigmatic Eğirdir, surrounded by shimmering Eğirdir Gölü (Lake Eğirdir) and ringed by steep mountains, lies hidden away from the heat and dust of Anatolia like some secret treasure. With its Byzantine fortress, unique Seljuk structures and crumbling old quarter ringed by beaches and fishing boats, the town makes an excellent base for the Lake District's sites and outdoor activities. Its family-run pensions offer inexpensive lodging and hearty, home-cooked meals.

Eğirdir stretches for several kilometres along the lake shore. Its centre is at the base of a promontory jutting into the lake, marked by an **Atatürk statue** and small otogar.

 ## Sights & Activities

HIZIR BEY CAMII
Mosque

Originally a Seljuk warehouse, this simple stone structure became a mosque in 1308.

DÜNDAR BEY MEDRESESI
Historic Building

In 1285 this grand stone structure – then a 67-year-old Seljuk caravanserai – was converted to a *medrese*. There's an onsite bazaar.

CASTLE
Ruin

A few hundred metres down the peninsula stand the massive walls of this ruined castle, which allegedly dates back to 5th-century BC Lydian King Croesus.

 ## Sleeping

Eğirdir's family-run pensions cluster around the castle ruins (close to the centre) and at the peninsula's far end, Yeşilada (1.5km north of the centre).

CHARLY'S PENSION
Pension €

(☎ 311 4611; www.charlyspension.com; Kale Mah, 4 Nolu Sokak; s/d/tr ₺35/55/65; 🛜) This family-run getaway, in a restored Ottoman-era house braced by the castle's western wall, offers cheerfully painted rooms with weathered wood floors and luminous curtains. The placid back balconies overlooking the lake are the venues for breakfast, dinner and sunbathing. A small beach lies below. Breakfast is ₺6.

MAVIGÖL HOTEL
Hotel €€

(☎ 425 1020; www.mavigolhotel.com; s/d ₺60/100; @ 🛜 ☎) If you seek swimming pools, safes and satellite TV, try Mavigöl, Eğirdir's only real hotel. Service is kind and attentive, and rooms are spotless. Billiards and table tennis add to the attractions for youngsters.

LALE PENSION
Pension, Hostel €

(☎ 311 2406; www.lalehostel.com; Kale Mahalessi 5 Sokak 2; s/d without breakfast ₺45/65; ✳ @) Near the castle, the long-established Lale consists of a quiet pension, with well-maintained modern rooms and rooftop lounge offering lake views, and a hostel. Breakfast is not included in the price, but meals can be enjoyed nearby in sister hotel Charly's Pension.

GÖL PENSION
Pension €€

(☎ 311 2370; ahmetdavras@hotmail.com; r ₺80-100; @) This family-run pension out on Yeşilada has spacious, clean and well-maintained rooms. Those on the top floor enjoy great lake views from the private terrace.

Beaches & Boat Trips

From Eğirdir's western shore by the castle, to the peninsula's tip at Yeşilada, several relaxing small **beaches** exist, some with changing cabins and food stalls. There are also beaches outside town; enquire at your pension or the Eğirdir Outdoor Center (p269), which also arranges **boat trips (per person ₺50)**. The seven-hour trip involves visiting hidden coves, swimming, sunbathing and a fresh fish lunch. Trips run from 15 June to 15 September.

Eğirdir

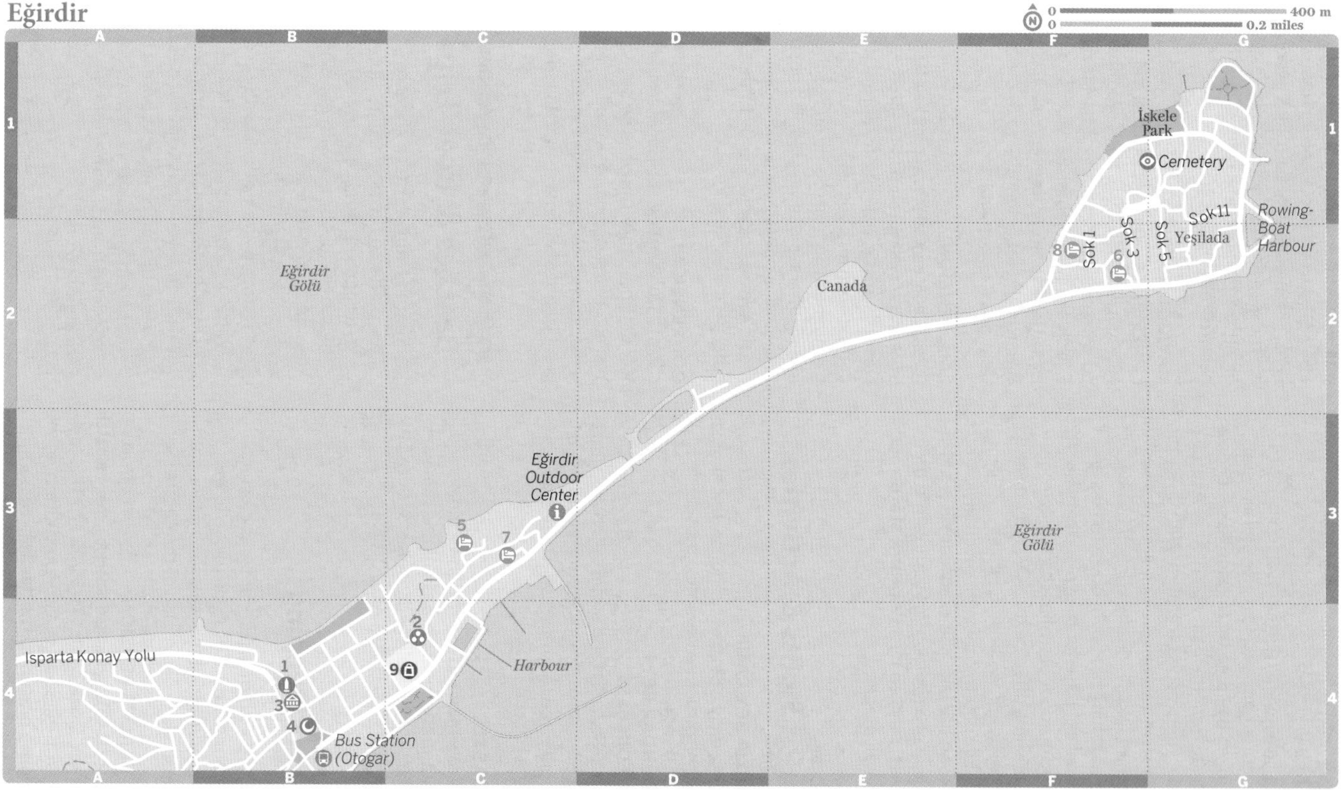
0 400 m
0 0.2 miles
A
B
C
D
E
F
G
1
2
3
4
İskele Park
Cemetery
Sok 11
Sok 1
Sok 3
Sok 5
Yeşilada
Rowing-Boat Harbour
8
6
Canada
Eğirdir Gölü
Eğirdir Outdoor Center
5
7
Eğirdir Gölü
2
9
Harbour
Isparta Konay Yolu
1
3
4
Bus Station (Otogar)

Eğirdir

🍴 Eating

Pension dinners are tasty and Yeşilada has good fish restaurants. Local specialities include *istakoz* (crayfish) and fish including the lake carp.

For caffeinated drinks, visit the Eğirdir Outdoor Center on the eastern waterfront.

EĞIRDIR MARKET　　　　　Market

Thursday market is held by the castle. On Sundays between August and October, you can buy apples, cheese and yoghurt from the Yörük Turks (p353), who descend from the mountains to hawk their wares.

ℹ Information

There are ATMs and banks in the centre.

Eğirdir Outdoor Center (📞 311 6688; www.egidiroutdoorcenter.com; Ata Yolu Üzeri) This all-in-one info centre and cafe is an excellent place for arranging local activities. It rents mountain bikes (₺5/45 per hour/day) and kayaks (₺25 per hour); and offers half-day and full-day boat trips (₺35 to ₺50), sunset cruises (₺20) and group-rate transport for day trips to locations including Sagalassos (₺180).

ℹ Getting There & Away

Eğirdir has frequent bus connections to İstanbul (₺55), Bursa, Antalya (₺30), Cappadocia (₺45), Denizli (for Pamukkale, ₺20) and İzmir (₺35). The frequency of buses is greater from Isparta, accessible by frequent minibuses (₺6, 30 minutes).

From the otogar, pensions by the castle are within walking distance, whereas Yeşilada is ₺1/10 by dolmuş/taxi. Most pension owners will retrieve you for free if you call ahead.

Sagalassos

To visit the sprawling ruins of **Sagalassos** (admission ₺5; ⏱ 7.30am-6pm), high amidst the jagged peaks of Ak Dağ (White Mountain), is to approach myth; indeed, the urban ruins set in stark mountains seem to illuminate the Sagalassian perception of a sacred harmony between nature, architecture and the great gods of antiquity.

With neither tour buses nor crowds, sometimes the visiting archaeologists or sheep wandering the mountains outnumber tourists. This is a place for feeling the raw Anatolian wind on your face, and, of course, for seeing some impressive ancient ruins. Take a few hours to linger, and take it all in from on high.

The oldest ruins date from the Hellenistic period that began when Alexander the Great conquered the city in 333 BC. Although most surviving structures are Roman, inscriptions are in Greek.

ℹ Information

Since Sagalassos sprawls upwards across steep, prickly terrain, wear sturdy shoes and long pants. Even on sunny days it's often windy, and clouds can suddenly arrive (bring an extra shirt or sweater). In summer, start early to avoid the midday sun on this exposed site.

It takes from 1½ to 3½ hours to do Sagalassos. Signage is excellent. From Monday to Thursday in summer, archaeologists will show you around.

The ticket office has informative pamphlets and sells drinks. Ağlasun (7km below) has small eateries; try the excellent pide at Tadim Pide ve Kebap Salonu (Fatih Caddesi; pides ₺5-9; ⏱ 9am-7pm).

ℹ Getting There & Away

The final 7km up to Sagalassos is on a narrow, winding road without guardrails; you may feel safer on an organised excursion.

An organised trip or shared taxi from Eğirdir costs from ₺50 to ₺80 per person. Enquire at your pension or Eğirdir Outdoor Center (p269).

Ankara

🎵 0312 / POP 4.5 MILLION

Turkey's 'other' city may not have any showy Ottoman palaces or regal facades, but the Turkish capital thrums to a vivacious, youthful beat unmarred by the tug of history. It's a dynamic and intellectual city, buzzing with student panache and foreign-embassy intrigue.

Many travellers transit Ankara; the main reason to linger is the Museum of Anatolian Civilisations. While here, spend some time in Kızılay's sidewalk cafes, frequented by hip students, bums and businessmen alike.

Sights

CITADEL   Neighbourhood
(Ankara Kalesi; Map p272; **M**Ulus) The imposing *hisar*, a well-preserved quarter of thick walls and intriguing winding streets, took its present shape in the 9th century AD, when the Byzantines constructed the outer ramparts. The inner walls date from the 7th century.

Opposite the main **Parmak Kapısı** (Finger Gate; Map p272) entry is the beautifully restored Çengelhan, housing the **Rahmi M Koç Industrial Museum** (Map p272; 🎵 309 6800; www.rmk-museum.org. tr; Depo Sokak 1; adult/child ₺6/3; ⏱10am-5pm Tue-Fri, to 6pm Sat-Sun). Inside, three floors cover subjects as diverse as transport, science, music and carpets; some displays have interactive features.

After you've entered Parmak Kapısı, and passed through a gate to your left, to your right a steep road leads to a flight of stairs to the **Şark Kulesi** (Eastern Tower; Map p272), with panoramic city views. Although harder to find, a tower to the north, **Ak Kale** (White Fort), also offers fine views.

Inside the citadel local people still live as they would in a traditional Turkish village; you'll see women beating and sorting skeins of wool.

FREE ANIT KABIR   Monument
(Atatürk Mausoleum and Museum; Map p271; Gençlik Caddesi; audio guide ₺5; ⏱9am-5pm May-Oct, to 4pm Nov-Apr; **M**Tandoğan) The monumental mausoleum of Mustafa Kemal Atatürk (1881–1938), the founder of modern Turkey, sits high above the city with its abundance of marble and air of veneration.

To the right of Atatürk's huge tomb, the extensive **museum** covers Atatürk and associated subjects such as the War of Independence.

Atatürk's lofty mausoleum is lined with marble and sparingly decorated with 15th- and 16th-century Ottoman mosaics. At the northern end stands an immense

Sagalassos ruins (p269)

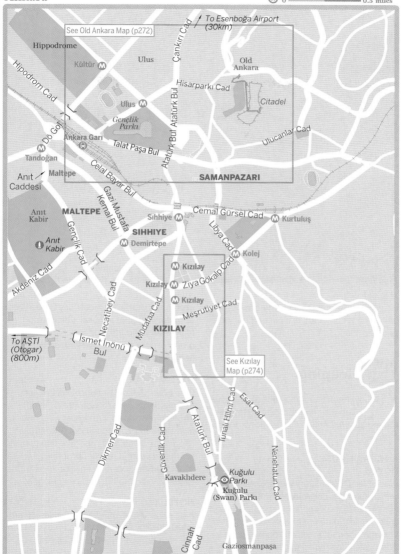

marble **cenotaph**, cut from a single piece of stone weighing 40 tonnes. The actual tomb is in a chamber beneath it.

It is virtually a pilgrimage site, so arrive early to beat the crowds; school groups frequently drop by midweek, especially in May, June and September.

The memorial straddles a hill in a park 1.2km south of Tandoğan metro station. A free shuttle zips up and down the hill from the entrance; alternatively,

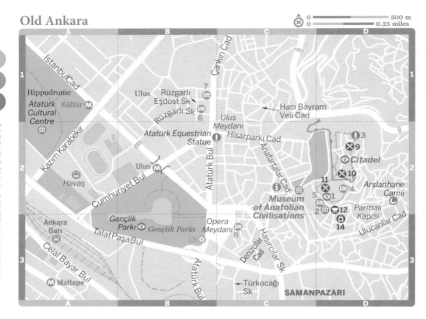

it's a 15-minute walk. Security checks, including a bag scan, are carried out on entry.

Sleeping

The following are in and around Ulus, the most convenient neighbourhood for the Museum of Anatolian Civilisations and the citadel.

ANGORA HOUSE HOTEL
Historic Hotel €€

(Map p272; ☎ 309 8380; www.angorahouse. com.tr; Kalekapısı Sokak 16; s/d/tr €50/69/75; ☎; Ⓜ Ulus) Its six spacious rooms infused with old-world atmosphere, this restored Ottoman house oozes subtle elegance. The walled courtyard garden is the perfect retreat from the citadel streets, and delightfully helpful staff add to the appeal.

DIVAN ÇUKURHAN
Historic Hotel €€€

(Map p272; ☎ 306 6400; www.divan.com.tr; Depo Sokak 3, Ankara Kalesi; s/d €130/150, ste €180-400; ☀ ☎; Ⓜ Ulus) This distinctive hotel offers a chance to soak up the historic ambience of the 16th-century Çukurhan caravanserai. Set around a dramatic glass-ceilinged interior courtyard, rooms blend ornate decadence with sassy contemporary style.

OTEL MITHAT
Hotel €

(Map p272; ☎ 311 5410; www.otelmithat.com. tr; Tavus Sokak 2; s/d/tr €25/40/50; ☀ ☎; Ⓜ Ulus) Revamped with groovy carpeting and sleek neutral bed linen, the Mithat's rooms are fresh and modern. The teensy bathrooms are a minor complaint. Unlike most budget hotels in Ankara, the Mithat takes its no-smoking policy seriously.

HOTEL TAÇ
Hotel €€

(Map p272; ☎ 324 3195; Çankırı Caddesi 35; s/d/ tr ₺70/90/110; ☀ ☎; Ⓜ Ulus) It may not look like much from outside, but the Taç is a solid midrange option. Cute floral rugs and nice art inject a bit of personality into the rooms, which have extras such as a kettle and hair dryer. Light sleepers should avoid the front rooms if possible.

HOTEL OĞULTÜRK
Hotel €€

(Map p272; ☎ 309 2900; www.ogulturk.com; Rüzgarlı Eşdost Sokak 6; s/d/tr €40/55/70;

Old Ankara

❄ 🅦; Ⓜ Ulus) The alleyway outside may be slightly seedy, but, inside, the smart Oğultürk has decent-sized rooms decked out in soft pastels and efficient, English-speaking staff.

 Eating

The following are in and around Ulus, the most convenient neighbourhood for the Museum of Anatolian Civilisations and the citadel. The southern end of Anafartalar Caddesi is the perfect hunting ground for cheap and cheerful *kebapçis* (kebap eateries).

ZENGER PAŞA KONAĞI Anatolian €€
(Map p272; ☎ 311 7070; www.zengerpasa. com; Doyran Sokak 13; mains ₺12-17; Ⓜ Ulus) Crammed with Ottoman ephemera, the Zenger Paşa at first looks like a deserted ethnographic museum, but climb up the rickety stairs and you'll find sweeping city views. Wealthy Ankaralıs love the pide (Turkish-style pizza), fine mezes and grills, cooked in the original Ottoman oven.

AND EVI CAFE Modern Turkish €€
(Map p272; ☎ 312 7978; İçkale Kapısı; mains ₺12-24; Ⓜ Ulus) This cafe, set into the citadel walls, is a winner for its cosy Ottoman-style interior and the terrace's panoramic city views. Tuck into a lunchtime crepe (₺11), sample a slice of the divine carrot

cake (₺6) with a latte, or choose one of the pasta dishes for dinner.

ÇENGELHAN Modern Turkish €€€
(Map p272; ☎ 309 6800; Depo Sokak 1; mains ₺16-30; ◷ Tue-Sun; Ⓜ Ulus) Inside an old caravanserai, the Rahmi M Koç Industrial Museum restaurant offers sleek dining in novel surroundings, with tables nestled between museum displays. Reservations are essential.

KINACIZADE KONAĞI Turkish €€
(Map p272; ☎ 324 5714; www.kinacizadekonagi. com; Kale Kapısı Sokak 28; mains ₺6-23; Ⓜ Ulus) This Ottoman house serves a range of kebaps alongside pide and *gözleme* (savoury pancakes). Eat in the shady courtyard, enclosed by picturesque timber-framed facades.

 **Drinking**

Kızılay is Ankara's cafe central, with terraces lining virtually every inch of space south of Ziya Gökalp Caddesi.

AYLAK MADAM Cafe
(☎ 419 7412; Karanfıl Sokak 2, Kızılay; ◷ 10am-late) A super-cool French bistro/cafe with a mean weekend brunch (10am to 2.30pm), plus sandwiches, cappuccinos and a jazz-fusion soundtrack.

KIRIT CAFE
Cafe

(Map p272; Koyunpazarı Sokak, Ankara Kalesi) With a ground-floor felt shop and quirky local art gracing the walls of the cafe upstairs, Kirit brews a decent coffee and the burgers, pasta and cheesecake hit the spot.

BIBAR
Bar

(Inkılap Sokak 19, Kızılay) Bibar attracts everyone from pale-faced student goths and alternative rockers to people who just want to boogie.

Entertainment

For a night out with Ankara's student population, head to Kızılay – particularly Bayındır Sokak, between Sakarya and Tuna Caddesis. The tall, thin buildings pack in multiple floors of bars, cafes and gazinos (nightclubs). Many clubs offer live Turkish pop music, and women travellers should feel OK in most.

ANKARA STATE OPERA HOUSE
Performing Arts

(Opera Sahnesi; Map p272; ☎ 324 6801; www. dobgm.gov.tr; Atatürk Bulvarı 20, Ulus) Hosts all the large productions staged by the Ankara State Opera and Ballet. The season generally runs from September to June.

Shopping

HISAR AREA
Handicrafts

(Map p272) The alleyways southwest of the Parmak Kapısı entrance to the citadel were traditionally the centre for trading Ankara's famous angora wool. Walk downhill from the dried-fruit stalls in front of the gate, and you'll come across copper-beaters and craftspeople, carpet and antique stores, small galleries and craft shops.

Information

Medical Services

Pharmacists take it in turns to open around the clock; look out for the nobetçi (open 24 hours) sign.

Bayındır Hospital (☎ 428 0808; Atatürk Bulvarı 201, Çankaya) An up-to-date private hospital.

Money

There are lots of banks with ATMs in Ulus and Kızılay.

Tourist Information

Tourist office (☎ 310 8789; Gazi Mustafa Kemal Bulvarı; ⏱ 9am-5pm Mon-Fri, 10am-5pm Sat) Staff are reasonably helpful and have lots of brochures. There are also (usually unmanned) branches at the otogar and train station.

Getting There & Away

Air

Domestic and international budget carriers serve Ankara's Esenboğa airport (p276).

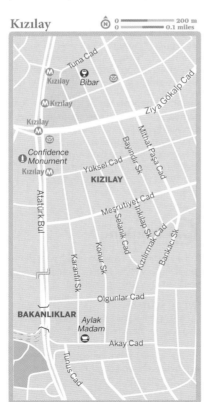

Kızılay

IZZET KERIBAR/GETTY IMAGES ©

Don't Miss **Museum of Anatolian Civilisations**

This superb museum in Ankara is the perfect introduction to the complex weave of Turkey's ancient past, housing artefacts cherry-picked from just about every significant archaeological site in Anatolia.

The museum is housed in a beautifully restored 15th-century *bedesten*. The 10-domed central marketplace houses reliefs and statues, while the surrounding hall displays exhibits from the earlier Anatolian civilisations: Palaeolithic, Neolithic, Chalcolithic, Bronze Age, Assyrian, Hittite, Phrygian, Urartian and Lydian. The downstairs sections hold classical Greek and Roman artefacts and a display on Ankara's history. Get there early to avoid the tour groups and school parties.

The exhibits are chronologically arranged in a spiral: follow it in an anticlockwise direction and visit the central room last.

NEED TO KNOW

Anadolu Medeniyetleri Müzesi; Map p272; ☎324 3160; Gözcü Sokak 2, Ulus; admission ₺15; ⊙8.30am-7pm Apr-Oct, to 5pm Nov-Mar; Ⓜ Ulus

---

Lufthansa, Pegasus Airlines and Qatar Airways offer international connections, while Anadolu Jet (www.anadolujet.com; THY Office, Atatürk Bulvarı 211) has direct flights to/from destinations including Antalya, Bodrum, İstanbul, İzmir and Van.

Bus

Every Turkish city or town of any size has direct buses to/from Ankara. The gigantic AŞTİ (Ankara Şehirlerarası Terminali İşletmesi; Mevlâna Bulvarı) otogar is at the western end of the Ankaray underground train line, 4.5km west of Kızılay. Services include İstanbul (₺40, six hours).

Apart from during public holidays, you can often turn up, buy a ticket and be on your way in less than an hour. The *emanet* (left-luggage room) charges ₺4 per item; you'll need to show your passport.

Detour:
Boğazkale, Hattuşa & Yazılıkaya

Mountainous **Hattuşa** (adult/student ₺5/free, also valid for Yazılıkaya; ☺9am-5pm) was the capital of the Hittite kingdom. At its apex this was a busy and impressive city with defensive walls over 6km in length, some of the thickest in the ancient world. Today, the site is strewn with ruined temples, forts and gates. The circuit is a hilly 5km loop; wear sturdy shoes and bring water, a hat and sunblock.

Yazılıkaya (Yazılıkaya Yolu Üzeri; admission included in Hattuşa ticket) means 'Inscribed Rock', and that's what you'll find in these two outdoor rock galleries, 3km from Hattuşa. Together they form the largest known Hittite rock sanctuary.

Touts have begun posing as 'compulsory guides' at both sites; ignore them, as this is a con. Ideally, tour the ruins early in the morning before the 21st century intrudes in the form of coaches and souvenir sellers.

Hattuşas Taxi (☏0535 389 1089; www.hattusastaxi.com) runs a full-day tour including Hattuşa and Yazılıkaya and the ruins at Alacahöyük (₺70 per person).

The best base is Boğazkale, a village 200km east of Ankara. It has some shops, a bank with an ATM and **Boğazkale Museum** (free audioguides available; ☺8am-5pm Tue-Sun), displaying Hittite artefacts including two sphinx statues.

Aşıkoğlu Hotel & Pension (☏452 2004; www.hattusas.com; Sungurlu Asfalt Caddesi; pension s/d ₺20/40, hotel s/d/tr ₺60/100/120;), 1km from the Hattuşa ticket kiosk, has simple, spick-and-span rooms, a terrace and restaurant (mains ₺5 to ₺20). The pension rooms are small and basic, but you can use the hotel facilities.

To reach Boğazkale by public transport, you'll need to go via Sungurlu. Many buses from Ankara to Sungurlu (₺12, three hours, hourly) are run by Mis Amasya (counter 23 at Ankara's otogar). Aşıkoğlu can organise taxi transfers from Sungurlu otogar (₺20) and Yozgat (convenient from Cappadocia; ₺40).

Train

Services between Ankara Train Station (Ankara Garı; Talat Paşa Bulvarı) and İstanbul have been cancelled until at least 2014.

The high-speed services to Eskişehir (economy/business class ₺25/35, 1½ hours, 10 daily) and Konya (economy/business class ₺25/35, two hours, eight daily) are comfortable, fast and efficient. Other destinations include İzmir and cities throughout eastern Anatolia.

ℹ Getting Around

To/From the Airport

Esenboğa airport (☏590 4000; www. esenbogaairport.com; Özal Bulvarı, Esenboğa) is 33km north of the city. Havaş (☏444 0487; www.havas.net; Gate B, 19 May Stadium, Kazım Karabekir Caddesi, Ulus) airport buses depart every half-hour between 2am and 10pm daily (₺10, 35 minutes). After 10pm buses leave according to flight departure times.

The same buses link the airport and the AŞTİ otogar (₺10, 60 minutes), leaving the otogar every half-hour between 1.30am and 9.30pm from in front of the passenger arrival lounge. Havaş has an information booth at the otogar.

Buses from the airport leave 25 minutes after each flight arrival. Don't pay more than ₺60 for a taxi between the airport and the city.

To/From the Otogar

The Ankaray metro line has a station at the AŞTİ otogar. Get off at Maltepe for the train station (a 10-minute walk). Change at Kızılay (to the metro line) for Ulus.

A taxi costs about ₺20 to the city centre.

Metro

Ankara's underground train network is the easiest way to get between Ulus and Kızılay and the transport terminals. Trains run from 6.15am to 11.45pm daily. A one-way fare costs ₺1.75. Tickets are available at all stations.

Taxi

Taxis are everywhere and they all have meters, with a ₺2.25 base rate. It costs about ₺10 to cross the centre; charges rise at night and the same trip will cost over ₺15.

Safranbolu

☑ 0370 / POP 41,954

Turkey's most thoroughly preserved Ottoman town is so gloriously dinky, it's as if it slid off the lid of a chocolate box. Safranbolu's Çarşı (old town) is a vision of red-tiled roofs and meandering alleys full of candy stores and cobblers. People flock here to recapture the heady scent of yesteryear within the muddle of timber-framed mansions now converted into quirky boutique hotels – all creaky wooden floors, exuberantly carved ceilings and traditional cupboard-bathrooms. A day at the hamam, browsing the market, and revelling in the cobblestone quaintness is about as strenuous as it gets.

Sights

FREE OTTOMAN HOUSES   Architecture
Virtually every house in Çarşı is an original, and what little modern development there is has been held in check. Many of the finest historic houses have been restored, and many more are being saved from deterioration and turned into hotels, shops or museums.

You can tour the Ottoman addresses of note, **Kaymakamlar Müze Evi** (Hıdırlık Yokuşu Sokak; admission ₺3; ☺9am-6pm) and **Kileciler Evi** (Manifaturacılar Sokak; adult/student ₺2/1; ☺9am-6pm), which are filled with period pieces and tableaux.

CINCI HANI   Architecture
(Eski Çarşı Çeşme Mahalessi; admission ₺1)
Çarşı's most famous and imposing structure is this brooding 17th-century caravanserai that's now a hotel. On Saturdays a market takes place in the square behind it.

Safranbolu

SALVATOR BARKI/GETTY IMAGES ©

 Sleeping

Safranbolu is popular with Turkish tourists during weekends and holidays. Prices may rise at particularly busy times, and it can be worth booking ahead.

GÜL EVI Historic Hotel €€€

(☎ 725 4645; www.canbulat.com.tr; Hükümet Sokak 46; s €75-90, d €100-120, ste €135-180; 🛜) Safranbolu's most striking reinterpretation of the Ottoman aesthetic, 'Rose House' is an affordable masterpiece where urban luxury mingles seamlessly with traditional Ottoman design. The rooms (spread over three houses) are all soft colours, gorgeous wood panelling and Turkman carpets. There's a tiny underground cave bar and private restaurant.

EFE BACKPACKERS PENSION Pension €

(☎ 725 2688; www.backpackerspension.com; Kayadibi Sokak 8; s/d/tr ₺45/70/80; 🛜) This hostel-cum-pension dishes up Ottoman charm, and stunning views from its terrace, at a smidgen of the cost of other accommodation. Being on a budget doesn't mean scrimping on quality, cleanliness or friendly efficiency, and the snug rooms mix local character with sparkly new bathrooms. Extras include free otogar transfers, dinners (₺10) and tours.

KAHVECILER KONAĞI Historic Hotel €€

(☎ 725 5453; www.kahvecilerkonagi.com; Mescit Sokak 7; s/d ₺60/120; 🛜) Kahveciler's large, minimalist-decorated rooms have whitewashed walls, glorious wood-panel ceilings and lovely views of red-tiled

Safranbolu – Çarşı

roofs. As a bonus for those less agile, the bathrooms are relatively big and require no climbing into cupboards.

SELVILI KÖŞK Historic Hotel €€
(☑712 8646; www.selvilikosk.com; Mescit Sokak 23; s/d/tr ₺100/160/200; 🛜) From the engraved banisters to the carved ceilings, this wonderful restoration job is a regal-feeling, romantic retreat. One of the most authentically Ottoman places in town.

BASTONCU PANSIYON Pension €€
(☑712 3411; www.bastoncupension.com; Hıdırlık Yokuşu Sokak; s/d/tr ₺60/90/120; 🛜) In a 300-year-old building, Bastoncu has a superb higgledy-piggledy feel. The friendly owners speak English and Japanese and appreciate travellers' needs.

Eating

TAŞEV Modern Turkish €€
(☑712 0680; www.tasevsanatvesarapevi.com; Hıdırlık Yokuşu Sokak 14; mains ₺11-23) This bonafide contemporary dining option delivers on thick steaks and creamy pasta dishes. Service is more aloof than elsewhere in town, but the wall art, multi-purpose exhibition space and extensive wine menu are alluring nonetheless.

ÇIZGI CAFE Anatolian €€
(Arasta Arkası Sokak; mains ₺7-15) Eat on the cushioned benches outside, or in one of the cosily intimate cubby-hole dining areas. Çızgi is an easygoing place where lo-

cal dishes such as *cevizli yayım* (macaroni topped with walnuts) and *mantı* (Turkish ravioli) are on the small menu, along with coffee and nargile (water pipe).

BIZIM CAFE Anatolian €
(Çeşme Mahallesi; mains ₺5-8) Deep in the old shopping district is this welcoming little family-run restaurant that serves whatever's on the stove. Locals love it.

KADIOĞLU ŞEHZADE
SOFRASI Turkish €
(☑712 5657; Arasta Sokak 8; mains ₺11-23; ⊙11.30am-10.30pm) It's all traditional Ottoman-style seating at this converted mansion restaurant. The huge, steaming-hot pide, *çorba*, grills and *zerde* (saffron dessert) are all great. The rooms are tacky but pretty large and service is swift.

HANIM SULTAN Anatolian €
(mains ₺5-10) Squirrelled away down a little alleyway, this place rustles up rustic, wholesome cooking. Try the divine pot of *etlı dolma* (vine leaves stuffed with meat) for a hearty, delicious lunch.

Drinking

SADE KAHVE Cafe
(Manifaturacılar Caddesi 17; coffee ₺4-6, desserts ₺4-8) Opposite a slew of tinkerers and metalbenders, this is a fabulous little find run by coffee fanatics who make a mean brew, Turkish or otherwise, and the most delicious waffles in town.

TÜRKÜ CAFE
Bar

(Musalla Mahallesi Han Arkası Sokak 16) On Safranbolu's equivalent of a bar strip, this friendly place is run by a cool mother-and-daughter team who pour ice-cold Efes with smiley efficiency. Also hosts regular live music.

Shopping

Safranbolu is a great place to pick up handicrafts, especially textiles, metalwork, shoes and wooden artefacts.

YEMENICILER ARASTASI
Market

(Peasant Shoe-Maker's Bazaar; Arasta Arkası Sokak) This restored *arasta* (row of shops by a mosque) is the best place to start looking for crafts. You may also see shops on nearby streets occupied by authentic working saddle-makers, felt-makers and other artisans.

Information

Çarşı has a bank, with an ATM, on Kazdağlıoğulu Meydanı.

Tourist office (712 3863; www.safranbolu.gov.tr; Kazdağlıoğulu Meydanı; 9am-5.30pm) Informed, multilingual staff can provide loads of tips and advice.

Getting There & Around

Most buses stop in Karabük first and then finish at Kıranköy otogar (upper Safranbolu), from where minibuses or a *servis* (shuttle bus) can deposit you in central Kıranköy, near the dolmuş stand for Çarşı. Dolmuşes/taxis between Kıranköy and Çarşı cost about ₺1.50/10.

There are several bus company offices along Sadrı Artunç Caddesi and just off Adnan Menderes Caddesi in Kıranköy, where you can buy tickets to destinations including Amasra (₺15, two hours), Ankara (₺25, three hours) and İstanbul (₺40, seven hours).

Amasya

0358 / POP 90,665

Amasya is a tale of two shores. On the north of the Yeşilırmak River, rows of half-timbered Ottoman houses sit squeezed together like chocolate cakes in a patisserie window. To the south, modern Turkey tries to get on with things in this narrow, rocky valley. Towering above the minarets and the *medreses* are pockmarks of Pontic tombs, etched into the high-rise bluff and guarded by a lofty citadel. Amasya's setting may evoke high drama, but life here unfolds as slowly as the train takes apples out of town via a mountain tunnel. In local folklore, these tunnels were dug by Ferhat, a star-crossed lover who was tragically in love with Sirin, the sister of a sultan queen.

The Kingdom of Pontus once dominated a large part of Anatolia from Amasya. It later prospered under the Romans and during the Ottoman era, when it became a centre of Islamic study.

Sights

TOMBS OF THE PONTIC KINGS
Tombs

(Kral Kaya Mezarları; admission ₺3; 8.30am-6.30pm May-Oct, to 4.45pm Nov-Apr) Looming above the northern bank of the river is a sheer rock face with the conspicuous cut-rock Tombs of the Pontic Kings. The tombs, cut deep into the limestone as early as the 4th century BC, were used for cult worship of the deified rulers.

The tombs have good panoramas of Amasya. The ticket office is near Harşena Otel.

HATUNIYE MAHALLESI
Historic Neighbourhood

The Hatuniye Mahallesi is Amasya's wonderful neighbourhood of restored Ottoman houses, interspersed with good modern reproductions to make a harmonious whole.

The **Hazeranlar Konağı** (Hazeranlar Sokak; admission ₺3; 8.30am-noon & 1pm-4.45pm Tue-Sun), constructed in 1865 and restored in 1979, has restored rooms beautifully furnished in period style.

FREE HARŞENA CASTLE
Citadel

(Kale) Perched precariously atop rocky Mt Harşena, the *kale* offers magnificent views down the valley. The remnants of the walls date from Pontic times.

Amasya

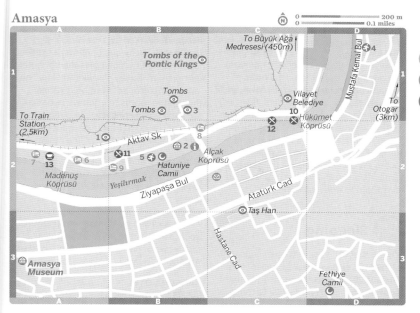

Amasya

⦿ Top Sights
Amasya Museum.....................................A3
Tombs of the Pontic Kings...................B1

⦿ Sights
1 Hatuniye Mahallesi..............................A2
2 Hazeranlar Konağı...............................B2
3 Tombs Ticket Office.............................B1

✪ Activities, Courses & Tours
4 Mustafa Bey Hamamı............................D1
5 Yıldız Hamamı.......................................B2

⦿ Sleeping
6 Emin Efendi Konağı..............................A2
7 Gönül Sefası..A2
8 Harşena Otel...B2
9 Şükrübey Konağı...................................B2

⊗ Eating
10 Amasya Şehir Derneği.........................C1
11 Eylül Buğusa Avlu................................B2
12 Strabon Restaurant.............................C2

⦿ Drinking
13 Seyran Cafe..A2

Travellers of either sex are advised not to go up unaccompanied later in the day. To reach the castle, turn left when you get to the Büyük Ağa Medresesi and follow the road for about 1km to a street on the left marked 'Kale'. It's 1.7km up the mountainside to a car park, then another steep 15-minute climb to the summit.

AMASYA MUSEUM Museum
(☑218 4513; Atatürk Caddesi; admission ₺3; ⊗8.15am-noon & 1-4.45pm) The 1st floor of this superb museum packs in beautifully laid out exhibits detailing Amasya and the surrounding area during the Bronze Age, Hittite, Pontic and Roman eras. Upstairs the extensive collection continues into later periods.

Housed in a separate room is a unique collection of mummies dating from the 14th-century İlkhan period. Be warned that none of it is suitable for squeamish or young eyes.

281

Activities

HAMAMS   Hamams

Amasya has several venerable hamams that are still in operation. The **Yıldız Hamamı** (Star Hamam; Hazeranlar Sokak; wash & massage ₺13) was built by the Seljuks in the 13th century and restored in the 16th century. On the southern side of the river is the Ottoman **Mustafa Bey Hamamı** (Mustafa Kemal Bulvarı; wash & massage ₺12), built in 1436. Both are open from about 6am to 10am and 4pm to 11pm for men; from 10am to 4pm for women.

Sleeping

GÖNÜL SEFASI   Guest House €€

(☏ 212 9461; Yalıboyu Sokak 24; s/d/tr ₺60/100/120) Antique farming equipment decorates the courtyard while Ottoman curios swing from every nook in the little restaurant, adding lots of local character to this family-run hotel. Upstairs the four large rooms are kept elegantly simple with comfy beds and modern bathrooms.

EMIN EFENDI KONAĞI   Historic Hotel €€

(☏ 213 0033; www.eminefendikonaklari.com; Hazeranlar Sokak 66-85; s/d ₺80/130; ❄ 🛜) Brought to life by one of Amasya's oldest families, the Emin Efendi is the hot hotel for northern Turkey's weekend elite. The lobby is a picture of stately elegance, though the rooms (eight have river views) are a mixed bag of classic and modern styling. The courtyard restaurant (mains ₺9 to ₺19) is the place for fine dining.

ŞÜKRÜBEY KONAĞI   Guest House €€

(☏ 212 6285; www.sukrubeykonagi.com.tr; Hazeranlar Sokak 55; s/d ₺60/120) A sweet family choice with simple, cosy rooms set around a courtyard, and a genuinely warm and welcoming atmosphere. Rooms lead out to narrow balconies with views of either the courtyard or the Yeşilırmak River.

HARŞENA OTEL   Historic Hotel €€

(☏ 218 3979; www.harsenaotel.com; Hatuniye Mahallesi; new house s/d/tr ₺95/160/180, old house s/d ₺180/220; ❄) Well-maintained and comfortable though the old house, backing onto the Yeşilırmak River, is the real star.

View of Amasya (p280)

Eating & Drinking

Amasya's best eating is found in its hotels but there are a few reasonable cafes and restaurants in Hatuniye Mahallesi and a smattering of more basic options around town.

STRABON RESTAURANT
Modern Turkish €€

(212 4012; Teyfik Havız Sokak; mains ₺7-16) Our favourite riverside deck in Amasya. The hot or cold mezes (₺5 to ₺9) are tasty and fresh; the meat grills and grilled *balık* (fish) are low on oil and literally fall off big serving plates. Also a fun venue for drinking booze.

AMASYA ŞEHIR DERNEĞI
Turkish €€

(Teyfik Havız Sokak; mains ₺8-16) Beloved by a suited-and-booted clientele, this popular restaurant has three tiers to choose from and a menu of typical Turkish grills.The balcony is the place to be, especially in the evening when the river views provide a respite from the live music 'entertainment' inside.

EYLÜL BUĞUSA AVLU
Turkish €€

(Hazeranlar Sokak; mains ₺8-15) It may have no view, but this shaded courtyard is a pleasant spot for a meal or a couple of beers. The menu sticks to Turkish staples and the soundtrack is a blast-from-the-past of '80s hits.

SEYRAN CAFE
Nargile Cafe

(Hazeranlar Sokak) The coveted seating is on the tiny balcony of this mellow cafe.

Information

Tourist office (Alçak Köprüsü)

Getting There & Away

The otogar (Atatürk Caddesi) has daily services to locations including Ankara (₺30, five hours), İstanbul (₺50, 11 hours) and Nevşehir (for Cappadocia, ₺50, nine hours).

Eastern Anatolia

Turkey's sparsely populated eastern reaches are its great, mostly undiscovered secret.
From the northeastern steppe and mountains, filmic backdrops for ruins such as Sumela Monastery, to the minarets above southeastern cities, experiences pile up like *lokum* (Turkish delight) in a bazaar.

With six neighbouring countries, it's a culturally diverse region, predominantly Kurdish in the southeast, with small Arabic and Christian pockets and, around the Black Sea and Kaçkar Mountains (Kaçkar Dağları), Laz and Hemşin people. Indeed, the wind-whipped ruins are poignant reminders that this has long been the case: Ani was the stately Armenian capital, a Commagene king built his burial mound atop Nemrut Dağı (Mt Nemrut), and the Urartians flourished near present-day Van.

For some serious history, one sight far predates even Mardin's atmospheric Mesopotamian lanes. Göbekli Tepe's Neolithic megaliths, constructed around 9500 BC, may be the world's first place of worship.

View of Mt Ararat (p314)

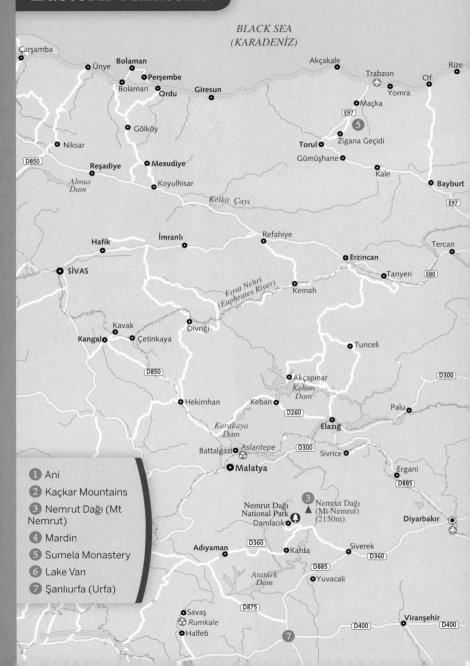

Eastern Anatolia

N 0 — 100 km
0 — 60 miles

*BLACK SEA
(KARADENİZ)*

Çarşamba

Ünye
Bolaman
Perşembe
Bolaman
Ordu
Giresun

Akçakale
Trabzon
Rize
Of
Yomra
Maçka
E97
5

Gölköy

Niksar
Torul
Zigana Geçidi
Gümüşhane
Kale
Bayburt

D850
Reşadiye
Mesudiye
*Almus
Dam*
Koyulhisar
Kelkit Çayı
E97

Hafik
İmranlı
Refahiye
Tercan
SİVAS
Erzincan
Tanyeri
E80
*Fırat Nehri
(Euphrates River)*
Kemah

Kavak
Divriği
Tunceli
Kangal
Çetinkaya
D850
D300

Akçapınar
*Keban
Dam*
Hekimhan
Keban
Palu
D260
*Karakaya
Dam*
Elazığ
Battalgazi
Aslantepe
D300
Sivrice
Malatya
Ergani
D885

1 Ani
2 Kaçkar Mountains
3 Nemrut Dağı (Mt Nemrut)
4 Mardin
5 Sumela Monastery
6 Lake Van
7 Şanlıurfa (Urfa)

Nemrut Dağı
National Park
3
Nemrut Dağı
(Mt Nemrut)
(2150m)
Damlacık
Diyarbakır

Adıyaman
D360
Kahta
Siverek
D360
*Atatürk
Dam*
D885
Yuvacali

Savaş
Rumkale
Halfeti
D875
Viranşehir
D400
7
D400

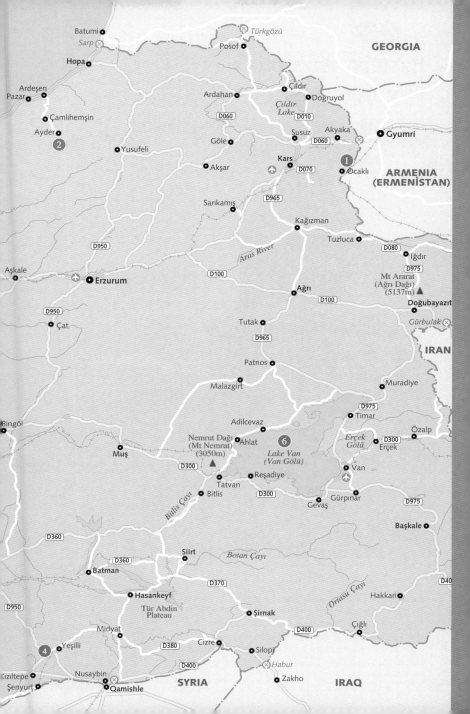

Eastern Anatolia's Highlights

1

Ani

A romantic scatter of ruins overlooking the Armenian border in a remote corner of the steppe, Ani (p308) was once a great capital and Silk Road hub. The city changed hands numerous times, as evinced by relics such as the restored Seljuk Palace and Armenian Church of the Redeemer. Above: Church of St Gregory; Top & Bottom Right: Ani's Cathedral

Need to Know

TOP TIP Visiting from Kars, tell your taxi driver you want 2½ to three hours at Ani. **ROCK-CUT HOUSES** Spot them in the river cliffs. **For further coverage, see p308**

Ani Don't Miss List

BY CELIL ERSOĞLU, GUIDE

1 CHURCH OF ST GREGORY

When this Gregorian church was built, Ani was an important Silk Road business centre, with over 100,000 inhabitants and no land available, so they built it on the valley slopes. It was built in 1215 by Tigran Honentz, one of Ani's wealthy merchants and self-styled 'barons'. The Georgians used it as a customs office and in 1255 the Seljuks gave it to the Armenians, who added the narthex and baptism room. The interior and facade were covered in frescoes, which remain some of the region's best preserved. Look out for the animal carvings.

2 CONVENT OF THE VIRGINS

Tigran Honentz also built this chapel, which is the next church you see perching dramatically above the Arpa Çay gorge. Nearby is a ruined Silk Road bridge; both are off limits but you get good views from the Menüçer Camii.

3 CATHEDRAL

Byzantine Orthodox missionaries built the imposing cathedral, Ani's largest building and a world-famous structure, for the Armenians. Begun in 989, it is the work of the celebrated medieval architect Trdat, who restored the dome of İstanbul's Aya Sofya. When the Seljuks took Ani in 1064, they converted and renamed the building Fethiye Camii (Victory Mosque), before building Menüçer Camii and returning the cathedral to the Armenians.

4 MENÜÇER CAMII

This is Anatolia's earliest Turkish mosque, built by the Seljuk Turks between 1064 and 1072. A dedication to Allah is inscribed in Koranic script on the octagonal minaret, and geometric, mythological and shamanistic symbols are carved in different coloured stones. It was built on the edge of the ravine, because the city was full of buildings.

5 İÇ KALE

At the southern end of Ani the ground rises to form this flat-topped hill, known as the 'Inner Fortress'. Behind it is the small church Kız Kalesi (Maiden's Castle). You have to look from a distance: the area is a forbidden military zone.

Kaçkar Mountains

Easily explored from Yusufeli or Ayder, the Kaçkars (p302) remain one of Turkey's less-visited gems. As well as fresh mountain air and numerous activities, the bucolic area offers cultural experiences including Hemşin cuisine, Georgian ruins, Ottoman humpback bridges and a taste of village life. Below: Rafting on the Çoruh River (p303); Top Right: Men in Yusufeli (p305); Bottom Right: Hiking in the Kaçkar Mountains (p302)

Need to Know

TOP TIP Many pensions close from October to April; book ahead in summer. **MONEY** Çamlıhemşin has the only ATM in the northern Kaçkars. **For further coverage, see p302**

Kaçkar Mountains Don't Miss List

BY NECMETTIN COŞKUN, RAFTING GUIDE

1 WHITE-WATER RAFTING

You can raft two 20km, three-hour stretches of the world-famous Çoruh River. Paddling down the river from Çamkertan to Yusufeli, you see two villages and castles, and it is suitable for beginners (level II to IV, depending on the volume of the river). The section from Yusufeli to İnanlı village is recommended for people who want some adrenaline: the High Tension, King Kong and Rock House rapids are very difficult and popular (level III to V). Alternatively, the 18km, two-hour section down the Barhal River from Sarıgöl Bridge to Yusufeli is very fast and technical (level III to IV) and takes you past two castles.

2 DÖRTKILISE

A great day walk from Yusufeli is the 14km to Dörtkilise (Four Churches), a picturesque ruined 9th-century Georgian monastery complex on a hillside. After 7km you reach Tekkale, where you can see village life and old wooden houses. Tekkale Castle, a ruined 10th-century Georgian castle, is on the right just before the village.

3 WALKING IN THE YAYLALAR

There are many day treks in the beautiful *yaylalar* (mountain pastures; see p302). In the southern Kaçkars, the ascent from Olgunlar to Dilber Düzü (Mt Kaçkar base camp) is popular. It's easy to find the correct route: you follow the stream coming down from Mt Kaçkar.

4 GEORGIAN VALLEYS

The area around Yusufeli was part of the medieval kingdom of Georgia and you can see many ruins on a day trip by car. In the hill village of İşhan, 34km east of Yusufeli, the 7th-century Church of the Mother of God has fine external reliefs and traces of blue frescoes. In Öşkvank village, off the Erzurum road south of Tortum Gölü (Tortum Lake), is an impressive late-10th-century cathedral – one of the region's grandest. The 10th-century church in Barhal (Altıparmak), the village at 1300m in the southern Kaçkars, is now used as a mosque.

Nemrut Dağı (Mt Nemrut)

Nemrut Dağı (p315) is one of Turkey's classic images: decapitated stone heads, toppled from statues erected by a less-than-modest pre-Roman king as part of his burial mound, atop a 2150m peak. Linger in the rugged surrounding park and you'll discover other ruins such as Karakuş Tümülüs, with eagle- and lion-topped columns, and Eski Kale, the ancient Commagene capital of Arsameia.

3

Mardin

4

Visit this magical southeastern outpost (p316) before the Turkish government (which plans to elevate Mardin to the same status as Ephesus) achieves its goal of attracting five million annual visitors here. Overlooking the Mesopotamian plains, stone houses cascade down the hillside, and donkeys remain a main form of transport in the bazaar. An ancient melting pot of Kurdish, Yezidi, Christian and Syrian cultures, there's simply nowhere else like Mardin. Minaret in Mardin

NEJDETDUZEN/GETTY IMAGES ©

Sumela Monastery

5

This striking Greek Orthodox monastery (p301), abandoned in 1923, nestles against the cliffs above a wooded valley. The external views of its improbable location are show-stealers, but there's also plenty to see inside the complex. The main chapel, cut into the rock, is the indisputable highlight, covered both inside and outside with colourful frescoes. The earliest examples date from the 9th century; most are 19th-century work.

6

Lake Van

This 3750-sq-km lake (p319), surrounded by stark Anatolian peaks, is lent further drama by Akdamar Island. King Gagik Artzruni built a palace, church and monastery on the island in AD 921, and the remaining church is one of the marvels of Armenian architecture, with masterful relief carvings. Near the lake's eastern shore, the city of Van makes a pleasant base with nightspots and a craggy ruined castle. Akdamar Kilisesi (p319) overlooking Lake Van

7

Şanlıurfa (Urfa)

This spiritual city (p309) was the setting for Abraham's (İbrahim) legendary brush with the Assyrian king Nimrod, in which God saved the great Islamic prophet from a funeral pyre. Indeed, the picturesque Gölbaşı area, with its rose garden and sacred carp ponds, is a symbolic recreation of this story. More history has been added to the pilgrimage town by the excavation of the Neolithic stone circle, Göbekli Tepe. 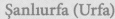 Dergah complex of mosques (p311)

Eastern Anatolia's Best...

Scenery

◦ **Kaçkar Mountains** (p302) Jagged peaks rising over 3000m, studded with alpine lakes and *yaylalar* (mountain pastures).

◦ **Doğubayazıt** (p314) Turkey's highest peak, Mt Ararat (5137m), towers above the surrounding steppe.

◦ **Lake Van** (p319) A blue sweep across mountainous southeastern Anatolia.

◦ **Nemrut Dağı** (p315) Ruin-dotted Mt Nemrut (2150m) surveys the Anti-Taurus Range.

◦ **Kars** (p306) Surrounded by expansive steppe and broad horizons.

Romantic Outposts

◦ **Mardin** (p316) Meandering lanes overlooking the hazy southern plains.

◦ **İshak Paşa Palace** (p314) Doğubayazıt's stunning palace gazes at Mt Ararat from its rocky perch.

◦ **Akdamar Kilisesi** (p319) The 10th-century Armenian church on an island in Lake Van.

◦ **Ani** (p308) Ruined city on the old Silk Road.

◦ **Sumela Monastery** (p301) Built into a cliff overlooking a misty mountain valley.

Mosques

◦ **Rızvaniye Vakfı Camii & Medresesi** (p311) Its arcaded wall overlooks Şanlıurfa's sacred pool, Balıklı Göl.

◦ **Ulu Camii** (p317) Mardin's 12th-century Iraqi Seljuk structure; minaret adorned with reliefs.

◦ **Menüçer Camii** (p289) First mosque built by Seljuk Turks in Anatolia (1072); Ani views from atop its octagonal minaret.

◦ **Mevlid-i Halil Camii** (p311) Ottoman mosque alongside a colonnaded courtyard in Dergah, Şanlıurfa.

Need to Know

Çay Stops

○ **Antik Sur** (p318)
Teahouses fill Mardin's restored caravanserai, where you can try local Assyrian wine.

○ **Kahvaltı Sokak** (p323)
Linger over a morning çay on Van's 'Breakfast Street'.

○ **Gümrük Hanı** (p311)
Backgammon and super-strong coffee, in a restored caravanserai in Şanlıurfa bazaar.

○ **Koza Caffe** (p299)
Meet Trabzon's students in Cocoon Cafe's funky medieval-style interior.

RESOURCES

○ **Kaçkar Mountains Trails** (http://cultureroutesinturkey.com/c/kackar-mountains-trails)

○ **Turku Tour** (www.turkutour.com)

○ **Economy Car Rentals** (www.economycarrentals.com)

○ **Harran-Nemrut Tours** (www.aslankonukevi.com)

○ **Nomad Tours Turkey** (www.nomadtoursturkey.com)

○ **Alkan Tours** (www.easternturkeytour.org)

GETTING AROUND

○ **Air** Flying from western Turkey recommended. Trabzon, Kars, Şanlıurfa, Mardin and Van connected to İstanbul and Ankara.

○ **Boat** Daily ferries cross Lake Van (Tatvan–Van; ₺10, four hours).

○ **Bus** A good way to cover the long distances between the major towns.

○ **Car** Great for localised travel. Hire in Trabzon, Şanlıurfa and Van.

○ **Dolmuş** Useful in rural areas like the Kaçkars.

○ **Tour** An easy way to visit remote sights.

BE FOREWARNED

○ **Kurds** Turkish–Kurdish relations are sensitive; most of the country's Kurds live in southeastern Anatolia.

○ **Islam** Eastern Anatolia is more pious than western Turkey, but non-Muslims are definitely welcome.

○ **Dress** Modest outfits recommended, especially when visiting mosques and pilgrimage places such as Dergah and Şanlıurfa.

○ **Bars** In pious cities, they often attract the local ne'er-do-wells.

○ **Distances** This is a vast area; focus on seeing one or two regions in depth.

○ **Car** Stick with major hire companies; many smaller companies don't provide insurance.

○ **Garages** Can be scarce; for Mt Nemrut, ensure you have fuel for 250km of normal driving (you have to drive in low gear).

○ **Accommodation** Expensive and in high demand in Mardin, Van and Trabzon.

○ **Şanlıurfa** Be careful what you eat, especially in summer, when the heat makes food poisoning more likely.

Left: İshak Paşa Palace (p314), Doğubayazıt;
Above: Mardin (p316)

Eastern Anatolia Itineraries

With exotic cities and ruins, mountain ranges and windblown steppe, eastern Anatolia is completely different from western Turkey. Don't try to see it all, but plan a doable route, and you will have a rewarding trip.

5 DAYS

SUMELA MONASTERY TO ANI
Mountains & Steppe

This tour of northeastern Anatolia's lyrical ruins and landscape begins at the Byzantine **(1) Sumela Monastery**, which clings to a cliff face above a forested valley. Approach on foot and appreciate the external views. Base yourself in nearby **(2) Trabzon**, which shows the Black Sea region's contemporary side on its buzzing main square and winding bazaar streets.

Next, just a few hours' journey along the coast are the **(3) Kaçkar Mountains**, a bucolic area of *yaylalar* and snowy peaks. White-water rafters may prefer Yusufeli, but twee Ayder arguably has more accessible alpine scenery. With your own car, drive up the Fırtına Valley, with its castle and Ottoman humpback bridges.

Next, continue east to **(4) Kars**, the disctinctive city where the Turkish Nobel laureate Orhan Pamuk set his novel *Kar (Snow)*. A castle overlooks the surprising rows of Russian belle époque mansions and Baltic architecture, built during the Russian occupation (1878–1920).

Finally, head across the steppe to one of Turkey's most romantic ruins, **(5) Ani**. This rubble-strewn field, dotted with circular churches, was a capital of both the Urartian and Armenian kingdoms.

Eastern Delights

Pilgrimage town **(1) Şanlıurfa (Urfa)** is a gateway to the Middle East, with calls to prayer resounding around its holy Gölbaşı area and Dergah mosque complex. The Ottoman bazaar and courtyards of gents playing backgammon are a fitting introduction to mystical southeastern Anatolia.

From Urfa, head 11km northeast to **(2) Göbekli Tepe**. The circular array of Neolithic megaliths has carvings of lions, foxes and vultures. Next, head to the Anti-Taurus Range, and the burial mound left by a hubristic Commagene king atop **(3) Nemrut Dağı (Mt Nemrut)**, its summit covered with stone statuary.

Unwind on the Mesopotamian plains, where honey-coloured **(4) Mardin** is a gorgeous heritage city with minarets rising from its lanes. Drift between mosques and museums, absorb the view from çay gardens and try local Assyrian wine.

Next, head northeast to mountain-ringed Lake Van, where motorboats buzz out to the 10th-century Armenian church on **(5) Akdamar Island**. Finish in **(6) Van**, a vibrant city with a whole street dedicated to Turkish breakfasts, and an excellent base for further lakeside adventures.

Bazaar area of Trabzon (p298)
DBIMAGES/ALAMY ©

Discover Eastern Anatolia

Yusufeli (p305)
IMAGEBROKER/ALAMY ©

BLACK SEA COAST

Trabzon
☎0462 / POP 239,700

The Black Sea coast's largest and arguably most sophisticated city, Trabzon mixes cosmopolitan buzz with, around the harbour, seedy port-town character. Local life is at its most vivid on Atatürk Alanı, the crazily busy main square in the eastern part of the city centre. Beeping dolmuşes (minibuses) hurtle around, events bring live music and dance performances to the square every summer weekend, and local students team headscarves with the Trabzonspor strip (the idolised local soccer team).

 Sights & Activities

Trabzon's main interest is as a base for visiting Sumela Monastery, but if you have some spare time here, or you are driving west from Trabzon, visit the **Aya Sofya Museum** (Aya Sofya Müzesi; ☎223 3043; www.trabzon muzesi.gov.tr; Aya Sofya Sokak; admission ₺5; ⊙9am-7pm Jun-Aug, 9am-6pm Apr-May & Sep-Oct, 8am-5pm Nov-Mar). Built in the late Byzantine period, between 1238 and 1263, the church has clearly been influenced by Georgian and Seljuk design. It is signposted uphill from the coastal highway, 4km west of the centre.

 Tours

EYCE TOURS Tour
(☎326 7174; www.eycetours.com; Taksim İşhanı Sokak 11) Day trips to Sumela (adult/student ₺25/20, 10am to 3pm) daily, and

Ayder (₺40, minimum five people) three days a week.

 **Sleeping**

OTEL HORON
Hotel €€

(☎ 326 6455; www.hotelhoron.com; Sıramağazalar Caddesi 125; s/d ₺90/140; ❄️🛜) A good central position and attractively decorated rooms with some of Trabzon's best showers and well-stocked minibars. The 5th-floor restaurant has city views.

NOVOTEL
Luxury Hotel €€€

(☎ 455 9000; www.novotel.com; Devlet Karayolu Caddesi 17, Yomra; r €125; ❄️@🛜🏊) Around 10km east of Trabzon, on the western side of Yomra, the Novotel has seafront vistas and four-star luxuries, including a sauna, fitness centre, private beach, landscaped gardens and air-conditioned bar-restaurant (mains ₺20). A taxi to Trabzon costs ₺35 to ₺40. Shuttles run to (but not from) Trabzon airport and the Forum mall.

HOTEL CAN
Hotel €

(☎ 326 8281; Güzelhisar Caddesi 2; s/d ₺30/50; ❄️🛜) There isn't much difference between the tall, thin 'Hotel Soul' and some of its more expensive neighbours. The friendly staff make this Trabzon's top budget choice.

ELIF OTEL
Business Hotel €€

(☎ 326 6616; Güzelhisar Caddesi 8; s/d ₺50/80; P🛜) Beyond its unimpressive reception, the friendly Elif's rooms are a good deal, with smart bathrooms and lumpy white duvets.

OTEL URAL
Business Hotel €€

(☎ 321 1414; Güzelhisar Caddesi 1; s/d ₺50/80; P❄️@🛜) With warm, chocolate-brown decor, flat-screen TVs and flash bathrooms, the Ural's spacious, spotless rooms raise the bar for Trabzon's hotel alley.

HOTEL NUR
Hotel €€

(☎ 323 0445; www.nurhotel.net; Cami Sokak 15; s/d ₺70/110; P❄️🛜) A long-standing travellers' favourite, with a lounge, travel agency and English-speaking staff. The nearby mosque doesn't skimp on the 5am call to prayer.

 Eating

Scores of eateries line Atatürk Alanı and the two streets running west. Uzun Sokak is great for sweet treats.

KALENDAR
Cafe, Turkish €

(Zeytinlik Caddesi; mains ₺8, salads ₺5; ⏱8.30am-9pm) Low tables and mood lighting give this welcoming cafe a cosmopolitan vibe. It's perfect for a coffee and brunch of *menemen* (scrambled eggs with peppers and tomatoes), *gözleme* (savoury pancake) or mixed plate of the daily dishes.

BORDO MAVI
International €€

(www.bordomavirestaurant.com; off Kahramanmaraş Caddesi, Trabzonspor Sadri Şener Tesisleri; mains ₺15) This cosmopolitan garden-cafe adjoins Trabzonspor's clubhouse, and the waiters wear the team strip. Pizzas, pastas and sandwiches are on the menu alongside Turkish meals and a range of drinks.

CEMILUSTA
Fish, Köfte €€

(Atatürk Alanı; mains ₺10) Trabzon's smart young professionals come to Cemilusta for house specialities fish and *köfte* (meatballs), and views of the square.

 Drinking & Entertainment

There are a few top-floor bars along Kahramanmaraş Caddesi. Most of the bars close by midnight.

KOZA CAFFE
Cafe

(1st floor, cnr Kunduracılar Caddesi & Sanat Sokak; 🛜) Opposite Şekerbank, studenty 'Cocoon Cafe' has a refreshingly funky interior with a mish-mash of fish tanks and faux medieval stylings. Grab a seat on one of the tiny outdoor balconies.

Trabzon – Bazaar Area

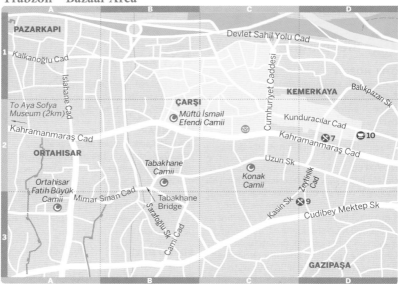

Trabzon – Bazaar Area

ℹ Information

Banks and ATMs are on and around Kahramanmaraş Caddesi.

Tourist office (📞326 4760; Cami Sokak; ⏰8am-5pm) English is usually spoken.

ℹ Getting There & Away

Air

Anadolu Jet (📞444 2538; www.anadolujet. com) To/from Ankara and İstanbul.

Onur Air (📞325 6292; www.onurair.com.tr) To/ from İstanbul and Northern Cyprus.

Pegasus Airlines (📞0850-250 0737; www. flypgs.com) To/from Ankara.

SunExpress (📞444 0797; www.sunexpress. com.tr) To/from Antalya, İstanbul, İzmir and European cities.

Turkish Airlines (0212-444 0849; www.thy.com) To/from Ankara and İstanbul.

Bus

Bus company offices including Metro and Ulusoy are scattered around Atatürk Alanı. Destinations include İstanbul (₺60, 18 hours) and Ankara (₺45, 12 hours).

For Ayder and the Kaçkar Mountains, catch a Hopa-bound bus and change at Pazar. If you miss

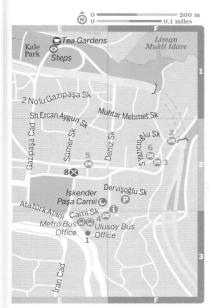

above evergreen forests. It's a mysterious place, especially when mists swirl in the tree-lined valley below and the call of a hidden mosque drifts ethereally through the forest. The monastery was founded in Byzantine times and abandoned in 1923, after the creation of the Turkish Republic quashed local Greek aspirations for a new state.

Visit early or late to avoid the hordes of Turkish tourists. Arriving when the site opens will beat the midmorning flow of tour groups. At the entrance to the **Altındere Vadısı Milli Parkı** (Altındere Valley National Park) there's a ₺15 charge for private vehicles. About 2km further on are riverside picnic tables and a restaurant.

The main trail to the monastery begins over the footbridge past the restaurant, and is steep but easy to follow, ascending 250m in about 30 to 45 minutes. Alternatively, follow the concreted road 1km uphill and across two bridges until you come to a wooden footbridge over the stream on the right. This trail is usually much quieter and takes the same time.

You can drive almost to the monastery ticket office; the 3km drive is challenging at busy times, with cars coming the other way on the narrow mountain road. En route are **waterfalls** and a **lookout point**, from where you can see the monastery suspended on a cliff face high above the forest.

After the ticket office, a steep flight of stairs leads to the monastery complex.

the daily bus to Kars (₺40, 10 hours), take one of the regular buses to Hopa or Erzurum for more services.

Car

You can hire a car to pick up, or drop off, in Trabzon or at the airport through Economy Car Rentals (www.economycarrentals.com). The following also have offices either in town or at the airport: Avis (322 3740; www.avis.com.tr), Dollar Rent A Car (www.dollar.com.tr; Taksim Caddesi), Europcar (444 1399; www.europcar.com. tr; Cikmaz Sokak 1a floor, 38, off Kunduracılar Caddesi) and National (325 3252; www. nationalcar.com.tr).

ⓘ Getting Around

A taxi to the airport, 5.5km east of the centre, costs about ₺25.

A taxi between the otogar (bus station), 3km east of the port, and Atatürk Alanı costs around ₺15.

Sumela Monastery

The Greek Orthodox **Monastery of the Virgin Mary** (admission ₺8; ☺9am-7pm) at Sumela, 46km south of Trabzon, clings improbably to a sheer rock wall, high

🍴 Eating

COŞANDERE TESISLERI RESTAURANT　　　　　Turkish €€
(0462-531 1190; www.cosandere.com; Sumela Yolu; mains ₺10) Located in Coşandere, a sleepy stream-fed village 5km south-east of Maçka en route to Sumela, this restaurant makes a pleasant lunch stop for köfte or saç kavurma (stir-fried cubed meat dishes), with outside tables and waitresses in traditional costume.

Sumela Monastery (p301)

IZZET KERIBAR/GETTY IMAGES ©

Getting There & Away

Bus

Eyce Tours (p298), Ulusoy and Metro run buses from Trabzon (₺25 return, one hour), leaving at 10am and departing Sumela at 1pm/2pm in winter/summer.

Car

Driving from Trabzon, take the Erzurum road and turn left at Maçka, 29km south of Trabzon. The monastery is also signposted as Meryemana (Virgin Mary).

NORTHEASTERN ANATOLIA

Kaçkar Mountains

The Kaçkar Mountains (Kaçkar Dağları) form a rugged range between the Black Sea and the Çoruh River, stretching roughly 30km northeast. Dense forest covers the lower valleys, but above about 2000m grasslands carpet the passes and plateaus, and the jagged ranges are studded with lakes and alpine summer *yaylalar* (mountain pastures).

Activities

Hiking

You can hike the higher mountain routes between mid-July and mid-August, when the snowline is highest. From May to mid-September there are plenty of walks on the lower slopes; conditions are more dependably dry and clear in June and September, and the autumn colours in September and October are beautiful.

Çamlıhemşin and Yusufeli are easily accessible, and public transport of varying frequency serves Ayder, Şenyuva, Çat, Barhal, Yaylalar and Olgunlar. High in the northwestern Kaçkars around 2000m, Yukarı Kavron, Amlakit, Palovit, Elevit and Avusor, all served by dolmuş (minibus) in summer, are good spots for day walks around the slopes and lakes. **Culture Routes in Turkey** (tinyurl.com/d6fld8l) has marked day walks around Barhal, Yaylalar and Olgunlar. Walks at lower altitudes, with or without a guide, are also stunning, with ancient Georgian churches and Ottoman bridges in the forests.

Many pensions can provide guiding services and give pointers. In the southern Kaçkars above Yusufeli, **Barhal Pansiyon** (☎0535 264 6765; Barhal; per person ₺50, half board ₺70, half board dm ₺30; 🛜), **Karahan Pension** (☎826 2071, 0538 351 5023; www.karahanpension.com; Altıparmak Köyü, Barhal; half board s/d ₺60/110) and **Çamyuva Pension** (☎0534 361 6959, 832 2001; www.kackar3937.com; Yaylalar; half board per person ₺80; 🛜) can arrange guides. **Turku Tour** (p304) offers day walks.

EAST TURKEY EXPEDITIONS   Hiking
(☎0543 480 4764; zaferonay@hotmail.com) Run by knowledgeable Zafer Onay.

CUMHUR BAYRAK   Hiking
(☎0537 562 4713; cumhurbayrak@hotmail.com; Yusufeli) Guide offering day walks around Yusufeli.

White-Water Rafting

The Çoruh River near **Yusufeli** is one of the world's best rafting rivers, with superb rapids and brilliant play holes. The river and its tributaries offer a wide range of rafting options for all skill levels, from beginners to level V. Rafting here is best between May and July.

Various local operators run day trips for about ₺100 per person (three or four people ₺70 per person) for around three hours of rafting. Reputable guides:

○ **Necmettin Coşkun** (☎0505 541 2522; www.coruhriver.com)

○ **Oktay Alkan** (☎811 3620; www.birolrafting.com; Greenpiece Camping & Pansiyon)

○ **Sırali Aydin** (☎811 3151, 0533 453 3179; www.coruhoutdoor.com)

Kaçkar Mountains

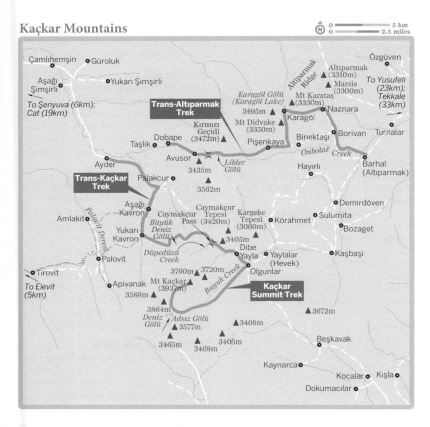

White-water rafting is also possible in July and August on the rapids around **Çamlıhemşin** (near Ayder). The rapids are smaller than the more exciting waters near Yusufeli, but the Black Sea region has arguably the more impressive scenery. There are operators on the Ardeşen–Çamlıhemşin road, including **Dağraft** (☏ 0464-752 4070; www.dagraft.com.tr; per person ₺40-60), which has routes geared towards rafters from amateurs to professionals (grades 1–2 and 3–4; 3km to 9km).

Ayder

Just beyond Çamlıhemşin, en route to Ayder from the coast, the road forks. The right fork leads up the Fırtına Valley; the left over the bridge and uphill to Ayder (17km). On both roads, you'll pass Ottoman humpback bridges.

About 4.5km below Ayder, you will pass through the entrance gate to the **Kaçkar Dağları Milli Parkı** (Kaçkar Mountains National Park; per vehicle ₺10).

The tourism hub of the Kaçkars, the high-pasture village of Ayder revels amidst a valley perched at 1300m. Snowy slopes slide towards its rooftops between woodland in various shades of green, waterfalls cascade to the river below, and traditional alpine-chalet structures dot the steep hillside. Sadly, however, Ayder is becoming more like a ski resort than a village. Nonetheless, it is worth visiting for an accessible taste of glorious Kaçkars scenery.

The village is still really only busy during the trekking season (mid-May to mid-September); at other times there may only be a few local families living here. During the Çamlıhemşin Ayder Festival (p43) accommodation can be almost impossible to secure, and over weekends in July and August, Turkish tourists fill most pensions by mid-afternoon.

The nominal village centre has restaurants, food shops, dolmuş and taxi stand. Accommodation and eateries are scattered for about 1km along the road either side of the centre.

 Activities

TURKU TOUR Hiking
(☏ 651 7230; www.turkutour.com; İnönü Caddesi 35, Çamlıhemşin) Mehmet Demirci, owner of pensions in Ayder and Çamlıhemşin, offers day walks, 4WD safaris, rafting, horse riding, cross-country skiing and photography. He runs a minibus up the Fırtına Valley on summer Saturdays and Thursdays, leaving Çamlıhemşin at 8am and heading up the valley to Amlakit (2000m), arriving at 11am and returning at 3pm.

KAPLICA Spa
(Hot Springs; ☏ 657 2102; www.ayderkaplicalari.com; admission ₺10, private bath ₺25; ⏱7.30am-7pm) Post-trek muscle relief is offered in marble environs at Ayder's spotless *kaplıca* (spa), where water temperatures reach 56°C.

 Sleeping

Most people opt for half-board accommodation at their pensions.

KUŞPUNI DAĞ EVI Pension €€
(☏ 657 2052; www.ayderkuspuniotel.com; per person ₺55, half board ₺75; ☎) This family-run chalet-pension has a stove-heated lounge and terrace with decent views, plus quaint rooms with traditional cupboard bathrooms and low slanted ceilings. Visitors rave about the food.

FORA PANSIYON Pension €€
(☏ 657 2153; www.forapansiyon.com; half board per person without bathroom ₺70) This hillside pension provides a cosy sitting room, pine-clad bedrooms with shared bathrooms, balconies and a laundry. Owner Mehmet Demirci also runs the equally wonderful Ekodanitap (p307; near Çamlıhemşin) – but he and his welcoming family spend more time here at Fora in season. Dinner on the view-laden terrace with the kids shouldn't be missed.

ZIRVE AHŞAP PANSIYON Pension €
(☏ 657 2177; mirayzirve@hotmail.com; per person ₺35; ☎) This solid budget option has two floors of spick-and-span rooms, both with and without bathroom. Views are lacking

but the old chairs in reception are great for chatting to friendly owner Sinem.

OTEL HAŞIMOĞLU
Hotel €€

(657 2037; www.hasimogluotel.com; s/d ₺50/100;) With facilities including a fitness centre, spa, riverside terraces and in-room minibar, you're losing the personal, family touch offered by smaller places, but these are Ayder's most comfortable digs.

YILMAZ CAFETERYA
Anatolian €

(mains ₺10, snacks ₺5) This family-run cafe offers chicken and fish dishes, plus local specialities like *muhlama* (a fondue-like Hemşin dish). The covered terrace has views down the main drag.

🛈 Getting There & Around

In summer, there are frequent dolmuşes to/from Pazar and Ardeşen (₺10) via Çamlıhemşin (₺5). Particularly above Çamlıhemşin, services are scarcer in winter; taxis from Çamlıhemşin to Ayder cost about ₺30. **Havaş** (325 9575; www.havas.net) operates shuttles between Pazar and Trabzon airport (₺15).

On summer mornings, dolmuşes run into the mountains (about ₺10) and return between roughly 2pm and 5pm, enabling day walks. Check locally for schedules.

Yusufeli

 0466 / POP 7000

This likeable riverside town and part of the nearby valley are, sadly, slated to vanish underwater due to the Yusufeli dam project. For now, the amicable country town is the gateway to the southern Kaçkars.

🛏 Sleeping

The following are all by the Barhal River.

OTEL ALMATUR
Hotel €€

(811 4056; www.almatur.com.tr; s/d ₺75/125;) Rooms have curvy lines, flat-screen TVs, fridges, big beds with white linen, and floor-to-ceiling windows with sweeping views. There's also a sauna and a 5th-floor restaurant, serving İskender kebap, *köfte* and mezes.

OTEL BARCELONA
Hotel €€

(811 2627; info@hotelbarcelona.com.tr; Arıklı Mahallesi; s/d €55/75, bungalow s/d €45/65; P ❄ 🔁) Restful Barcelona has a bar-restaurant, hamam and fitness centre;

Ayder region of the Kaçkar Mountains

SALVATOR BARKI/GETTY IMAGES ©

smart rooms with black-and-white tiled floors, stylish furniture and flat-screen TVs; and relatively simple bungalows (well, wooden cabins). The Turkish-Spanish owners are clued up on the area.

GREENPIECE CAMPING & PANSIYON
Pension €

(☏ 811 3620; www.birolrafting.com; Arıklı Mahallesi; s/d excl breakfast ₺35/50, breakfast ₺10; P @ 🛜) This laid-back pension in a peaceful spot has rooms in three blocks, including a traditional wooden, chalet-style unit. Those above the pleasant riverside bar benefit from views of the gurgling Barhal. Rafting trips can be organised.

Eating

KÖŞK CAFE & RESTAURANT
Turkish €

(mains ₺7-10) This jolly venture above the tourist office, with a good view of Yusufeli's main drag, serves simple breakfasts, fish and chicken dishes, burgers, *tost* (toasted sandwich) and rice pudding.

ÇARDAK DÖNER RESTAURANT
Anatolian €

(mains ₺7.50; ⊘ breakfast & lunch) Ramazan works the döner spit while wife Sevgi and daughters rustle up fresh, organic, traditional daily specials. Choose between goodies such as *kahvaltı* (breakfast), *hazır yemek* (ready-made food) and home-made baklava.

ⓘ Information

Yusufeli has banks with ATMs, a petrol station and tourist office (⊘ 8am-9.30pm May-Oct, 8am-5.30pm Mon-Fri Nov-Apr).

ⓘ Getting There & Away

Yusufeli's central otogar is near the tourist office.

There are morning buses to Artvin (₺15), Erzurum (₺20, three hours) and the Black Sea coast. You can also take a dolmuş (₺4) or taxi (₺25) to the petrol station on the Artvin–Erzurum road and catch passing buses, including the Kars bus, which passes at about 1pm (₺30).

To reach Barhal, Yaylalar or Olgunlar in the morning for a day walk, you will likely have to hire a taxi (₺100 between Barhal and Yusufeli or Yaylalar).

Driving into the Kaçkars, the road is surfaced from Yusufeli to Sarıgöl (about 18km). Continuing to Barhal (about 10km), about 60% is surfaced; thereafter, the road is unsurfaced. If it's dry, the winding, narrow road can be braved by confident drivers, in an ordinary car with good clearance (and without sentimental value), all the way up to Olgunlar. Allow plenty of time, seek local advice before setting off, and beware rockfalls and landslides in wet weather and when the snow is melting; springtime is risky. The road is particularly rocky above Yaylalar.

Kars

☏ 0474 / POP 76,928

With its stately, pastel-coloured stone buildings, dating from the Russian occupation (1878–1920), and its well-organised

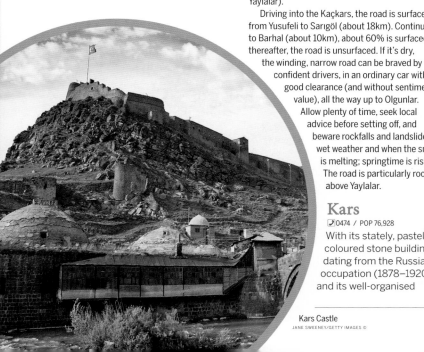

Kars Castle
JANE SWEENEY/GETTY IMAGES ©

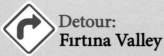

Detour:
Fırtına Valley

This beautiful and atmospheric river valley is a wonderful place to experience traditional Hemşin life.

Don't cross the bridge in the village of **Şenyuva**, 6km from Çamlıhemşin, but continue along the river and into the hills for 6km to reach the spectacularly situated **Zil Castle** (Zil Kale). It's a tough but scenic walk.

The road disintegrates at the castle, but it's navigable in a normal car. Another 15km takes you to the riverside hamlet Çat (1250m), and the start of even rougher mountain roads. A further 3.5km uphill, **Çat summer village** (1800m) is well worth the walk for the *yaylalar* (mountain pastures), overlooked by snowy peaks. Turn left after the humpback stone bridge **Çılanç Köprüsu**.

Accommodation is available at **Ekodanitap** (651 7787; www.ekodanitap.com; half board per person Hemşin house/tree house ₺90/75;), with traditional Hemşin (p353) houses and tree houses hidden up a winding road (coming from the coast, just before Çamlıhemşin on the right); and at the friendly riverside **Otel Doğa** (651 7455; Şenyuva Yolu; half board per person ₺55;), about 4.5km up the valley from Çamlıhemşin. In Çamlıhemşin, **Publik Bistro** (651 7270; İnönü Caddesi 35, Çamlıhemşin; meals ₺10; winter 8am-5pm, summer to 10pm; @) serves kebaps, pasta, *muhlama* (fondue-like Hemşin dish) and kingly breakfasts on its riverside terrace.

In summer, Turku Tour (p304) runs a twice-weekly minibus up the valley. Taxis (Şenyuva/Çat ₺15/60) and dolmuşes (Çat ₺15) also run from Çamlıhemşin.

grid plan, Kars looks like a slice of Russia teleported to northeastern Anatolia. And the city's mix of influences – Azeri, Turkmen, Kurdish, Turkish and Russian – adds to its distinct feel. No wonder it provided the setting for Orhan Pamuk's novel *Kar (Snow)*.

As well as visiting nearby Ani, explore the city centre's **Russian monuments** and walk up to **Kars Castle** (Kars Kalesi; admission free) for views over the city and steppe.

 Sleeping

GÜNGÖREN OTEL
Hotel €€

(212 6767; www.gungorenhotel.com; Millet Sokak; s/d/tr ₺70/120/150;) At this travelling-circuit stalwart, the smart, creamy rooms have flat-screen TV, fridge and tiled bathroom. The friendly staff speak some English, there's a restaurant and the copious breakfast features local cheese and honey.

GRAND ANI HOTEL
Hotel €€€

(223 7500; www.grandani.com.tr; Ordu Caddesi; s/d/tr/ste €80/100/120/150;) The Grand Ani's impressive facilities include an indoor pool, sauna, hamam, fitness centre, licensed restaurant, lobby bar, subterranean parking and even a barber. The comfortable rooms have shiny-clean bathroom, flat-screen TV and huge bed. Book ahead.

KAR'S OTEL
Boutique Hotel €€€

(212 1616; www.karsotel.com; Halit Paşa Caddesi; s/d €99/139;) This eight-room boutique hotel, housed in a 19th-century Russian mansion, feels like a luxurious cocoon, though some might find the white colour scheme rather too clinical. With its contemporary furnishings and mood lighting, the licensed Italian restaurant is ideal for romantic meals.

MIRAÇ OTEL Hotel €
(212 3768; Cengiz Topel Caddesi 19; s/d/tr
₺30/50/70;) At the Ascension, next to
Yapı Kredi bank, staircases with worn carpets lead ever-upwards to small, simple
rooms, which are reasonably clean with
shower. Atop the tall, thin building, a spiral
staircase climbs to the breakfast room for
views of the hills. A good budget option
for women.

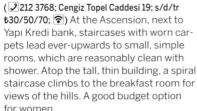

Eating & Drinking

Kars is noted for its excellent honey and
kaşar peyniri (a mild yellow cheese); perfect ingredients for a picnic on the steppe.

The best of the licensed hotel
restaurants is at the Grand Ani (p307). It
specialises in Turkish classics, prepared
to perfection and served in modern
surrounds (mezes ₺5, mains ₺15).

OCAKBAŞI RESTORAN Turkish €€
(212 0056; www.kaygisizocakbasi.com;
Atatürk Caddesi 276; mains ₺10-15;) This
40-year-old favourite serves unusual
Turkish dishes, such as its house specialities *ali nazık* (eggplant purée with yoghurt
and beef tenderloin; ask for *et siz* for
the vegetarian version) and *ejder kebap*
(sesame bread stuffed with meat, cheese,
parsley, nuts and eggs).

ANI OCAKBAŞI Anatolian, Kebap €€
(www.aniocakbasi.com; Kazım Paşa Caddesi 128;
mains ₺10) This smart restaurant is held
in high esteem locally, offering a wide
menu, from salads and soups to *köfte* and
local dishes. You can't go wrong with the
kebabs and grills.

DÖNERISTAN ET LOKANTASI Turkish €
(Atatürk Caddesi 50; mains ₺6-10;) There's
a lot to like about this clean, bright eatery,
patronised at lunchtime by locals from
office workers to cops. The döner kebab
is a perennial favourite.

BARIŞ TÜRKÜ CAFE PUB Pub, Cafe
(Atatürk Caddesi) Housed in a historic mansion, this atmosphere-laden cafe-bar-
disco attracts students of both sexes,
with live music most nights.

ⓘ Information

The **tourist office** (212 1705; cnr Faik Bey &
Gazi Ahmet Muhtar Paşa Caddesi; ⊙8am-5pm
Mon-Fri) has Kars and Ani maps and brochures.

ⓘ Getting There & Away

Air

A taxi to/from the airport costs about ₺15 to ₺18.
◦ **Anadolu Jet** (www.anadolujet.com) Flies daily
to/from Ankara.
◦ **Sun Express** (www.sunexpress.com.tr) İstanbul
daily; İzmir thrice weekly.
◦ **Turkish Airlines** (www.thy.com) Ankara and
İstanbul daily.

Bus

Kars' otogar is 2km southeast of the centre.
Servises ferry passengers to/from the bus
companies' city-centre offices, which are mostly
on and around Faik Bey Caddesi. **Metro** (www.
metroturizm.com.t) daily services include Amasya
(₺60) and İstanbul (₺70).

Minibuses to local towns leave from
the **minibus terminal** (Küçük Kazım Bey
Caddesi). Destinations include Iğdır (₺15, for
Doğubayazıt).

Trabzon Iğdırlı Turizm (0476 227 2877; www.
igdirliturizm.com.tr) and Aydoğan have daily
services (₺45), leaving at 12.30pm.

Van Turgutreis (cnr Faik Bey & Atatürk Caddesis)
has a daily service at 8.30am (₺50).

Yusufeli Take a bus or minibus bound for Artvin
or the Black Sea coast and ask to be dropped at
the nearest junction, about 10km from Yusufeli
on the Artvin–Erzurum road. Dolmuşes run from
there to Yusufeli.

Ani

Your first view of **Ani** (admission ₺8;
⊙8.30am-6pm May-Sep, to 3pm Oct-Apr),
45km east of Kars, is stunning: the
earthquake-damaged hulks of great stone
buildings adrift on a sea of undulating
grass are landmarks in a ghost city that
was once the stately Armenian capital.
The poignant ruins, the windswept plateau overlooking the Turkish–Armenian
border, and the total lack of crowds make
for an eerie ambience. In the silence

Ani

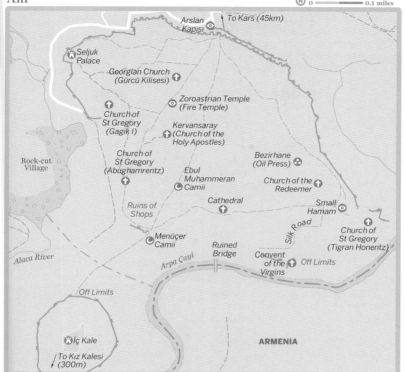

Ani

0 ─── 200 m
0 ─── 0.1 miles

To Kars (45km)
Arslan Kapısı
Seljuk Palace
Georgian Church (Gürcü Kilisesi)
Zoroastrian Temple (Fire Temple)
Church of St Gregory (Gagik I)
Kervansaray (Church of the Holy Apostles)
Church of St Gregory (Abughamrentz)
Ebul Muhammeran Camii
Bezirhane (Oil Press)
Church of the Redeemer
Rock-cut Village
Ruins of Shops
Cathedral
Small Hamam
Menüçer Camii
Ruined Bridge
Church of St Gregory (Tigran Honentz)
Alaca River
Arpa Çayi
Convent of the Virgins
Off Limits
Off Limits
İç Kale
To Kız Kalesi (300m)
ARMENIA
Silk Road

broken only by the gurgling river, ponder what went before: the thriving kingdom; the solemn ceremony of the Armenian liturgy; and the travellers, merchants and nobles bustling about their business in this Silk Road entrepôt.

From the entrance, follow the path to the left and tour the churches in clockwise order. Not all the site is open to visitors; some parts are off limits. Allow at least 2½ hours here. There are toilets and a small shop at the gate, with a cafe possibly opening, but play it safe and bring food and water.

For more about Ani, see p289.

ℹ️ Getting There & Away

The easiest option is a taxi minibus to the site (50 minutes), organised by **Celil Ersoğlu** (📞0532 226 3966; celilani@hotmail.com). One

person will pay roughly ₺140, two pay ₺70 each, three pay ₺45 each and four to six pay ₺35 each. If there are other travellers around, you will share the ride and the expense. This includes 2½ hours' waiting time.

SOUTHEASTERN ANATOLIA
Şanlıurfa (Urfa)
📞0414 / POP 515,000

Şanlıurfa (the Prophets' City; also known as Urfa) is a pilgrimage town and spiritual centre. This is where the prophets Job and Abraham left their marks, and your first sight of the Dergah complex of mosques and the holy Gölbaşı area, soundtracked by the call to prayer, will be a magical moment.

Şanlıurfa (Urfa)

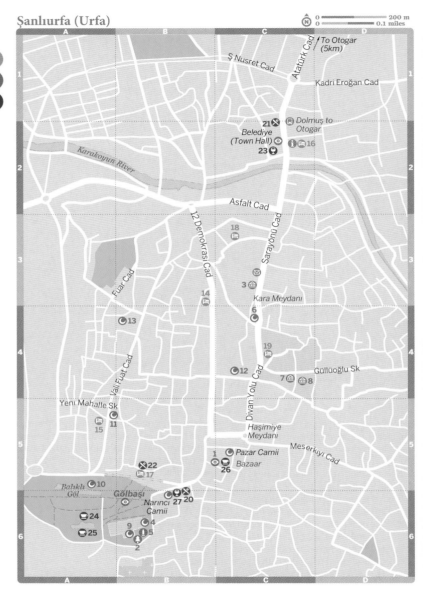

In Urfa you'll feel you've reached the Middle East. Women cloaked in black elbow their way through the odorous crush of the bazaar, and moustached gents swill tea and click-clack backgammon pieces in shady courtyards.

Sights & Activities

For tours to sights including Göbekli Tepe, Mt Nemrut and Mardin, try **Harran-Nemrut Tours** (📞 0542 761 3065, 215 1575;

Şanlıurfa (Urfa)

EASTERN ANATOLIA ŞANLIURFA (URFA)

www.aslankonukevi.com; Demokrasi Caddesi 12), **Mustafa Çaycı** (313 1340, 0532 685 2942; musma63@yahoo.com; Hotel Uğur, Köprübaşı Caddesi 3) or **Nomad Tours Turkey** (0533 747 1850; www.nomadtoursturkey.com; per person B&B €30, with full board €35), which also offers homestays in a Kurdish village en route to Mt Nemrut.

GÖLBAŞI   Historic Area

This picturesque area is a symbolic re-creation of the story of the great Islamic prophet Abraham's (İbrahim) battle in old Urfa with Nimrod, the local Assyrian king. Two rectangular pools of water (**Balıklı Göl** and **Ayn-i Zeliha**) are filled with supposedly sacred carp, while west of the **Hasan Padişah Camii** is a rose garden. **Rızvaniye Vakfı Camii & Medresesi** – the mosque and *medrese* (seminary) with a much-photographed arcaded wall – over-looks Balıklı Göl.

BAZAAR   Market

(Mon-Sat) Urfa's bazaar is a jumble of streets, some covered, some open, selling everything from sheepskins and pigeons to jeans and handmade shoes. Women should be on guard for lustful hands.

One of the most interesting areas is the **bedesten (covered market)**, an ancient caravanserai where silk goods have long been sold. The courtyard of the neighbouring restored caravanserai, **Gümrük Hanı (Customs Depot; Urfa bazaar; coffee ₺3)**, is always full of tea- or coffee-swilling moustached gents playing backgammon. Ask for *kahve mirra*, the super-strong and bitter local style of Turkish coffee.

DERGAH   Park

Southeast of Gölbaşı is the Dergah complex of mosques and parks sur-rounding the colonnaded courtyard of the **Hazreti İbrahim Halilullah (Prophet Abraham's Birth Cave; admission ₺1)**, built and rebuilt over the centuries as a place of pilgrimage. Its western side is marked by the **Mevlid-i Halil Camii**, a large Ottoman-style mosque. At its southern side is the entrance to the cave where Abraham was reputedly born.

This is still a place of pilgrimage and prayer, with separate entrances for men and women. To visit these important places of worship you should be modestly dressed.

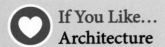# If You Like...
Architecture

Şanlıurfa has been a spiritual city for centuries, with many venerable mosques to show for it. Delve into the backstreets and you'll also find examples of Urfa's distinctive limestone houses, with protruding bays supported on stone corbels.

1 **ULU CAMII**
(Divan Yolu Caddesi) This Syrian-style mosque dates from 1170–75. Its spacious forecourt has a tall tower topped by a clock with Ottoman numerals.

2 **HÜSEYIN PAŞA CAMII**
(Kara Meydanı) A late-Ottoman construction, built in 1849.

3 **SELAHATTIN EYUBI CAMII**
(Vali Fuat Caddesi) Enormous and beautifully restored, it was once St John's Church, as evidenced by the altar.

4 **YENI FIRFIRLI CAMII**
(Yeni Fırfırlı Camii) This finely restored building was once the Armenian Church of the Twelve Apostles.

5 **GÜZEL SANATLAR GALERISI**
(⊙8am-5.30pm Mon-Fri, noon-4pm Sat) Although many of the city's distinctive limestone houses are falling into decay, a few have been restored. This house is now an art gallery.

6 **ŞURKAV**
(Balıklı Göl Mevkii) This local government building, its courtyard draped with greenery, is a good example of local architecture.

7 **İL ÖZEL İDARESI KÜLTÜR VE SANAT MERKEZI**
North of the market area (take 1001 Sokak), this splendid restored house was once a church.

8 **İLKÖĞRETIM OKULU**
This stately, historic building now houses a school.

# Sleeping

MANICI HOTEL _Historic Hotel €€€_
(☎215 9911; www.manici.com.tr; Balıklı Göl Mevkii; s/d ₺110/180; ❄️ 🛜) The opulent Manici has beautifully restored rooms that effortlessly fulfil any expectations of a romantic getaway. The shared public areas are relaxed and calm-inducing, and there's an excellent licensed restaurant.

OTEL URHAY _Historic Hotel €€_
(☎0544 215 7201, 216 2222; www.otelurhay.com; Sarayönü Caddesi, Beyaz Sokak; s/d ₺50/100; ❄️ 🛜) A quiet inner courtyard and cool kilim-decorated lounge/restaurant combine with simple whitewashed rooms. Weddings and parties are sometimes hosted on weekends.

ASLAN KONUK EVI _Pension €€_
(☎0542 761 3065, 215 1575; www.aslankonukevi.com; Demokrasi Caddesi 12; r ₺90-120; ❄️ @ 🛜) Simple but spacious high-ceilinged rooms are arranged around a shared courtyard in a heritage Urfa building. Run by English teacher Özcan Aslan, with good food and cold beer in the rooftop restaurant.

HOTEL UĞUR _Hotel €_
(☎0532 685 2942, 313 1340; musma63@yahoo.com; Köprübaşı Caddesi 3; per person with shared bathroom ₺20; ❄️ 🛜) Rooms are sparsely decorated and relatively compact, but clean and spotless. There's a great travellers' vibe, enhanced by a few cold beers on the terrace. Rates exclude breakfast, but there's a good _kahvaltı salonu_ (breakfast restaurant) downstairs.

Eating

Local specialities include the Urfa kebap (skewered chunks of lamb served with tomatoes, sliced onions and hot peppers), _çiğ köfte_ (minced uncooked mutton), _şıllık_ (crepes filled with walnuts and syrup) and pomegranate dressing.

MARION BULL/ALAMY ©

Don't Miss **Göbekli Tepe**

Catapulted to international fame after a *National Geographic* cover story in 2011, this fascinating archaeological site is thought to be the world's first place of worship. Around 11km northeast of central Urfa, the circular array of Neolithic megaliths at 'Pot Belly Hill' is estimated to date back to 9500 BC, around 6500 years before Stonehenge. The stone pillars have exquisitely stylised carvings of lions, foxes and vultures.

A return taxi from Şanlıurfa is about ₺25 to ₺30, and the site can also be visited with Harran-Nemrut Tours (p310), Mustafa Çaycı (p311) and Nomad Tours Turkey (p311).

NEED TO KNOW
www.gobeklitepe.info

MANICI HOTEL Turkish €€
(☏ 215 9911; Balıklı Göl Mevkii; mezes ₺6-8, mains ₺15-20) With excellent mezes and traditional Turkish mains, this fully licensed restaurant is an elegant affair framed by paintings of Ottoman sultans.

BEYAZ KÖŞK Kebap €
(Akarbaşı Göl Cadessi 20; mains ₺6-10) Turkey's best *lahmacun* (Arabic-style pizza) restaurants reputedly huddle in Gölbaşı's labyrinth of lanes, and this is a great place to try plate-covering pizza studded with spicy *ızot* (dried flaked peppers). Also served is *ciğer* kebap (grilled skewered liver).

GÜLHAN RESTAURANT Turkish €€
(Atatürk Caddesi; mains ₺8-14) Razor-sharp waiters; well-presented food that impresses rather than threatens; slick and salubrious surrounds; a pictorial menu with English translations – all good ingredients. For dessert, don't miss the *şıllık* (crepes filled with walnuts and syrup).

 **Drinking**

For a cup of tea in leafy surrounds, head for the **çay bahçesis** (tea gardens) in the Gölbaşı park. For a cold beer, head

313

Detour:
Doğubayazıt

Doğubayazıt's setting is superb. On one side, the talismanic **Mt Ararat** (Ağrı Dağı, 5137m), Turkey's highest mountain, hovers majestically over the horizon. On the other side, **İshak Paşa Palace** (İshak Paşa Sarayı; admission ₺5; ⏱8am-7pm), a breathtakingly beautiful fortress-palace-mosque complex, surveys town from its rocky perch.

Located 6km uphill southeast of town, the palace embodies *One Thousand and One Nights* romanticism. Built between 1685 and 1784, its architecture is an amalgam of Seljuk, Ottoman, Georgian, Persian and Armenian styles.

Doğubayazıt itself is a friendly, predominantly Kurdish place with an appealing sense of border-town wildness. Accommodation is available at **Hotel Grand Derya** (☎312 7531; fax 312 7833; Dr İsmail Beşikçi Caddesi; s/d ₺70/120; ❄🛜) and **Hotel Ararat** (☎312 4988; www.hotelararatturkey.com; Belediye Caddesi 16; s/d/tr ₺35/60/85; 🛜). **Simurg** (Meryemana Caddesi 19; mains ₺5-13; 🔌) serves dishes including spaghetti, pizza, chicken schnitzel and köfte.

From the otogar, 2km west of town on the D100 to Ağrı, you'll often have to travel via Erzurum (₺25, four hours) for long-distance destinations; for Kars, via Iğdır (₺7, 45 minutes, every 30 minutes). Van minibuses normally leave between 6.30am and 2pm daily (₺15, three hours).

Taxis charge ₺10 to ₺15 to the palace; ₺20 to ₺25 return, including a one-hour wait.

to the **Altin Kupa** (Köprübaşı Kişla Caddesi 4) pub (probably a tad blokey for single female travellers), or have dinner at the Aslan guesthouse (nonguests, book in the morning) or Manici Hotel.

ŞAMPIYON VITAMIN Juice Bar
(Akarbaşi Göl Cadessi; juices from ₺2) Fresh juice bar on the edge of the bazaar.

Entertainment

Raucous *sıra geceleri* (live music evenings) are held in the *konuk evi* (charming 19th-century stone mansions, converted into restaurants and hotels) such as **Cevahir Konuk Evi** (☎215 4678; www.cevahirkonukevi.com; Yeni Mahalle Sokak; mains ₺10-15; ❄🛜) and **Yıldız Sarayı Konukevi** (☎215 9494; www.yildizsarayikonukevi.com; Yıldız Meydanı, 944 Sokak; mains ₺8-12; ❄), usually at weekends. Guests sit, eat, sing and dance in *şark odası* (Ottoman-style lounges).

ℹ Information

Harran-Nemrut Tours (p310) and Mustafa Çaycı (p311) can usually provide city maps and English-language information.

ℹ Getting There & Away

Air

The airport is 45km from Urfa on the road to Diyarbakır. Ask about the Havaş airport bus at **Kalıru Turizm** (☎215 3344; www.kaliruturizm.com.tr; Sarayönü Caddesi; ⏱8.30am-6.30pm).

Turkish Airlines (www.turkishairlines.com) Daily flights to/from Ankara (from ₺84) and İstanbul (₺105).

Pegasus Airlines (www.flypgs.com) Regular flights to/from Ankara (from ₺100), İstanbul (from ₺100) and İzmir (from ₺100).

Bus

Urfa's otogar is 5km north of town off the Diyarbakır road. Some buses will drop passengers at a roundabout around 300m from the otogar. Taxis usually ask ₺20 to the otogar.

Daily services include Ankara (₺60, 13 hours), İstanbul (₺75, 20 hours), Mardin (₺30, three hours) and Van (₺45, nine hours).

Car

For car hire (around ₺80 per day) try Mustafa Çaycı (p311) or Harran-Nemrut Tours (p310).

Nemrut Dağı National Park

The spellbinding peak of Nemrut Dağı (Mt Nemrut) rises to a height of 2150m in the Anti-Taurus Range (not to be confused with the Nemrut Dağı near Lake Van).

The **summit** (admission ₺8; ☉dawn-dusk) was created when a megalomaniac pre-Roman local king cut two ledges in the rock, filled them with colossal statues of himself and the gods (his relatives – or so he thought), then ordered an artificial mountain peak of crushed rock 50m high to be piled between them. The king's tomb and those of three female relatives are reputed to lie beneath those tonnes of rock.

Earthquakes have toppled the heads from most of the statues, and now many of the colossal bodies sit silently in rows, with the 2m-high heads watching from the ground.

Plan to visit between late May and mid-October, and preferably in July or August; the road to the summit becomes impassable with snow at other times. Even in high summer it will be chilly and windy on top of the mountain, especially at sunrise.

 Tours

From Şanlıurfa, tours are available with **Harran-Nemrut Tours** (☎0414-215 1575; www. aslankonukevi.com; Demokrasi Caddesi 12, Aslan Konak Evi),

€50 per person, minimum two; Mustafa Çaycı (p311; ₺130 per person, minimum two) and Nomad Tours Turkey (p311; €100 per person).

Companies in Cappadocia offer two- to three-day minibus tours.

🍴 Eating

Pensions on the roads to the summit serve food, including **Karadut Pension** (☎0532 566 2857, 0416-737 2169; www.karadut pansiyon.net; Karadut; d per person ₺35; ❄@), where meals are available in the alfresco terrace bar, and **Hotel Euphrat** (☎0416 737 2175; www.hoteleuphratnemrut.com; s/d/tr with half board €45/58/68; ❄🏊), with spectacular views from the restaurant terrace.

ℹ Getting There & Away

Approaching the summit from the southern side, you pass through Karadut, a village some 12km from the top, before embarking upon the last few kilometres to the car park.

The path to Mt Nemrut's peak
WU SWEE ONG/GETTY IMAGES ©

Nemrut Dağı Area

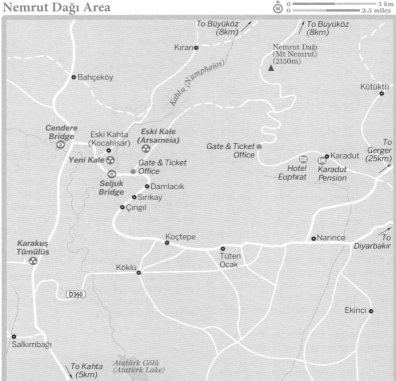

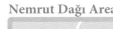

From the southwestern side, a secondary road passes Eski Kale (Arsameia) and climbs steeply for about 10km until it merges with the Karadut road, some 6km before the car park at the summit. This secondary road is quite rough in parts, and should only be attempted by confident drivers; it can be bypassed from Kahta by taking the D360 via Narince.

Be prepared for the rough, steep last 3km up to the summit.

Mardin

✏ 0482 / POP 88,000

Mardin is an addictive and unmissable spot. Minarets emerge from a baked brown labyrinth of meandering lanes, a castle dominates the old city, and stone houses cascade down the hillside above the Mesopotamian plains. As a melting pot of Kurdish, Yezidi, Christian and Syrian cultures, it also has a fascinating cultural mix.

With regular flights from İstanbul, you'll see lots of Turkish visitors in summer, and the government plans to promote Mardin internationally.

 Sights

SAKIP SABANCI
MARDIN CITY MUSEUM   Museum
(Sakıp Sabancı Mardin Kent Müzesi; www.sabanci muzesimardin.gov.tr; Eski Hükümet Caddesi; admission ₺3; ⊙8am-5pm Tue-Sun) Showcases Mardin's cosmopolitan and multicultural past, with an art gallery downstairs.

SULTAN İSA (ZINCIRIYE)
MEDRESESI   Mosque
(Cumhuriyet Caddesi; admission ₺2) The 14th-century complex's highlight is the imposing recessed doorway, but make sure you

wander through the pretty courtyards, and onto the roof to enjoy the cityscape. The tea garden is a top spot to sit and survey Mardin's beauty.

BAZAAR Market

Mardin's rambling commercial hub parallels Cumhuriyet Caddesi one block down the hill. Donkeys are still a main form of transport; look out for saddle repairers.

Delicate reliefs adorn the minaret of the secluded **Ulu Camii**, a 12th-century Iraqi Seljuk structure that suffered badly during the Kurdish rebellion of 1832.

 Sleeping

The city's boutique hotels are atmospheric, but rooms are often small and lack natural light; ask the right questions when you book. Summer weekends are busiest.

ŞAHMERAN OTANIK PANSIYON Pension €

(☏ 213 2300; www.sahmeranpansiyon. com; Cumhuriyet Caddesi, 246 Sokak 10; per person with/without bathroom ₺40/35; ⏾) Old Mardin's best-value historic option is arrayed around a honey-coloured stone courtyard. Kilims and heritage features punctuate the rustic and simply furnished rooms. Breakfast is an additional ₺5.

REYHANI KASRI Boutique Hotel €€€

(☏ 212 1333; www.reyhanikasri.com.tr; Cumhuriyet Caddesi; s/d ₺150/190; ❄ ⏾) Sleek and modern rooms are concealed within a lovingly restored historic mansion, with multiple floors cascading down the hillside. Have a drink at its remarkable 'Sky Terrace' bar for the best views in town.

ANTIK TATLIEDE BUTIK HOTEL Boutique Hotel €€

(☏ 213 2720; www.tatlidede.com.tr; Medrese Mahallesi; s/d/tr ₺100/150/200; ❄ ⏾) In a quiet location near Mardin's bazaar, this labyrinthine heritage mansion's rooms

♥ If You Like... History

Settled by Assyrian Christians during the 5th century, and later ruled by Arab, Seljuk Turkish, Kurdish, Mongol, Persian and Ottoman overlords, Mardin is steeped in history with numerous ancient buildings.

1 FORTY MARTYRS CHURCH
(Kırklar Kilisesi; Sağlık Sokak) This church dates back to the 4th century and was renamed in the 15th century to commemorate Cappadocian martyrs, who are now remembered in the fine carvings above the entrance.

2 MARDIN MUSEUM
(Mardin Müzesi; Cumhuriyet Caddesi; admission ₺5; ⏾8am-5pm Tue-Sun) With a small but well-displayed collection, this superbly restored late-19th-century mansion sports carved pillars and elegant arcades on the upper floor.

3 OLD MARDIN HOUSE
The three-arched facade of this ornately carved house is a fabulous example of Mardin's domestic architecture.

4 POST OFFICE
(Cumhuriyet Caddesi) The former post office is housed in a 17th-century caravanserai covered with carvings.

5 ŞEHIDIYE CAMII
(Cumhuriyet Caddesi) This 14th-century mosque's elegant, slender minaret is superbly carved.

6 LATIFIYE CAMII
This 14th-century mosque's shady courtyard has a central şadırvan (ablutions fountain). Nearby, the eye-catching **Hatuniye** and **Melik Mahmut Camii** have been fully restored.

7 EMIR HAMAMI
(Cumhuriyet Caddesi; treatments from ₺20; ⏾men 6.30am-noon & 6-10pm, women noon-5.30pm) This hamam's history goes back to Roman times. After a sauna and massage, take in the great views from the terrace.

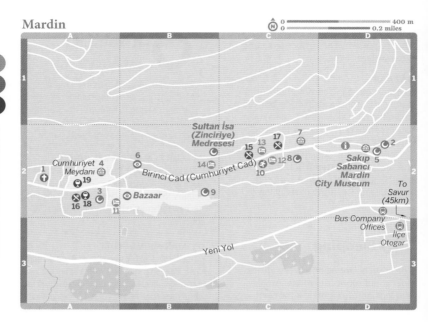

are filled with a rustic mix of old kilims and antique furniture. Most are fairly spacious. The expansive lobby flows to terraces with views across the plains.

ZINCIRIYE BUTIK HOTEL
Boutique Hotel €€

(212 4866; www.zinciriye.com; Sok 243, Medrese Mahallesi; s/d ₺90/140; ❄ 🛜) Just off the main drag, with small but quaintly decorated rooms with centuries-old stone walls. Some lack windows downstairs; try and head upstairs, where there's also a shared terrace with superb views.

 Eating & Drinking

KAMER CAFE MUTFAK
Anatolian €€

(Cumhuriyet Caddesi; mains ₺10-15) Operated by a support organisation for women who are victims of domestic violence, this terrific restaurant serves local cuisine.

CERCIS MURAT KONAĞI
Anatolian €€€

(213 6841; Cumhuriyet Caddesi; mains ₺20-25; ⏱noon-11pm) Occupies a finely decorated traditional Syrian Christian home with a terrace with stunning views. The *mekbuss* (eggplant pickles with walnut), *kitel raha* (Syrian-style meatballs) and *dobo* (lamb with garlic, spices and black pepper) are highlights. Book ahead. Wine and beer are served.

ANTIK SUR
Restaurant €€

(Cumhuriyet Caddesi; mains ₺10-15) Ease into the shaded surrounds of this restored caravanserai. Turkish tourists love the authentic local flavours and Assyrian wine. Live music kicks off around 8pm most weekends, and laid-back teahouses fill the upper level.

ABBABAR BAR
Bar

(www.abbabarbar.com; Cumhuriyet Caddesi) Retire to the expansive terrace for views all the way to Syria, or grab an indoor table and wait for the live Turkish music to kick off.

SHILUH
Wine Bar

(www.suryanisarabi.com; Cumhuriyet Caddesi) Local Syriac Christian communities have practised viticulture for over 5000 years, and wines are available for sampling and purchase here.

Mardin

ⓘ Information

Tourist office (Cumhuriyet Caddesi; ⏱8.30am-5.30pm; @) Free internet and maps and brochures.

ⓘ Getting There & Away

Air

A taxi from Mardin airport, some 20km south of town, to old Mardin is around ₺25.

Turkish Airlines (www.turkishairlines.com) Daily to/from İstanbul (from ₺92) and Ankara (from ₺64).

Bus

Most buses leave from the **İlçe Otogar** east of the centre. For long-distance destinations, buses stop in front of the bus company offices in the old town and in new Mardin. Services include Şanlıurfa (₺25, three hours).

Lake Van

The most conspicuous feature on the map of southeastern Turkey, this 3750-sq-km lake was formed when a volcano (Nemrut Dağı) blocked its natural outflow. The vast expanse of water is surrounded by snowcapped mountains.

Sights

AKDAMAR KILISESI   Church

(Church of the Holy Cross; admission ₺3; ⏱8am-6pm) One of the marvels of Armenian architecture is this carefully restored church, perched on an island 3km out in the lake. In 921 Gagik Artzruni, King of Vaspurkan, built a palace, church and monastery on the island. Little remains of the palace and monastery, but the church walls are in superb condition and the wonderful relief carvings are among the masterworks of Armenian art. There are also some frescoes inside.

Eating

AKDAMAR RESTAURANT   Restaurant €€

(✆0542 743 1361, 214 3479; www.akdamar restaurant.net; mains ₺15; ⏱Apr-Sep) This licensed restaurant, opposite the ferry departure point for Akdamar Island, has a terrace with lake views. A speciality is *kürt tavası* (meat, tomato and peppers cooked in a clay pot).

ⓘ Getting There & Away

The easiest way to visit from Van is with Alkan Tours (p321).

Below: Akdamar Kilisesi (p319), Lake Van; **Right:** Van Castle

(LEFT) IZZET KERIBAR/GETTY IMAGES ©; (BELOW) DENNIS COX/ALAMY ©

Boats to Akdamar Island (₺8) run as and when visitor numbers warrant it (minimum 15 people). From May to September, boats fill up on a regular basis. Outside of the summer, you may need to charter your own boat (around ₺120).

Van

📞 0432 / POP 353,500

More urban, more casual and less rigorous, Van is very different in spirit from the rest of southeastern Anatolia. Young couples walk hand in hand on the main drag, live bands knock out Kurdish tunes in pubs, and a resilient population coping with the impact of two earthquakes in 2011 inspire a satisfying urban buzz.

Sights

VAN CASTLE (VAN KALESI) & ESKI VAN   Ruin

About 4km west of the centre, **Van Castle** (Rock of Van; admission ₺3; ⏰9am-dusk) domi-

nates the view of the city. Try to visit at sunset for great views across the lake.

The site is fairly spread out, something to bear in mind when it's scorching hot. At the northwestern corner of the rock are the ticket office and a tea garden.

From the summit the foundations of **Eski Van** (the old city) reveal themselves on the southern side of the rock. The flat space punctuated by the grass-covered foundations of numerous buildings was the site of the old city, destroyed during WWI. The Ottomans destroyed it before the Russians occupied it in 1915.

VAN MUSEUM   Museum

(Van Müzesi; Kişla Caddesi; admission ₺3; ⏰8am-noon & 1-5pm Tue-Sun) This compact museum was closed at the time of writing following the 2011 earthquakes, and a potential move to near Van Castle was also rumoured.

The museum boasts an outstanding collection of Urartian exhibits, including exquisite gold jewellery, and an array of

bronze belts, helmets, horse armour and terracotta figures.

 Tours

ALKAN TOURS   Travel Agency
(☏ 0530 349 2793, 215 2092; www.easternturkey tour.org; Ordu Caddesi) Guided day trips (per person €20) take in Akdamar Island, the spectacular 17th-century Kurdish castle at Hoşap and the Urartian site at Çavuştepe. More in-depth tours exploring the region's Armenian heritage are available, as well as excursions to Kars, Doğubayazıt and elsewhere.

 Sleeping

ELITE WORLD HOTEL   Hotel €€€
(☏ 0212-444 0883; www.eliteworldhotels.com. tr; Kazım Karabekir Caddesi 54; s/d €85/95; ❄ @ 🛜 ⛱) Opened in 2012, Elite World has business traveller-friendly features

including a bar, nonsmoking rooms, spa and sauna. Posted rates are high; search online for discounts.

BÜYÜK ASUR OTELI   Hotel €€
(☏ 216 8792; www.buyukasur.com; Cumhuriyet Caddesi, Turizm Sokak; s/d ₺100/150; ❄ 🛜) This reliable midrange venture has colourful rooms complete with fresh linen, TV and well-scrubbed bathrooms. English is spoken and the hotel can organise local tours including Akdamar Island and Hoşap Castle.

AKDAMAR OTEL   Hotel €€
(☏ 214 9923; www.otelakdamar.com; Kazım Karabekir Caddesi; s/d ₺120/160; ❄ 🛜) The popular Akdamar is centrally located close to good restaurants and pastry shops, with flat-screen TVs and spacious bathrooms. The young, English-speaking staff have lots of recommendations.

CEMIL HOTEL   Hotel €
(☏ 215 1520; PTT Caddesi, opposite the Hacı Osman Camii; s/d ₺25/30) This good-value central spot is a simple pension with shared

bathrooms, and numerous restaurants just metres away. From Van's main drag, walk 100m down the lane between Simit Sarayı and the Adi Güzel gold shop.

Eating

TAMARA OCAKBAŞI — Steakhouse €€
(Yüzbaşıoğlu Sokak; mains ₺15-20; ⏲5pm-late) A meal here is dizzying, especially for carnivores. In the Hotel Tamara, the dining room eatery features 40 *ocak* – each table has its own grill. High-quality meat and fish dishes feature prominently, but the mezes are equally impressive.

KERVANSARAY — Anatolian €€
(Cumhuriyet Caddesi; mains ₺12-18) Upstairs from Cumhuriyet Caddesi, Kervansaray is Van's go-to spot for a more elegant and refined dining experience. Dive into a few shared plates of excellent mezes as you peruse a menu containing more than a few local specialities.

KEBABISTAN — Kebap €€
(Sinemalar Sokak; mains ₺8-15) Kebabistan's kitchen turns out expertly cooked kebaps (go for the *kuşbaşı*, with little morsels of beef). A second branch, across the street, specialises in pides. It's in a side street where men sit on low chairs playing backgammon and drinking tea.

HALIL İBRAHİM SOFRASI — Turkish €€
(Cumhuriyet Caddesi; mains ₺8-15) This downtown hot spot's eclectic food is well presented and of high quality, with service to match, served in sleek surrounds. Try the rich and tender İskender kebap, or the generous 'pide special', with a bit of everything.

🍷 Drinking & Entertainment

HALAY TÜRKÜ BAR — Live Music, Bar
(Kazım Karabekir Caddesi) Multiple floors add up to multiple ways to enjoy Van's low-key nightlife scene. Kick off with tasty mezes and grilled meat before graduating to draught beer, local spirits and live music.

NORTH SHIELD — Pub
(Yüzbaşıoğlu Sokak, Hotel Tamara) Perfect for a cold pint in an English pub–type atmos-

Akdamar Kilisesi (p319), overlooking Lake Van

BRUNO MORANDI/GETTY IMAGES ©

phere, with an excellent grill restaurant upstairs.

ℹ Information

Tourist office (☎ 216 2530; Cumhuriyet Caddesi; ⏰ 8.30am-noon & 1-5.30pm Mon-Fri) English is spoken and there are good maps and brochures.

ℹ Getting There & Away

Air

A taxi to the airport costs about ₺30.

Pegasus Airlines (www.flypgs.com) Six weekly flights to/from Ankara (from ₺130); daily to/from İstanbul (from ₺80).

Turkish Airlines (www.turkishairlines.com) Together with Anadolu Jet (www.anadolujet.com) has frequent daily flights to/from İstanbul (from ₺85) and Ankara (from ₺70).

Bus

Bus company offices are found at the intersection of Cumhuriyet and Kazım Karabekir Caddesis. They provide *servises* to/from the otogar on the northwestern outskirts.

Daily services include Ankara (₺90, 17 hours), Şanlıurfa (₺60, 11 hours) and Trabzon (₺75, 15 hours).

Breakfasts of Champions

Van is famed for its tasty *kahvaltı* (breakfast). Skip your usually bland hotel breakfast and head to pedestrianised Eski Sümerbank Sokak, also called 'Kahvaltı Sokak' (Breakfast St). Here, a row of eateries specialises in full Turkish breakfasts (₺12 to ₺15).

On summer mornings the street heaves with punters sampling local cheese, honey from the highlands, olives, *kaymak* (clotted cream), butter, tomatoes, cucumbers and *sucuklu yumurta* (omelette with sausage).

Minibuses to Doğubayazıt depart from a dusty car park down a side street on the right of the northern extension of Cumhuriyet Caddesi.

Car

Avis (☎ 214 6375; www.avis.com.tr; Cumhuriyet Caddesi), near the tourist office, rents cars for about ₺100 per day. Other rental agencies line Cumhuriyet Caddesi.

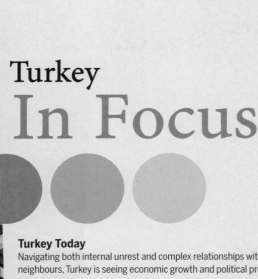

Turkey
In Focus

Güllüdere (Rose Valley), Göreme National Park (p249)
PHOTOGRAPHER: RAINER MIRAU

Turkey Today

The Bosphorus (p11), İstanbul

> *Turks are optimistic about the future, and witnessing their love for this nation is uplifting*

ethnic groups
(% of population)

70 Turkish

20 Kurdish

10 Other

if Turkey were 100 people

80 would be Muslims
19 would be Alevi Muslims
1 other religions

population per sq km

TURKEY   USA   UK

= 30 people

Continental Junction

The very heart of the world during the Ottoman and Byzantine empires, Turkey remains pivotal on the global stage. Its position at the meeting of Europe and Asia informs its political bent: the secular country has a moderate Islamic government and good relations with the West, for which Turkey is a key ally in the Middle East.

Cross-Border Tensions

With eight neighbouring countries including Iran, Iraq and Greece, cross-border tensions are a fact of life for the Turkish government. In 2012 its biggest concern was the unrest in Syria. Refugee camps sprung up along the border in southeastern Anatolia, accommodating over 100,000 Syrian refugees. Tensions between the countries continued, with Turkey returning fire after stray Syrian shells hit the Turkish border town Akçakale and killed five civilians.

Meanwhile, efforts to normalise Turkish–Armenian diplomatic relations, long strained over the alleged massacre of Ottoman

MURATKOC

15 million Kurds; freedom of speech; and EU discomfort about embracing a 99% Muslim country. In 2012 no chapters had been opened for two years; Turks resented the stalemate, especially given Turkey's economic boom and Eurozone woes.

The Kurdish Question

Domestically, Turkey's most pressing problem is the Kurdish issue, which sparked a near civil war between the military and the Kurdistan Workers Party (PKK), classed internationally as a terrorist group by organisations including the EU and US government, in the 1980s and '90s. The situation has simmered down, but skirmishes continue in southeastern Anatolia, where the PKK stepped up attacks during the Syrian unrest. The creation of an independent Kurdistan is unlikely; the Kurds remain suspicious of promises from nationalistic politicians, and point to Iraq's semi-autonomous Kurdish region as a way forward.

Political Progress

Prime Minister Erdoğan's Justice and Development (AKP) government has ushered in a broadly positive era for Turkey. Decades of military coups have given way to stability and economic growth matching China's. The 2010 referendum on constitutional reform, in which Turkey voted for change, will hopefully lead to greater democracy. The all-party constitutional conciliation commission appointed to draft the new constitution has made some progress. However, efforts have been slowed by problems such as the Syrian unrest and fighting with the PKK in southeastern Anatolia, and Erdoğan has threatened to bypass the commission. Nevertheless, most Turks are optimistic about the future, and witnessing their love for this dynamic, booming nation is refreshing and uplifting.

Armenians during WWI, have faltered despite the two countries' increasing cultural and trade ties. The border remains closed, and Turkey was furious when France tabled a law that would have criminalised denying that the events were an act of 'genocide'. The French court later annulled the law. Most Turks maintain that there was no such genocide; you may also see museum exhibits concerning atrocities that Armenian militias supposedly perpetrated against Turks. It remains a matter of national pride and an extremely sensitive issue. Discussing it is illegal in Turkey, under the law against insulting the Turkish nation.

EU Ambitions

Turkey's bid to join the European Union (EU) continues; accession talks started in 2005 and discussions relating to 13 of the 35 policy chapters have opened. Obstacles include Turkey's refusal to recognise EU member Cyprus; the marginalisation of its

History

Cave painting depicting a hunting scene, Çatalhöyük

 DEA / M. SEEMULLER/GETTY IMAGES

From the world's first city to the Ottoman Empire's fluctuating fortunes, Turkish history has produced a stream of episodes and characters worthy of a thriller. The Hittites, Romans, Byzantines and Seljuks were a few of the great dynasties that fought over Anatolia, where their castles and palaces, mosques and cathedrals are still scattered over the steppe. The tumultuous early 20th century finally put paid to empires, and Atatürk founded today's Republic.

First Cities

Çatalhöyük, which arose around 6500 BC, was perhaps history's first-ever city – a centre of innovation, where locals developed crop irrigation, domesticated pigs and sheep, and created distinctive pottery. Larger settlements, often fortified, sprung up, and by 3000 BC advances in metallurgy led to the creation of various Anatolian kingdoms, including one at Alacahöyük. It showed Caucasian influ-

1800 BC
The Hittites establish their great capital at Hattuşa and create the first Anatolian empire.

ence, which is evidence of trade beyond the Anatolian plateau.

On the west coast, trade was also increasing, with Troy trading with the Aegean islands and mainland Greece. Around 2000 BC the Hatti people established a capital at Kanesh (Kültepe, near Kayseri), ruling over a web of trading communities. Here, for the first time, Anatolian history materialises from archaeological conjecture, with clay tablets providing written records of dates, events and names.

Hittites & Troy

The Hatti soon declined and the Hittites swallowed their territory, leaving a legacy that includes their state archives (cuneiform clay tablets) and distinctive artistic styles. They were warlike, yet also displayed imperial trappings such as a sense of ethics and occasional diplomacy. They overran Ramses II of Egypt in 1298 BC, then patched things up by marrying him to a Hittite princess.

The Hittite Empire was harassed in later years by subject principalities, including the new dynasty at Troy, which established itself as a regional power. The encroachment of the iron-smelting Greeks, generally known as the 'sea peoples', hastened the Hittites' demise and led to the Trojan War in 1250 BC.

Anatolian Kingdoms

Post-Hittite Anatolia was a patchwork of peoples, including the Urartians, who forged a kingdom near Lake Van, and the Phrygians, who created a capital at Gordion (near Ankara) under King Gordius (of Gordian knot fame). The Lycians established a confederation of city states on the western Mediterranean coast, and the Lydians dominated western Anatolia from Sardis (near İzmir), creating history's first-ever coinage.

Meanwhile, Greek influence spread from the burgeoning Greek colonies on the Mediterranean coast: the Lycians borrowed the legend of the Chimera, for example, and Lydian art combined Greek and Persian styles. The Greeks derided most Anatolian people as 'barbarians', with some exceptions; they were so impressed by the wealthy Lydian king Croesus that they coined the expression 'as rich as Croesus'.

The Persians later checked the expansion of coastal Greek colonies and Hellenic influence, subdued the interior and ended the era of home-grown Anatolian kingdoms.

The Best...
Ancient Capitals

1 İstanbul (p51)

2 Ephesus (p156)

3 Ani (p308)

4 Hattuşa (p276)

5 Xanthos (p208)

6 Amasya (p280)

547 BC
Cyrus, emperor of Persia, invades Anatolia, defeating the Lydians and extending control to the Aegean.

323 BC
Alexander the Great dies in Babylon and a flurry of civil wars soon divides his empire.

133 BC
King Attalus III dies, bequeathing Pergamum to Rome; a beachhead for Rome's embrace of Anatolia.

Alexander & After

In 334 BC, Alexander the Great and his Macedonian adventurers crossed the Dardanelles, intent on liberating Anatolia from the Persians. They rolled the Persians near Troy, besieged Halicarnassus (modern-day Bodrum), swept eastwards and vanquished another Persian force on the Cilician plain.

Alexander conclusively removed Persian influence and brought Anatolia within the Hellenic sphere. Pergamum (now Bergama) became the most notable settlement in the network of municipal communities that spread across Anatolia, driven by trade, and the Greek language eventually extinguished native Anatolian languages.

The cauldron of Anatolian cultures continued to produce various flavour-of-the-month kingdoms, including Celtic Galatia, the Armenians and the kingdom of Pontus, respectively centred on Ankara, the Lake Van region and Amasya.

Rome & Christianity

The Romans arrived in 190 BC and, by 65 BC, had overcome all resistance and extended their rule to Armenia, on the Persian border.

Tradition states that in the 1st century AD St John retired to Ephesus to write the fourth Gospel, bringing Mary with him. St Paul used the Roman road system to spread the word across Anatolia. In the late 3rd century AD Diocletian tried to steady the empire by splitting it into eastern and western administrative units, simultaneously attempting to wipe out Christianity. Both endeavours failed. The religion continued to spread, albeit clandestinely and subject to persecution.

Diocletian's reforms, meanwhile, resulted in a civil war, won by the Christian convert Constantine – said to have been guided by angels to build a 'New Rome' on the ancient Greek town of Byzantium. The city came to be known as Constantinople (now İstanbul) and, by the end of the 4th century, Christianity was the Roman Empire's official religion.

Byzantium

Under Justinian, Byzantium (the Eastern Roman Empire) became a distinct entity, although sentimental attachment to the idea of Rome remained: the Greek-speaking Byzantines called themselves Romans, and the Turks later referred to them as 'Rum'.

Justinian's ambition overstretched the Byzantine Empire, which was battered by plague, encroaching Avars and Slavic tribes, and a drawn-out struggle with those age-old rivals, the Persians. This made Anatolia's eastern provinces easy prey for the Arab armies exploding out of Arabia, who brought a new language, civilisation and religion: Islam.

On the western front, Goths and Lombards advanced, pushing Byzantium back into the Balkans and Anatolia by the 8th century. Though the Macedonian emperors

129 BC

Ephesus becomes capital of the Roman province of Asia Minor.
Ephesus (p156)

527–65 AD

Emperor Justinian builds the Aya Sofya, codifies Roman law and extends the Byzantine Empire's boundaries.

chalked up victories against Islamic Egypt, the Bulgars and Russia, but Basil II's death in 1025 marked the end of Byzantine expansion.

Seljuks

From about the 8th century, the nomadic Turks moved ever-westward from Central Asia. They encountered the Persians and converted to Islam en route, swallowed parts of the Abbasid empire and built their own empire centred on Persia. The Turkish Seljuk clan began raiding Byzantine territory and, in 1071, faced down a Byzantine army at Manzikert. This laid Anatolia open to wandering Turkic bands and began the Byzantine Empire's demise.

In the 12th and 13th centuries, Crusader incursions set the Seljuks back. The Crusaders established short-lived statelets at Antioch (modern-day Antakya) and Edessa (now Şanlıurfa), and sacked Constantinople, although the Christian Byzantines were ostensibly their allies. Meanwhile the Seljuk empire, riven by power struggles, fragmented.

The Seljuk legacy persisted in the Sultanate of Rum, centred on Konya. Celaleddin Rumi, the Sufi mystic who inspired the Mevlevi (whirling dervish) order, exemplified the Seljuks' cultural and artistic achievements. Although ethnically Turkish, they were purveyors of Persian culture and art, introducing woollen rugs and remarkable architecture to Anatolia. Seljuk buildings were Anatolia's first truly Islamic art forms, and became the prototypes for Ottoman art.

The warlike Mongols ended the Seljuk era and Anatolia fractured into a mosaic of Turkish *beyliks* (principalities).

Ottoman Beginnings

The Ottoman story begins modestly with the Turkish *bey* (tribal leader) Osman (1258–1326), whose bands flitted around the borderlands between Byzantine and formerly Seljuk territory. Once galvanised, however, the Ottomans moved with zeal. In an era of destruction and dissolution, they provided an ideal that attracted legions of followers, and they in turn embraced all Anatolian cultures. Their traditions became an amalgam of Greek and Turkish, Islamic and Christian elements.

The Best...
Dramatically Located Ruins

1 İshak Paşa Palace (p314)

2 Akdamar Kilisesi (p319)

3 Nemrut Dağı (p315)

4 Sumela Monastery (p301)

5 Bergama Acropolis (p138)

6 Basilica Cistern (p65)

IN FOCUS HISTORY

654–669
Arab forces take Ankara and besiege Constantinople.

1326
The Ottomans establish their capital at Bursa, moving it to Adrianople (now Edirne) in 1365.

1396
Sultan Beyazıt trounces the armies of the last Crusade at Nicopolis (Bulgaria).

Seemingly invincible, the Ottomans forged west and expanded into Europe. By 1371 they had reached the Adriatic and in 1389 they defeated the Serbs at Kosovo Polje, effectively taking control of the Balkans. The Ottomans neatly absorbed the area's Christian communities, by recognising minorities and allowing them to govern their own affairs.

The Road to Constantinople

Sultan Beyazıt disastrously taunted the Tatar warlord Tamerlane, leading to his capture and defeat. Ottoman expansion halted as Tamerlane lurched through Anatolia, and Beyazıt's sons wrestled for control. Mehmet I emerged victorious and the Ottomans regained their mojo, scooping up the rest of Anatolia, rolling through Greece, making a first attempt at Constantinople and beating the Serbs again.

Mehmet II again set Ottoman sights on Constantinople; he built a fortress on the Bosphorus, imposed a naval blockade and amassed his army. On 29 May 1453, the Ottomans took the city. Christendom shuddered at the seemingly unstoppable empire, and Mehmet, now known as Mehmet the Conqueror, was declared a worthy successor to the great Roman and Byzantine emperors.

The Alexander Sarcophagus, displayed in İstanbul's Archaeology Museum (p68)

LEEMAGE/GETTY IMAGES ©

1451

Mehmet II becomes sultan; Ottoman territory now surrounds Constantinople, the last redoubt of the Byzantines.

1453

After seven weeks of siege, the Ottomans seize Constantinople.

1683

The siege of Vienna, the Ottomans' final (failed) tilt at expansion.

Golden Years

The Ottoman war machine rolled on. The janissary system, which converted and trained Christian youths for the military, meant that the Ottomans had the only standing army in Europe. Selim the Grim captured the Hejaz, Mecca and Medina in the early 16th century, making the Ottomans the venerated guardians of Islam's holiest places. It wasn't all mindless militarism, however: demonstrating the empire's multicultural nature, Jews expelled by the Spanish Inquisition were invited to Constantinople in 1492.

The Ottoman golden age came during Süleyman the Magnificent's reign (1520–66). A remarkable figure, Süleyman was noted for codifying Ottoman law; his legal code was a visionary amalgam of secular and Islamic law. His patronage of the arts saw the Ottomans reach their cultural zenith, and there were of course further military successes. The empire enjoyed victories over the Hungarians and absorbed the Mediterranean coast of Algeria and Tunisia.

Where his predecessors had enjoyed the comforts of concubines, Süleyman fell in love and became the first Ottoman sultan to marry. Sadly, monogamy did not make for domestic bliss. Palace intrigues brought about the death of his first two sons, and the period after his wife Roxelana's ascension became known as the 'Sultanate of Women'.

**The Best...
Castles**

1 Kızkalesi Castle (p226)

2 Castle of St Peter (p173)

3 Van Castle (p321)

4 Mamure Castle (p223)

5 Uçhisar Castle (p258)

6 Rumeli Hisarı (p85)

Weak Sultans

Some historians pinpoint Süleyman's death as the moment when the Ottoman rot began to set in. The remarkable line of Ottoman sovereigns could not continue indefinitely. Süleyman's successors were not up to the task, beginning with his son by Roxelana, Selim, known disparagingly as 'the Sot'. He lasted only eight years as sultan (1566–74), and oversaw the naval catastrophe at Lepanto, which spelled the end of Ottoman naval supremacy.

Furthermore, Süleyman was the last sultan to lead his army into the field. Later rulers were coddled and sequestered in the fineries of the palace, gaining minimal experience of everyday life and having little inclination to administer the empire. This, coupled with the inertia that was inevitable after 250 years of unfettered expansion, caused the Ottomans' once-irresistible military might to decline.

The late-17th and 18th centuries were a downward spiral for the Ottoman establishment. The empire remained vast and powerful, but slowly fell behind the

1799
Napoleon's swashbuckling Egypt campaign indicates that an emboldened Europe is willing to challenge the Ottomans.

1878
Romania, Montenegro, Serbia and Bosnia break away from the Ottoman Empire; Russia occupies Kars.

1908
The 'Young Turks' (CUP) force Sultan Abdülhamid to abdicate and reinstate the Ottoman constitution.

Anatolia's Armenians

The Ottoman Empire's final years saw widespread human misery, but nothing has proved as enduringly controversial as the fate of Anatolia's Armenians. The tale begins in 1915, with Ottoman army units marching Armenian populations towards the Syrian desert. It ends with an Anatolian hinterland virtually devoid of Armenians. What happened in between remains an unresolved issue. Armenians maintain that, in an orchestrated 'genocide', 1.5 million Armenians were executed or killed on death marches. Turkey, meanwhile, says the order had been to 'relocate' Armenians, and the deaths were due to disease and starvation, caused by the chaos of war.

West socially, militarily and scientifically. The Habsburgs in central Europe and the Russians became increasingly assertive, and Western Europe was rich after centuries of colonising the 'New World'.

Declining Empire

One Western development in particular quickened the Ottoman demise: nationalism. For centuries manifold ethnic groups had coexisted relatively harmoniously in the empire, but the creation of Western European nation states sparked a desire among subject peoples to throw off the Ottoman 'yoke'. Greece attained its freedom in 1830 and other countries followed.

Attempts at reform were too little, too late. In 1876 Abdülhamid allowed the creation of an Ottoman constitution and the first-ever Ottoman parliament, but he soon annulled the constitution and returned to authoritarianism. Educated Turks were looking for ways to improve their lot, for example, by creating the Committee for Union and Progress (CUP) in Macedonia. Reform-minded and influenced by the West, the CUP came to be known as the 'Young Turks'.

European Wars

The First Balkan War (1912–13) removed Bulgaria and Macedonia from the Otto-man map, with Bulgarian, Greek and Serbian troops advancing rapidly on İstanbul. European diplomats plotted how to cherry-pick the choicest parts of the once-mighty empire, now deemed the 'sick man of Europe'.

A triumvirate of ambitious, nationalistic CUP *paşas* (generals) took de facto control of the ever-shrinking empire, pushed back the unlikely alliance of Balkan armies and

1915–16

Over 100,000 soldiers die on the Gallipoli Peninsula in one of WWI's bloodiest episodes. Gallipoli cemetery

1920

The humiliating Treaty of Sèvres dismembers the Ottoman Empire, leaving the Turks a sliver of steppe.

saved İstanbul. However, they chose the losing side in WWI. The Ottomans had to fend off the Allies on multiple fronts: Greece in Thrace, Russia in northeast Anatolia, Britain in Arabia and a multinational force at Gallipoli. It was during this tumultuous period that the Armenian tragedy unfolded.

By the end of WWI, the French held southeast Anatolia, the Italians controlled the western Mediterranean, the Greeks occupied İzmir, and Armenians, with Russian support, controlled parts of northeast Anatolia.

Birth of Modern Turkey

At the head of a slowly building Turkish nationalist movement, Mustafa Kemal (later called Atatürk) began organising Turkish resistance and established a national assembly in Ankara, far from opposing armies and meddling diplomats.

Meanwhile, a Greek force pushed out from İzmir, intent on using Turkish disorder to realise their *megali idea* (great idea) of re-establishing the Byzantine Empire. They soon took Bursa and Edirne and pushed towards Ankara. This was just the provocation that Mustafa Kemal needed to galvanise Turkish support. The two sides clashed at the battles of İnönü and Sakarya before the Turks savaged the Greeks at Dumlupınar. The Greeks retreated in panic towards İzmir, where they were expelled from Anatolia.

Mustafa Kemal emerged as the hero of the Turkish people, realising the dream of the 'Young Turks' of years past: to create a modern Turkish nation state. The Treaty of Lausanne in 1923 undid recent humiliations and saw foreign powers leave Turkey. The borders of the modern Turkish state were set and the Ottoman Empire was no more.

Dynamic Republic

The Turks consolidated Ankara as their capital and abolished the sultanate. Assuming the newly created presidency of the secular republic, Mustafa Kemal's energy was apparently limitless in pursuing his vision of placing Turkey, devastated after years of war, among the modern, developed countries of Europe.

The Atatürk era was one of enlightened despotism. Atatürk established the institutions of democracy while never allowing any opposition to impede him. Although he worked tirelessly for the betterment of his people and country, one aspect of the Kemalist vision has caused ongoing fallout: the insistence that the state be solely Turkish. Encouraging national unity made sense, considering the nationalist separatist movements that had bedevilled the Ottoman Empire, but in doing so a cultural existence was denied the Kurds. Within a few years a Kurdish revolt erupted in southeast Anatolia, beginning the fighting that continues today.

The desire to create homogenous nation states on the Aegean also prompted population exchanges between Greece and Turkey: Greek-speaking communities from Anatolia were shipped to Greece, while Muslim residents of Greece were transferred to Turkey. It was a melancholy episode, bringing great disruption and the creation of ghost villages, vacated and never reoccupied.

1923
Foundation of the Republic of Turkey, with Mustafa Kemal (Atatürk) as its first president.

1938
Atatürk dies aged 57, and is succeeded by İsmet İnönü.

1971
Military coup. The army returns power to the state in 1973.

In Atatürk's zeal for modernisation, everything from headgear to language was scrutinised and reformed. Throughout the 1920s and 1930s Turkey adopted the Gregorian calendar (as used in the West), reformed its alphabet (adopting the Roman script), standardised the Turkish language, outlawed the fez, instituted universal suffrage and decreed that Turks should take surnames.

Political Unrest

Though reform proceeded apace, Turkey remained economically and militarily weak, and avoided involvement in WWII. Following the war, the country allied itself with the USA. A strategically important bulwark against the Soviet bloc, Turkey also fought with the Americans against the Communist powers in Korea, receiving significant US aid and becoming a NATO member.

Meanwhile, democratic reform gained momentum and in 1950 the Democratic Party swept to power. However, they became increasingly autocratic and the army intervened in 1960 to remove them. Army rule lasted only briefly, but it set the tone for years to come. The military considered themselves the guardians of Atatürk's pro-Western, secular vision and felt obliged to step in when necessary.

The 1960s and 1970s saw the creation of political parties of all stripes, but the profusion did not make for a happy democracy. The decades of unrest finally ended in 1983, when Turgut Özal, leader of the Motherland Party (ANAP), won a majority and set Turkey back on course. An astute economist and pro-Islamic, Özal made vital economic and legal reforms that brought Turkey in line with the international community and sowed the seeds of its current vitality.

Atatürk

Many Western travellers remark on the Turks' devotion to Atatürk. He appears on stamps, banknotes, statues, and seemingly every house where he stayed is a museum. In response, the Turks simply say that the Turkish state is a result of his energy and vision, that without him there would be no Turkey. From an era that threw up Stalin, Hitler and Mussolini, Atatürk (his name literally means 'Father Turk') stands as a beacon of statesmanship and proves that radical reform, deftly handled, can be hugely successful. Any perceived insult to Atatürk is considered highly offensive and is also illegal.

1980
Military coup. The army re-establishes order by creating the highly feared National Security Council.

1993–96
Tansu Çiller is Turkey's first and only female prime minister to date.

1999
PKK leader Abdullah Öcalan's capture offers an opportunity (largely unrealised) to settle the Kurdish question.

Gulf War Onwards

In 1991 Turkey played a supporting role in the allied invasion of Iraq and, after decades in the wilderness, affirmed its place in the international community and as an important US ally. At the end of the Gulf War millions of Iraqi Kurds fled north into southeast Anatolia. This brought the Kurdish issue into the spotlight, and saw the establishment of a Kurdish safe haven in northern Iraq. The Kurdistan Workers' Party (PKK) stepped up their terrror campaign, aimed at creating a Kurdish state in Turkey's southeast. With an iron-fisted response from the Turkish military, the southeast effectively endured a civil war.

Following Turgut Özal's sudden death in 1993, various weak coalition governments and a cast of figures flitted across the political stage. The religious Refah (Welfare) Party formed a government, but made Islamist statements that angered the military for transgressing the constitutional ban on religion in politics. Faced with what some dubbed a 'postmodern coup', the government resigned and Refah was disbanded.

A new political force arose in the new millennium: Recep Tayyip Erdoğan's moderately Islamic Justice & Development Party (AKP) has overseen societal reforms and capitalised on the improved economy. The AKP has sought to pursue Turkey's entry to the EU; end military intervention in politics; and improve relations with neighbouring countries.

Turkish flag and statue of Atatürk, Kaş
IMAGE SOURCE/GETTY IMAGES ©

2002
The newly formed AKP party wins a landslide victory in the general election.

2010
Turkey votes for change in the referendum on constitutional reform.

2011
The AKP enters its third term, with grand plans for the republic's centenary (2023).

Family Travel

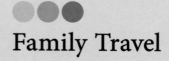

SAFFRON BLAZE/GETTY IMAGES ©

Travelling in family-focused Turkey is a blessing with çocuklar (children) big and small: waiters play with babies, strangers entertain and indulge, and free or discounted entry to sights is common. Your travels will be peppered with cries of Maşallah (glory be to God) and your child clutched into the adoring arms of new Turkish friends. Just bear in mind that facilities are often lacking and safety consciousness rarely meets Western norms.

Children's Highlights

There are numerous opportunities for children to interact with Turkey's fascinating history. Older children and teenagers will enjoy major sights such as Ephesus (Efes), while ruins including İstanbul's Hippodrome offer space for toddlers to expend energy.

Cappadocia's fantastical landscape of fairy chimneys (rock formations) and underground cities will thrill older children, as will cave accommodation. This is a safe, relaxing rural area with activities including horse riding and hot-air ballooning, and teenagers will enjoy walking here and in other scenic areas such as the Kaçkar Mountains.

The western Mediterranean has beaches and activities including water sports, tandem paragliding, boat trips and sea kayaking over submerged ruins. For younger children, holiday towns such as Kaş offer picturesque lanes and sandy beaches. The Aegean region has more beaches, and ruins for older children. Holiday spots including Kuşadası and the Bodrum Peninsula offer sights, facilities, water sports and glorious coastline. Bozcaada island offers safe swimming and good cycling.

Sweet treats include baklava, *dondurma* (ice cream) and *lokum* (Turkish delight). If teenagers are inspired, cooking courses are available in İstanbul and elsewhere.

Planning

Accommodation

Many hotels have family suites; those in tourist areas can often arrange a babysitting service.

Facilities

Many Turkish women breastfeed in public; you could do the same, provided you are covered and discreet. Playgrounds are common, but check the equipment for safety.

Health

Consider giving children the BCG tuberculosis vaccine. They should avoid dogs and other mammals because of the risk of rabies and other diseases. Double-check drugs and dosages prescribed by doctors and pharmacists.

Products

Pasteurised UHT milk is widely available in cartons; fresh milk is harder to find. Consider bringing a supply of baby food; what little you find here, your baby will likely find inedible. Migros supermarkets have the best range, and most supermarkets stock vitamin-fortified rice cereal and (very expensive) formula.

Transport

İstanbul's antique tram, ferries (also in İzmir) and funicular railways are novelties. Free travel on public transport within cities, and discounted tickets for longer journeys, are common. Most car-rental companies can provide child-safety seats for an extra charge. Buses often do not have functioning toilets, but stop every few hours.

The Best...
İstanbul Sights for Kids

1 Rahmi M Koç Museum (p97)

2 Basilica Cistern (p65)

3 Rumeli Hisarı (p85)

4 İstanbul Modern (p88)

IN FOCUS FAMILY TRAVEL

Need to Know

○ **Changing facilities** Rare.

○ **Cots** Increasingly common; ask hotels in advance.

○ **Highchairs** Uncommon, but increasingly widespread in tourist areas (apart from İstanbul).

○ **Kids' menus** Uncommon, but special dishes often prepared for children.

○ **Nappies (diapers; *bebek bezi*)** Readily available; Prima and Huggies are best.

○ **Strollers** With dangerous drivers and uneven surfaces, a 'baby backpack' is more useful.

Architecture

Aya Sofya (p69), İstanbul

SALVATOR BARK/GETTY IMAGES ©

Settled over millennia by countless civilisations, Turkey boasts a dizzying array of architectural styles. Crumbling castles and soaring mosques alike display their creators' cultural influences, technical prowess and engineering techniques. Significant buildings and sites range from Ephesus (Efes), Turkey's pre-eminent example of Roman city construction, to imperial Ottoman mosques. Recently, a restoration wave has swept the country, adding sheen to towns such as Safranbolu with its Ottoman mansions.

Ancient

Anatolia's earliest architectural remains are those of mud-brick constructions at history's first city, 8500-year-old Çatalhöyük. By the time Troy was established, classical temple design was beginning to develop. The Hittite remains at Hattuşa include hefty gates, stone walls and earthen ramparts.

Greek & Roman

Ancient Greek architects displayed increasing sophistication in city planning, design and construction, incorporating vaults and arches. The later-arriving Romans established a comprehensive road network. Common classical buildings seen at Greco-Roman sites include amphitheatres, agoras, forums and temples. In addition to Ephesus, good places to see classical architectural remains include Bergama (Pergamum), Hierapolis, Afrodisias, Sagalassos and Behramkale.

Byzantine

The Byzantines developed church and basilica design, particularly dome construction (exemplified by İstanbul's Aya Sofya), and tackled new media including brick and plaster. Antakya's Hatay Archaeology Museum and Church of St Peter have fine examples of the Byzantines' famous mosaics. İstanbul's Basilica Cistern and Kariye Museum (Chora Church) respectively highlight Byzantine engineering skills and frescoes.

Meanwhile, Armenian stonemasons developed a distinctive style, seen at the ruins of Ani, and at the 10th-century church, Akdamar Kilisesi.

Seljuk

Seljuk architecture reveals Persian influences, with decorative flourishes such as Kufic lettering and intricate stonework. Cosmopolitan Seljuk art and architecture mixed nomadic Turkic design traditions, Persian know-how and Mediterranean-influenced Anatolian Greek elements.

Central Anatolia has the best of the Seljuks' magnificent mosques, *medreses* (seminaries), caravanserais and conical *türbe* (tombs). Many caravanserais can be seen at roadsides in and around Cappadocia, and Amasya and Eğirdir have impressive Seljuk structures.

The Best...
Greek & Roman Ruins

1 Ephesus (Efes; p156)

2 Bergama (Pergamum; p131)

3 Hierapolis (p263)

4 Miletus (p174)

5 Didyma (p174)

6 Priene (p174)

Ottoman

The Ottomans were influenced by Byzantine styles, especially ecclesiastical architecture and dome construction. Mixing these and Persian influences produced the T-shape plan, for which Edirne's Üç Şerefeli Cami became a model. Imperial Ottoman mosques, especially those designed by Mimar Sinan, remain Turkey's most impressive. Sinan's great works include Edirne's Selimiye Camii and the Süleymaniye Mosque in İstanbul.

The Ottomans also built distinctive multistorey houses, with protruding upper floors balanced on carved brackets. Common features include *haremlik* and *selamlık* (women's and men's areas), intricate woodwork detailing on ceilings and joinery, ornate fireplaces and expansive rooms. These houses are best seen in Safranbolu, Amasya and Kaleiçi.

Pleasure-seeking later Ottomans built *yalı* (wooden seaside summer mansions) and pavilions. Also visible on Bosphorus cruises is the extravagant Dolmabahçe Palace, exemplifying 'Turkish baroque', a rococo and baroque pastiche of hammed-up curves, frills, scrolls, murals and fruity excesses.

Neoclassical & Modern

From the 19th century, foreign influences led to an eclectic neoclassical blend, mixing European architecture, Turkish baroque and Ottoman elements. Notable examples include Ankara's central post office and İstanbul's Sirkeci train station.

During the 1940s and 1950s, the nationalist architecture movement searched for a homegrown style to honour the new republic, resulting in sturdy edifices such as the Çanakkale Şehitleri Anıtı (Martyrs' Memorial) on the Gallipoli Peninsula. In recent decades, Turks have taken more notice of their pre-republic heritage, restoring buildings nationwide, often for use as hotels. For example, Tuvana Hotel, located in Antalya's historic Kaleiçi quarter, occupies six restored Ottoman houses.

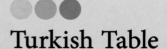

Turkish Table

Baklava

AHMET GUL/GETTY IMAGES ©

Afiyet olsun (bon appétit)! Turkish cuisine is much more than mere belly fuel: it's a celebration of community and life. Kebaps are succulent, yaprak dolması (stuffed vine leaves) are filled with subtly spiced rice, and seasonal produce quickly makes its way from ground to table. Turkey's diverse dishes mix elements developed on the Central Asian steppes with ingredients from Greece, Persia, Arabia and the Balkans, all absorbed during the Ottoman Empire.

Eating Through the Day
Breakfast

Typical Turkish *kahvaltı* (breakfast), served at every hotel, consists of white bread, jam or honey, black olives, slices of cucumber and tomato, hard-boiled eggs, *beyaz peynir* (salty white cheese made from ewe's or goat's milk) and sweetened black çay. *Menemen* (scrambled eggs with peppers, tomatoes and sometimes cheese) is a hearty breakfast dish.

Lunch

Many locals eat *öğle yemeği* (lunch) in a *lokanta*, where *hazır yemek* (ready-made food) is kept warm in bains-marie. Point to what you want: you can order one portion (*bir porsiyon*), a *yarım* (half) *porsiyon* or a plate with a few different choices – you'll be charged by the *porsiyon*.

Staples include *çorba* (soup), typically *mercimek* (lentil), *ezo gelin* (red lentil and rice) and *domates* (tomato), plus a range of meat and vegetable dishes, *pilavs* (rice dishes) and *dolmas* (vegetables stuffed with rice or meat).

Dinner

There are plenty of options for *akşam yemeği* (dinner). In a *meyhane* (Turkish tavern), customers usually enjoy a selection of mezes followed by a fish main. Go to a *kebapçı* (kebap restaurant) to sample kebaps (meat grilled on a skewer), and a *köfteci* to try *köfte* (meatballs). Both usually serve mezes to start the meal. *Ocakbaşı* (fireside) *kebapçıs* are the most fun, with patrons sitting around a grill where their meat is cooked. Most *restorans* (restaurants) serve mezes and kebap, *köfte* and fish dishes.

What's on the Menu?

Mezes

Turkey's version of tapas and hors d'oeuvre is a whole eating experience. In *meyhanes* and restaurants, waiters heave around enormous trays or trolleys of cold mezes that customers can choose from; hot mezes are usually ordered from the menu. Mezes are usually vegetable-based, though seafood dishes also feature.

Meat

Turks are huge meat eaters, preparing beef, lamb, mutton, liver and chicken in a number of ways. Classic dishes are kebaps – döner (lamb slow-cooked on an upright revolving skewer, shaved off and stuffed into bread or pide) and *şiş* (small pieces of lamb grilled on a skewer); *köfte, saç kavurma* (stir-fried cubed meat dishes) and *güveç* (meat and vegetable stews cooked in a terracotta pot).

The spicy beef sausage *sucuk* is popular; garlicky *pastırma* (pressed beef preserved in spices) is a common accompaniment to egg dishes, and served with warm hummus as a meze. *Mantı* (Turkish ravioli stuffed with beef mince and topped with yoghurt, garlic tomato and butter) is perfect in winter, but can be overly rich and heavy in hot weather.

Regional Kebaps

Particularly when it comes to kebaps, every regions has its specialities. In Cappadocia, many restaurants serve *testi kebapı* (kebap in a mushroom and onion sauce slow-cooked in a sealed terracotta pot that is broken open at the table). In the calorie-laden İskender (Bursa) kebap, döner lamb is served on a bed of crumbled pide and yoghurt, then topped with tomato and burnt butter sauces. The Adana kebap consists of spicy

Confrontational Choices

Like most countries, Turkey has some dishes that only a local could love, notably *kokoreç* (seasoned lamb or mutton intestines wrapped around a skewer and grilled over charcoal).

İşkembe (tripe) soup reputedly wards off a hangover; it's even more popular than *kelle paça* (sheep's trotter) soup.

Locals seeking extra-sexual stamina swear by spicy *koç yumurtası* (ram's 'eggs'), and often resort to *boza,* a mucous-coloured beverage made from water, sugar and fermented barley.

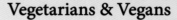

Vegetarians & Vegans

The concepts of vegetarianism and veganism may be foreign here, but vegetarian *(vejeteryen)* dishes are reasonably common, and usually dominate the meze spread. Salads, soups, pastas, omelettes, pides, *böreks* (filled pastries) and hearty vegetable dishes are also readily available. Ask *'etsiz yemek var mı?'* ('is there something to eat that has no meat?').

The main source of inadvertent meat eating is *et suyu* (meat stock), which is often used in otherwise vegetarian *pilav,* soup and vegetable dishes. Your hosts may not even consider *et suyu* to be meat; ask *'et suyu var mı?'* ('is there meat stock in it?') to check.

köfte wrapped around a flat skewer and barbecued, then served with onions, sumac, parsley, barbecued tomatoes and pide.

Fish

Fish is wonderful, but can be pricey. In a *balık restoran* (fish restaurant), copy the locals and choose your fish from the display. This is important, as the occasional dodgy restaurant may try to serve you old fish. Ask the approximate price: the fish will be weighed, and the price computed at the day's per-kilogram rate.

Fish is typically cooked over coals and served unadorned, accompanied by salads.

Popular fish include *hamsi* (anchovy), *lüfer* (bluefish; avoid when this overfished species is small), *kalkan* (turbot), *levrek* (sea bass), *lahos* (white grouper), *mezgit* (whiting), *çipura* (gilthead bream) and *palamut* (bonito).

Vegetables & Salads

Turks love vegetables, eating them fresh in summer and pickled *(turşu)* during winter. There are two particularly Turkish ways of preparing vegetables: *zeytinyağlı* (sautéed in olive oil) and *dolma* (stuffed with rice or meat). The Turks' beloved *patlıcan* (aubergine) is cooked in every conceivable manner; look out for the famous dish *imam bayıldı* ('the imam fainted'; aubergines slow-cooked in olive oil with tomatoes, onion and garlic).

Simplicity is the key to Turkish *salata* (salads), with crunchy fresh ingredients, adorned with oil and vinegar at the table, eaten as a meze or accompaniment to a main. The most popular summer salad is colourful *çoban salatası* (shepherd's salad; chopped tomatoes, cucumber, onion and pepper).

Sweets

Turks prefer fruit for dessert, but will often visit a *muhallebici* (milk pudding shop), *pastane* (patisserie) or *baklavacı* (baklava shop) for a mid-afternoon sugar hit. Turkish sweets worth sampling are honey-drenched, pistachio-studded baklava, *fırın sütlaç* (rice pudding; tasting of milk, sugar and a hint of exotic spices), *dondurma* (the local ice cream), *kadayıf* (syrup-soaked dough, topped with cream) and *künefe* (*kadayıf* layers cemented together with sweet cheese, doused in syrup and served hot with a sprinkling of pistachio).

Fast Food

Turkey's favourite fast food is undoubtedly the döner kebap. Possible accompaniments include soggy cold French fries, green chillies, garlicky yoghurt, salad and a sprinkling of slightly sour sumac.

Also hugely popular is pide (Turkish pizza), its canoe-shaped base topped with *peynir* (cheese), *yumurta* (egg) or *kıymalı* (minced meat). A *karaşık* pide has a mixture of toppings. You can eat in a *pideci* (pizza parlour) or order it *paket* (wrapped to go). *Lahmacun* (Arabic-style pizza) has a thinner crust than pide and is usually topped with chopped lamb, onion and tomato.

Börek are sold, usually in the morning only, at *börekçi* (small takeaway outfits). They come in square, cigar or snail shapes and are filled with *peynir, ispanak* (spinach), *patates* (potatoes) or *kıymalı*. Bun-shaped *poğaca* are glazed with sugar or stuffed with cheese and olives. *Su böreği* (melt-in-the-mouth lasagne-like layered pastry laced with white cheese and parsley) is the most popular of all *börek* styles.

Gözleme (thin, savoury pancakes cooked with cheese, spinach or potato) are also great snacks. Turkey's favourite fast-food chain is Simit Sarayı, which sells the country's much-loved *simit* (sesame-encrusted bread ring), mostly around breakfast time.

Etiquette

In rural Turkey locals usually eat two meals a day, at around 11am and in the early evening. In the cities three meals a day is the norm. Most Turks eat with a spoon *(kaşık)* and fork *(çatal)*, and rarely with a knife *(bıçak)*.

Turkish meze platter

CLIVE STREETER/GETTY IMAGES ©

In restaurants, it's not considered important that everyone eats the same courses at the same pace, so dishes are delivered when they are ready: it's normal for all the chicken dishes to arrive and then, five minutes later, the lamb. You don't have to wait for everyone's food to arrive before eating.

Turkish waiters have a habit of snatching plates away before the diner has finished. Saying *'kalsın'* ('let it stay') may slow them down. If the waiter does not take your plate, say *'biti, alabilirsin'* ('finished, you can take it').

Try to avoid blowing your nose in public; sniff or excuse yourself if you need to do this.

Local Tipples

Alcoholic Drinks

In tourist-heavy destinations along the coast virtually every restaurant serves alcohol. The same applies to more expensive restaurants in the big cities. In smaller towns, there's usually at least one restaurant where alcohol is served.

Turks have a fairly relaxed attitude towards alcohol, but public drunkenness is frowned upon.

Similar to Greek ouzo, the Turks' beloved rakı (aniseed brandy) is served in long thin glasses – neat or with water, which turns the clear liquid chalky white. Add the water before the ice *(buz),* as dropping ice straight into rakı kills its flavour. Rakı is best accompanied by melon and *beyaz peynir* mezes and seafood.

Bira (beer) is also popular. The local pilsener, Efes, comes in bottles, cans and on tap.

Turkey makes its own *şarap* (wine), which has improved in quality over the past decade but is expensive. Head to Cappadocia or the Aegean island of Bozcaada to taste-test.

The major producers of *kırmızı* (red) and *beyaz* (white) wine are the Doluca Company (www.doluca.com; look out for its labels Sarafin, Karma, Kav Tuğra and DLC); and

Man cutting döner kebaps
DAVID FORMAN/GETTY IMAGES ©

Kavaklidere (www.kavaklidere.com), known for its labels Ancyra, Prestige, Pendore – the red *boğazkere* (one of several Turkish varietals) is particularly good – and quaffable Çankaya white blend. Smaller producers such as Vinkara (www.vinkara.com) and Kayra (www.kayrasaraplari.com) are starting to build a reputation with wines such as Kayra's *buzbağ*.

Nonalcoholic Drinks

Drinking çay is the national pastime. Sugar cubes are the only accompaniment and you'll find these are needed to counter the effects of long brewing, although you can always try asking for it *açık* (weaker). In hotels and Western-style cafes it's acceptable to ask for *süt* (milk).

The wholly chemical, caffeine-free *elma* (apple) çay is mainly for tourists.

Surprisingly, *türk kahve* (Turkish coffee) isn't widely consumed. A thick and powerful brew, it's drunk in a couple of short sips. If you order a cup, you will be asked of you want it *çok şekerli* (very sweet), *orta şekerli* (middling), *az şekerli* (slightly sweet) or *şekersiz or sade* (not at all). A glass of water should accompany the coffee, to clear your palate before sampling the heady brew.

Taze portakal suyu (fresh orange juice) and other juices are popular and cheap; delicious *nar suyu* (pomegranate juice) can be ordered in season.

Refreshing *ayran* (yoghurt whipped with water and salt) is the traditional accompaniment for kebaps.

Hot milky *sahlep*, made from wild orchid bulbs and reputedly an aphrodisiac, takes off the winter chill. The first gulp of *şalgam suyu* is a revolting salty shock, but persevere and you may grow fond of this turnip concoction.

The Best...
Culinary Hotspots

1 Beyoğlu, İstanbul (p94)

2 Bodrum (p172)

3 Şanlıurfa (Urfa; p312)

4 Mardin (p318)

5 Antakya (Hatay; p230)

6 Cappadocia (p254)

Arts

Turkey's artistic traditions are rich and diverse, displaying influences of the many cultures and civilisations that have waxed and waned in Anatolia over the centuries. The art form most synonymous with Turkey is the carpet, and most travellers visit a carpet shop, but you can also appreciate Turkish culture through everything from belly-dancing shows to fusion albums. For more book, film and music recommendations, see p47.

Carpets

Turkish carpets are the culmination of a textile-making tradition dating back over 2000 years to the goat-hair tents and woollen saddle bags woven by Turkic nomads on the Central Asian steppes. Incorporating Persian motifs and Chinese cloud patterns into their robust floor coverings and Islamic prayer rugs, by the 12th century the Turks had introduced hand-woven carpets to Anatolia, where regional designs evolved. Uşak carpets, with star and medallion motifs, attracted European attention, and carpet-making contributed significantly to the Ottoman economy.

Village women still weave carpets, but usually work to fixed contracts for shops. Where cooperatives produce carpets, their quality makes up for any losses in individuality; most silk Hereke carpets are mass-produced, but to standards that make them highly sought-after. Keep an eye out for 'project carpets', usually of high quality, that are produced by projects to revive traditional weaving and dyeing methods in western Turkey.

Literature

Historically, Turkish literature was all about poetry: warrior epics passed down orally, Sufi mystical verses by the likes of Rumi, and the legends and elegies of wandering *aşık* (minstrels).

Yaşar Kemal's gritty stories of rural life were the first Turkish novels to attract international attention. *Memed, My Hawk,* a tale of the desperate plight of Anatolian villagers, has won Kemal nomination for the Nobel Prize for Literature on several occasions. Irfan Orga's books, including *The Caravan Moves On,* recounting his travels with Yörük nomads in the Taurus Mountains (Toros Dağları), were also published in the 1950s.

Notable contemporary writers include Elif Şafak; *The Flea Palace* is a wordy novel about an elegant İstanbul apartment building fallen on hard times, and *The Bastard of Istanbul* is a coming-of-age saga bristling with eccentric characters. Ayşe Kulin's *Last Train to İstanbul* follows Turkish diplomats' attempts to save Jewish families from the Nazis, and *Farewell* is set during the post-WWI Allied occupation of Turkey. Jewish-Turkish writer Moris Farhi's *Young Turk* is pacy and episodic, and Latife Tekin's *Dear Shameless Death* is a heady whirl of Anatolian folklore and magic realism.

Music

Pop, Rock & Experimental

With its skittish rhythms, shimmering sounds and strident vocals, Turkish pop is energetic and distinctive. Sezen Aksu is widely regarded as the queen of Turkish pop, while the hip-swivelling pop star Tarkan is a household name in Turkey.

The percussionist Burhan Öçal's *New Dream* is a funky take on classical Turkish music, and his Trakya All-Stars albums are a Roma-Balkan investigation of the music of Thrace. Mercan Dede's albums incorporate traditional instruments and electronic beats; similarly, BaBa ZuLa create a fusion of dub, *saz* (Turkish lute) and pop, accompanied by belly dancing at their performance 'events'.

Mixing metal, rock and Anatolian folk styles on their 2012 album *e-akustik,* maNga appeared in Eurovision 2010.

Orhan Pamuk

The biggest name in Turkish literature is Orhan Pamuk, an inventive prose stylist who juggles elaborate plots and finely sketched characters with the weighty issues confronting Turkey. He won the Nobel Prize for Literature in 2006 – the only Turk to have won a Nobel Prize.

Pamuk's novels are mostly set in İstanbul, including the existential whodunit *Black Book* and the 16th-century murder mystery *My Name is Red.* The nonfiction *İstanbul: Memories and the City* explores Pamuk's relationship with the city, where he has opened a museum (p88) inspired by his novel *The Museum of Innocence.*

Folk & Arabesk

Turkish folk ensembles typically consist of *saz,* drums and flutes, producing arrangements with plaintive vocals and swelling choruses. Big names include the female Kurdish singers Aynur Doğan and Rojin, whose hit 'Hejaye' has a singalong chorus.

You'll hear skittish *fasıl,* a lightweight version of Ottoman classical, at *meyhanes* (taverns), usually played by gypsies using clarinet, *kanun* (zither), *darbuka* (hourglass-shaped drum), *ud* (six-stringed Arabic lute) and *keman* (violin). Wandering minstrels play the *zurna* (pipe) and *davul* (drum) in bus stations to send off cadet conscripts.

The biggest names in arabesk, an Arabic-influenced blend of crooning backed by string choruses and rippling percussion, are Orhan Gencebay and the Kurdish former construction worker İbrahim Tatlıses.

Cinema

Turkey is a popular location for foreign filmmakers; the James Bond pic *Skyfall* (2012) was shot here. The homegrown film industry came of age in the 1960s and 1970s, when political films were made alongside lightweight Bollywood-style movies – collectively labelled *Yeşilçam* movies.

The uncompromising Yılmaz Güney was the first Turkish filmmaker to attract international attention. *Yol,* which explores the dilemmas of men on weekend-release from prison, was banned in Turkey until 2000, and the late director endured prison and exile. More recent political films include Yeşim Ustaoğlu's İstanbul-set *Güneşe Yolculuk* (Journey to the Sun), in which a Turk mistaken for a Kurd endures injustices. Fatih Akın's hard-hitting *Duvara Karsi* (Head On) and *Edge of Heaven* examine Turkish immigrant life in Germany; his documentary *Polluting Paradise* covers Turkey's environmental shortcomings.

Internationally, Nuri Bilge Ceylan has the highest profile, having won awards at Cannes for *Uzak* (Distant), a bleak meditation on migrants' lives in Turkey, and *Üç*

Dervish musician

Maymun (Three Monkeys). *İklimler* (Climates), which he also starred in, explores male-female relationships. *Once Upon a Time in Anatolia* (2011), an intriguing all-night search for a corpse in the Turkish backwoods, features Ceylan's trademark long landscape shots, brooding silences and minimal dialogue.

Other directors of note include Semih Kaplanoğlu (*Bal*), Yılmaz Erdoğan (*Vizontele* and *Vizontele Tuuba*), Reha Erdem (*Kosmos*) and Ferzan Özpetek (*Hamam* and *Harem Suare*).

Visual Arts

Turkey has a long tradition of textile- and carpet-making, *ebru* (paper marbling), calligraphy and ceramics, all of which can be glimpsed in bazaars nationwide. İznik became a centre for tile production from the 16th century, producing the exuberant tiles that adorn Ottoman-era interiors.

Educated Ottomans were influenced by European-style painting, and in the Republican era, government-backed academies promoted 'modern' secular art in place of the religious art of the past. İstanbul galleries (p88) are the best places to see modern Turkish art.

Dance

Turks are enthusiastic dancers, swivelling their hips and shaking their shoulders in ways entirely different from Western styles. Turkey's folk dances include Anatolian *halay*, led by a handkerchief-waving dancer and often seen in İstanbul *meyhanes;* and the Black Sea region's *horon*, which involves dramatic Cossack-style kicking.

The *sema* (whirling dervish ceremony) is not unique to Turkey, but this is a good place to see it performed. Belly dancing may not have originated here, but Turkish performers, who you can see at folk shows in İstanbul, reputedly dance with the least inhibition and the most revealing costumes.

The Best...
Music Venues

1 Aspendos (p212)

2 Bodrum Ancient Theatre (p149)

3 Babylon (p99)

4 Ankara State Opera House (p274)

5 Munzur Cafe & Bar (p99)

6 Şanlıurfa (Urfa) *konuk evis* (p314)

IN FOCUS ARTS

People

Men drinking tea and playing a board game

PATRICK SYDER IMAGES/GETTY IMAGES

Turkey has a population of almost 80 million, the majority of whom are Muslim and Turkish. Kurds form the largest minority, but there are various other groups, leading some to say Turkey is comprised of 40 nations. Since the 1950s, people have steadily moved from rural to urban areas, with 70% of the population now in cities. Nonetheless, all the peoples of Turkey tend to be family-focused, easy-going, hospitable, gregarious and welcoming.

Turks

The modern Turks are descendants of Central Asian tribal groups that began moving westward through Eurasia over 1000 years ago. As such, the Turks retain cultural and linguistic links with various peoples through southern Russia, Azerbaijan, Iran, Central Asia and western China. Turkish is in the family of Turkic languages, spoken by over 150 million people across Eurasia.

The predecessors of the modern Turks encountered the Persians and converted to Islam, before the Seljuks established the Middle East's first Turkic empire. Over the following centuries, Anatolia became the heartland of the Ottoman Empire and the core of the modern Turkish Republic. Owing to Ottoman imperial expansion, today there are people of Turkish ancestry in Cyprus, Iraq, Macedonia, Greece, Bulgaria and Ukraine.

Kurds

Turkey's significant Kurdish minority is estimated at over 15 million people, with about eight million in southeastern Anatolia. Kurds have lived for millennia in the mountains where the modern borders of Turkey, Iran, Iraq and Syria meet.

Kurds retain a distinct culture, folklore and language (related to Persian and, distantly, Indo-European tongues). Most Turkish Kurds are Sunni Muslims. The Kurds have their own foundation myth, associated with Nevruz, the Persian New Year (21 March).

Unlike the Greeks, Jews and Armenians, the 1923 Treaty of Lausanne did not guarantee the Kurds rights as a minority group. The Turkish state was decreed to be unitary, or inhabited solely by Turks. Denying the Kurds a cultural existence swiftly caused problems; fighting between the Kurdistan Workers Party (PKK), classed internationally as a terrorist group, and Turkish military continues in southeastern Anatolia.

Previous Turkish governments have refused to recognise the existence of the Kurds, calling them 'Mountain Turks'. Even today, census forms and identity cards do not allow anyone to identify as Kurdish. However, progress is being made, with debate about how Turkey can accommodate a Kurdish identity, and Kurdish language courses are allowed at government schools.

Muslim Minorities

Turkey is home to numerous minorities, most are regarded as Turks, but they nonetheless retain aspects of their culture and their native tongue.

Laz & Hemşin

The Laz mainly inhabit the valleys between Trabzon and Rize: you can't miss the women in their vivid maroon-striped shawls. Once Christian, the Laz are a Caucasian people speaking a language related to Georgian.

The Hemşin were also originally Christian, and speak a language related to Armenian. They mainly come from the far-eastern end of the Black Sea coast, although perhaps no more than 15,000 Hemşin still live there; most have migrated to the cities, where many work as bread and pastry cooks. Around Ayder, Hemşin women wear eye-catching leopard-print scarves coiled into elaborate headdresses.

Others

The last link to the wandering Turkic groups who arrived in Anatolia in the 11th century, the Yörük maintain a nomadic lifestyle around the Taurus Mountains (Toros Dağları).

Islam in Turkey

Turkey is a 99% Muslim country, but many Turks take a relaxed approach to religious duties and practices. Fasting during Ramazan is widespread and Islam's holy days and festivals are observed, but Islamic holidays are the only times many Turks visit a mosque. You can also tell by the many bars that Turks like a drink or two. Turkish Muslims have gradually absorbed and adapted other traditions; it's not uncommon to see Muslims praying at Greek Orthodox shrines or monasteries, while the Alevi minority has developed a tradition combining elements of Anatolian folklore, Sufism and Shia Islam.

The Best...
People Watching

Around the Syrian border, there are Arabic-speaking communities. There are also groups that came from the Caucasus and the Balkans towards the end of the Ottoman Empire, including Circassians, Abkhazians, Crimean Tatars, Bosnians and Turkic Uighurs (from China).

Non-Muslim Groups

The Ottoman Empire had large Christian and Jewish populations, and some remain. Today, Turkey's Jews mostly live in İstanbul, and some still speak the Judaeo-Spanish language Ladino.

Armenians have long been in Anatolia; a distinct Armenian people existed by the 4th century, when they became the first nation to collectively convert to Christianity. About 70,000 Armenians still live in Turkey, mainly in İstanbul, and in isolated pockets in Anatolia. Turkish-Armenian relations remain tense (see boxed text, p334), but there are signs of rapprochement.

Large Greek populations once lived throughout the Ottoman realm, but after the population exchanges of the early Republican era and acrimonious events in the 1950s, the Greeks were reduced to a small community in İstanbul. Southeastern Anatolia is also home to ancient Christian communities.

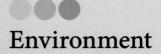

Environment

With snowcapped mountains, rolling steppe, vast lakes and 7200km of coastline, Turkey is a stupendously diverse country. In this continental meeting point at the junction of Europe and Asia, the environment often loses out to Turkey's economic boom. However, away from its highly populated and industrialised areas, the vast country still features many glorious corners from beaches to mountain ranges.

Land

The country comprises two parts, Anatolia (Asian Turkey) and Eastern Thrace (European Turkey), which respectively make up 97% and 3% of the 769,632-sq-km land area. The two parts are separated by İstanbul's Bosphorus strait, the Sea of Marmara and the Dardanelles.

Geographic Regions

The Aegean coast overlooks the Aegean islands, which mostly belong to Greece. Inland, western Anatolia has the vast Lake District and Uludağ (Great Mountain; 2543m), one of over 50 Turkish peaks above 2000m. Central Anatolia is characterised by a vast high plateau of rolling steppe and Cappadocia's valleys of fairy chimneys (rock formations). The Mediterranean coast is mostly backed by mountains, including the Taurus range.

The Black Sea coast is also frequently rugged, vertiginous and hemmed in by mountains, including the Kaçkar range, with its glaciers, mountain lakes and *yaylalar* (mountain pastures). The rest of northeastern Anatolia is also mountainous and wildly beautiful, not least Mt Ararat (Ağrı Dağı; 5137m), Turkey's highest peak. Southeastern Anatolia offers windswept steppe, jagged outcrops of rock, and the alkaline, mountain-ringed Lake Van (Van Gölü).

Animals

If you're trekking, in theory you could see bears, deer, jackals, caracal, wild boars and wolves in the wild.

People wandering off the beaten track, especially in eastern Turkey, are sometimes startled by Kangal dogs, originally bred to protect sheep from wolves and bears on mountain pastures. These huge, yellow-coated, black-headed animals sometimes have a spiked collar to protect against wolves. Their mongrel descendants live on Turkey's streets.

Birds

Some 400 bird species are found in Turkey, and about 250 of them migrate from Africa to Europe. Spring and autumn are good times to see feathered commuters, and it's particularly easy to spot eagles, storks, (beige) hoopoes, (blue) rollers and (green) bee-eaters. Other species include the *Geronticus eremita* (eastern bald ibis), purple gallinule and flamingos.

Endangered Species

Anatolia's lions, beavers and Caspian tigers are extinct, and its lynx, striped hyena and Anatolian leopard have all but disappeared. The beautiful, pure-white Van cat, often with one blue and one amber eye, has also become endangered in its native Turkey.

Rare loggerhead turtles still nest on Mediterranean beaches, and a few rare Mediterranean monk seals live around Foça (north Aegean). Turkey has been criticised by Greenpeace for not following international fishing quotas relating to Mediterranean bluefin tuna, which is facing extinction.

Dolphins survive in İstanbul's Bosphorus, and the Anatolian wild sheep, unique to the Konya region, is making a comeback.

Plants

As one of the world's most biodiverse temperate-zone countries, Turkey produces an incredible range of fruit and vegetables and has an exceptionally rich flora: over 9000 species, 1200 of them endemic, with a new species reportedly discovered every week (on average).

Common trees and plants are pine, cypress, myrtle, laurel, rosemary, lavender, thyme and, on the coast, purple bougainvillea.

Southwest Turkey has some of the last remaining populations of *Phoenix theophrastii* (Datça palm) and *Liquidambar orientalis* (frankincense trees).

The Best...
National Parks

1 Göreme National Park (p249)

2 Kaçkar Mountains National Park (p302)

3 Nemrut Dağı National Park (p315)

4 Saklıkent National Park (p199)

5 Gallipoli National Historic Park (p120)

Parks & Reserves

Turkey has 13 Ramsar sites (wetlands of international importance), 33 *milli parkıs* (national parks), 16 nature parks and 35 nature reserves. Its 58 'nature monuments' are mostly protected trees, including 1500- to 2000-year-old cedars in Finike, southwest of Antalya.

Sometimes regulations are carefully enforced in parks and reserves, but in other cases problems such as litter-dropping picnickers persist. Tourism is not well developed in the national parks, which rarely have clearly marked footpaths, camping spots or other facilities.

Beach cleanliness, however, is prominent, with 352 beaches and 19 marinas qualifying for Blue Flag status. Visit www.blueflag.org for the complete list.

Nuclear Energy

Despite Turkey's seismic vulnerabilities, three nuclear power plants are planned, with the aim of aiding economic growth and reducing dependency on natural gas supplies from Russia and Iran. Construction is set to begin in 2013 at Akkuyu on the eastern Mediterranean coast, a controversial site 25km from a seismic fault line. Another proposed location is the Black Sea town of Sinop.

Earthquake Danger

At least three active earthquake fault lines run through Turkey – the North Anatolian, East Anatolian and Aegean – and the country has recorded more than 25 major earthquakes, measuring up to 7.8 on the Richter scale, since 1939.

In 1999 a 7.6-magnitude quake hit İzmit (Kocaeli) and Adapazarı (Sakarya) in northwestern Anatolia, killing more than 18,000 people. A 7.1-magnitude earthquake shook the Van area in 2011, killing more than 600, injuring over 4000 and causing massive structural damage, with some 60,000 locals left homeless.

If a major quake struck İstanbul, it is believed much of the city would be devastated, due to unlicensed, jerry-built construction.

Environmental Issues

Balancing environmental management with rapid economic growth and urbanisation is a major challenge for Turkey. To date the environment has fallen a long way down its list of priorities, but there are glimmers of improvement, largely due to the country's desire to join the EU.

The government aims to harmonise all environmental legislation with the EU, and the European Commission reported in 2011 that Turkey had made good progress on waste management. However, it reported limited progress in areas including air and water quality, climate change, and industrial pollution control and risk management; and no progress on nature protection.

The Bosphorus

Over 45,000 vessels pass along İstanbul's Bosphorus strait annually; around 10% are tankers, which carry over 100 million tonnes of hazardous substances through every year.

Accidents have already occurred; the 1979 *Independenta* collision with another vessel killed 43 people and spilt and burnt some 95,000 tonnes of oil (around 2½ times the amount spilt by the *Exxon Valdez* in 1989). As well as existing and planned pipelines, proposed solutions include a US$12 billion canal to divert tankers, which would also see the creation of two new cities by the Bosphorus.

Construction & Dams

Building development is taking a huge toll on the environment, especially along the Aegean and Mediterranean coasts, where former fishing villages such as Kuşadası and Marmaris have been near swamped by urban sprawl.

Short of water and electricity, Turkey is one of the world's major builders of dams: there are already more than 600, with many controversial projects afoot. The gigantic Southeast Anatolia Project, known as GAP, is one of Turkey's major construction efforts. Harnessing the headwaters of the Tigris and Euphrates Rivers, it is causing friction with the arid countries downstream that also depend on this water.

Hasankeyf, which was a Silk Road commercial centre on the border of Anatolia and Mesopotamia, is slated to be drowned by the İlisu Dam Project in 2015. Opposition is ongoing, but the ruins look set to vanish, along with their atmospheric setting on the Tigris River and dozens of villages, displacing up to 70,000 people.

Survival
Guide

A diver off the coast of Kaş (p207)
PHOTOGRAPHER: BORUT FURLAN

Directory

●●●

Accommodation

Turkey has accommodation options to suit all budgets, with concentrations of good, value-for-money hotels, pensions and hostels in places most visited by independent travellers, such as İstanbul and Cappadocia.

Rooms are discounted by about 20% during the low season (October to April), but not during the Christmas and Easter periods and major Islamic holidays. Places within easy reach of İstanbul and Ankara may hike up their prices during summer weekends.

If you plan to stay a week or more in a coastal resort, check package-holiday deals. British, German and French tour companies in particular often offer money-saving flight-and-accommodation packages to the South Aegean and Mediterranean.

Accommodation options in more Westernised spots such as İstanbul often quote tariffs in euros; in less-touristy locations, they generally quote in lira. Many places will accept euro (or even US dollars in İstanbul). We've used the currency quoted by the business being reviewed.

APARTMENTS

Outside İstanbul and a few Aegean and Mediterranean locations, apartments for holiday rentals are often thin on the ground, but they represent good value for money, especially for families and small groups.

WEBSITES

- www.holidaylettings.co.uk
- www.ownersdirect.co.uk
- www.perfectplaces.com
- www.turkeyrenting.com
- www.vrbo.com

HOTELS
BUDGET

- Good, inexpensive beds are readily available in most cities and resort towns.

- Difficult places to find good cheap rooms include İstanbul, Ankara, İzmir and package-holiday resort towns such as Alanya and Çeşme.

- The cheapest hotels typically charge from around ₺35/40 for a single room with shared/private bathroom, including breakfast.

- The cheapest hotels are mostly used by working-class Turkish men; not suitable for solo women.

MIDRANGE

- One- and two-star hotels are less oppressively masculine in atmosphere, even when clientele is mainly male.

- Such hotels charge around ₺80 to ₺125 for an en suite double, including breakfast.

- Three-star hotels are generally used to cater for female travellers.

- Hotels in more traditional towns normally offer only Turkish TV, Turkish breakfast and none of the 'extras' commonplace in pensions.

- In many midrange hotels, a maid will not make your bed and tidy your room unless you ask in reception or hang the sign on the doorknob.

- Prices should be displayed in reception.

- You should never pay more than the prices on display, and will often be charged less.

- Often you will be able to haggle.

- Out east, couples are often given a twin room even if they ask for a double.

- The cheaper the hotel, and the more remote the location, the more conservative its management tends to be.

Book Your Stay Online

For more accommodation reviews by Lonely Planet authors, check out http://hotels. lonelyplanet.com. You'll find independent reviews, as well as recommendations on the best places to stay. Best of all, you can book online.

BOUTIQUE HOTELS

○ Old Ottoman mansions, caravanserais and other historic buildings refurbished, or completely rebuilt, as hotels.

○ Equipped with all mod cons and bags of character.

○ Most in the midrange and top-end price brackets.

○ Many reviewed at **Small Hotels** (www. boutiquesmallhotels.com).

PENSIONS

In destinations popular with travellers you'll find *pansiyons* (pensions): simple, family-run guesthouses, where you can get a good, clean single/double from around ₺40/70. Many also have triple and quadruple rooms.

In touristy areas in particular, there are advantages to staying in a pension, as opposed to a cheap hotel, including:

○ A choice of simple meals

○ Laundry service

○ International TV channels

No Vacancy

Along the Aegean, Mediterranean and Black Sea coasts, and in parts of Cappadocia, the majority of hotels, pensions and camping grounds close roughly from mid-October to late April. Before travelling to those regions in the low season, check if there is accommodation available.

Price Ranges

Ranges are based on the cost of a double room. The rates quoted in this book are for high season (June to August, apart from İstanbul, where high season is April, May, September and October). Unless otherwise mentioned, they include tax (KDV), an en suite bathroom and breakfast. Listings are ordered by preference.

İSTANBUL

€	less than €70 (₺165)
€€	€70 (₺165) to €180 (₺425)
€€€	more than €180 (₺425)

REST OF TURKEY

€	less than ₺80
€€	₺80 to ₺170
€€€	more than ₺170

○ Staff who speak at least one foreign language

EV PANSIYONU

In a few places, old-fashioned *ev pansiyonu* (pension in a private home) survive. These are simply rooms in a family house that are let to visitors at busy times of the year.

TOUTS

In smaller tourist towns such as Selçuk, touts may approach you as you step from a bus and offer you accommodation. Some may string you a line about the pension you're looking for, in the hope of reeling you in and getting a commission from another pension. Taxi drivers also play this game.

It's generally best to politely decline these offers, although touts sometimes work for newly opened establishments offering cheap rates. Before they take you to the pension, establish that you're only looking and are under no obligation to stay.

Activities

Turkey offers a wide array of activities, from the hair-raising to the serene. Want to sail over archaeological remains? Check out a Turkish ski resort? Explore Cappadocia on horse-back? No problem. It's all here.

WALKING

Turkey is excellent for walking, with day walks in scenic areas such as Cappadocia and the Kaçkar Mountains. In the western Mediterranean, you can walk sections of the way-marked Lycian Way (509km) and St Paul Trail (500km). Visit www.trekkinginturkey. com and cultureroutesinturkey .com for more information.

WATER SPORTS

For divers, Turkey offers a choice of reefs, drop-offs, caves, amphorae and broken pottery from ancient shipwrecks. The waters are generally calm, with no tides or currents, and visibility averages a reasonable 20m. Small reef species are prolific, the standard of facilities is high and there are sites for all levels of proficiency. Top dive spots include Kuşadası, Kaş and Ayvalık.

Sea kayaking and canoeing are the best ways to experience the Turquoise Coast's breathtaking scenery and access pristine terrain. You might see flying fish, turtles and even frolicking dolphins. Top paddling spots include Kekova and Patara, both on the western Med.

The 18km-long Saklıkent Gorge is renowned for canyoning and can be reached on day trips from Mediterranean towns such as Fethiye. In the same area, head to Ölüdeniz and Kaş for paragliding and parasailing, and to Fethiye and Olympos for *gület* (traditional wooden yacht) cruises. For white-water rafting, the Kaçkar Mountains are the best destination, along with

Activity Zones

○ **South Aegean** Bring your swimsuit to spots such as Bodrum, where operators offer boat trips, diving and waterskiing.

○ **Antalya & the Turquoise Coast** The western Mediterranean offers the widest array of activities, including sea kayaking, boat trips, diving, two waymarked walking trails, canyoning, rafting and paragliding.

○ **Cappadocia** Excellent for a half- or full-day hike, with a surreal landscape. There are also white-water rafting opportunities, horse riding, and skiing on Erciyes Dağı (Mt Erciyes).

○ **Eastern Anatolia** Head to the eastern wilds, especially the northern part, for serious adrenaline fixes: white-water rafting, skiing, hiking, snowboarding and snowshoeing.

Saklıkent Gorge and Köprülü Kanyon (near Antalya).

On the Çeşme Peninsula (near İzmir), Alaçatı is a world-class windsurfing (and kitesurfing) destination.

Business Hours

Most museums close on Monday; from April to October, they shut 1½ to two hours later than usual. The following also experience seasonal variation: a bar is likely to stay open later in summer than in winter; and tourist offices in popular locations open for longer hours and at weekends during summer.

The working day shortens during the holy month of Ramazan, which currently falls during summer. More Islamic cities such as Şanlıurfa (Urfa) virtually shut down during noon prayers on Friday (the Muslim sabbath); apart from that, Friday is a normal working day.

○ **Information** 8.30am-noon & 1.30-5pm Mon-Fri

○ **Eating** breakfast 7.30-10am, lunch noon-2.30pm, dinner 7.30-10pm

○ **Drinking** 4pm-late

○ **Nightclubs** 11pm-late

○ **Shopping** 9am-6pm Mon-Fri (longer in tourist areas and big cities – including weekends)

○ **Government departments, offices and banks** 8.30am-noon & 1.30-5pm Mon-Fri

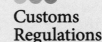

Customs Regulations

Turkish Ministry of Customs & Trade (www.gumruk.gov.tr) has more information.

IMPORTS

Items valued over €1500 will be liable for import duty. Jewellery valued over US$15,000 should be declared, to ensure you can take it out when you leave. Goods including the

Food

This book uses the following price ranges, based on the cost of a main course.

İSTANBUL

€ less than ₺15
€€ ₺15 to ₺25
€€€ more than ₺25

REST OF TURKEY

€ less than ₺9
€€ ₺9 to ₺18
€€€ more than ₺18

following can be imported duty-free:

- 600 cigarettes
- 200g of tobacco
- 2kg of coffee, tea, chocolate or sugar products
- 1L of spirits (over 22%)
- 2L of wine and beer (under 22%)
- 600mL of perfume
- One camera with five films
- One video camera
- One laptop
- One GSM mobile phone
- One GPS
- Unlimited currency
- Souvenirs/gifts worth up to €430 (€150 if aged under 15)

EXPORTS

- Buying and exporting genuine antiquities is illegal.
- Carpet shops should be able to provide a form certifying that your purchase is not an antiquity.
- Ask for advice from vendors you buy from.
- Keep receipts and paperwork.

Discount Cards

The **Museum Pass İstanbul** (www.muze.gov.tr/museum_pass) offers a possible ₺36 saving on entry to the city's major sights, and allows holders to skip admission queues.

The **International Student Identity Card** (ISIC; www.isic.org), **International Youth Travel Card** (IYTC; http://tinyurl.com/25tlbv7)

and **International Teacher Identity Card** (ITIC; http://tinyurl.com/25tlbv7) get discounts on accommodation, eating, entertainment, shopping and transport in Turkey.

Electricity

230V/50Hz

230V/50Hz

Gay & Lesbian Travellers

Homosexuality is legal in Turkey and attitudes are changing, but prejudice remains strong and there are sporadic reports of violence towards gay people – the message is discretion.

İstanbul has a flourishing gay scene, as does Ankara. In other cities there may be a gay bar or two.

Kaos GL (www.kaosgl.com) The Ankara-based LGBT rights organisation publishes a gay-and-lesbian magazine; its website has news and information in English.

Pride Travel Agency (www.turkey-gay-travel.com) Gay-friendly travel agent, with useful links on the website.

Health
BEFORE YOU GO

RECOMMENDED VACCINATIONS

Consult a doctor four to eight weeks before departure. Vaccinations for the following are recommended as routine for all travellers, regardless of the region they are visiting.

- diphtheria
- measles
- mumps
- pertussis (whooping cough)
- polio
- rubella
- tetanus
- varicella (chicken pox)

Vaccinations for the following are also recommended for travellers to Turkey:

o hepatitis A and B

o typhoid

MEDICAL CHECKLIST

Consider packing the following in your medical kit:

o acetaminophen/ paracetamol (Tylenol) or aspirin

o adhesive or paper tape

o antibacterial ointment (eg Bactroban) for cuts and abrasions

o antidiarrhoeal drugs (eg loperamide)

o antihistamines (for hay fever and allergic reactions)

o anti-inflammatory drugs (eg ibuprofen)

o bandages, gauze and gauze rolls

o insect repellent for the skin that contains DEET

o insect spray for clothing, tents and bed nets

o oral rehydration salts (eg Dioralyte)

o pocket knife

o scissors, safety pins and tweezers

o steroid cream or cortisone (for allergic rashes)

o sunblock (it's expensive in Turkey)

IN TURKEY

Prevention is the key to staying healthy while travelling in Turkey. Infectious diseases can and do occur here, but they are usually associated with poor living conditions and poverty, and can be avoided with a few simple precautions.

AVAILABILITY & COST OF HEALTH CARE

Getting Treated

If you need basic care for problems such as cuts, bruises and jabs, you could ask for the local *sağulık ocağuı* (health centre), but don't expect anyone to speak anything but Turkish.

The travel assistance provided by your insurance may be able to locate the nearest source of medical help. In an emergency, contact your embassy or consulate.

Standards

The standard of Turkish healthcare varies. Although the best private hospitals in İstanbul and Ankara offer world-class service, they are expensive. Elsewhere, even private hospitals don't always have high standards of care.

Hospitals & clinics Medicine, and even sterile dressings or intravenous fluids, may need to be bought from a local pharmacy. Nursing care is often limited or rudimentary.

Dentists Standards vary and there is a risk of hepatitis B and HIV transmission via poorly sterilised equipment, so watch the tools in use carefully.

Pharmacists For minor illnesses, such as diarrhoea, pharmacists can often provide advice and sell over-the-counter medication, including drugs that would require a prescription in your home country. They can also advise when more specialised help is needed.

INFECTIOUS DISEASES

In addition to the ailments mentioned under Recommended Vaccinations, the rare skin disorder leishmaniasis (spread by the bite of an infected sandfly or dog) is found in Turkey; as is leptospirosis (spread by the excreta of infected rodents), malaria (found in a few areas

Traveller's Diarrhoea

To prevent diarrhoea, stick to bottled water and avoid tap water unless it has been boiled (for 10 minutes), filtered or chemically disinfected (with iodine or purification tablets). Eat fresh fruit or vegetables only if they're cooked or you have peeled them yourself, and avoid dairy products that might contain unpasteurised milk. Buffet meals are risky since food may not be kept hot enough; meals freshly cooked in front of you in a busy restaurant are more likely to be safe.

If you develop diarrhoea, drink plenty of fluids, and preferably an oral rehydration solution containing salt and sugar. In severe cases, take an antidiarrhoeal agent (such as loperamide) – or if that's not available, an antibiotic (usually a quinolone drug) – and seek medical attention.

near the Syrian border) and tuberculosis (spread through close respiratory contact and, occasionally, infected milk or milk products). The risk of contracting these maladies is extremely low.

Rabies

Rabies, spread through bites or licks on broken skin from an infected animal, is endemic in Turkey. However, vaccination is not recommended unless you are travelling to remote areas, where a reliable source of post-bite vaccine is not available within 24 hours. Vaccination does not provide immunity, it merely buys you more time to seek medical help.

Any bite, scratch or lick from a warm-blooded, furry animal should immediately be thoroughly cleaned. If you have not been vaccinated and you get bitten, you will need a course of injections starting as soon as possible after the injury.

ENVIRONMENTAL HAZARDS
Heat Illness

Causes Sweating heavily, fluid loss and inadequate replacement of fluids and salt. Particularly common when you exercise outside in a hot climate.

Symptoms & effects Headache, dizziness and tiredness.

Prevention Drink sufficient water (you should produce pale, diluted urine).

Treatment Replace fluids by drinking water, fruit juice or both, and cool down with cold

Practicalities

- Turkey uses the metric system for weights and measures.
- Electrical current is 230V AC, 50Hz.
- You can buy plug adaptors at most electrical shops.
- Take a surge protector.
- A universal AC adaptor is also a good investment.
- **Today's Zaman** (www.todayszaman.com) is an English-language newspaper. **Hürriyet Daily News** (www.hurriyetdailynews.com) and **Sabah** (www.sabahenglish.com) have English editions.
- **Cornucopia** (www.cornucopia.net) is a glossy magazine in English about Turkey.
- Turkish Airlines' in-flight monthly, **Skylife** (www.thy.com), is worth a read.
- TRT broadcasts news daily, in languages including English, on radio and at www.trt-world.com.
- Digiturk offers numerous Turkish and international TV channels.

water and fans. Treat salt loss by consuming salty fluids, such as soup or broth, and adding a little more table salt to foods.

Heatstroke

Causes Extreme heat; high humidity; dehydration; drug or alcohol use; or physical exertion in the sun.

Symptoms & effects An excessive rise in body temperature, sweating stops, irrational and hyperactive behaviour, and eventually loss of consciousness and death.

Treatment Rapidly cool down by spraying the body with water and using a fan. Emergency fluids and replacing electrolytes by intravenous drip is usually also required.

Insect Bites & Stings

Causes Mosquitoes, sandflies (located around the Mediterranean beaches), scorpions (frequently found in arid or dry climates), bees and wasps (in the Aegean and Mediterranean coastal areas, particularly around Marmaris).

Symptoms & effects Mosquitoes can cause irritation and infected bites, and may carry malaria in southeastern Anatolia. Sandflies have a nasty, itchy bite, and can carry leishmaniasis. Turkey's small white scorpions can give a painful sting that will bother you for up to 24 hours.

Prevention DEET-based insect repellents.

Snake Bites

Prevention Do not walk barefoot or stick your hands into holes or cracks when exploring nature or even touring overgrown ruins and little-visited historic sites.

Treatment If bitten, do not panic. Half of those bitten by venomous snakes are not actually injected with poison (envenomed). Immobilise the bitten limb with a splint (eg a stick) and bandage the site with firm pressure, similar to applying a bandage over a sprain. Do not apply a tourniquet, or cut or suck the bite. Get the victim medical help as soon as possible so that antivenene can be given if necessary.

Insurance

○ A travel insurance policy covering theft, loss and medical expenses is recommended.

○ Some policies exclude 'dangerous activities', which can include scuba diving, motorcycling and even trekking.

○ Some policies may not cover you if you travel to regions of southeastern Anatolia where your government warns against travel.

○ If you cancel your trip on the advice of an official warning against travel, your insurer may not cover you.

○ Look into whether your regular health insurance and motor insurance will cover you in Turkey.

○ Worldwide travel insurance is available at www.lonelyplanet.com/bookings/insurance.do. You can buy, extend and claim online anytime – even if you're already on the road.

Internet Access

○ Throughout Turkey, the majority of accommodation options of all standards offer wi-fi.

○ Wi-fi networks are also found at locations from travel agencies and carpet shops to otogars (bus stations) and ferry terminals.

○ In this book, the wi-fi access icon (📶) indicates that a business offers a network.

○ Internet access icon (@) indicates that an establishment provides a computer with internet access for guest use.

○ Internet cafes typically open roughly from 9am until midnight, and charge around ₺1.50 an hour (İstanbul ₺3).

Legal Matters

Technically, you should carry your passport at all times. There have been cases of police stopping foreigners and holding them until someone brings their passport. In practice, you may prefer to carry a photocopy.

There are laws against lese-majesty (insulting the Turkish state and its founder, Atatürk), buying and smuggling antiquities, and illegal drugs.

Money

Turkey's currency is the Türk Lirası (Turkish lira; ₺). The lira comes in notes of five, 10, 20, 50, 100 and 200, and coins of one, five, 10, 25 and 50 kuruş and one lira.

After decades of rampant inflation, the lira is now stable. Because hyperinflation led to Turkish lira having strings of zeros, many people, confusingly, still work in thousands and millions. Don't

---

Insurance

Turkish doctors generally expect payment in cash. Find out in advance if your insurance plan will make payments directly to providers or reimburse you later for overseas health expenditures. If you are required to pay upfront, make sure you keep all documentation. Some policies ask you to call a centre in your home country (reverse charges) for an immediate assessment of your problem. It's also worth ensuring your travel insurance will cover ambulances and transport – either home or to better medical facilities elsewhere. Not all insurance covers emergency medical evacuation home by plane or to a hospital in a major city, which may be the only way to get medical attention in a serious emergency.

be alarmed if you're buying items worth, say, ₺6 and the shopkeeper asks you for ₺6,000,000.

Lack of change is a constant problem; try to keep a supply of coins and small notes for minor payments.

ATMS

ATMs dispense Turkish lira, and occasionally euros and US dollars, to Visa, Master-Card, Cirrus and Maestro card holders. Machines are found in most towns.

It's possible to get around Turkey using only ATMs if you draw out money in the towns to tide you through the villages that don't have them. Also keep some cash in reserve for the inevitable day when the machine throws a wobbly.

CREDIT CARDS

Both Visa and MasterCard are widely accepted by hotels, shops and restaurants, although often not by pensions and local restaurants outside the main tourist areas. You can also get cash advances on these cards. Amex is less commonly accepted outside top-end establishments. Inform your credit-card provider of your travel plans; otherwise, transactions may be stopped, as credit-card fraud does happen in Turkey.

FOREIGN CURRENCIES

Euros and US dollars are the most readily accepted foreign currencies. Foreign currencies are accepted in shops, hotels and restaurants in many tourist areas, and taxi drivers will take them for big journeys.

Climate

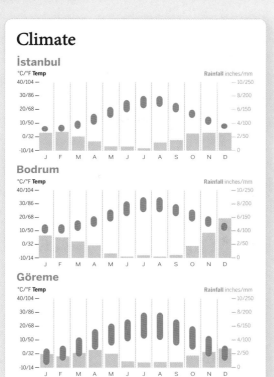

İstanbul

Bodrum

Göreme

MONEY CHANGERS

The Turkish lira is weak against Western currencies, and you will probably get a better exchange rate in Turkey than elsewhere. The lira is virtually worthless outside Turkey.

US dollars and euros are the easiest currencies to change, although many exchange offices and banks will change other major currencies such as UK pounds and Japanese yen.

You'll get better rates at exchange offices, which often don't charge commission, than at banks. Exchange offices operate in tourist and market areas, with better rates often found in the latter, and some post offices (PTTs), shops and hotels. They generally keep longer hours than banks.

TIPPING

Turkey is fairly Western in its approach to tipping and you won't be pestered with demands for baksheesh. Tipping is customary in restaurants, taxis, midrange and top-end hotels, and optional elsewhere. Tip 10% to 15% in midrange and top-end restaurants; a few coins in budget eateries. Some more expensive restaurants automatically add the *servis ücreti* (service charge) to your bill. Give 3% of the room price in midrange and top-end hotels, and a few lira to caretakers who open historical and archaeological sites for you; round up metered taxi fares to the nearest 50 kuruş (not expected in dolmuşes – minibuses); masseurs may appreciate 10% to 20%.

Public Holidays

○ **New Year's Day** (Yılbaşı; 1 January)

○ **National Sovereignty & Children's Day** (Ulusal Egemenlik ve Çocuk Günü; 23 April) Commemorates the first meeting of the Turkish Grand National Assembly in 1920.

○ **International Workers' Day** (May Day; 1 May) Features marches through İstanbul. Thousands gather around Taksim Sq, where the Taksim Square Massacre happened on 1 May 1977.

○ **Youth & Sports Day** (Gençlik ve Spor Günü; 19 May) Dedicated to Atatürk and Turkish youth.

○ **Şeker Bayramı** (Sweets Holiday; see table) Also known as Ramazan Bayramı, it celebrates the end of Ramazan.

○ **Victory Day** (Zafer Bayramı; 30 August) Commemorates the republican army's victory over the invading Greek army at Dumlupınar during the War of Independence.

○ **Kurban Bayramı** (Festival of the Sacrifice; see table) The most important holiday, marking İbrahim's near-sacrifice of İsmael on Mt Moriah (Quran, Sura 37; Genesis 22). Transport and accommodation fill up fast.

○ **Republic Day** (Cumhuriyet Bayramı; 28 to 29 October) Commemorates the proclamation of the republic by Atatürk in 1923.

Safe Travel

Turkey is not a safety-conscious country: holes in pavements go unmended; precipitous drops go unguarded; safety belts are not always worn; lifeguards on beaches are rare; dolmuş drivers negotiate bends while counting out change.

The two areas to be most cautious are İstanbul, where various scams operate, and southeastern Anatolia, where the PKK (Kurdistan Workers

Party) carries out terrorist activities.

The Kurdish issue occasionally also leads to violence in western Turkey; in 2010 a suicide bomber injured 32 people on Taksim Sq, İstanbul.

Sexual assaults have occurred against travellers of both sexes in hotels in central and eastern Anatolia. Make enquiries, check forums and do a little research in advance, especially if you are travelling alone.

FLIES & MOSQUITOES

In high summer, mosquitoes are troublesome even in İstanbul; they can make a stay along the coast a nightmare. Some hotel rooms come equipped with nets and/or plug-in bugbusters, but it's a good idea to bring some insect repellent and mosquito coils.

LESE-MAJESTY

The laws against insulting, defaming or making light of Atatürk, the Turkish flag, the Turkish people, the Turkish Republic and so on are taken very seriously. Turks have been known to claim derogatory remarks were made in

Major Islamic Holidays

The rhythms of Islamic practice are tied to the lunar calendar, which is slightly shorter than its Gregorian equivalent, so the Muslim calendar begins around 11 days earlier each year. The following dates are approximate.

ISLAMIC YEAR	NEW YEAR	PROPHET'S BIRTHDAY	RAMAZAN	ŞEKER BAYRAMI	KURBAN BAYRAMI
1434	16 Nov 2012	25 Jan 2013	10 Jul 2013	8 Aug 2013	15 Oct 2013
1435	5 Nov 2013	14 Jan 2014	29 Jun 2014	28 Jul 2014	4 Oct 2014
1436	25 Oct 2014	3 Jan 2015	18 Jun 2015	17 Jul 2015	23 Sep 2015
1437	14 Oct 2014	23 Dec 2014	7 Jun 2015	6 Jul 2015	12 Sep 2015

the heat of a quarrel, which is enough to get the foreigner arrested.

SCAMS & DRUGGINGS

In a notorious İstanbul scam, normally targeted at single men, a pleasant local guy befriends you in the street and takes you to a bar. After a few drinks, and possibly the attention of some ladies, to whom you offer drinks, the bill arrives. The prices are astronomical and the proprietors can produce a menu showing the same prices. If you don't have enough cash, you'll be frogmarched to the nearest ATM. If this happens to you, report it to the tourist police; some travellers have taken the police back to the bar and received a refund.

A less common variation on this trick involves the traveller having their drink spiked. Single men should not accept invitations from unknown folk in large cities without sizing the situation up carefully. You could invite your new-found friends to a bar of *your* choice; if they're not keen to go, chances are they are shady characters.

The spiking scam has also been reported on overnight trains, with passengers getting robbed. Turks are often genuinely sociable and generous travelling companions, but be cautious about accepting food and drinks from people you are not 100% sure about.

ANTIQUITIES

Do not buy coins or other artefacts offered to you at ancient sites. It is a serious crime here, punishable by long prison terms, and the touts are likely in cahoots with local policemen.

SHOE CLEANERS

In Sultanahmet, İstanbul, if a shoe cleaner walking in front of you drops his brush, don't pick it up. He will insist on giving you a 'free' clean in return, before demanding an extortionate fee.

VAT

Various VAT (value-added tax) scams operate. When buying a precious item such as a carpet, do not pay on the understanding that you will receive a VAT refund at the airport, even if you are asked to sign an official-looking Turkish document. The document may be a statement that you have received your refund, leaving you out of pocket when you reach the airport.

Some shops have signs indicating that they offer tax-free shopping. In most cases, the best policy is to assume you will not receive a refund and pay a price that you are happy with. Do not sign any paperwork unless you can understand it and, if you suspect a vendor of underhand dealings, take your business elsewhere.

SMOKING

Smoking in enclosed public spaces is banned, and punishable by a fine. Hotels, restaurants and bars are generally smoke-free, although bars sometimes relax the rules as the evening wears on. Off the tourist trail in budget and midrange hotels, the ban is enforced in public areas but more leniently in rooms. Public transport is meant to be smoke-free, although taxi and bus drivers sometimes smoke at the wheel.

TRAFFIC

As a pedestrian, note that Turks are aggressive, dangerous drivers; 'right of way' doesn't compute with many motorists, despite the little green man on traffic lights. Give way to vehicles in all situations, even if you have to jump out of the way.

Telephone

Türk Telekom (www.turktelekom.com.tr) has a monopoly on phone services, and service is efficient if costly. Within Turkey, numbers starting with 444 don't require area codes and, wherever you call from, are charged at the local rate.

KONTÖRLÜ TELEFON

If you only want to make one quick call, it's easiest to look for a booth with a sign saying *kontörlü telefon* (metered telephone). You make your call and the owner reads the meter and charges you accordingly. In touristy areas you can get rates as low as ₺0.50 per minute to Europe and beyond.

MOBILE PHONES

o   Reception is excellent across most of Turkey.

o   Mobile phone numbers start with a four-figure number beginning with 05.

o   Major networks are **Turkcell** (www.turkcell.com.tr), the most comprehensive, **Vodafone** (www.vodafone.com.tr) and **Avea** (www.avea.com.tr).

PAYPHONES & PHONECARDS

◦ Türk Telekom payphones can be found in most major public buildings and facilities, public squares and transport terminals.

◦ International calls can be made from payphones.

◦ All payphones require cards that can be bought at telephone centres or, for a small mark-up, at some shops. Some payphones accept credit cards.

◦ The telephone cards come in units of 50 (₺3.75), 100 (₺7.50), 200 (₺15) and 350 (₺19).

◦ Fifty units are sufficient for local calls and short intercity calls; 100 units are suitable for intercity or short international conversations.

INTERNATIONAL PHONECARDS

◦ Cards can be used on landlines, payphones and mobiles.

◦ Stick to reputable phonecards such as IPC.

◦ With a ₺20 IPC card you can speak for about 200 minutes to Europe and beyond.

◦ Cards are available in the tourist areas of major cities.

Time

◦ Standard Turkish time is two hours ahead of GMT/UTC.

◦ During daylight saving (summer time), the clocks go forward one hour, and Turkey is three hours ahead of GMT/UTC.

◦ Daylight saving runs from the last Sunday in March until the last Sunday in October.

◦ Turkish bus timetables and so on use the 24-hour clock, but Turks rarely use it when speaking.

◦ Visit www.timeanddate.com for more on time differences.

Toilets

Most hotels have sit-down toilets, but hole-in-the-ground models – with a conventional flush, or a tap and jug – are common. Toilet paper is often unavailable, so keep some with you. Many taps are unmarked and reversed (cold on the left, hot on the right).

In most bathrooms you can flush paper down the toilet, but in some places this may flood the premises. This is the case in much of İstanbul's old city. Signs often advise patrons to use the bin provided. This may seem slightly gross to the uninitiated, but many Turks (as well as people from other Middle Eastern and Asian countries) use a jet spray of water to clean themselves after defecating, applying paper to pat dry. The used paper is thus just damp, rather than soiled. Where a bin is provided and paper is used to clean (rather than just dry), it's best to place the first used sheets in the toilet and later sheets in the bin.

Public toilets often require a payment of around 50 kuruş. In an emergency it's worth remembering that mosques have basic toilets (for both men and women).

Tourist Information

Every Turkish town of any size has an official tourist office run by the **Ministry of Culture and Tourism** (www.goturkey.com). Tour operators, pension owners and so on are often better sources of information.

Travellers with Disabilities

Turkey is a challenging destination for disabled (*engelli* or *özürlü*) travellers. Ramps, wide doorways and properly equipped toilets are rare, as are Braille and audio information at sights. Crossing most streets is particularly challenging, as everyone does so at their peril.

Airlines and the top hotels and resorts have some provision for wheelchair access, and ramps are beginning to appear elsewhere. Dropped kerb edges are being introduced to cities, especially in western Turkey – in places such as Edirne, Bursa and İzmir they seem to have been sensibly designed. Selçuk, Bodrum and Fethiye have been identified as relatively user-friendly towns for people with mobility problems because their pavements and roads are fairly level. In İstanbul, the tram and the metro are the most wheelchair-accessible forms of public transport.

Turkish Airlines offers 25% discounts on domestic flights to travellers with minimum 40% disability and their companions. Some Turkish trains have disabled-accessible lifts, toilets and other facilities.

ORGANISATIONS

Businesses and resources serving travellers with disabilities include the following:

Access-Able (www.access -able.com) Includes disabled travellers' reports and a small list of tour and transport operators in Turkey.

Apparleyzed (www. apparelyzed.com) Features a report on facilities in İstanbul under 'Accessible Holidays'.

Hotel Rolli (www.hotel-rolli. de) Specially designed for wheelchair users.

Mephisto Voyage (www. mephistovoyage.com) Special tours for mobility-impaired people, utilising the Joëlette wheelchair system.

Visas

○ Nationals of countries including Denmark, Finland, France, Germany, Israel, Italy, Japan, New Zealand, Sweden and Switzerland don't need a visa to visit Turkey for up to 90 days.

○ Nationals of countries including Australia, Austria, Belgium, Canada, Ireland, the Netherlands, Norway, Portugal, Spain, the UK and USA need a visa, but it is just a sticker bought on arrival at the airport or border post.

○ The above nationals are given a 90-day multiple-entry visa.

○ Nationals of countries including Slovakia and South Africa are given a one-month multiple-entry visa on arrival.

○ Check the **Ministry of Foreign Affairs** (www. mfa.gov.tr) for the latest information.

○ The cost of the visa varies. At the time of writing, Americans paid US$20 (or €15), Australians and Canadians US$60 (or €45) and British citizens UK£10 (or €15 or US$20).

○ At major entry points such as İstanbul Atatürk International Airport, it is possible to pay with Visa and MasterCard. Many land border crossings are less equipped, with no ATMs or money-changing facilities. In all cases it is worth having the fee ready in one of the above currencies, in hard-currency cash. Try to have the correct amount as you may not receive change.

Women Travellers

Travelling in Turkey is straightforward for women, provided you follow some simple guidelines.

ACCOMMODATION

The cheapest hotels, as well as often being fleapits, are generally not suitable for lone women. Stick with family-oriented midrange hotels.

If conversation in the lobby grinds to a halt as you enter, the hotel is not likely to be a great place for a woman.

If there is a knock on your hotel door late at night,

don't open it; in the morning, complain to the manager.

CLOTHING

Tailor your behaviour and your clothing to your surrounds. Look at what local women are wearing. On the streets of Beyoğlu in İstanbul you'll see skimpy tops and tight jeans, but cleavage and short skirts without leggings are a no-no everywhere except nightclubs in İstanbul and heavily touristed destinations along the coast.

Bring a shawl to cover your head when visiting mosques.

On the street, you don't need to don a headscarf, but in eastern Anatolia long sleeves and baggy long pants should attract the least attention.

EATING & DRINKING

Restaurants and tea gardens aiming to attract women and children usually set aside a special room (or part of one) for families. Look for the term *aile salonu* (family dining room), or just *aile*.

HOLIDAY ROMANCES

It is not unheard of, particularly in romantic spots such as Cappadocia, for women to have holiday romances with local men. As well as fuelling the common Middle Eastern misconception that Western women are more 'available', this has led to occasional cases of men exploiting such relationships. Some men, for example, develop close friendships with visiting women, then invent sob stories, such as their mother has fallen ill, and ask them to help out financially.

REGIONAL DIFFERENCES

Having a banter with men in restaurants and shops in western Turkey can be fun, and many men won't necessarily think much of it. In contrast, eastern Anatolia is not the place to practise your Turkish (or Kurdish) and expect men not to get the wrong idea; even just smiling at a man or catching his eye is considered an invitation. Keep your dealings with men formal and polite, not friendly.

TRANSPORT

When travelling by taxi and dolmuş, avoid getting into the seat beside the driver.

On the bus, lone women are often assigned seats at the front near the driver. There have been cases of male passengers or conductors on night buses harassing female travellers. If this happens to you, complain loudly, making sure that others on the bus hear, and repeat your complaint on arrival at your destination.

Transport

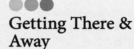

Getting There & Away

Flights, cars and tours can be booked online at lonelyplanet.com.

ENTERING THE COUNTRY

The main idiosyncrasy to be aware of is that most visitors need a 'visa' – really just a sticker in their passport, issued at the point of entry.

Travellers arriving from a yellow fever–infected country (and people who have been in such a country recently) need to show proof of vaccination before entry.

PASSPORT

Make sure your passport will still have at least six months' validity after you enter Turkey.

 AIR

It's a good idea to book flights months in advance if you plan to arrive in Turkey any time from April until late August. If you plan to visit a resort, check with travel agents for flight and accommodation deals. Sometimes you can find cheap flights with Turkish carriers and less-usual airlines.

AIRPORTS

The main international airports are in western Turkey:

İstanbul Atatürk (www.ataturkairport.com) Turkey's principal international airport.

İstanbul Sabiha Gökçen (www.sgairport.com) Served by many European budget carriers.

Antalya International Airport (www.aytport.com)

İzmir International Airport (www.adnanmenderesairport.com)

Bodrum International Airport (www.bodrum-airport.com)

Dalaman International Airport (www.atmairport.aero)

Ankara International Airport (www.esenbogaairport.com)

 SEA

Departure times change between seasons, with fewer ferries generally running in the winter. The routes available also change from year to year. A good starting point for information is **Ferrylines** (www.ferrylines.com).

Day trips on ferries to Greece are popular. Remember to take your passport, and check you have a multiple-entry Turkish visa so you can get back into the country at the end of the day. (Tourist visas issued on arrival in Turkey normally allow multiple entries.)

Getting Around

 AIR

AIRLINES

Turkey is well connected by air throughout the country, although many flights go via the hubs of İstanbul or Ankara. Internal flights are a good option in such a large country, and competition between the following keeps tickets affordable.

AnadoluJet (☏ 444 2538; www.anadolujet.com) The Turkish Airlines subsidiary serves some 30 airports in its parent company's network.

Atlasjet (☏ 0850-222 0000; www.atlasjet.com) A limited network including Antalya, Bodrum, Dalaman, İstanbul and İzmir.

Onur Air (☏ 0850-210 6687; www.onurair.com.tr) Flies from İstanbul to destinations including Antalya, Bodrum, Dalaman, İzmir and Trabzon.

Pegasus Airlines (☏ 0850-250 0737; www.pegasusairlines.com) A useful network of some 20 airports, including most of the locations mentioned in the above listings plus less-usual spots such as Kayseri (for Cappadocia) and Van.

Sun Express (☏ 444 0797; www.sunexpress.com.tr) The Turkish Airlines subsidiary has a useful network of about 15 airports, with most flights from Antalya, İstanbul and İzmir.

Turkish Airlines (☏ 0850-333 0849; www.thy.com)

State-owned Turkish Airlines provides the main domestic network, covering airports from Çanakkale to Kars.

🚲 BICYCLE

Hazards These include Turkey's notorious road-hog drivers, rotten road edges and, out east, stone-throwing children, wolves and ferocious Kangal dogs. Avoid main roads between cities; secondary roads are safer and more scenic.

○ **Hire** You can hire bikes for short periods in tourist towns along the coast and in Cappadocia.

○ **Maps** The best map for touring by bike is the *Köy Köy*

Türkiye Yol Atlası, available in bookshops in İstanbul.

○ **Parts and service** Good-quality spare parts are generally only available in İstanbul and Ankara. **Delta Bisiklet** (www.deltabisiklet.com), which has branches in İstanbul, Ankara, İzmir and Antalya, services bicycles and can send parts throughout the country.

○ **Transport** You can often transport your bike by bus, train or ferry free of charge, although some buses will charge for the space it takes up.

🚢 BOAT

İstanbul Deniz Otobüsleri (p102) operates passenger and car ferries across the

---

Ferries to/from Greece & Northern Cyprus

○ Ayvalık (north Aegean) – Lesvos, Greece (see www.jaletour.com)

○ Alanya (eastern Mediterranean) – Girne (Kyrenia), Northern Cyprus (www.fergun.net)

○ Bodrum (south Aegean) – Kos and Rhodes, Greece (www.bodrumferryboat.com and www.bodrumexpresslines.com)

○ Çeşme (north Aegean) – Chios, Greece (www.erturk.com.tr)

○ Datça (south Aegean) – Rhodes and Simi, Greece (www.knidosyachting.com)

○ Kaş (western Mediterranean) – Meis (Kastellorizo), Greece (www.meisexpress.com)

○ Kuşadası (south Aegean) – Samos, Greece (www.meandertravel.com)

○ Marmaris (south Aegean) – Rhodes (www.yesilmarmaris.com)

○ Taşucu (eastern Mediterranean) – Girne (Kyrenia; www.akgunler.com.tr)

○ Turgutreis (south Aegean) – Kos (www.bodrumferryboat.com)

Sea of Marmara, with routes including:

○ İstanbul Kabataş–Çınarcık (west of Yalova)

○ İstanbul Yenikapı–Bandırma, Bursa and Yalova.

 BUS

Turkey's intercity bus system is as good as any you'll find, with modern, comfortable coaches crossing the country at all hours and for very reasonable prices. On the journey, you'll be treated to hot drinks and snacks, plus liberal sprinklings of the Turks' beloved *kolonya* (lemon cologne).

COMPANIES

Try to stick to the major bus companies. The smaller operators are less dependable, and sometimes drop passengers on the road outside town rather than taking them all the way to the otogar.

These are some of the best companies, with extensive route networks:

Kamil Koç (☏ 444 0562; www.kamilkoc.com.tr) Serves most major cities throughout western and central Turkey.

Metro Turizm (☏ 444 3455; www.metroturizm.com.tr) Serves most major cities and towns throughout Turkey.

Ulusoy (☏ 444 1888; www.ulusoy.com.tr; İnönü Caddesi 59) Serves most major cities and towns, particularly in western and central Turkey, going as far east as Erzurum.

Varan Turizm (☏ 444 8999; www.varan.com.tr) Mostly focuses on western Turkey, going as far east as Ankara and Trabzon.

COSTS

Bus fares are subject to fierce competition between companies. Prices reflect what the market will bear, so the fare from a big city to a village is likely to be different from the fare in the opposite direction.

TICKETS

Although you can usually walk into an otogar (bus station) and buy a ticket for the next bus, it's wise to plan ahead on public holidays, at weekends and during the school holidays from mid-June to early September. You can reserve seats online with some of the companies listed.

○ **At the otogar** When you enter bigger otogars, prepare for a few touts offering buses to the destination of your choice. It's usually a good idea to stick to the reputable big-name companies. You may pay a bit more, but you can be more confident the bus is well maintained, will run on time, and will have a relief driver on really long hauls. For shorter trips, some companies have big regional networks.

○ **Men and women** Unmarried men and women are not supposed to sit together, but the bus companies rarely enforce this in the case of foreigners. You may be asked if you are married, without having to produce any proof of your wedlock, or both travellers may find their tickets marked with *bay* (man).

○ **Refunds** Getting a refund can be difficult; exchanging it for another ticket with the same company is easier.

○ **Seats** All seats can be reserved, and your ticket will bear a specific seat number.

The ticket agent will have a chart of the seats with those already sold crossed off. They will often assign you a seat, but if you ask to look at the chart and choose a place, you can avoid sitting in the following black spots:

○ **At the front** The front row of seats behind the driver has little legroom, plus you may have to inhale his cigarette smoke and listen to him chatting to his conductor.

○ **Above the wheels** Can get bumpy.

○ **In front of the middle door** Seats don't recline.

○ **Behind the middle door** Seats have little legroom.

○ **At the back** Can get stuffy, and may have 'back of the cinema' connotations if you are a lone woman.

OTOGAR

Most Turkish cities and towns have a bus station, called the otogar, *garaj* or *terminal,* generally located on the outskirts. Besides intercity buses, otogars often handle dolmuşes (minibuses that follow prescribed routes) to outlying districts or villages. Most bus stations have an *emanetçi* (left luggage) room, which you can use for a nominal fee.

Particularly in eastern Anatolia, don't believe taxi drivers at otogars who tell you there is no bus or dolmuş to your destination; they may be trying to trick you into taking their taxi. Check with the bus and dolmuş operators.

SERVIS

Because most bus stations are some distance from the town or city centre, the bus companies provide free *servis* shuttle minibuses. These take you to the bus company's office or another central location. Ask '*Servis var mı?*' ('Is there a *servis*?') Rare cities without such a service include Ankara.

○ **Leaving town** Ask about the servis when you buy your ticket at the bus company's central office; they will likely instruct you to arrive at the office an hour before the official departure time.

○ **Drawbacks** This service saves you a taxi or local bus fare to the otogar, but involves a lot of hanging around. If you only have limited time in a location, a taxi fare may be a good investment.

○ **Scams** Pension owners may try to convince you the private minibus to their pension is a bus company *servis*. Taxi drivers may say the *servis* has left or isn't operating in the hope of convincing you that their cab is the only option. If you do miss a *servis*, enquire at the bus company office; they normally run regularly.

CAR & MOTORCYCLE

Bear in mind that Turkey is a huge country and spending time in the car travelling long distances will eat up your time and money. Consider planes, trains and buses for covering long journeys, and cars for localised travel.

Public transport is a much easier and less stressful way of getting around the traffic-clogged cities.

AUTOMOBILE ASSOCIATIONS

Motorcyslist website **Horizons Unlimited** (www.

horizonsunlimited.com/country/turkey) has Turkey-related information and contacts.

Motorcyclists may want to check out **One More Mile Riders Turkey** (www.ommriders.com), a community resource for riding in Turkey.

CHECKPOINTS

Roadblocks are increasingly common in Turkey, with police checking vehicles and paperwork are in order. As well as their licence and vehicle papers, foreign drivers occasionally need to show their passport. In southeastern Anatolia, you may encounter military roadblocks – part of operations against the PKK (Kurdistan Workers Party). They will likely check your ID and vehicle papers before waving you on, although roads in the region are sometimes closed completely if there is trouble ahead.

DRIVING LICENCES

Drivers must have a valid driving licence. Your own national licence should be sufficient, but an international driving permit (IDP) may be useful if your licence is from a country likely to seem obscure to a Turkish police officer

FINES

You may be stopped by blue-uniformed *trafik polis,* who can fine you on the spot for speeding. If you know you have done nothing wrong and the police appear to be asking for money, play dumb. You'll probably have to pay up if they persist, but insisting on proof of payment may dissuade them from ex-

tracting a fine destined only for their pocket. If the police don't ask for on-the-spot payment, contact your car-rental company (or mention the incident when you return the vehicle), as it can pay the fine and take the money from your card. Do the same in the case of fines for other offences, such as not paying a motorway toll. Note that you get a discount for early payment.

FUEL

Turkey has the world's second-highest petrol prices (Norway tops the list). Petrol/diesel cost about ₺4/4.70 per litre. There are petrol stations everywhere, at least in western Turkey, and many are mega enterprises. In the vast empty spaces of central and eastern Anatolia, it's a good idea to have a full tank when you start out in the morning.

HIRE

You need to be at least 21 years old, with a year's driving experience, to hire a car in Turkey. Most car hire companies require a credit card. Most hire cars have standard (manual) transmission; you'll pay more for automatic. The majority of the big-name companies charge hefty one-way fees, starting at around ₺150 (eg pick up in İstanbul and drop off in İzmir) and climbing to hundreds of euros (eg pick up in eastern Anatolia and drop off in İstanbul).

The big international companies – including Avis, Budget, Europcar, Hertz, National and Sixt – operate in the main cities, towns and most airports. Particularly in eastern Anatolia, stick to the major companies, as the local agencies often do not have insurance. Even some of the major operations are actually franchises in the east, so you should always check the contract carefully; particularly the section relating to insurance. Ask for a copy in English.

If your car incurs any accident damage, or if you cause any, do not move the car before finding a police officer and obtaining a *kaza raporu* (accident report). The officer may ask you to take an alcohol breath-test. Contact your car-rental company as soon as possible. In the case of an accident, your hire-car insurance may be void if it can

be shown you were operating under the influence of alcohol or drugs, were speeding, or if you did not submit the required accident report within 48 hours to the rental company.

Because of high local fuel prices, agencies generally deliver cars with virtually no fuel, unless you specifically request otherwise.

Economy Car Rentals (www.economycarrentals.com) Gets excellent rates with other companies, including Budget and National; recommended.

Car Rental Turkey (www. carrentalturkey.info) İstanbul-based car hire.

Green Car (☎ 0232-446 9060; www.greenautorent.com; Mithatpaşa Caddesi 57, Karataş, İzmir) This local company is one of the largest in the Aegean region.

CarHireExpress.co.uk (www.carhireexpress.co.uk/turkey/) A booking engine.

INSURANCE

When hiring a car, 100%, no-excess insurance is increasingly the only option on offer. If this is not the only option, the basic, mandatory insurance package should cover damage to the vehicle and theft protection – with an excess, which you can reduce or waive for an extra payment. You may be offered personal accident insurance; your travel insurance should cover any personal accident costs in the case of a crash.

As in other countries, insurance generally does not cover windows and tyres. You

will likely be offered cover for an extra few euros a day.

PARKING

Parking is easy to find in most towns and smaller settlements, and you can generally park next to accommodation and sights outside Turkey's main centres. Space is at a premium in cities and some towns, but there are normally plenty of car parks where you can park cheaply for an hour or so, or safely leave your car overnight. You will often have to leave your keys with car park attendants.

● **Accommodation** Top-end and a handful of midrange hotels offer undercover parking for guests, and most midrange and budget options have a roadside parking place or two that is nominally theirs to use. If they don't, parking will be close by in an empty block overseen by a caretaker, or on the road; in both cases you have to pay a fee. Your best bet is to set it up in advance when you book your room.

○ **Clamping** Park in the wrong place and you risk having your car towed away, with the ensuing costs and hassle.

ROAD CONDITIONS

Road surfaces and signage are generally good – on the main roads, at least. The most popular route with travellers, along the Aegean and Mediterranean coasts, offers excellent driving conditions. There are good *otoyols* (motorways) from Edirne to İstanbul and Ankara, and from İzmir around the coast to Antalya.

Elsewhere, roads are being steadily upgraded, although

they still tend to be worst in the east, where severe winters play havoc with the surfaces. In northeastern Anatolia, road conditions change from year to year; seek local advice before setting off on secondary roads. There are frequent roadworks in the northeast; even on main roads traffic can crawl along at 30km/hr. The new dams near Yusufeli will flood some roads, and the construction causes waits of up to half an hour. Ask locally about the timing of your journey; on some roads, traffic flows according to a regular timetable, posted at the roadside.

In winter, be careful of icy roads. In bad winters, you will need chains on your wheels almost everywhere except along the Aegean and Mediterranean coasts. In mountainous areas such as northeastern Anatolia, landslides and rockfalls are a danger, caused by wet weather and snow-melt in spring. Between İstanbul and Ankara, be aware of the fog belt around Bolu that can seriously reduce visibility, even in summer.

ROAD RULES

In theory, Turks drive on the right and yield to traffic approaching from the right. In practice, they often drive in the middle and yield to no one. Maximum speed limits, unless otherwise posted, are 50km/h in towns, 90km/h on highways and 120km/h on *otoyols*.

SAFETY

Turkey has one of the world's highest motor-vehicle accident rates. Turkish drivers are impatient and incautious; rarely use their indicators and pay little attention to anyone else's; drive too fast both on the open road and through towns; and have an irrepressible urge to overtake – including on blind corners.

To survive on Turkey's roads:

○ Drive cautiously and defensively.

○ Do not expect your fellow motorists to obey road signs or behave in a manner you would generally expect at home.

○ As there are only a few divided highways and many two-lane roads are serpentine, reconcile yourself to spending hours crawling along behind slow, overladen trucks.

○ Avoid driving at night, when you won't be able to see potholes, animals, or even vehicles driving without lights, with lights missing, or stopped in the middle of the road. Drivers sometimes flash their lights to announce their approach.

○ Rather than trying to tackle secondary, gravel roads when visiting remote sights, hire a taxi for the day. It's an extra expense, but the driver should know the terrain and the peace of mind is invaluable.

○ The US embassy in Ankara has a page of safety tips for drivers at http://turkey.usembassy.gov/driver_safety_briefing.html.

TOLLS

You must pay a toll to use the major *otoyols*. You can buy green-and-orange toll cards and place *kontör* (credit) on them at the offices near mo-torway toll gates. The offices are not open 24 hours; most close on Sunday. There is a ₺100 fine for nonpayment, which takes about two weeks to come through.

DOLMUŞES & MIDIBUSES

As well as providing transport within cities and towns, dolmuşes run between places. Ask, '[Your destination] *dolmuş var mı?'* (Is there a dolmuş to [your destination]?) Some dolmuşes depart at set times, but they often wait until every seat is taken before leaving. To let the driver know that you want to hop out, say *'inecek var'* (someone wants to get out).

Midibuses generally operate on routes that are too long for dolmuşes, but not popular enough for full-size buses.

LOCAL TRANSPORT

BUS

For most city buses you must buy your *bilet* (ticket) in advance at a special ticket kiosk. Kiosks are found at major bus terminals and transfer points, and sometimes attached to shops near bus stops. The fare is normally about ₺2.

LOCAL DOLMUŞ

Dolmuşes are minibuses or, occasionally, *taksi dolmuşes* (shared taxis) that operate on set routes within a city. They're usually faster, more comfortable and only slightly more expensive than the bus. In larger cities, dolmuş stops are marked by signs; look for a 'D' and text reading '*Dolmuş İndirme Bindirme Yeri'* (Dolmuş Boarding and Alighting Place).

Stops are usually conveniently located near major squares, terminals and intersections.

METRO

Several cities now have underground or partially underground metros, including İstanbul, İzmir, Bursa and Ankara. These are usually quick and simple to use, although you may have to go through the ticket barriers to find a route map. Most metros require you to buy a *jeton* (transport token; around ₺2) and insert it into the ticket barrier.

TAXI

If your driver doesn't start his meter, mention it right away by saying '*saatiniz*' (your meter). Check your driver is running the right rate. The *gece* (night) rate is 50% more than the *gündüz* (daytime) rate, but some places, including İstanbul, do not have a night rate.

Some drivers, particularly in İstanbul, try to demand a flat payment from foreigners. In this situation, drivers sometimes offer a decent fare; for example to take you to an airport. It is more often the case that they demand an exorbitant amount, give you grief, and refuse to run the meter. If this happens find another cab.

Generally, only when you are using a taxi for a private tour involving waiting time should you agree on a set fare, which should work out cheaper than using the meter. Taxi companies normally have set fees for longer journeys written in a ledger at the rank; they can be haggled down a little. Always confirm such fares in advance to avoid argument later.

Locals usually round up the fare to the nearest 0.5TL.

TRAM

Several cities have *tramvays* (trams), which are a quick and efficient way of getting around, and normally cost around ₺2 to use.

TOURS

Every year we receive complaints from travellers who feel they have been fleeced by local travel agents, especially some of those operating in Sultanahmet, İstanbul. However, there are plenty of good agents alongside the sharks. Figure out a ballpark figure for doing the same trip yourself using the prices in this book, and shop around before committing.

OPERATORS

Amber Travel (www.ambertravel.com) British-run adventure travel company specialising in hiking, biking and sea kayaking.

Bougainville Travel (p207) Long-established English-Turkish tour operator offering a range of Mediterranean activities plus tailor-made nationwide tours.

Crowded House Tours (p119) Tours to the Gallipoli Peninsula and other areas including Cappadocia and Ephesus.

Dragoman (www.dragoman.com; UK) Overland itineraries starting in İstanbul.

Eastern Turkey Tours (p321) Also known as Alkan

Tours, this recommended Van-based outfit specialises in eastern Anatolia.

Fez Travel (www.feztravel.com) Tours around Turkey, including the Gallipoli Peninsula.

Hassle Free Travel Agency (p119) Tours to the Gallipoli Peninsula plus itineraries including other parts of western and central Turkey.

Imaginative Traveller (www.imaginative-traveller.com; UK) Various overland adventures through Turkey.

Intrepid Travel (www.intrepidtravel.com.au) Offers a variety of small-group tours, for travellers who like the philosophy of independent travel but prefer to travel with others.

Kirkit Voyage (www.kirkit.com) Cappadocia specialists offering customised tours around Turkey, including İstanbul and Ephesus. French spoken too.

🚆 TRAIN

Train travel through Turkey is becoming increasingly popular as improvements are made, with high-speed lines appearing.

CLASSES

Turkish trains typically have several seating and sleeping options. Most have comfortable reclining Pullman seat carriages. Some have 1st- and 2nd-class compartments, with six and eight seats respectively; sometimes bookable, sometimes 'first come, best seated'.

COSTS

Train tickets are usually about half the price of bus tickets. A return ticket is 20% cheaper than two singles. Seniors (60 years plus; proof of age required) get a 20% discount. Children under eight travel free.

InterRail, Balkan Flexipass and Eurodomino passes are valid on the Turkish railway network, but Eurail passes aren't.

NETWORK

The **Turkish State Railways** (www.tcdd.gov.tr) network covers the country fairly well, with the notable exception of the coastlines. For the Aegean and Mediterranean coasts you can travel by train to either İzmir or Konya, and take the bus from there.

While the line running into Anatolia from İstanbul's Haydarpaşa station is being upgraded, trains running southeast from the city have been cancelled until 2014 or 2015. Trains to eastern Anatolia now depart from Ankara, easily reached from İstanbul by bus.

Useful routes include:

○ Ankara–Konya (high speed)

○ İstanbul–İzmir (including ferry to/from Bandırma)

○ İzmir–Selcuk

RESERVATIONS

Most seats on the best trains must be booked in advance.

Weekend trains tend to be busiest.

You can buy tickets at stations, through an agency, or with a credit card at www.tcdd.gov.tr as much as 14 days before departure; www.seat61.com/Turkey2.htm gives step-by-step instructions for navigating the transaction.

TIMETABLES

You can double-check train departure times, which do change, at www.tcdd.gov.tr.

Timetables usually indicate stations rather than cities; most refer to Haydarpaşa and Sirkeci rather than İstanbul, and to Basmane and Alsancak in İzmir.

Language

Pronouncing Turkish is pretty simple as most Turkish sounds are also found in English. If you read our coloured pronunciation guides as if they were English, you'll be understood. Note that, in our pronunciation guides, **ew** is pronounced as the 'ee' in 'see' with rounded lips, **uh** as the 'a' in 'ago', and that **r** is always rolled. The stressed syllables are indicated with italics.

To enhance your trip with a phrasebook, visit **lonelyplanet.com**. Lonely Planet iPhone phrasebooks are available through the Apple App store.

BASICS

Hello.
Merhaba.   mer·ha·ba
Goodbye.
Hoşçakal./Güle güle.   hosh·cha·kal/gew·le gew·le
(said by person leaving/staying)
Yes./No.
Evet./Hayır.   e·vet/ha·yuhr
Excuse me.
Bakar mısınız.   ba·kar muh·suh·nuhz
Sorry.
Özür dilerim.   er·zewr dee·le·reem
Please.
Lütfen.   lewt·fen
Thank you.
Teşekkür ederim.   te·shek·kewr e·de·reem
How are you?
Nasılsınız?   na·suhl·suh·nuhz
Fine, and you?
İyiyim, ya siz?   ee·yee·yeem ya seez
Do you speak English?
İngilizce   een·gee·leez·je
konuşuyor   ko·noo·shoo·yor
musunuz?   moo·soo·nooz
I don't understand.
Anlamıyorum.   an·la·muh·yo·room

How much is it?
Ne kadar?   ne ka·dar
It's too expensive.
Bu çok pahalı.   boo chok pa·ha·luh

ACCOMMODATION

Do you have a single/double room?
Tek/İki kişilik   tek/ee·kee kee·shee·leek
odanız var mı?   o·da·nuz var muh
How much is it per night/person?
Geceliği/Kişi   ge·je·lee·ee/kee·shee
başına ne kadar?   ba·shuh·na ne ka·dar

EATING & DRINKING

I'd like (the menu).
(Menüyü)   (me·new·yew)
istiyorum.   ees·tee·yo·room
Cheers!
Şerefe!   she·re·fe
That was delicious!
Nefisti!   ne·fees·tee
The bill, please.
Hesap lütfen.   he·sap lewt·fen

I don't eat ...
... yemiyorum.   ... ye·mee·yo·room
  eggs   *Yumurta*   yoo·moor·ta
  fish   *Balık*   ba·luhk
  red meat   *Kırmızı et*   kuhr·muh·zuh et

EMERGENCIES

Help!
İmdat!   eem·dat
I'm ill.
Hastayım.   has·ta·yuhm
Call a doctor!
Doktor çağırın!   dok·tor cha·uh·ruhn
Call the police!
Polis çağırın!   po·lees cha·uh·ruhn

DIRECTIONS

Where is ...?
... nerede?   ... ne·re·de

bank	*banka*	ban·ka
hotel	*otel*	o·tel
market	*pazar*	pa·zar
post office	*postane*	pos·ta·ne
restaurant	*restoran*	res·to·ran
toilet	*tuvalet*	too·va·let
tourist office	*turizm*	too·reezm
	bürosu	bew·ro·soo

Behind the Scenes

Author Thanks

JAMES BAINBRIDGE

Çok teşekkürler to all my Local Knowledge interviewees for generously sharing your expertise and passion. I was blown away by your willingness to patiently engage with my questions, demands and deadlines. Thanks especially to Celil Ersoğlu (when I next visit Kars, the *ejder kebaps* are on me), and to Ufuk and Phil in Kaş for stepping into the breach. Finally, a big shout-out to Brigitte Ellemor, Cliff Wilkinson and everyone at Lonely Planet, and to my wife Leigh-Robin.

Acknowledgments

Climate map data adapted from Peel MC, Finlayson BL & McMahon TA (2007) 'Updated World Map of the Köppen-Geiger Climate Classification', *Hydrology and Earth System Sciences,* 11, 163344.

Illustrations pp70-1, pp74-5 and pp158-9 by Javier Zarracina.

Cover photographs: Front: Blue Mosque at dawn, Sultanahmet, İstanbul, Diego Lezama/Getty Images. Back: Görkündere (Love Valley), Cappadocia, Izzet Keribar/ Getty Images.

This Book

This 1st edition of Lonely Planet's *Discover Turkey* guidebook was researched and written by James Bainbridge, Brett Atkinson, Chris Deliso, Steve Fallon, Will Gourlay, Jessica Lee, Virginia Maxwell and Tom Spurling.

This guidebook was commissioned in Lonely Planet's London office, and produced by the following:

Commissioning Editor Clifton Wilkinson

Coordinating Editor Briohny Hooper

Coordinating Cartographer Alex Leung

Coordinating Layout Designer Carlos Solarte

Managing Editors Brigitte Ellemor, Martine Power, Angela Tinson

Managing Cartographer Adrian Persoglia

Managing Layout Designer Chris Girdler

Assisting Editors Janet Austin, Anne Mulvaney, Gina Tsarouhas

Assisting Cartographers Mick Garrett, Corey Hutchison, Samantha Tyson

Cover Research Naomi Parker

Internal Image Research Aude Vauconsant

Language Content Branislava Vladisavljevic

Thanks to Penny Cordner, Ryan Evans, Larissa Frost, Jane Hart, Jouve India, Laura Jane Trent Paton, Raphael Richards, Wibowo Rusli, Joseph Spanti, Gerard Walker

Index

000 Map pages

000 Map pages

000 Map pages

How to Use This Book

These symbols will help you find the listings you want:

- ⊙ Sights
- 🏖 Beaches
- 🏃 Activities
- 🎓 Courses
- 🎯 Tours
- 🎉 Festivals & Events
- 🛏 Sleeping
- 🍴 Eating
- 🍷 Drinking
- ☆ Entertainment
- 🛍 Shopping
- ℹ Information/ Transport

Look out for these icons:

| FREE | No payment required |
| 🌿 | A green or sustainable option |

Our authors have nominated these places as demonstrating a strong commitment to sustainability – for example by supporting local communities and producers, operating in an environmentally friendly way, or supporting conservation projects.

These symbols give you the vital information for each listing:

- ☎ Telephone Numbers
- ⊙ Opening Hours
- P Parking
- ⊖ Nonsmoking
- ❄ Air-Conditioning
- @ Internet Access
- 📶 Wi-Fi Access
- 🏊 Swimming Pool
- 🥗 Vegetarian Selection
- 📖 English-Language Menu
- 👪 Family-Friendly
- 🐾 Pet-Friendly
- 🚌 Bus
- ⛴ Ferry
- Ⓜ Metro
- Ⓢ Subway
- 🚊 Tram
- 🚆 Train

Reviews are organised by author preference.

Map Legend

Sights
- 🏖 Beach
- 🏛 Buddhist
- 🏰 Castle
- ✝ Christian
- 🕉 Hindu
- ☪ Islamic
- ✡ Jewish
- ❶ Monument
- 🏛 Museum/Gallery
- 🏛 Ruin
- 🍷 Winery/Vineyard
- 🐾 Zoo
- ⊙ Other Sight

Activities, Courses & Tours
- 🤿 Diving/Snorkelling
- 🛶 Canoeing/Kayaking
- ⛷ Skiing
- 🏄 Surfing
- 🏊 Swimming/Pool
- 🚶 Walking
- 🏄 Windsurfing
- ➕ Other Activity/ Course/Tour

Sleeping
- 🛏 Sleeping
- ⛺ Camping

Eating
- 🍴 Eating

Drinking
- ☕ Drinking
- ☕ Cafe

Entertainment
- 🎭 Entertainment

Shopping
- 🛍 Shopping

Information
- ✉ Post Office
- ℹ Tourist Information

Transport
- ✈ Airport
- ⊗ Border Crossing
- 🚌 Bus
- 🚠 Cable Car/ Funicular
- 🚴 Cycling
- ⛴ Ferry
- 🚝 Monorail
- P Parking
- Ⓢ S-Bahn
- 🚕 Taxi
- 🚉 Train/Railway
- 🚊 Tram
- ⊖ Tube Station
- Ⓤ U-Bahn
- Ⓜ Underground Train Station
- • Other Transport

Routes
- Tollway
- Freeway
- Primary
- Secondary
- Tertiary
- Lane
- Unsealed Road
- Plaza/Mall
- Steps
- Tunnel
- Pedestrian Overpass
- Walking Tour
- Walking Tour Detour
- Path

Boundaries
- International
- State/Province
- Disputed
- Regional/Suburb
- Marine Park
- Cliff
- Wall

Population
- ◉ Capital (National)
- ◉ Capital (State/Province)
- ● City/Large Town
- ● Town/Village

Geographic
- 🏠 Hut/Shelter
- 🗼 Lighthouse
- 👁 Lookout
- ▲ Mountain/Volcano
- 🌴 Oasis
- 🌳 Park
-)(Pass
- 🏕 Picnic Area
- 💧 Waterfall

Hydrography
- River/Creek
- Intermittent River
- Swamp/Mangrove
- Reef
- Canal
- Water
- Dry/Salt/ Intermittent Lake
- Glacier

Areas
- Beach/Desert
- Cemetery (Christian)
- Cemetery (Other)
- Park/Forest
- Sportsground
- Sight (Building)
- Top Sight (Building)

WILL GOURLAY

History, Architecture, Arts, People A serial visitor to Turkey, Will has been leaving his home base of Melbourne on regular Turkish forays for more than 20 years. As a backpacker, English teacher and writer he has explored all corners of Anatolia, the more remote the better. His most recent trips have been with his wife and children in tow, although they usually stay on the beach while he rummages around in the backwoods or takes the train into Iran. He is currently researching a PhD on Turkish politics and society.

JESSICA LEE

Cappadocia & Central Anatolia Jessica spent four years traversing the breadth of Turkey as a tour leader. In late 2011 she returned to live and this edition saw her researching the Seljuk splendour and Hittite ruins of central Anatolia and the surreal scenery of Cappadocia. Jessica has authored many guidebooks to destinations in the Middle East and her travel writing has appeared in several international newspapers and magazines.

VIRGINIA MAXWELL

İstanbul, Turkish Table Although based in Australia, Virginia spends much of her year researching guidebooks in the Mediterranean countries. Of these, Turkey is unquestionably her favourite. As well as working on five previous editions of the *Turkey* country guide, she is also the author of Lonely Planet's *İstanbul* city and pocket guides and writes about the city for a host of international magazines and websites. Virginia usually travels with partner Peter and son Max, who have grown to love Turkey as much as she does.

Read more about Virginia at:
lonelyplanet.com/members/virginiamaxwell

TOM SPURLING

Gallipoli & the North Aegean Tom lives in Perth with his wife Lucy and their two children, Oliver and Poppy. He has coauthored a number of editions of *Turkey* and worked in five continents for Lonely Planet. When not travelling he teaches high-school English and is currently completing a Masters in International Education Policy. Advice for first-time travellers to Turkey? Çay, hamam, çay. Repeat daily.

Our Story

A beat-up old car, a few dollars in the pocket and a sense of adventure. In 1972 that's all Tony and Maureen Wheeler needed for the trip of a lifetime – across Europe and Asia overland to Australia. It took several months, and at the end – broke but inspired – they sat at their kitchen table writing and stapling together their first travel guide, *Across Asia on the Cheap*. Within a week they'd sold 1500 copies. Lonely Planet was born.

Today, Lonely Planet has offices in Melbourne, London, Oakland and Delhi, with more than 600 staff and writers. We share Tony's belief that 'a great guidebook should do three things: inform, educate and amuse'.

Our Writers

JAMES BAINBRIDGE

Coordinating Author, Eastern Anatolia, Turkey Today, Plan, Survival Guide Coordinating a number of Lonely Planet *Turkey* guides, media assignments and extracurricular wanderings have taken James to most of Turkey's far-flung regions. He lived in İstanbul (Cihangir to be exact) while coordinating the previous edition of this book, and learnt to love suffixes on a Turkish-language course. For this book, discovering northeastern Anatolia's mountains and steppe, ruins and Caucasian ambience showed him yet another side of this multifaceted and endlessly intriguing country. When he's not missioning to Kaçkar *yaylalar* (high-altitude pastures) or tucking into Black Sea cuisine, he lives in Cape Town, South Africa. Visit James' website at www.jamesbainbridge.net.

Read more about James at:
lonelyplanet.com/members/james_bains

BRETT ATKINSON

Antalya & the Mediterranean Coast, Eastern Anatolia Since first visiting Turkey in 1985, Brett has returned regularly to one of his favourite countries. For his third Lonely Planet trip to Turkey, he explored the Kurdish heartland of southeast Anatolia and reignited an interest in archaeology along the stunning Mediterranean coast. Brett is based in Auckland, New Zealand, and has covered more than 40 countries as a guidebook author and travel and food writer. See www.brett-atkinson.net for what he's been eating recently and where he's travelling to next.

CHRIS DELISO

Ephesus, Bodrum & the South Aegean, Cappadocia & Central Anatolia Chris first experienced İstanbul's total sensory overload in 1999, during an Oxford MPhil dedicated to Turkey's Byzantine incarnation. Since then he's travelled widely throughout Turkey, from the Iran–Iraq border area and the lush Black Sea coast to semitropical Aegean beaches in the west. Having developed a deep affection for this ever-surprising country, Chris was delighted to return to Western Anatolia and the South Aegean for this book. He also writes about nearby Greece, Bulgaria, Romania and Macedonia for Lonely Planet.

Read more about Chris at:
lonelyplanet.com/members/chrisdeliso

STEVE FALLON

Antalya & the Mediterranean Coast With a house in Kalkan, Steve treats Turkey like a second home. And this assignment kept him pretty much in his own backyard – Lycia – from the riverine turtle town of Dalyan to pulsating Antalya, capital of Turkey's Mediterranean coast. OK, OK...*Türkçe'yi hala mağara adamí gibi konuşuyor* (he still speaks Turkish like a caveman), but no Turk has called him Tarzan – yet.

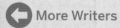

More Writers

Published by Lonely Planet Publications Pty Ltd
ABN 36 005 607 983
1st edition – June 2013
ISBN 978 1 74220 282 2
© Lonely Planet 2013   Photographs © as indicated 2013
10 9 8 7 6 5 4 3 2
Printed in China